Over-the-Road
Wireless
FOR
DUMMIES®

Over-the-Road Wireless FOR DUMMIES®

by E. Phil Haley

WILEY

Wiley Publishing, Inc.

Over-the-Road Wireless For Dummies®

Published by
Wiley Publishing, Inc.
111 River Street
Hoboken, NJ 07030-5774

www.wiley.com

Copyright © 2006 by Wiley Publishing, Inc., Indianapolis, Indiana

Published by Wiley Publishing, Inc., Indianapolis, Indiana

Published simultaneously in Canada

For general information on our other products and services, please contact our Customer Care Department within the U.S. at 800-762-2974, outside the U.S. at 317-572-3993, or fax 317-572-4002.

For technical support, please visit www.wiley.com/techsupport.

Wiley also publishes its books in a variety of electronic formats. Some content that appears in print may not be available in electronic books.

Library of Congress Control Number: 2006924030

ISBN-13: 978-0-471-78403-6

ISBN-10: 0-471-78403-6

Manufactured in the United States of America

10 9 8 7 6 5 4 3 2 1

1B/RX/QX/QW/IN

WILEY

About the Author

E. Phil Haley is a truck driver and equipment operator living in Anchorage, Alaska, and writes articles about wireless Internet access and security. Phil first started driving trucks in September 1979, and his most recent over-the-road experience has been with Leavitt's Freight Service of Springfield, Oregon, where he enjoyed the challenge of hauling long loads. During his over-the-road adventures, he travels with two laptops (one for work and one for fun), a handful of wireless adapters, more antennas than any one person should own, and a wireless signal amplifier (just in case). When he's not driving or surfing the Web, he can usually be found in one truck stop or another extolling the virtues of wireless Internet access to anyone in earshot or helping a new convert get set up for wireless Net surfing. Phil also maintains (or, more often, fails to maintain) theCyberTruckStop.com.

Dedication

This book is dedicated to the memory of Darrell R. Meyer; friend, mentor and trucker extraordinaire. 1948 - 2004

Author's Acknowledgments

A lot of people at Wiley Publishing worked as hard, or harder, than I did to produce a book that provides solid, accurate, useful, and usable information. Acquisitions Editor Melody Layne presented me with the opportunity to author this book and, for that, I'll be forever grateful. Further, the initial guidance of Melody Layne, Editorial Manager Leah Cameron, and Project Editor Becky Huehls, each of them giving me important pointers, got this book started off on the right foot. I feel particularly fortunate to have had Becky Huehls assigned as the Project Editor. To say that I'm thankful for the work she so skillfully performed, and for her guiding hand, is an understatement of immense proportion.

A few others at Wiley Publishing to whom I'm grateful for their contribution of hard work and application of skill include Senior Copy Editor Barry Childs-Helton, Copy Editor Heidi Unger, and Copy Editor Virginia Sanders. They all made sure that, among many other things, my misuses of the English language got put right and rendered readable. Technical Editor Steven Fletcher pointed me back toward the path of accuracy whenever I strayed. Project Coordinator Jennifer Theriot ensured the illustrations and layout went smoothly, while Ms. Brooke Graczyk took my chicken scratch drawings and turned them into useful works of art. (I don't know *how* she did that.)

Flying J Communications, Bill Bingaman of Highway Hotspots, Michael Ginsberg of EVDOinfo.com, Bill Adams of InternetAnywhere.us, Max Mattia of OrbitalEnterprises.net, Brian Shaffer representing RaySat, Rebecca Schnall at Sirius Radio, and Fritz Roland Bjorklund at the Drivers Daily Log, all made contributions and my thanks go out to them.

Finally, I'm thankful for, and grateful to, my wife; Sue Ann Haley. There's just no way I could've completed this book without her help and support. She never lost faith in my abilities, even when I was sure she was imagining their existence. I thank God for her every day.

Publisher's Acknowledgments

We're proud of this book; please send us your comments through our online registration form located at www.dummies.com/register/.

Some of the people who helped bring this book to market include the following:

Acquisitions, Editorial, and Media Development

Project Editor: Rebecca Huehls

Acquisitions Editor: Melody Layne

Senior Copy Editor: Barry Childs-Helton

Technical Editor: Steven Fletcher

Editorial Manager: Leah P. Cameron

Media Development Manager: Laura VanWinkle

Editorial Assistant: Amanda Foxworth

Sr. Editorial Assistant: Cherie Case

Cartoons: Rich Tennant (www.the5thwave.com)

Composition Services

Project Coordinator: Jennifer Theriot

Layout and Graphics: Claudia Bell, Carl Byers, Andrea Dahl, Lauren Goddard, Brooke Graczyk, Stephanie D. Jumper, Barbara Moore, Barry Offringa, Alicia South

Proofreaders: John Greenough, Leeann Harney

Indexer: Techbooks

Special Help: Heidi Unger, Virginia Sanders

Publishing and Editorial for Technology Dummies

Richard Swadley, Vice President and Executive Group Publisher

Andy Cummings, Vice President and Publisher

Mary Bednarek, Executive Acquisitions Director

Mary C. Corder, Editorial Director

Publishing for Consumer Dummies

Diane Graves Steele, Vice President and Publisher

Joyce Pepple, Acquisitions Director

Composition Services

Gerry Fahey, Vice President of Production Services

Debbie Stailey, Director of Composition Services

Contents at a Glance

Table of Contents

Introduction

The other day I was watching *The Andy Griffith Show*. It was an episode I've probably seen ten thousand times. (You think I'm exaggerating, don't you? There's a reason I own *TAGS* on DVD.) Andy was using a phone stuck on the wall in his kitchen to talk with Aunt Bea, who was in Mt. Pilot. In order to let Opie talk to her, Andy had to lift him up to the mouthpiece. When I first started lugging a laptop around the country with me, I felt kind of like Andy and Opie; I had to bring the laptop to the phone if I wanted to connect to the Internet — and the phone wasn't always located in the most comfortable or convenient places.

All that changed for me when truck stops began offering the possibility of making a wire-free connection to the Internet. Suddenly, from almost anywhere in the facilities or on the lot, I could get online easily (what a concept).

I love the freedom afforded me by having the option of making a wireless connection to the Internet — and now, whether you're traveling the highways in a truck or RV, using the facilities of (say) a campground or truck stop, it's possible for you to enjoy that freedom, too.

About This Book

There are, quite literally, millions of books — and they collectively contain more information than any one person could ever hope to comprehend. Just for the sake of argument, though, let's say you had, in fact, both read and comprehended all that information. . . . So what? Knowledge is only half the battle. At some point in time, for knowledge to be an asset, you've got to get up out of your chair, walk out of the classroom, and actually *do* something with that information.

Among this book's goals is a dual purpose: (1) providing you with both the information you need about the whys and wherefores of making a wireless Internet connection in an over-the-road environment, and (2) showing you some ways you can use that knowledge to meet specific Wi-Fi needs in the real world.

By the way, this book does make reference to a lot of Wi-Fi paraphernalia — including hardware, software, and services that can make your over-the-road lifestyle easier, better, or more fun (at least where computers or electronics are concerned). But don't think you absolutely must have everything all at once. I recognize that everyone's needs and desires are different; you might need or want some items now, some later, and some never. I offer all these marvels for your consideration — and I do my best to provide enough information so you can decide whether any product, program, or service deserves a place in your Internet toolbox.

Foolish Assumptions

Ever since I was a kid — after my dad first showed me how the word "assume" breaks down — I've been hesitant to make assumptions, believing them all to be foolish. But I'm going out on a limb here; for the sake of writing a useful book, I assume that

- ✔ You're seriously considering the inclusion of a computer in the list of equipment that accompanies you in your over-the-road travels.

- ✔ Your computing experience ranges from "Yes, I'm aware that computers do exist" to "I use a computer at home and in my business every day."

- ✔ You want to make secure, wire-free connections to the Internet from various locations on or near the highways and byways of our great country.

How This Book Is Organized

I first read John Steinbeck's *The Grapes of Wrath* while in high school and, since that time, I've wanted to write The Great American Novel. This isn't it, but that's okay, because it isn't a novel (great or otherwise), and you don't have to read it like one. If you like, you can start at the end or read the chapters you find most interesting first. The whole book is a beginning, of sorts — and, as such it doesn't really have an ending as long as your over-the-road adventure goes on. (Whoa. Deep.) I did, however, organize the parts and chapters in a way that builds logically, to a certain extent, from one subject to another — so if you're a beginner (or just new to Wi-Fi), you might want to read the book one chapter after the other.

Additionally, even if you're relatively experienced, you might want to read chapters containing information that you're familiar with. After all, in the words of R. Buckminster Fuller, "You can never learn less; you can only learn more."

This book is broken up into seven parts, each part is made up of two to four chapters — and that'd be them coming up now. . . .

Part 1: The Wonderful World of Wireless Fidelity

If you're just getting your feet wet with wireless Internet connectivity, you may have questions ranging from "How does wireless work?" to "How do I get started?" In this part, I help you to

- ✔ Discover the basics of wireless Internet access, as well as ways in which it can enhance your over-the-road computing experience (Chapter 1).
- ✔ Identify the various wireless standards and decide which standard most suits your needs (Chapter 2).
- ✔ Find and buy hardware devices that are especially well suited for use in your over-the-road environment (Chapter 3).
- ✔ Get your wireless gear set up and running smoothly (Chapter 4).

Part 11: Surfing the Net Unplugged

After you've got your gear sorted out and set up, you're ready to surf the Net without wires. In this part, I help you to

- ✔ Identify and use the directories and devices that can get you to friendly locations from which to make a wireless connection to the Internet (Chapter 5).
- ✔ Set up an account, get connected at the hotspot of your choice, and handle issues like troubleshooting and e-mail (Chapter 6).

Part 111: Bridging the Wireless Gap

Even though wireless Internet access is a rapidly spreading phenomenon, there are still a few gaps in coverage. In this part, I take a look at some methods you can use to make an alternate connection. For example, I help you to

- ✔ Discover some ways cellular data services and equipment can help you connect your computer to the Internet when there's not a hotspot — or even a building — in sight (Chapter 7).

✔ Use dialup effectively, efficiently, and enjoyably when it's your only hope of getting connected. I also tell you about a product that can make dialup a lot more convenient to use. (It's all in Chapter 8.)

✔ Explore the potential of using a satellite to make your connection to the Internet (Chapter 9).

Part IV: Securing Your Information

When you've made a wireless Internet connection, it's nice to know there are steps you can take to make it secure. In this part I show you how to

✔ Identify and neutralize threats to your security (Chapter 10).

✔ Easily encrypt your data and information (Chapter 11).

✔ Make a secure connection, from a remote location, to a computer at your home or office (Chapter 12).

Part V: Taking Care of Business

Communication and paperwork are tenets of business — and, by using your computer and the Internet, your over-the-road office can help you be more efficient and increase your profits. In this part, I explore:

✔ Making low-cost calls over the Internet (Chapter 13).

✔ Finding and using various tools that can help you increase your income, save time, save more money, and maintain records (Chapter 14).

Part VI: Entertaining Electronics

You can't spend *all* your time working! In this part, I help you find a few ways to relax and have some fun with your electronic devices. For example, I tell you a little bit about

✔ Getting and using satellite radio (Chapter 15).

✔ A few ways to use your computer as an audio-and-video entertainment center (Chapter 16).

Part VII: The Part of Tens

Every *For Dummies* book includes a Part of Tens, and this one's no exception. In Chapters 17 and 18, I take a look at ten (or so) ways to accessorize your over-the-road electronics and ten free software applications that can enhance your computing experience. Check 'em out.

Conventions Used in This Book

Fortunately, for both you and me, the editors of this book have taken great pains to ensure that certain *conventions* are consistently applied throughout this book. Conventions assist in avoiding confusion by standardizing certain elements of a book. A few of the conventions used here include the following:

✔ New terms — such as *conventions* — are presented in italics and then either defined or explained in the text that follows.

✔ A *URL* (Web address), or anything you need to type into a text-entry field, is presented in monofont; like this: `www.jiwire.com`.

✔ Italics are also used as placeholders in a URL, and might look like this: `www.somewebsite.com`.

✔ Arrows indicate a continuity of activity, usually a sequence of mouse clicks. Choose File⇨New, for example, means to click the File menu and then choose the New option on that menu.

Icons Used in This Book

The Tip icon marks tips (duh!) and shortcuts that you can use to make finding, buying, setting up, or using Wi-Fi-related hardware, software, utilities, or accessories easier.

The Remember icons mark information that's especially important to know. To siphon off the most important information in each chapter, just skim through these icons.

The Technical Stuff icon marks information of a highly technical nature that you can normally skip over (until things get, well, *technical*).

The Warning icon tells you to watch out! It marks information that may save you headaches, heartaches, time, or even money.

Part I
The Wonderful World of Wireless Fidelity

"Yes, it's wireless, and yes, it weighs less than a pound, and yes, it has multiuser functionality...but it's a stapler."

In this part . . .

The central theme is getting set up with all the gear you need to make a wireless Internet connection. Of course, before you dash out the door on your hunt for hardware, you want to have a basic understanding of the way Wi-Fi (wireless fidelity) works. Although my well-informed and highly entertaining sock puppets refused to assist me (something about putting pens in their mouths), I promise that by the time you get done reading Chapters 1 and 2, you'll know more about Wi-Fi than do most people (or sock puppets). Armed with this knowledge (and with the help of Chapter 3), you can plunk down your cash with confidence. After you get your money spent and bring the doodads home, you can use Chapter 4 to get everything set up and fully operational.

Chapter 1

Taking the Wi-Fi Highway

In This Chapter

▶ Discovering Wi-Fi on the highway

▶ Looking at your choices

▶ Breaking down the parts of wireless access

▶ Meeting your over-the-road wireless needs

*E*ven though I think anybody choosing an over-the-road lifestyle has got to have adventurer's, explorer's, or maybe even pirate's blood running through their veins, I appreciate the fact that few are those who blaze new trails through unknown territory. Myself, I'm no Captain Kirk; adventure or not, I prefer to go where at least a few people have gone before. I always get a little nervous when kids come running out of their houses to watch the big truck go by. Well, the Wi-Fi highway's been paved, the kids have become bored with the passing traffic, and it looks like it's here to stay.

If it's new to you, then you might feel a little anxious about taking the on-ramp. Don't be; the weather's great, the curves and slopes are gentle, and the scenery's always interesting. Some parts of the highway — even though it's fairly new — are being repaired and improved upon; other parts, though passable, are still under construction. Just think of me, someone who's been down this road before, as a fellow traveler.

Why Wireless?

In the sociology of science, there are two competing theories regarding technological development. One of them, the *genius theory,* holds the view that inventors or scientists make discoveries independent of any outside influences, just because they're so darn smart. The other theory, known as *deterministic theory,* holds the view that social and environmental forces, the needs and desires of the people, *require* that inventions or discoveries be made, and that the individual making them is incidental to the process.

Personally, I think a combination of genius and environment — both social and technological — must be necessary for invention.

For example, wireless technology — from home phones to cellphones to computers — has been developed (if not by geniuses, then at the very least by people a whole lot smarter than me) in response to the unmet needs and desires of those wishing to roam freely while staying connected. Wireless phone handsets meet the needs of those who want to leave the kitchen or bedroom while conversing; cellphones meet the needs of those desiring freedom of travel while maintaining their ability to reach out and touch — or be touched by — someone. That's environment and genius coming together, meeting the needs of the populace; so it is with Wi-Fi.

Exploring the advantages

I'm thinking that shortly after the first phone cord was connected to a computer (tethering both it and the user to a small and specific radius), somebody — possibly an ungrateful son or a meddling daughter-in-law — began trying to figure out how to cut the cord. When the first laptops hit the market, the movement toward a wireless Internet connection hit high gear. Included among the needs and desires that wireless Internet connection technology strives to meet are the following:

- ✔ **Convenience:** I think this is the most attractive of all wireless Internet attributes. When using a dialup connection, it's sometimes difficult to find a suitable spot from which to connect the cord. Because Wi-Fi does away with the cord or cable, everyplace within range of the wireless access point is suitable for use. (I explain wireless access points later in this chapter.)

- ✔ **Privacy:** To a certain extent, this attribute goes hand-in-hand with freedom and convenience. I've seen RV parks that require dialup computer users to sit in the office or laundry room, and truck stops usually relegate dialup users to a noisy coffee shop or noisier TV room. When using Wi-Fi you can, if you choose, sit comfortably in the privacy of your own home on wheels.

- ✔ **Speed:** Download speeds for wireless broadband Internet connections are typically as much as ten to twenty times faster than dialup. In Chapter 2, I discuss Wi-Fi data-transfer speeds in greater detail.

- ✔ **Ease of use:** Yeah, okay, I hear you: "If it's so easy to use, why do I need a book?" Well, it really is easy to set up and use, but as with anything, there's a learning curve. Besides, I've got to make a living somehow.

- ✔ **Reasonable cost:** If you've already got a laptop or PDA, you can easily and inexpensively adapt it for wireless Internet access. (I tell you more about this in Chapters 3 and 4.) And Internet services, which I talk about in Chapter 6, are usually reasonably priced, too.

So . . . what, no disadvantages?

Well, yes, I have to admit that for all its affirmative attributes, Wi-Fi does have a few disadvantages. Among them, the following three are primary:

- ✔ **Range:** Because of federally mandated power limitations — as well as the attributes of a high-frequency radio signal — Wi-Fi has a limited range. Another factor influencing range is interference; in a truck stop or RV park, that's the usual result when signals are blocked or bounced by trucks, trailers, and other RVs. I discuss increasing effective range in Chapter 3.

- ✔ **Roaming:** Unlike cellphone providers, most of those providing wireless Internet access have no roaming agreements. When, for example, you sign up for service with Flying J, you need to be in or near a Flying J facility in order to access the Internet. Flying J and others do provide access in areas other than their own facilities — and they're working on other solutions as well. You get a look at the details of connecting to hotspots (and examples of different plans) in Chapters 6.

- ✔ **Security:** Okay, you're sending data using a radio signal, which means someone could intercept your transmissions. It is possible, but in Part IV, I discuss in detail methods of maintaining security and privacy.

Examining your options

If the allure of an untethered connection to the Internet beckons you forward, you might wonder about your choices and options. Currently, the primary methods of connecting to the Internet that are free from the tether of a phone cord include the following:

- ✔ **Wi-Fi:** Believe it or not, even though it's fully functional — and its use and availability are rapidly expanding — this technology's still in development. Wi-Fi uses a high-frequency, low-power radio signal to transmit and receive data. To use Wi-Fi, you must be within range of the access point transceiver, which is known as a *hotspot.* I tell you more about this in the next few sections.

- ✔ **High-speed cellular:** On a cellphone, data's often carried separately from voice; usually you need a data-service subscription in addition to your voice-service subscription. I tell you more about cellular data service in Chapter 7.

- ✔ **Satellite:** Requiring the use of some fairly expensive and specialized equipment (not to mention a commitment to a hefty monthly subscription), this option is most popular with those living full-time in their RVs. I tell you more about satellite Internet in Chapter 9.

Taking the plunge

Of all the options available to you, the easiest and least expensive method of making a wireless connection to the Internet is Wi-Fi. In order to get started down the Wi-Fi highway, you need the following:

- **Wi-Fi-enabled computer:** There are two methods for enabling a laptop or PDA for use in a wireless environment:

    - *Wi-Fi adapter:* By using an inexpensive adapter, wireless capability can be added to almost every laptop and most PDA devices. I tell you more about finding adapters in Chapter 3 and more about setting them up in Chapter 4.

    - *Integrated card:* Most new laptop computers, and quite a few PDA devices, come equipped with a built-in wireless card. If you're shopping for a new computer, I give you some helpful hints in Chapter 3.

- **Hotspot proximity:** You need to be within the coverage area of the radio transceiver, or access point, that has a wired or satellite connection to the Internet. (I introduce hotspots in the "What the heck is a hotspot?" section later in this chapter, and Chapter 5 explains how you can find them.)

- **Wireless Internet service provider:** Better known as and often referred to as a WISP, most hotspot operators are WISPs or they contract with WISPs for service. In most cases, you can buy an hourly, daily, monthly, or annual subscription to a WISP — as you discover in Chapter 6.

The Nuts and Bolts of Wi-Fi

To put it very simply, Wi-Fi uses a two-way radio signal instead of wires to complete the connection between your computer and the wired connection to the Internet. Also, instead of using slow dialup, the business end of a wireless Internet connection is usually high-speed DSL, cable, or T-1 line.

CB radios for computers

Sometime in the late '50s or early '60s, a couple of truckers stuck CB radios in their rigs so they could irritate each other while heading down the highway. Obviously, for radio communication to occur, both drivers had to install radios — and each radio had to be capable of both transmitting and receiving a signal. Such is the case with Wi-Fi. A few of the attributes and elements of Wi-Fi radios are as follows:

- ✔ **Transceiver:** The ability to both transmit and receive as well as the ability to set and determine the circumstances under which each task is to be performed.

- ✔ **Antenna:** As with a CB radio, the antenna must be capable of both receiving and transmitting a signal in a specific bandwidth. Most antennas are integrated into wireless cards, but in some cases, it's possible to add an external antenna. (I talk more about antennas in Chapters 3 and 4.)

- ✔ **Code/Decode:** Known as a *codec,* this is the method by which (among other things) digital data is converted into a radio signal and vice versa.

- ✔ **Spread-spectrum signal:** High-frequency radio signals used by Wi-Fi are both low-powered and susceptible to interference. Wide-band, spread-spectrum radio signals aren't as sensitive to interference as narrow-band signals — and they're quite efficient at getting the most out of the limited power. They also help in avoiding traffic jams among radio signals, which makes it possible for several Wi-Fi transceivers to operate at the same time.

What have an actress and composer got to do with Wi-Fi?

For all of you who believe the abilities of entertainers begin and end with their musical or acting talents, read this: Just prior to the American entry into World War II, George Antheil, an American composer, and Hedy Kiesler Markey — better known by her stage name, Hedy Lamarr — got into a discussion over dinner regarding torpedo guidance. Seems like standard entertainer table talk. Ms. Lamarr, who'd been married to an Austrian arms merchant, was interested in the problems surrounding torpedo guidance, and Mr. Antheil understood multichannel synchronization (It's a long story, involving propellers and player pianos). Together they developed — and in August 1942 were granted a patent for — what they called a "Secret Communication System." They hoped the SCS would eliminate,

through the use of "frequency hopping," the possibility that the enemy might jam torpedo radio-guidance systems.

Frequency-hopping technology, which couldn't be used until radio technology caught up to it in the early '60s, formed the foundation for the spread-spectrum radio transmissions that all the Wi-Fi standards use. The first 802.11 standard employed frequency-hopping spread spectrum (FHSS), and the 802.11b standard uses direct-sequence spread spectrum (DSSS). Building on these concepts, orthogonal frequency-division multiplexing (OFDM), on which the 802.11g standard is based, was developed and implemented. (Try saying *that* five times fast.)

What the heck is a hotspot?

The basic definition of a *hotspot* is a wireless local-access network (WLAN) that's open to the public. So, what, you ask, is a WLAN? It is — and I'll never understand why the acronym gods didn't call it a LAWN — nothing more than two or more computers networked together using Wi-Fi. There are two primary types of WLANs:

- ✔ **Ad-hoc:** Also known as *peer-to-peer networks,* computers in an ad-hoc WLAN communicate with each other directly. By switching your Wi-Fi cards to ad-hoc mode, you and a nearby neighbor can create a WLAN to play games, for example.

- ✔ **Infrastructure:** This is the type of WLAN all hotspots use. It's also the most commonly used form of WLAN in home or business and is sometimes referred to as a *client-server* WLAN. There are two basic elements to an infrastructure WLAN, as shown in Figure 1-1.

    - *Client:* Any computer included in the WLAN, accessing the Internet via the access point, is known as a *client.*

    - *Access point:* An *access point* is a Wi-Fi transceiver that's connected directly or by satellite to the Internet. The access point serves, or distributes, the Internet connection to the client computers within the network.

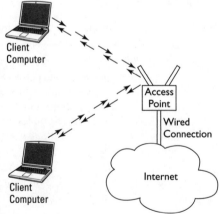

Figure 1-1:
Two client computers communicate with the access point, which connects to the Internet.

Hotspots are WLANs open to the public, but you typically need to provide a password before you can open a hotspot's gateway to the Internet. You can think of an access point like a castle that freely drops the drawbridge over the moat, allowing entry into the gateway tunnel, but opening the gate to the interior only after the visitor gives the proper password.

Deciding on the Best Route

One thing I've found in my experience with over-the-road types is that everybody's situation is vastly different. Because of that, I'm not likely to come up with a universal solution to the question of how long any Wi-Fi subscription should be, which WISP you should subscribe to, whether you should maintain a dialup account, or whether you should choose to sign up with a cellular carrier for data service.

What I *can* do is give you as much information as possible so that, hopefully, it'll become clear which route is the most beneficial and economical to you. I can also get you started in your decision process.

If you're a trucker

For years upon years, I've been told by countless truckers that they don't spend much time in truck stops. Right. All those trucks I see clogging the lots must be mirages, merely Fig Newtons of my amalgamation. Face it; trucks stop at truck stops. You and I might *prefer* to spend time elsewhere, but the last time I checked, almost no one else wants a truck parked in their lots any longer than it takes to unload the products necessary for them to do business.

That means a truck stop WISP will probably provide you with the best Wi-Fi service. Still, depending on whether you haul peaches or couches, the plan and provider best suited to you might be drastically different. For example, are you a trucker . . .

- ✔ **With a dedicated route?** If you haul the same freight over the same route week after week, year after year, it's likely that you make the same stops. Are the truck stops you frequent all in the same chain? If they are, signing up for an annual Wi-Fi subscription can save you some money over the long term. If your stops run the gamut of travel plaza chains, could you alter your stops so that an annual subscription might be feasible?

- ✔ **Traveling far and wide?** If you're never heading in the same direction two weeks in a row, or you rarely spend three nights a week in a truck stop of the same chain, you might consider paying for Wi-Fi by the day, using dialup as a backup. If, however, you can plan to be in a position to use the same WISP three or four nights a week, you can save a few bucks by signing up for a monthly or annual plan. (I talk more about using dialup as a backup in Chapter 8.)

- ✔ **Hauling over-dimensional loads?** Having hauled over-dimensional freight (think WIDE LOAD), I know how hard it can be to park within sight of the facilities. Because that's where the access point is most often located, you might be parked, quite often, too far away to make a connection. If that's the case, you might want to investigate a high-speed cell data plan. (See Chapter 7 for more information.)

The level of Internet access that you *require* each day, week, or month is a primary consideration in determining the type and level of wireless Internet service you subscribe to. If, for example, you check your e-mail or surf the Net a couple of times a week, you might want to pay by the day. You also might, however, want to spin through the chapters in Parts V and VI for ways to get more use out of your computer and the Internet.

In Chapter 6, among other things, I compare the plans and costs offered by the major truck stop WISPs. Surprisingly, some of the most competitively priced and widely available Wi-Fi in the nation is provided by the truck-stop and travel-plaza chains.

If you're an RVer

How you use your RV as well as the frequency with which you need access to the Internet are the two most important considerations when determining how wireless Internet access fits into your plans. The type and level of service best suited to your needs is different depending on whether (for example) you're

- ✔ **On vacation:** If you're only away from home for a couple of weeks, or maybe, a month, it makes no sense whatsoever to sign up with a single service for more than one or two days. Using dialup as a back-up, though, does make sense — so you might want to check out Chapter 8 for some ideas about getting the most out of dialup on the road.

- ✔ **On an extended trip:** For trips longer than a month, it might be worth your while to plan your trip in such a way that you can take advantage of a month-to-month subscription. In Chapter 5, I tell you about some ways to find RV-friendly hotspots, and in Chapter 6, I provide information about the major WISPs servicing RV parks and campgrounds.

- ✔ **Living in your RV:** Especially if you need consistent and regular access to the Internet, you might well consider investing in a satellite Internet system, which I cover in Chapter 9.

Chapter 2

Selecting a Standard

*W*henever I deal with computer-related technology, I'm constantly confronted with a confusing array of choices filled with ever-present abbreviations, acronyms, and standards. It sometimes seems (at least to me) that the menu of available solutions far exceeds the corresponding list of problems. If the problem is (say) lunch, sooner or later you have to order up — and that means finding your way around the menu.

That's why this chapter helps you decide which wireless standard best suits your over-the-road needs. Along with demystifying the mind-numbing menagerie of wireless standards you face, I explain how you can be sure any and all of the equipment you buy will work wherever you go. I'll also help you separate the wheat from the chaff when you're deciding on a standard.

Matching Purpose to Standard

Okay, a word about *standards:* They're guidelines that keep computer equipment and software reasonably consistent in the way they work. That's why (for example) you can make a good wireless connection regardless of who made your equipment. It makes good sense to use the standard that best meets your needs. And that means paying attention to some everyday details.

When I'm faced with a myriad of choices, I find it helpful to first focus on my purpose — the goal I'm trying to achieve or the problem I'm trying to solve. After that's clearly identified, I can investigate various ways to meet those goals and solve those problems. For example, when I'm picking up freight requiring multiple deliveries, I've got to load it so the last product on is the first product off. But I've also got to load it so each set of axles is weighted in accordance with laws and standards. The first order of business is to get loaded; but how do you decide what part of the problem to tackle first?

Defining your primary purpose

I'm going to guess that at least one reason (likely the primary reason) you're interested in Wi-Fi is that you want to connect to the Internet from the quiet and comfort of your truck or RV. You want to browse the Web, send and receive e-mail, or conduct business without the noise and distraction of a coffeehouse or restaurant.

So, if that's the case (I'll go out on a limb and assume it is), then your primary goal is to connect to the Internet, from nearly anywhere, minus the quarter-mile of telephone cord. Yeah, that was my main goal, too — but a few other qualifying factors also enter into consideration. Those pesky industry standards, for example. . . .

Identifying secondary goals

A tale from days of old — before personal computers (hard to believe, isn't it?) — shows how technology standards can influence your goals. Back when home video was just starting to catch on, two competing standards fought to dominate the videocassette market: Beta and VHS. Beta produced higher-quality images than VHS, but VHS became the most widely accepted standard — for reasons that had nothing to do with image quality.

Both VHS and Beta fulfilled the primary purpose — transferring video to tape — but as VHS became more common, producers stopped putting out Beta versions of their movies. It was far more likely, then inevitable, that anything you rented, borrowed, bought, or lent would be VHS. Beta (with its high quality) was doomed. At that point, secondary considerations influenced the choice between Beta and VHS: You had to put up with somewhat lower video quality to have home video at all, because VHS was *available* and *compatible* with most equipment on the market.

Okay, back to the future (that is, now): As wireless-connection equipment crops up everywhere, standards are all over the map — and going through their own struggle for dominance. So here are a couple of questions you'll want to answer for yourself as you settle on a Wi-Fi standard:

✔ **Where will you be using your wireless connection?** If you're using only the hotspots in places like truck stops, coffee shops, motels, or RV parks, then you can narrow your standard choices pretty drastically. If you'll be mixing your use between highway, home, and office, you'll need a standard that can handle all three. You'll also need to make certain that any equipment you purchase conforms to a standard that's in wide use and is *interoperable* (that is, plays nice) with other equipment that conforms to the same standard.

✔ **Will you be using Wi-Fi for purposes other than connecting to the Internet?** If connecting to the Internet to use e-mail or download basic travel information is your one and only goal, then you'll probably choose a different standard than you would if (for example) you were looking to get into head-to-head gaming or transferring large files (such as music or video) from one computer to another.

Answering questions like these can give you a good grasp on why you want wireless capabilities in your life in the first place. Then you can move ahead with selecting a Wi-Fi standard that does the job for you.

Focusing on the Front-Runners

Although approximately 13 standards for wireless connectivity exist, fortunately, you don't need to become familiar with each and every standard. As you delve deeper into the wireless world, the standards referenced most often are 802.11a, 802.11b and 802.11g. Another standard that you'll run across — yet to be ratified but lurking on the horizon — is 802.11n. These four standards define the protocols and specifications used to transfer data via radio signals — so they're the only ones for which you need a good working knowledge. Here's the short course:

✔ The 802.11a standard specifies operation in the 5.0GHz band.

✔ The 802.11b, g, and n standards specify operation in the 2.4GHz frequency band.

✔ Because 802.11a operates at a higher frequency, it has a shorter range and it's more likely to be adversely affected by obstructions. Consequently, this standard has found its niche in the wall-free world of corporate cubicles.

So which of these standards can do the job for you? Well, the following sections offer a brief rundown of the major attributes of the standards you'll encounter most often.

By getting a basic handle on standards, you can make better choices when you're buying wireless gear. Armed with the information in this chapter, you can march to Chapter 3 for details of getting geared up.

802.11a: Connecting over short distances

This standard covers the 5GHz band; devices that comply with it are incompatible with the 2.4GHz-band b, g, and n standards. 802.11a is most commonly found in businesses that require a high-speed wireless network connection to transfer files between desktop or laptop computers. If your primary goal is connecting to the Internet at hotspots — without getting all business-obsessed about it — you can safely ignore this standard.

802.11b: Opting for the basic standard

802.11b is the standard that started the boom — and it's best-suited for connecting to the Internet or for streaming audio or video.

- ✔ The theoretical maximum *bandwidth* (in effect, how fast data can be transferred or transmitted) is 11 Mbps (See the following section for a detailed explanation.)
- ✔ This is the standard hotspots currently use most often.
- ✔ Both the 802.11g and 802.11n standards are, or will be, backward-compatible with this standard.

  Backward compatibility — a requirement of the 802.11 standard — means that any new versions must be designed to work and play well with older versions.

802.11g: The speedier standard

Ratified in 2003, this standard is quickly becoming the favorite for folks setting up home networks (and yes, a RV counts as "home" — but you knew that).

- ✔ The theoretical maximum bandwidth is 54 Mbps.
- ✔ It's most commonly found in home or business networks as well as newly established hotspots. Some owners of established hotspots are upgrading aging 802.11b equipment with new equipment that conforms to 802.11g as well.
- ✔ It's backward-compatible with the 802.11b standard.
- ✔ 802.11g is, maybe, more than a home user needs, but it's still well-suited for connecting to the Internet for basic information. It also gets high

marks for streaming audio and video, head-to-head gaming, and transfer-ring large files between computers on the same network.

✔ You can also go for 802.11g "enhanced." This is sometimes called *pre-n*, *enhanced g*, and by proprietary names such as SpeedBooster, Super G, Xtreme G, and so on. It isn't a standard in its own right; rather, it's a variation of the 802.11g standard.

- Theoretical maximum advertised speeds up to 108 Mbps.

- Most often found in home networks.

- Generally compatible with the 802.11b and g standards, although it's not ideal for use in mixed-standard environments (the enhanced abilities are usually lost).

  If a hotspot uses, say, an access point conforming to 802.11g, but client computers that conform to 802.11b, g, or even "enhanced g" can still connect to it, it's a *mixed-standard environment*.

- It's best-suited for use in integrated "enhanced-g" networks. It's overkill for a basic Internet connection, but it shines at handling streaming audio and video, gaming, and huge file transfers.

Connecting 802.11b and g devices in the same network won't adversely affect the speed of b-standard devices, but it will slow down the general performance of the g-standard devices.

The difference in price between 802.11b- and 802.11g-standard equipment is negligible. The use and popularity of the 802.11g standard is also beginning to eclipse the older 802.11b standard. For these reasons — and because it offers faster speeds in certain situations — 802.11g seems to be dominating in availability, compatibility, and utility.

802.11n: Looking to the future

This yet-to-be-ratified standard specifies a data-transfer rate of 100 Mbps — equaling that of the wired Ethernet networks businesses use today. It will be backward-compatible with both b and g.

Ensuring Compliance and Compatibility

Technology isn't all innovation — when you get to the marketplace, it's also about consistent quality. You have to be able to trust it to do what it was

Who's in charge here?

My guess is that as soon as the second computer was completed, someone started figuring out how to get the first one to communicate with it. It's also a pretty good bet that if any two separate engineers developed devices to do that job, the widgets they built would be completely different and entirely incompatible. After all, computer engineers are resourceful and innovative — in every possible direction. How else could they come up with so many different ways to achieve a single goal? Well, a quick spin down the byway of history can clarify how we got to this point.

Fortunately, the engineers themselves have long recognized the importance of achieving not only solutions to problems, but also solutions that work and play well together.

Problems of compatibility (and their solutions) go way back. In 1963, the American Institute of Electrical Engineers (AIEE) and the Institute of Radio Engineers (IRE) merged to form the Institute of Electronics and Electrical Engineers (IEEE). It would be difficult to imagine a better-qualified group leading the charge to set technology standards that serve as the foundation for developing a wide variety of compatible computer-related devices.

The task of creating the first wireless standard was placed in the capable hands of an IEEE working group laboring under the name (well, okay, number) 802.11. In 1997, when the structure of the first standard was fully defined, developed and ratified, the working group, beaming with the pride of a proud papa, named it after themselves.

A couple of years later, with the birth (just as proudly announced) of the fraternal twins 802.11a and 802.11b, the alphabet soup of standards was well on its way to rivaling the confusion brought about by naming all the sons in the Foreman family George.

Actually, each letter refers to a smaller group within the 802.11 working-group, assigned the task of expanding and enhancing, in very specific ways, the specifications of the original 802.11 standard. To date 13 different task groups, ranging from 802.11a to 802.11n, have been formed.

Okay, I can see you flipping fingers up as you go through the alphabet, and those of you with your socks off have discovered that from *a* to *n* there are 14 letters. This is true. There will never be an 802.11 l; that's to avoid the possibility of confusing the letter *l* with the letter *i* and the number *1*.

designed to do. For instance, when I was a kid my mom and dad wouldn't think of buying a lamp or toaster without the world-famous Underwriters Laboratories seal of approval. UL developed, and still develops safety standards for a wide variety of products — and then certifies, through extensive product testing, that manufacturers meet those standards. By purchasing products certified safe by Underwriters Laboratories, my folks could rest assured that unless our Dachshund chewed through a cord, my sister and I wouldn't be zapped out of existence. Products that merited UL certification also had to be of good-enough quality to keep it. Well, where quality and certification are concerned, the world of Wi-Fi is no less in need of a watchdog organization.

Wireless networking was just starting to peek out of the corporate box at the end of the last century. So, to promote wireless networking by giving the public some confidence in the products they purchased, the computer industry formed a trade group known as the Wireless Ethernet Compatibility Alliance (WECA) in 1999. WECA certifies that products manufactured under various wireless standards have the specs to meet those standards — and that they're interoperable with each other.

Somewhere along the line some sharp individual got the bright idea to trademark the catchy name *Wi-Fi*. One thing led to another and, presto change-o, WECA became the Wi-Fi Alliance — new name, same job. Wi-Fi Certified products can be identified by looking for the Wi-Fi CERTIFIED logo, shown in Figure 2-1.

Figure 2-1:
The Wi-Fi
Certified
logo.

The logo also includes a bit of information concerning which standard the device meets and with which standards the device is compatible. Here's the gist:

✔ Products displaying the Wi-Fi CERTIFIED logo are guaranteed to be interoperable with other Wi-Fi CERTIFIED products built to the same or compatible standards.

✔ Products built to the 802.11a standard (which doesn't specify compatibility with any other standard) don't have to be compatible with those built to the 802.11g standard in order to be Wi-Fi certified.

✔ Products built to the 802.11g standard must be compatible with 802.11b. In addition, because the Wi-Fi Alliance has certified their compliance with the g standard, they're guaranteed to interoperate with b-standard products.

Speed Limits on the Cyberhighway

It's true: After you finish a day of driving on our nation's actual streets and highways — wisely restricted by various speed limits — you'll be facing similar limits on the cyberhighway. Unlike federal, state, and local authorities, however, the people in charge of the cyberhighway are constantly searching for ways to let us go *faster*.

What limits speed on the cyberhighway is the performance limit of internal protocols and the wireless environment. So here's a look at a few things that limit speed — and a way to put it all into perspective: comparing real-world speeds with typical Internet-connection speeds.

Measuring speeds in cyberspace

You can measure your speed on the highway by looking at a speedometer indexed in miles per hour, kilometers per hour, or (sometimes) both. Traveling at sixty miles per hour means you're covering a distance of 1,056 inches every second — and, because you can easily tell an inch from a mile, this measurement has meaning.

Data-transmission rates are commonly measured in *bits per second* (bps). So what's a bit? It's both symbolic and real: In mathematical terms, it's either a 1 or a 0; in electrical terms, it's a state of being (respectively) either on or off.

By its lonesome, a bit is pretty insignificant — but if you put eight bits together in a string, you get a *byte* — and then there are 256 possible combinations of ones and zeros. That's enough to represent all the individual letters, numbers, spaces, and symbols necessary for communication.

It takes 32 bits of data (that is, 4 bytes), to represent a number such as 5828, the number on the front of my house. If you wanted me to put a comma between the 5 and the first 8, however, it would take eight more bits — another byte — and I'd have to head for the hardware store to look for a copper comma.

Now, the 802.11b standard specifies a data-transmission rate of 11 Mbps — and the *M* represents *mega* (a million). 11 Mbps, then, means data can be transmitted at a rate of *eleven million bits per second*. If you put that in terms of inches per second, that'd be like traveling down the highway at a speed of 625,000 miles per hour. (Oh yeah, that'd be a ticket.)

K (kilo) or *M* (mega) can be used in reference to communication or storage — and there's a slight difference in the value that depends on how it's used. When I'm talking about data-transmission rate, *kilo* means *one thousand* and *Mega* means *one million*. If, however, I'm talking about a storage device — say, your hard drive — then *kilo* refers to *1024* and *mega* refers to *1,048,576*.

A small *b* used in an abbreviation refers to a bit; a capital *B* represents a byte.

Comparing advertised and actual wireless speeds

So you're thinking that the 11Mbps speed of 802.11b is pretty fast, right? Yeah, me too — but that's a *theoretical* maximum speed. 11 Mbps won't be the *actual* speed at which data is sent. No, it isn't a matter of truth in advertising. Not exactly, anyway. Here's why:

✔ **The data isn't all that's traveling.** A whole bunch of those bits being blasted through the air form a virtual envelope, a sort of logical container known as a *packet*. Your data is broken down into chunks, placed in these packets, and sent. Each packet includes a lot of information about where the data came from, where it's going, how to reassemble it, and so on. Believe it or not, this extra information — known as *protocol overhead* — can take up 30 or 40 percent of the data stream.

✔ **Speed varies depending on the environment the signal is traveling through.** The actual speed may, for a number of reasons, drop to as little as 1 Mbps. Due to distance or interference, the quality of the signal might not be sufficient to support a bandwidth of 11 Mbps. In that case, the specifications of the standard mandate the use of *dynamic rate shifting* — which cuts the transmission speed in half, to 5.5 Mbps. If the conditions still aren't sufficient to support the 5.5Mbps speed, then the data gets slowed down (by dynamic rate shifting) until it reaches a data-transmission rate that can be supported.

When all is said and done, no matter which standard you end up utilizing, you shouldn't count on achieving more than 50 percent of the theoretical maximum data-transmission rate. In reality it'll probably be even less than that. Okay, now that I've got you sufficiently bummed out, I've got some good news (no, I didn't save a bundle on insurance): A real-world speed of 4, 3, 2 or even 1 Mbps is still faster than you'll probably need for most of the things you're going to want to do with Wi-Fi — such as (for example) connecting to the Internet.

Comparing common Internet-connection speeds

Many moons ago (ah, to be younger, dumber, and blessed with more hair), I tried connecting my laptop to the Internet by using my cellphone as a dialup modem. I fried phone after phone before I finally gave up on that idea. Why the fry (sorry about that)? The main reason was that the Internet download speeds were only 19 Kbps. That was good enough for e-mail, but if I wanted to surf the Net, I was out of luck: The simplest of Web sites appeared at glacial speed, if at all. (On more than one occasion, I fell asleep while waiting.)

My cellphone created a bottleneck through which data, no matter how fast it'd been moving before it got to my phone, could only travel at no more than 19 Kbps.

No matter how fast any part of a connection might be, the overall speed of the *entire* connection will be limited to the slowest portion.

It's a pretty safe bet that the greatest limit on the performance you experience with Wi-Fi will be the method used to connect the hotspot's access point to the Internet. Here's a look at the most common connection scenarios:

- ✔ **Dialup:** Most of you are probably familiar with the earliest of Internet connection methods. I, at one time, had a dialup connection rated at 28 Kbps (some of the earliest were between 7 and 10 Kbps), but for the most part, dialup connections move data at a maximum rate of 56 Kbps.

- ✔ **Broadband:** Taking the form of a cable or DSL connection, broadband speeds are typically in the 700Kbps range. Whenever I've checked my cable connection speed, I've found it varies quite a bit. The lowest rate I measured was 238 Kbps — and the highest was 768 Kbps. The DSL providers in my area offer similar speeds.

- ✔ **Satellite:** Also known as Very Small Aperture Terminal (VSAT), a connection via satellite can take on many forms. Depending on the carrier and connection plan, connection speeds can range from around 500 Kbps to as high as 2 Mbps.

- ✔ **T-1 line:** Although not at the absolute top of the heap when it comes to speed, a T-1 connection moves data at a pretty respectable rate — 1.544 Mbps. These connections can be pretty speedy; they're found, most commonly, as a connection for hotspots and businesses.

There are a few other, faster, methods of connecting to the Internet — but the chances that you'll ever run across a hotspot using one of them (say, a T-3 or OC3 connection) is about equal to my chances of winning the Daytona 500 or the Kentucky Derby: Don't hold your breath.

Anyway, most hotspots you'll encounter, like truck stops and large RV parks, use either a high-speed satellite connection or a T-1 line as the method of connecting the main access point to the Internet. Some of the smaller mom-and-pop-operated hotspots, though, often employ a broadband cable or DSL connection. For now, at least, it does the job. We'll probably laugh about it one of these days.

Picking the Standard That Meets Your Needs

Here we get back to the issues raised in the first portion of this chapter: After you've identified your primary reason for wanting a wireless connection — and reviewed what the various standards can (and can't) do for you, you can make an informed decision among the standards and choose one that works.

Here are some examples of identified needs and the standards that best meet those needs:

- ✔ **Connecting to the Internet at a hotspot.** Almost every hotspot is connected to the Internet at a rate no faster than about 1.5 Mbps. For that reason, most of them utilize equipment (such as access points and antennas) built around the 802.11b standard. Taking this into consideration, 802.11b starts to look like the standard most likely to meet your needs if your primary objective is making a basic connection to the Internet.

- ✔ **Hotspot Internet connections and connecting within a home network.** Because many home networks are built around the 802.11g standard (and considering that 802.11g is backward-compatible with the 802.11b standard in use at most wireless hotspots), it follows that the 802.11g standard might well be a good choice here.

Of course, you're not necessarily locked in to any one standard for all the ways you use the Internet. Take a look at Chapter 3 to see the ways a laptop can be adapted for more than one standard.

Chapter 3

Gearing Up

● ●

In This Chapter

▶ Evaluating your OTR environment

▶ Choosing a laptop or a PDA

▶ Picking out a wireless adapter

▶ Extending wireless capacity

● ●

*J*oining in the fun and excitement of the Wi-Fi revolution may mean purchasing some really cool computer gear. If you're like me, just the thought of buying computer-related equipment sends shivers of excitement down your spine. (I even get those shivers at the thought of *you* buying some cool stuff.)

In this chapter, I help you shop for your gear by pointing out the major pieces of equipment you need, as well as any features you should look for. I look at ways to integrate the two most travel-friendly PCs — laptop and handheld — into the freedoms and limitations of your over-the-road surroundings, and enhance their capabilities to meet your needs better.

Surveying Your Needs Before You Shop

Before you run off to the CompuMart, take some time to think about what equipment will best suit your over-the-road computing needs. (For example, look at Chapters 13 and 14 if you're still trying to figure out what those needs are!) With your computing requirements in mind, think about matching the conditions of your over-the-road (OTR) environment to the characteristics of the equipment.

Because you're traveling the highways in a vehicle that affords you more room than those poor unfortunates trapped in the confines of an airplane seat, your criteria for choosing a computing device and accessories will be less constrained than theirs. You can have that laptop that weighs ten pounds *and* sports a wide screen. You don't need to limit yourself to a tiny ultra-portable; you can have a big, full-featured, truck-size *desktop replacement.*

On the other hand, no matter the size of your rig, perhaps you've already got stuff crammed into every nook, cranny, and cubbyhole. You've got a TV and DVD player. You always seem to park so far from the truck-stop coffee shop that you've considered strapping a scooter to the frame. Or you just don't want *another* shoulder-strap bag to carry into the truck stop or motel. But you do want access to e-mail *and* browse the Web — so the Personal Digital Assistant (PDA) might be just what you're looking for.

Of course, choosing between laptop and PDA is just one piece of the puzzle. You also need to think about issues and equipment that affect wireless connectivity and usability. When it's decision time, size up the contenders and their offerings by how they fit with your honest evaluation of your workspaces and habits. The following list can help you sift the details:

- **Durability:** Whatever equipment you choose to use will be doing duty in an OTR environment; make certain that it'll stand up to the job. The device doesn't need to be armor-plated, but do some research into make, model, and manufacturer reputation for durability.

  Laptops and PDAs are designed for travel, but durability isn't necessarily a given. Over the years, I've found the reviews, user ratings, and opinions at Web sites such as www.cnet.com and www.epinions.com to be excellent tools for judging roadworthiness.

- **Adaptability:** Whether you're adapting a device, laptop or palmtop for wireless, GPS, or any other function, you'll need expandability via various slots and ports. Most laptops have at least one PCMCIA slot and two USB ports — but twice as many would be really nice. The minimum requirement for a PDA is a single Secure Digital or Compact Flash Type II slot. If you can get both, great — and if you can get a USB port, even better! (I dig into Wi-Fi adaptability later in this chapter, under the heading "Adapting Your Laptop or PDA for Wireless"; Chapter 13 tackles GPS.)

  Even if you choose a computer with built-in Wi-Fi, you may have to use a wireless adapter when you're on the road. Here's why: Integrated wireless capability has proven more than adequate for use in busy airports and coffee shops, where you often find those same fine folks from Silicon Valley who designed 'em (coincidence? I think not). Apparently they never figured out that some travelers enjoy a wireless Internet connection while relaxing in the bunk of a truck or reclining on a couch in an RV — sometimes parked in the back forty.

- **Compatibility:** Any device you choose has to be completely compatible with *every* aspect of your OTR environment — not only the 802.11b/g standards in use at the various hotspots, but also with *you*. Before buying anything — whether PDA or laptop — give it a good going over at a local retailer. Type on the keyboard, maneuver the mouse, and use as many of the features (those enabled by the store, anyway) as you possibly can. It's your money; make sure you're spending it on something you really like.

- **Usefulness:** Most likely, you'll want to extend computer use beyond just staying in touch. You can equip a laptop or PDA with a host of software and components, ranging from voice recognition to GPS. Do you want to watch DVDs? With a DVD drive, a large, wide-aspect-ratio LCD screen, and a set of external speakers, your laptop becomes a home theater. Or maybe you want to play games or catch up on your bills. Your computer is a useful tool, but with some imagination, it can be a whole lot more.

- **Convenience:** It's entirely possible to get excited about a product that may not be as convenient as one would hope. A good example of this might be an outdoor mounted directional antenna. (I tell you more about antennas in a later section, "Extending Your Range.") While the performance of one of these antennas might be outstanding, consider whether you'll *really* want to set it up after a long day of driving.

- **Memory and storage capacity:** More is better, especially when it comes to laptops. It's possible to get by with minimum requirements, but most people quickly outgrow a laptop system that's configured with only 128 MB of RAM (Random-Access Memory) and a hard drive holding no more than 20 GB. Look for at least 64 MB of RAM in a PDA. (I talk about PDA memory and storage in the section headed "Keeping Life Compact with a PDA," later in this chapter.)

The speed and capacity of your laptop's RAM (Random-Access Memory) will have a greater impact on its overall performance than any other factor. If you're considering the purchase of a laptop and you're going to splurge on any one item, choose to buy more RAM.

You may have noticed that I haven't mentioned desktop computers for use in a truck or RV. There's a good reason for this. Aside from the room they take up, desktop PCs are designed for use in a stationary home environment. Unless you live on the San Andreas Fault, they're not likely to move around much, let alone be subjected to the jolts and vibrations of highway travel. A few diehard folks have tried using a desktop in a truck or RV — you can too, if you really insist — but by and large, resist the urge.

Living Large with a Laptop

If you find yourself interested in purchasing a laptop, you're not alone. Laptop sales have skyrocketed, surpassing those of desktops, as more and more people are finding themselves attracted to the convenience of a truly portable computer. After seeing an ever-increasing number of people in truck stops toting laptops or PDAs, I made the decision to purchase a laptop of my own.

Initially, my anticipated computer use didn't extend far beyond maintaining e-mail communication with my family and friends. Even though I was really excited to join the ranks of laptop-toting truckers, there was no way I envisioned just how indispensable my portable PC would become. Before I knew it, I'd found tons of things I could do with my laptop and I couldn't imagine leaving home without it. For example, besides just e-mailing and Web surfing, I use my laptop to

✔ **Download music:** And, after amassing quite an eclectic collection, I can burn some *really* entertaining CDs. (More about this in Chapter 16.)

✔ **Maintain my OTR office:** With the addition of a few software applications, I can find freight, keep a digital log book, balance my checkbook, pay my bills, budget my income, and file my income tax returns. I can even use my laptop as a phone. (Find out more about these subjects in Chapters 13 and 14.)

✔ **Find destinations:** I used to call every shipper and receiver that I hadn't previously visited to get directions. After installing a GPS receiver and mapping software, I've saved a ton of cellphone minutes that are better used calling people I really want to talk with (even some who want to speak with me!). I still make occasional calls to confirm appointments but directions are a done deal. (More about GPS in Chapter 14.)

✔ **Watch movies on DVD:** I don't download a lot of movies but I do rent quite a few from Netflix. It usually works out pretty well. I take the movies with me, drop 'em in the mail after viewing, and when I get home, new ones are waiting. Blockbuster has a similar online service.

If you're considering the purchase of a laptop as a way to enhance the enjoyment of time spent traveling the highways, take a look at the next sections for ideas to keep in mind while shopping.

Ensuring wireless capability

It's hard to find a new laptop these days that doesn't come with integrated 802.11b or 802.11g wireless capability (check out Chapter 2 for a full explanation of wireless standards) — built-in wireless isn't a strict necessity. Almost every laptop has a standard PCMCIA (PC card) slot or USB port that allows easy adaptation to wireless connectivity. Chances are good that the laptop you choose will be equipped with multiple PC card slots and USB ports. Not that you *need* a whole bunch of slots and ports to get connected the wireless way, but having 'em can work to your advantage.

For example, using a wireless adapter that fits into one of your PC's extra slots can actually improve your ability to access a wireless signal. When you're parked in a space far, far away from the access point, the Wi-Fi signal may be too weak for your integrated wireless to detect. If you plug a more powerful adapter card into an extra laptop slot, you can probably pull in those weak signals. (So what kind of adapter card do you need? Glad you asked! Check the criteria for choosing a wireless adapter in "Adapting Your Laptop or PDA for Wireless," later in this chapter.)

Employing a Wi-Fi-friendly operating system

Windows XP with Service Pack 2 (SP2) is the operating system you really want installed on your laptop. Could you get by with Windows 98, SE, ME or 2000? You could but XP does everything the older systems do, with regard to wireless Internet access, and much more. Additionally, many wireless adapters and security programs aren't compatible with the older operating systems.

By employing Windows XP with SP2 as your operating system you assure yourself that the hardware or software you purchase, at least for the foreseeable future, will be compatible with your system. And Windows SP2 provides an enhanced security infrastructure that defends against viruses, worms and hackers.

Here's one thing to keep in mind: Windows XP requires more memory than do the Windows 98, SE, ME or 2000 operating systems. Microsoft indicates that you need a minimum of 128MB of RAM to run Windows XP, but my recommendation is that you consider 256MB to be your rock bottom minimum.

Purposeful laptop abuse tests durability

A couple of years ago, a PC-focused magazine tested a handful of laptops to determine which would stand up to the most abuse. Innocent and unsuspecting laptops got dropped from a desk, frozen, cooked, and kicked. I suspect the testing staff enjoyed it; they spilled coffee on the keyboards, slammed the lids, and inflicted a host of other tortures. (Okay, maybe they didn't bounce the poor laptops down the road in the cab of a truck or drop 'em out the door of a Freightliner, but I've taken care of both those tests.) Result: Every one of the laptops passed the tests. Some took longer than others to recover from the ordeal, but recover they did. Laptops, at least the top brand names, are becoming more and more durable as technology progresses.

Scouting out durability

If you locate a laptop that looks and feels sturdy, has a special hard-drive-protection system and sports a good set of latches, you may have found a laptop suitable for traveling the road with you.

I'm asking you to trust your instincts here. If the lid and the case look flimsy to you, then chances are that the machine isn't the best choice for travel in a truck or RV. If the outside looks wimpy, you've really got to wonder how tough the inside is.

Take the time to check out your purchases for features that scream *durability*. The following list gives you a couple of specifics to look for:

- **Hard-drive protection systems:** Manufacturers offer different types of systems designed to protect a laptop's hard drive. Active systems such as IBM's APS (Active Protection System) and Toshiba's EasyGuard focus primarily on safeguarding machines that are dropped, bumped, or experience excessive vibration while in use. Dell's StrikeZone is a passive system, which surrounds the drive bay with rubber shock absorbers in an attempt to protect the hard drive from bumps and bruises when the laptop is in use or in transit. Check out Table 3-1 for a rundown of some models and their spin on hard-drive protection.

- **LCD screen protection:** The main protection for the fragile LCD screen is the laptop lid. I sometimes have to dig my laptop out from under a pile of junk before using it, so its sturdy case and well-designed lid serve to protect the fragile (did I mention it's fragile?) LCD screen. When you're shopping for a new laptop, look closely at the construction and quality of the lid and latches. For example, one nice feature of IBM ThinkPad lids is the double latch; with a latch near each corner, the lid can't be bent at the corners when it's closed, and the display screen can't be distorted. You can see that the lid has a direct impact on how well the LCD screen is protected; better protection helps ensure screen longevity.

Table 3-1	Laptop Models with Hard-Drive Protection Systems	
Manufacturer / Model	*Protection System*	*What It Does*
IBM / ThinkPad	Active Protection System (APS)	Uses motion sensing to detect rapid acceleration that occurs in a fall; temporarily parks the hard-drive head until the system is stabilized.

Manufacturer / Model	Protection System	What It Does
Toshiba / Tecra	EasyGuard	Uses active motion sensing to park the hard-drive head if the laptop falls. Other protective features include a spillproof keyboard tray.
Dell / Latitude	StrikeZone	Uses a passive system that surrounds the hard-drive bay with rubber shock absorbers to dampen motion.
HP / Compaq	Basic design (no catchy name here!)	Mounts the hard drive directly to the frame so the frame dissipates some of the shock of being dropped, bounced, or vibrated.

When you're shopping for a laptop, you would do well to place Dell Latitude, Toshiba Tecra, HP Compaq, and IBM (Lenovo) ThinkPad laptops near the top of your shopping list. Each of these manufacturers offers a measure of protection for the hard drive that goes beyond (in some cases, far beyond) the protection afforded by the outer shell of the laptop itself.

Another laptop line at which you might want to look closely is manufactured by TwinHead and sold under the Durabook brand. The model N15RI, for example, features a magnesium case with rubber protection surrounding both the LCD screen and hard disk drive. The keyboard and touchpad are also spill-resistant. You can get more information at `http://usa.twinhead.com`.

You may also want to check out *Laptops For Dummies* (Wiley Publishing, Inc.) for more valuable information about what to consider, and what to ignore, when purchasing a laptop.

Keeping Life Compact with a PDA

The original purpose of the PDA (Personal Digital Assistant), also known as a handheld or palmtop, was simply PIM (Personal Information Management). I've always been just a little bit jealous of people who found it necessary to carry a PDA around with them. They always seem to live such full and interesting lives. I mean, just ask someone who owns one to join you for lunch, or even coffee. The very first thing your friend does is whip out a PDA to check that busy schedule. After this consultation comes the overcommitted response.

(You know: "Sorry, ohhhhh, it looks like I'm scheduled to change the air in my tires, give my cat a bath, and apply for astronaut training this afternoon. Maybe we can get together after I get back from the moon.")

Whatever . . . my life's just never been so busy that I felt the need to schedule it minute by minute, so if PIM were all that a PDA was really good for, I wouldn't even include it here for your consideration. With better screens, faster processors, more memory, and greater expandability, these PDAs (such as the one shown in Figure 3-1) have become a whole lot more than digital card catalogs and calendars.

To get the full use and benefit of a PDA, it's really necessary to have a computer at home. Most software programs, for example, must be loaded onto a PC and then transferred, by means of a USB cable or cradle, in a process known as *syncing*.

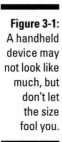

Figure 3-1: A handheld device may not look like much, but don't let the size fool you.

That's not to say that the PIM function of a PDA is a total waste of time — quite the contrary. But these handy and compact devices are capable of that and a whole lot more — for example, a well-equipped PDA can

- ✔ **Browse the Web:** With a decent Web browser (I discuss PDA Web browsers later in this section) and an Internet connection you can surf the Web and e-mail with a PDA in a fashion similar to (although maybe not exactly the same as) that of a laptop or desktop PC.

- ✔ **Recognize handwriting:** My dad was a math whiz. He communicated best by scribbling equations on restaurant napkins while we sipped coffee. I usually only made it through the first napkin. If he could've written on a PDA, we'd have saved several trees (and I could have taken the equations to a math professor to explain what my dad was telling me). If you write a lot of napkin notes, then you'll love this feature.

✔ **Recognize your voice:** Okay, this isn't *Star Trek* (you'll probably feel more like Captain Dork than Captain Kirk while talking to your PDA) but you've got to admit it's a cool idea. Several application programs, for both laptops and PDAs, will get you an answer to the salutation "Computer . . ." (even if you don't want to do it too often in public).

✔ **Get directions to your destination:** Some PDAs (like those built by Garmin) are GPS-mapping devices first and foremost; most others can be easily adapted for GPS capability, a wide variety of mapping applications are available for both Palm and Windows Mobile platforms.

✔ **Play games and download music and video:** Your PDA can do double duty as a miniature entertainment center. In addition to tons of games, you can use software applications to listen to favorite tunes, watch TV, and show movies. Get ready to squint, though. Those tiny screens won't provide you with an experience anything like you can get with a PC.

✔ **Store and sort business and personal info:** This is where the PIM function of a PDA really shines. I've always carried a little black book (well, actually the cover had a "Marvin the Martian" theme) with phone numbers, addresses, and driving directions; a PDA makes it no longer necessary.

If you've decided, for whatever reason, that a PDA sounds like the answer to your prayers, then carefully consider the ideas covered in the following sections as you begin shopping for the perfect PDA.

Deciding on an operating system

The operating system (OS) you choose will, to some extent, determine the brand of handheld device you choose. For some obscure reason, those PDAs that use the Palm OS are known by the generic term *PDA* while a device designed to use the Windows Mobile OS is called a *Pocket PC.* These two operating platforms dominate the market. There are others, like BlackBerry and Symbian, but they're largely utilized by the makers of a variation on the PDA known colloquially as the *smartphone.*

As you might expect, PDAs manufactured by Palm use the Palm OS — but so do those made by Sony and Garmin. Pocket PCs, using the Windows Mobile 2003SE (or the latest iteration, Windows Mobile 5.0) OS are manufactured by Asus, Dell, Fujitsu, HP and Toshiba, among others.

You might think I'm going to recommend one of these operating systems. You might be wrong. For good reason — each operating system has a vast following of fiercely loyal fans. Okay, I wasn't overly impressed with the early iterations of the Windows Mobile OS, but the two newer versions (2003SE and 5.0) are both strong competition for the Palm OS.

When you're choosing an operating system, keep the following items in mind:

✔ The Windows Mobile platforms, since they're diminutive versions of the Windows desktop OS, will be quite familiar to those who already have experience with a Windows-based laptop or desktop. The Palm platform, on the other hand, is simple to use and said by many to be intuitive. Being somewhat dense, myself, I usually don't find any operating systems (or program applications for that matter) to be intuitive — I have to commit the complete user manual to memory. That being said, even I find the Palm OS extremely simple to use.

✔ Microsoft produces both Windows Mobile OS and Microsoft Office applications (such as Outlook, Word, and Excel), so it makes sense that Pocket PCs can interface easily with these applications. Palm, however, also offers several PDAs that work almost equally well with these applications. If you happen upon a model that doesn't, an application such as Dataviz Documents to Go can ease compatibility problems.

All program applications written for PDAs and Pocket PCs are intended for use on those devices. You can't use desktop programs on a PDA or Pocket PC, and their program applications aren't compatible with desktops or laptops. Some programs, however, are being released in both desktop and handheld versions so you can enter information into one device and sync it with the other.

✔ Time was, many more software applications were written for the Palm OS than for the Windows Mobile platform — but that difference has dwindled until it's no longer a relevant issue. Both platforms are compatible with a wide variety of games and software applications. Many, if not all, of these are exclusive to one OS or another. So if there's a game or application you just can't live without, make sure it's supported by the OS you're favoring.

Before choosing between the Palm and Windows Mobile OS, I strongly suggest you test-drive several models loaded with each platform. That's really the only way to know for sure which one you're more comfortable with.

Picking a PDA

After choosing an operating platform for your PDA (see the previous section), you have to choose a handheld device to run it. Pay special attention to

✔ **Synchronization:** Be sure that any device you consider comes with a synchronization cable or cradle, along with sync software. A PDA is a self-contained unit, but you do need access to a desktop (or laptop) PC to perform synchronization. Most applications, for example, must first be downloaded to a PC and then synchronized (*synced*) to your handheld.

✔ **The display screen:** Because the screen is the largest single feature on any handheld device, it makes sense to consider it carefully:

- **Size:** Be certain that the size of the screen isn't going to cause you to strain your eyes while reading e-mail, browsing the Web, playing games, and so on.

- **View:** Many older PDAs and Pocket PCs operated only in what's known as a *portrait view* (long side vertical), but sometimes browsing the Web, playing games, viewing photos, or watching video can be more enjoyable with a *landscape view* (long side horizontal). Shop for a device that can offer both views.

- **Color of the display:** Most handheld devices made these days have a color display, but some lower-cost units still employ a monochrome screen (fine for PIM and e-mail but that's about it).

- **Resolution:** The higher the screen resolution, the better the viewing experience. PDAs can be found with resolutions ranging from 160×160 pixels up to 640×480 pixels. If you see a PDA advertised with a VGA (Video Graphics Array) screen, it boasts the 640×480 resolution; if you find a QVGA (Quarter VGA) screen, its resolution is 320×240. Higher resolution often translates into higher price, so go look at screens of varying resolution to determine your rock-bottom minimum.

Make certain, no matter the size, view, or resolution that the PDA you choose has an *active-matrix* screen, making it viewable at an angle. Most these days are so equipped but a few still persist with the *passive-matrix* technology, which makes viewing the screen difficult from any angle other than head-on.

✔ **Memory and data storage:** Because the Windows Mobile operating systems are bulkier than the Palm OS, a Pocket PC will take up more memory than a Palm-based PDA. Every application you add to your device though, no matter the OS, will soak up available RAM.

Newer PDA devices use a combination of Flash ROM (or even a hard drive) and RAM. The operating system comes loaded in ROM, and it shares a bit of RAM, leaving a portion accessible to the user. This *user-accessible memory* is the important number to look at when shopping for a PDA (or, for that matter, any computer — handheld, laptop, or desktop). Get the most built-in user-accessible memory you can afford.

Look for a device equipped with a *non-volatile* or *persistent* memory that doesn't let your data disappear if the power fails. That way, if your PDA runs completely out of power, your data remains perfectly safe.

✔ **Expandability:** You might find three expansion slots or ports on a hand-held device: Compact Flash (CF), Secure Digital (SD), and USB. Some have one, some have none, and some have all three. Make sure any device you fancy is equipped with, at the very least, one CF or SD slot, as shown in Figure 3-2.

- **Compact Flash (CF) type II:** The types of additions you can make to a PDA via a CF type II slot range from adding wireless connectivity to increasing available memory. Flash memory is a type of solid-state technology so, unlike RAM, it doesn't need a constant power source.

- **Secure Digital (SD):** This method of expansion, which is also solid-state, is a *secure alternative* (meaning it supports Digital Rights Management) to the multimedia card. If the SD slot is input/output-capable (SDIO), it can also be fitted with an SDIO wireless adapter. (I tell you more about this in "Adapting Your Laptop or PDA for Wireless," later in the chapter.)

- **USB:** A USB port enables you to connect a wide variety of peripheral devices to your PDA — including, but not limited to, GPS receivers, digital cameras, and miniature hard drives.

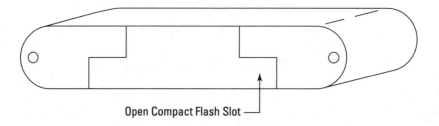

Open Compact Flash Slot —

Top View of a typical PDA/Pocket PC

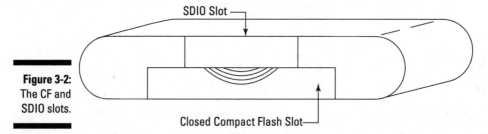

SDIO Slot —

Figure 3-2:
The CF and
SDIO slots.

Closed Compact Flash Slot—

Not every PDA or Pocket PC can be adapted for wireless connectivity; a few PDAs equipped with an SDIO slot *do not* support Wi-Fi. Before you buy a handheld device that doesn't have integrated Wi-Fi, *be absolutely certain* that its expansion slot (whether CF or SDIO) and OS will allow it to be adapted.

To save space in RAM, you can load certain program applications or files onto SD or CF memory cards. If you save important or confidential files and applications to removable memory cards, and keep them separate from your PDA, you still have that data if your PDA is lost, damaged, or stolen.

Considering your wireless options

A PDA or Pocket PC with an open CF type II or SDIO slot (see the previous section) can, in all likelihood, be easily adapted for wireless capability. However, several manufacturers are offering an increasing number of units with integrated wireless capabilities. This, as Martha Stewart would say, is a good thing.

Having built-in wireless connectivity can considerably simplify your Web surfing experience and, even though it might add a bit to the bottom line at the outset, I believe the extra convenience is well worth the extra cost. Besides, if you decide to go with a unit that lacks integrated wireless, you're still faced with purchasing a wireless adapter, and they don't just give 'em away.

Another good reason to choose a Pocket PC or PDA with integrated wireless capability is that your expansion slots will remain free for other purposes.

If you choose, however (like so many others before you), to ignore my sage advice and purchase a PDA or Pocket PC lacking built-in wireless connectivity, never fear. I explain how to make that device Wi-Fi-capable in "Adapting Your Laptop or PDA for Wireless," later in this chapter.

Customizing with a browser, mouse, and keyboard

You can choose from a wide variety of hardware and software options to make your PDA a trusted and worthy traveling companion — so you might as well start with a Web browser, a mouse, and a keyboard.

Web browsers installed on handheld devices are somewhat different from those on PCs. Because the screen is so small, it's difficult (if not impossible) to squeeze the contents of a Web page into the tiny space in a way that renders it readable. Several solutions have been tried, with varying success. Your browsing options depend on the operating system on your device:

✔ **A Pocket PC with the Windows Mobile OS:** On a new Pocket PC, at least, your default browser is Pocket Internet Explorer (PIE). If you've got a Pocket PC with WM 2003SE installed, you can choose from several good alternate browsers, including NetFront 3.2, ThunderHawk, and Skweezer. (I'm sure that other alternative versions, such as NetFront 3.3, will soon be available for WM 5.0 as well.)

✔ **PDA with the Palm OS:** Palm takes a different approach and installs browsers that are device-specific. For example, the Palm TX utilizes the Blazer 4.3 Web browser and the Palm LifeDrive comes with Blazer 4.1.

I haven't really found an alternate browser for Palm-powered devices that I think is any better than their standard installed browser. I can't say the same for PIE, although the version included with Windows Mobile 5.0 is a bit better than the version supplied with older WM iterations.

In addition to choosing a browser, you may want to add a keyboard or mouse, too. Yes, I know — the reason you're probably attracted to a PDA in the first place is because it's ultra-portable and if you wanted a keyboard you could just get a laptop. Well, what can I say? You might be right, but the nice thing about a PDA keyboard is that you don't *have* to carry it everywhere you go — and when they're not in use, many portable keyboards can fold up.

Personally, I can't use the tiny keyboards found on some devices, and I don't really like the idea of tapping on the screen with a stylus to enter information into a PDA. But I wouldn't consider being without a portable keyboard — and if I'm going to have one, I might as well have a mouse, right? You think I'm getting carried away? I think not. When you need it, you've got it; when you don't, just fold it and stow it. As a matter of fact, Stowaway is the brand name of the mouse and keyboard I recommend you look at first; they're manufactured by Think Outside.

Getting more PDA info

For more information about handheld devices, check out either *Palm For Dummies,* 2nd Edition (Wiley Publishing) or *Pocket PCs For Dummies,* 2nd Edition (Wiley Publishing). I've also found the following Web sites useful:

✔ **BargainPDA.com** (www.bargainpda.com)**:** With lots of news, reviews, and price comparisons, this is a good site to visit if you're considering a Palm OS PDA.

✔ **MobileTechReview.com** (www.mobiletechreview.com)**:** Featuring information and reviews of PDAs, Pocket PCs, and more cyber-stuff than you can shake a high-tech stick at.

✔ **Pocket PC magazine** (www.pocketpcmag.com)**:** Featuring a buyer's guide, forum, tips, and reviews, this is a good place to visit if you're considering a Pocket PC. My favorite section is "Best Software Awards." You can even get the magazine delivered to your door! (What a concept.)

Adapting Your Laptop or PDA for Wireless

If your laptop or palmtop isn't equipped with an integrated wireless connectivity solution — or you're trying to increase the capability of a laptop that is — you're in the market for a wireless adapter.

A *wireless adapter* is, basically, a radio transceiver that (after the appropriate software is loaded) enables a PC or PDA to send and receive radio signals that carry data. The adapter is powered through the particular interface slot or port that it's designed to use. It's like a CB radio for your laptop or PDA — except it has to follow very specific standards and protocols (see Chapter 2) and, of course, there's no trash talk.

When you're searching for a wireless adapter, you find several possible solutions:

✔ **PCMCIA card adapter:** The Personal Computer Memory Card International Association has developed standards for the PCMCIA card, known as the *PC card*. These cards (Figure 3-3 shows an example) are available for various purposes and come in three different sizes. The Type II card (5.0mm thick) is the size most often used to provide input/output capability for laptops. PC cards can adapt a laptop for (among other things), fax, dial-up, Ethernet, and Wi-Fi.

Another adapter card standard, known as an ExpressCard/34 (to reflect its 34mm width) has been developed by PCMCIA. So far no wireless adapter cards conforming to this standard are available, but the port is beginning to show up on laptops like the Apple Macintosh MacBook Pro and some Dell models. I expect to see wireless card adapters showing up on shelves soon. If you want more info you can visit www.expresscard. org/web/site.

✔ **USB adapter:** The Universal Serial Bus has quickly become the most used and useful port on a laptop. It's also beginning to show up on quite a few PDA devices. Although I don't yet know of any USB 802.11b/g adapters for handheld devices, several are available for laptops (most of which look like a broken lighter). If you happen to have an empty USB port, you can always plug in a USB-powered cup warmer to keep the coffee in your favorite *Star Trek* mug piping hot (I *told* you it was a useful port).

Figure 3-3:
I'm tired of hearing these adapters described as credit-card size, but I can't come up with a better description.

✔ **Secure Digital I/O Adapter:** You use this adapter (shown in Figure 3-4) with a PDA or Pocket PC, and it fits into an SDIO slot. If you want to give a Palm PDA wireless capability, first be certain that it's equipped with an SDIO expansion slot. Not all are, so check the specs. SDIO slots are also beginning to supplant Compact Flash slots on Pocket PCs.

✔ **Compact Flash Adapter:** Type I and Type II CF slots are beginning to disappear from Pocket PC handheld devices these days, but enough of them are still around that you might be able to adapt your handheld with a CF wireless adapter (like the one shown in Figure 3-5).

Figure 3-4:
A Secure Digital wireless adapter.

Figure 3-5:
An example
of a
Compact
Flash
wireless
adapter.

Looking at enhanced-performance laptop adapters

Because over-the-road environments, as well as the OTR traveler's needs, differ from those of the average business traveler, it stands to reason that the criteria for choosing an adapter will also be a bit different. For example, most folks owning a laptop with integrated wireless wouldn't recognize a potential need for *also* owning a Wi-Fi adapter. But here are a few things to consider while you're out shopping for an adapter:

✔ **Look for an adapter with enhanced capability:** Several adapters on the market excel at pulling in weak signals and connecting with distant access points. (I focus on these devices later in this section.)

✔ **If your laptop has an integrated wireless solution, give it a good test drive:** Before you shop for a high-powered adapter to use in place of your built-in wireless solution, take your laptop with you on a road trip. You might find that your usual OTR environment doesn't pose a problem when you access the Internet. If it ain't broke, don't fix it!

✔ **Don't be overly concerned with shopping for the fastest standard:** Okay, some people in the market for a wireless laptop adapter are obsessed with the adapter's speed and standard, but this is only relevant if you also plan to use the adapter extensively within a home network. The available speed under the 802.11b standard is plenty quick for connecting to the Internet. (For the details on standards, see Chapter 2.)

If you do decide to purchase a laptop adapter, you may as well get one that can improve your ability to make a connection. An adapter can accomplish this job in two ways:

✔ **Increased power:** The average output of a standard laptop wireless adapter is between 31.6mW and 63.2mW — sufficient for surfing the Net while sipping latte — but when you're berthed in the back row and there's an ocean of trucks or RVs between you and the access point, more power may be the answer. Fortunately, several adapter models, all seemingly built around the same basic design, boast an output of 200mW.

When shopping for an adapter, you're bound to see power rated in two ways: *milliwatts* (mW) and in *decibels* above or below 1mW (dBm). You'll also see antenna gain referenced, usually, as decibels relative to a theoretical isotropic antenna (dBi). Sounds a bit like *Star Trek,* doesn't it? But here's the practical gist: When you're comparing two devices, remember that an increase of 3 dBm (or 3 dBi) indicates a *doubling* of the power level (also called *antenna gain*); a decrease of 3 dBm (or 3 dBi) means a *halving* of the power level. For example 31.6mW is expressed as 15 dBm, 63.2mW is expressed as 18 dBm, and 200mW is expressed as (approximately) 23 dBm, which is pretty powerful either way.

You may find, while wandering the World Wide Web, wireless adapters that claim a power output of 300mW or higher. *These adapters aren't meant for use in a laptop.* Higher power means higher heat; you could fry your laptop's delicate innards like a shoe-leather steak.

✔ **Increased antenna gain:** A high-gain antenna uses a more focused energy to pull in signals that a standard antenna may not even be able to detect. I don't fully understand antenna gain — and only a handful of people (mainly employed by NASA) can claim to know someone who does — but I'm content if it works as advertised.

Several laptop adapters currently available incorporate one, or both, of the methods that improve adapter performance. Some are PC-card adapters; others are USB adapters. Whichever you use is purely your own preference. I prefer to travel with a PC-card adapter; you may, for any number of reasons, want a USB-powered device. Table 3-2 lists some of these adapters in no particular order. (Okay, bias being what it is, my favorite *is* listed first!)

Table 3-2	Performance-Enhancing Adapters	
Adapter	*Power and/ or Increased Antenna Gain*	*Highlights*
SMC2532W-B (Yes, it's my favorite PC card adapter.) 802.11b standard	This high-output card boasts 200mW (23 dBm) of power and comes standard with a removable 5.5 dBi high-gain antenna, combining both methods of performance enhancement. For more	Other PC card adapters assembled by other manufacturers are based around the same Prism 2.5 chipset, but I like this SMC adapter best. One reason, its superb performance notwithstanding, is that it's widely available from

Adapter	Power and/ or Increased Antenna Gain	Highlights
	about the advantages of having a removable antenna, see "Extending your range," later in this chapter.	online discount retailers (I got mine from Amazon.com), and it's even sold in some truck stop c-stores for about the same price.
Hawking HWC54D PC card 802.11g standard	One of the most innovative adapters on the market today, the outer end of the card, which sticks out a couple inches, is a 6dBi, directional, high-gain antenna that flips up and rotates toward the signal source. (I talk about antennas in "Extending your range," later in this chapter.)	Reports and reviews indicate this card has the ability to connect with a hotspot at two to three times the distance of a standard 'g' card or integrated 'b' solution. Make sure that, if you decide to buy this adapter, you get version 2.0 because it includes some really cool (and useful) LED signal-strength indicator lights.
Hawking HWU54D USB 802.11g	Like its PC-card cousin, uses a 6 dBi high-gain directional antenna that can be aimed toward the signal source to increase the strength of a connection.	The big advantage this USB adapter offers is the high-gain directional antenna that significantly increases signal strength.
Netgate EUB-362 (EXT) USB 802.11b/g	This is the only high-power-output USB adapter (at least that I know of) on the market today. With this version, you can remove the standard antenna and easily add an external antenna of your choice (that's what the EXT is all about).	Claiming to be completely compatible with the 802.11b/g standard, the adapter is built to the proprietary Super G (108 Mbps) standard. Of course this is a *theoretical* data-transfer rate (see Chapter 2), and the highest *actual* transfer rates would only be achieved within a Super G network. When it's operating in an 802.11b or g network, the power output is rated at 200mW (23 dBm).

Perusing PDA adapters

If you've decided to ignore my sage advice (see "Picking a PDA," earlier in this chapter) and have purchased a handheld that lacks integrated wireless connectivity, then your choice for a compatible adapter will be driven by the type of expansion slots built into your device. Unfortunately, there just aren't a lot of Wi-Fi adapters available on the market today — and none of them offers any sort of enhanced capability. Here are a couple of representative PDA/Pocket PC adapters that offer standard output:

- ✔ **Socket Go Wi-Fi! E300:** A low power consumption SDIO card that's compatible with Windows Mobile 2003, 2003SE or 5.0 operating systems. Socket also makes a CF card known as the Go Wi-Fi! P500.

- ✔ **Palm P10952U:** Manufactured by Palm and built to the 802.11b standard, this SDIO card (as one might guess) can be used in Palm devices that support wireless connectivity.

- ✔ **Linksys WCF54G:** Compatible with most Pocket PC devices that are equipped with a Compact Flash expansion slot, this Compact Flash wireless card complies with the 802.11g standard.

Extending Your Range

I don't know how many times I've read generic Wi-Fi tips suggesting that if you're having trouble getting a decent signal at the hotspot of your choice, you move closer to the source of the signal. Right.

I don't know about you, but when I'm searching for a truck-stop parking space, I usually take what I can get and hope I'll fit. I don't remember the last time I was able to pick and choose or move around at random. The real solution (other than more parking spaces) is extending the range of your laptop. PDAs need not apply. I don't know of a way to increase the range of a PDA wireless-connection device.

Enhanced-capability laptop adapters go a long way toward alleviating the problem of being too far from an access point. You can use them to enhance your ability to access a hotspot with your laptop. Before rushing right out to purchase all the pieces and parts mentioned in this chapter, give one of the enhanced-capability laptop adapters a good test. If you're still having problems obtaining or maintaining a connection, then you can come back and try one of the following ways to extend your wireless radio-transceiver range:

- ✔ **Increasing antenna gain:** If you've purchased one of the laptop adapters that has a removable antenna, then you can attach an external high-gain antenna. Most standard laptop adapters are equipped with an antenna rated at somewhere around 2 dBi — but even those equipped with high-gain antennas can do better with an *external* high-gain antenna. There are two types of high-gain antennas:

- **Omnidirectional:** Most antennas are omnidirectional — covering a 360-degree area — and that includes the most common high-gain antennas that are suitable for travel. Note, however, that an omni-directional signal is *not* spherical.

- **Directional:** The difference between omnidirectional and directional antennas is like the difference between (respectively) a lantern and a flashlight. A lantern casts light in a full circle; a flashlight focuses its light as a narrow beam.

The phrase *antenna gain* refers to the focus of the signal or field. A high-gain antenna has a tightly focused field; a low-gain antenna has a widely focused field. A high-gain antenna, therefore, isn't necessarily more powerful than a standard-gain antenna. In fact, there's really no energy increase connected with a high-gain antenna — it's just that the existing energy is more focused.

✔ **Amplifying output:** If you've found that a high-output 200mW laptop adapter doesn't quite cut the mustard (or you're just plain power-hungry), there are several wireless amplifiers on the market that range in output from 200mW to 1000mW (1 Watt).

Do not — I repeat, *do not* — attempt to amplify the output of a high-output adapter. You'll only fry the amplifier. Amplifiers are designed to handle the input power of a standard wireless adapter — that is, with a range of 32mW to 63mW.

✔ **Combining increased output and gain:** By far the most powerful configuration for extending your Wi-Fi range is the combination of a high-output amplifier and a high-gain antenna. You'll be happy to know that several vendors sell complete kits that include the adapter, the amplifier, and a high-gain antenna.

Comparing directional and omni-directional antennas

A directional antenna, as its name suggests, picks up and transmits a signal from — and in — a particular direction. Here are some attributes typical to a directional antenna:

✔ **Focused beam width:** With its energy directed into a relatively narrow vertical and horizontal beam width, a directional antenna can be extremely efficient — it's a high-gain antenna almost by definition. The higher its rated gain, the more narrowly focused the beam width.

✔ **Reduced interference:** Because interference may be centered in an area not covered by the narrow beam width, and because the energy is more

> focused (or dense), a directional antenna may be less affected by any local interference.
>
> ✔ **Need to be aimed:** As with a flashlight beam, a directional antenna has to be aimed at the target. This need to be aimed — and the fact that the beam width narrows as the gain increases — makes the accuracy of the aim more critical as gain increases. Thus you may want to avoid using a directional antenna with a rated gain in excess of 10 to 12 dBi.

After reading the preceding information, you might be all set to run out the door in search of a directional antenna. Well, wait just a second there partner — there's more to this story. Everything I've said about a directional antenna is true, *but* (you just knew a "but" was coming, didn't you?) when you're traveling, you might not be able to get a clear shot at the signal source. That's especially true if the source is coming from behind and you've got a big ol' trailer between you and it. High trailers, especially metallic trailers, can serve as outstandingly effective barriers to wireless signals.

You might be well advised to seriously consider choosing a less discriminating omnidirectional antenna that encompasses a much wider area. So here are some attributes typical to omnidirectional antennas:

> ✔ **360-degree horizontal beam width:** Because energy is being expended throughout a 360-degree circumference around the antenna, the beam is somewhat less efficient than that of a directional antenna. As the gain of an omnidirectional antenna increases, the vertical beam width becomes narrower and more focused — but (of course) its 360-degree horizontal beam width is maintained.
>
> ✔ **Susceptible to interference:** At least it's more susceptible than a directional antenna might be in the same environment. While the hotspot signal may be coming from one direction, interference in another area may be picked up as well. A high-gain omnidirectional antenna is, however, less susceptible to interference than its low-gain cousin.
>
> ✔ **No aiming:** The real beauty of an omnidirectional antenna is that it doesn't need to be precisely aimed — so it might detect signals that would otherwise be blocked from a directional antenna's line of sight.

Choosing an indoor versus an outdoor antenna

When you're choosing an external high-gain antenna for use with your high-power adapter, you'll have to decide whether you'll want to use a directional or omnidirectional antenna — and whether you want an antenna designed for indoor or outdoor use. Consider the following:

✔ **Indoor antennas:** Indoor antennas are the most commonly available that are suitable for use in a truck or RV. One nice thing about an indoor antenna is that you don't need to run a whole bunch of cable through a window, vent, or other such opening in your vehicle. There are also a few other advantages and disadvantages associated with indoor antennas:

- • The single biggest advantage of an indoor antenna (relating strictly to directional antennas) is that you can aim it without much trouble. You can sit right next to your laptop and watch the signal strength indicator as you move the antenna. Outdoor mounted antennas, by contrast, can be extremely difficult, even dangerous (read: nearly impossible) for a single person to aim.

- • All other things being equal, a directional antenna usually outperforms an omnidirectional antenna. If I were choosing an indoor antenna, my leading candidates would be directional (especially since I already own an SMC2532W-B adapter card that comes standard with a 5.5 dBi omnidirectional antenna).

- • You can, in most cases, permanently (or semipermanently) mount an indoor antenna in your vehicle, but that isn't necessary. You can store the antenna in an out-of-the-way nook or cranny when it's not in use, and then place it in a suitable position when it's needed.

- • If you're having difficulties getting connected, one problem might be too many obstructions. Unfortunately, you may not be able to raise an indoor antenna — which is restricted by your roof, walls and doors — above the obstructions.

✔ **Outdoor antennas:** Large numbers of outdoor high-gain antennas are available, but only a fraction of them are designed for mobile use. With a little ingenuity, you can get some of the antennas designed mainly for static use to work quite nicely — especially for RVs. Here are some major pros and cons regarding outdoor antennas:

- • Possibly the greatest advantage to using an outdoor is that you can mount it high enough to clear most, if not all, obstructions. Another advantage to this type of mounting is that the roof of the vehicle might well act as a *ground plane* (in effect, a kind of electrical shield against interference), further optimizing the performance of the antenna.

- • An outdoor antenna requires a more permanent mount, which sometimes requires the drilling of tiny little holes. Antenna cable will also need to be run from the outside to the inside and secured.

Once all that's done (at least for an omnidirectional antenna), it's pretty darn convenient to use.

If I were going to purchase an outdoor antenna, it would be omnidirectional. And, yes, an outdoor antenna can be a pain to mount in a tidy fashion, but once that job's done, it'll usually outperform indoor antennas with a similar rated gain. Just put it up as high as you can get it and it does its job.

- Several companies manufacture and sell mobile antennas with the familiar magnetic mount. That's not much help if you've got an aluminum or fiberglass cab, or if your RV has FRP body panels, but if you're still living in the Iron Age, they can be handy.

- There are, really, no outdoor directional antennas designed to be permanently mounted on a moving vehicle. To employ an outdoor directional antenna, a mount must be fashioned that allows removal of the antenna before vehicle travels.

Checking out example antennas

Most of the major wireless manufacturers carry a line of external high-gain antennas. If you're in the market for an indoor antenna, you might begin your search at Hawking Technology (www.hawkingtech.com), Buffalo Technology (www.buffalotech.com/products/wireless.php), or SMC (www.smc.com). Here are a few good examples of available antennas:

- ✔ **Hawking HAI6SDP:** This is an outstanding 6 dBi directional antenna designed for indoor use. The HAI6SDP uses a Reverse Polarity-SMA connector so if you want to connect it to the SMC2532W-B PC card you'll need to obtain an RP-MMCX to RP-SMA pigtail as an adapter. (More about cables and connectors in the next section.)

- ✔ **Hawking HAI7SIP:** Its slightly higher 7 dBi-rated gain would put it at the top of my list if I were going to purchase an indoor omnidirectional antenna. It comes with an RP-SMA connector so an RP-MMCX to RP-SMA pigtail will be needed to adapt it for use with the SMC2532W-B card. (Again, I cover the connectors next.)

- ✔ **Buffalo WLE-DA2:** Buffalo Technology manufactures some very high-quality and well-reviewed wireless products; the WLE-DA2 9 dBi directional (indoor) antenna is a good example. The vertical and horizontal beam width is 75 degrees, so it's not terribly difficult to aim. The only problem you might run into is in adapting the connectors for use with an SMC2532W-B PC card.

- ✔ **SMCHMANT-6:** Manufactured by SMC this 6 dBi directional (indoor) antenna is similar to the Hawking HAI6SDP. Its beam width is 80 degrees on both the horizontal and vertical planes, so it's a bit more forgiving than a much-higher-dBi directional antenna might be. Now, you might think that (since it's manufactured by SMC) that the connector would be compatible with the SMC2532W-B — but no. Like the Hawking Technology antennas, this one needs an RP-MMCX to RP-SMA pigtail.

✔ **Trucker & RV +7 dBi:** WarDrivingWorld.com offers this 7 dBi omnidirectional (outdoor-mount) antenna that includes an integrated ground plane. It comes with seven feet of cable and you can get additional cable from them. It mounts directly into pre-drilled CB antenna holes, or you can buy an optional mirror mount. You can choose the RP-MMCX connector for use with the SMC2532W-B adapter card.

✔ **HyperGain HG2409UM-KIT:** Offered by HyperLink Technologies, this 8.5 dBi Omni-directional antenna is designed for use in a marine environment and is suitable for use on a truck or RV. The package includes a four-way marine mount, allowing the antenna to be folded flat for travel. The connector is an RP-SMA, so (surprise, surprise) you need an RP-MMCX to RP-SMA pigtail for use with an SMC2532W-B adapter card. (See the next section for more.)

Getting cables and connectors

When you're adding an external antenna to a device like your wireless adapter, you may need to adapt the connection. The SMC2532W-B uses an MMCX connection (for example), and the antenna you desire might be equipped with a SMA connector. This is a minor irritation; in almost all cases, it can be easily remedied. You can traipse down to your local electronics geek shop for a solution or check out one of these online vendors:

✔ **WarDrivingWorld.com:** These are the folks from whom I obtained my RP-MMCX to RP-SMA pigtail for use with my SMC2532W-B card. When you go to their site in search of a pigtail you need only find the subheading "Cables & Pigtails" under the main heading "Store home" and follow that link. This online store also carries other Wi-Fi-related gear that's tailored to a mobile environment.

✔ **WirelessNetworkProducts.com:** Under the heading "More Info," look for the subheading "Pigtail Picker" and follow that link. You will be taken to a page that lets you specify the exact connectors you need on either end of your custom pigtail. They also offer many other products you might be interested in.

✔ **RadioLabs.com:** Follow the link titled "Wireless" on top of the page, and then follow the link titled "Cables." You find other links for "WiFi Cables," "Wi-Fi Connectors," and "Wireless Pigtail cables." Somewhere within this site lies the solution to your problems. RadioLabs.com is a site to bookmark and return to often.

Okay, all you know for sure is that the two ends don't connect. Your best bet is to take the two pieces down to a local electronics shop that sells connectors. They can identify the tiny offenders and probably sell you a pigtail or bullet adapter to mate them. Failing that, call RadioLabs.com, at the toll-free number listed on the top of their Web pages, and tell them which pieces you're tying to connect. They'll be able to help and you can buy what you need from them.

Combining power and sensitivity in a kit

If your deepest desire is to amplify your power output to the maximum, then you, my friend, are in the market for a Wi-Fi kit. Most of these kits include a wireless adapter card, a high-gain omnidirectional (outdoor) antenna, and (of course) an amplifier.

You can, if you so choose, buy an amplifier as a standalone device — but I highly recommend that you resist that temptation. There are several obscure (and not-so-obscure) FCC regulations that apply; by purchasing a kit, you avoid breaking those regulations.

Both kits that I recommend here incorporate a 500mW amplifier. Yes, you could purchase a 1000mW amplifier, but — depending on the rated gain of your antenna — you could easily exceed the maximum power output allowed by the FCC (36dB). You might also become a source of interference, causing problems for neighboring trucks and RVs.

Several manufacturers offer 802.11b/g wireless amplifiers; quite a few of them package these items in complete kits. Here are two of those kits that I think offer excellent performance and good value:

- **RadioLabs Trucker Wireless Internet Antenna Kit:** This is a kit put together by the good folks at RadioLabs.com. It's got everything you might need, including a 12V cigarette-lighter jack for powering the amplifier. The total power output of the 500mW (27 dBm) amplifier and 7 dBi antenna is approximately 34dB, falling safely inside the maximum of 36dB allowed by the FCC.

- **HyperLink Marine MAX Range Wi-Fi Kit:** This kit, offered by HyperLink Technology is (okay) a bit more complicated to install. The kit includes an 802.11g (b/g) 500mW amplifier and 12V-power supply, 8.5 dBi marine antenna and mount, 802.11b PC card, and connecting cables. The total power output is a barely-legal 35.5dB.

Chapter 4

Putting Your Gear Together

*W*hen you've gone out and got yourself a bunch of stuff, it's time to get it all set up and running. Most Wi-Fi gear is relatively simple to set up and install. Believe me, if I can do it, anyone can do it — and you (you lucky dog) can benefit from my vast experience (read: ocean of errors).

In this chapter, I walk you through the process of installing and operating a wireless adapter in your laptop or PDA. I also give you some tips, pointers, and instructions for setting up and mounting an external antenna.

Getting Ready to Install a Wireless Adapter

I usually want to get whatever new gadget I've purchased installed as fast as I can. I rip off the cellophane, tear open the box, and start grabbing goodies. But hold on a minute. Even though getting Wi-Fi gear set up and operating smoothly is really pretty simple, it still takes a little forethought and preparation. There aren't a lot of things that cause serious problems as you get your laptop or PDA Wi-Fi-ready and running efficiently, but the few that crop up can be frustrating, to say the least. Here, my goal is to help you avoid frustration by employing the Boy Scout motto: "Be Prepared."

If you've got a laptop with an integrated Wi-Fi card, follow these three steps before you install an additional adapter:

1. **Read the instructions.**

2. **Disable the Wireless Zero Configuration utility.**

3. **Disable your wireless radio.**

If your laptop has no integrated wireless capability, then you can (obviously) skip the final step — and if you've got a PDA, then you can skip the last two — but the first item applies to one and all. In the following sections, I explain each step in detail.

Read the instructions

Steven Wright, one of my favorite comedians, once said: "Experience is something you don't get until just after you need it." While that's true to a certain extent, at least you can benefit from the experience of others. I've learned (after enough repetitive "lessons") that manufacturers print these instructions for a reason. These days (finally) I read the instructions — completely — before I begin the assembly or installation of anything. Pretty radical, isn't it? But reading the instructions can head off some frustrating or annoying surprises, because you start off knowing

✔ Whether or not your operating system is compatible.

✔ Whether you need to install the drivers before inserting the card, or vice versa.

✔ What needs to be turned off and what needs to be running.

✔ That you're going to need a cup of coffee before you start.

Addressing the Wireless Zero Configuration utility

Windows XP provides a Wireless Zero Configuration (WZC) utility to manage the connection of PDAs or laptops to wireless networks. That is, the utility displays the wireless networks in range, along with their status, and performs the computer gymnastics necessary to make a connection to your network of choice. It also remembers the network and any configurations, like a security password or whether or not you allow an automatic connection.

Unfortunately, WZC doesn't always work well with wireless adapters. For example, it seems to work well enough with the Buffalo Technology WLI-CB-G54A adapter — but if your adapter is a SMC2532W-B, you may note that the user guide strongly recommends turning off the WZC and using the adapter's configuration utility instead. In general, no matter the adapter, I prefer to use a connection utility other than the WZC.

In all cases, if you're using a connection utility or manager other than the Windows Zero Configuration utility — such as the one provided by the adapter's manufacturer — the WZC must be disabled, preferably *before* you install any drivers or other software associated with your adapter card. You want to eliminate any chance of conflict between configuration utilities.

The good news: Disabling the WZC is easy. You can do it in several different ways, all equally effective. My preferred method is as follows:

1. **Choose Start➪Control Panel➪Switch to Classic View (assuming Category View is the current default view).**

    The Classic View Control Panel opens.

2. **Double-click the Administrative Tools icon.**

    The Administrative Tools window opens.

3. **Double-click the Services icon.**

    The double-pane Services window opens, as shown in Figure 4-1.

4. **In the right pane of the Services window, scroll down to Wireless Zero Configuration and click it.**

    The item is highlighted; in the upper-left corner, you see the heading *Wireless Zero Configuration*, which lists two choices: Stop the Service and Restart the Service.

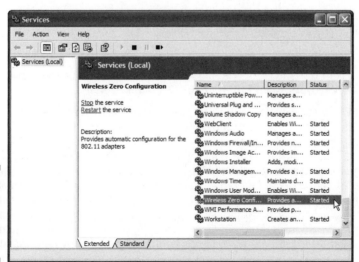

Figure 4-1:
Stop the service in the Services dialog box.

5. **Click Stop the Service.**

   The previous two choices disappear. They are replaced by a single choice (Start the Service), which means your choice is acknowledged.

6. **Move the cursor over to the highlighted Wireless Zero Configuration item and right-click it. From the context menu that appears, choose Properties.**

   The Wireless Zero Configuration Properties dialog box opens, as shown in Figure 4-2.

7. **Click the General tab (if it isn't already showing).**

   In the center of the dialog box, you see *Startup Type: Automatic.*

Figure 4-2:
Disabling
the service
in the
Properties
dialog box.

8. **From the Startup Type drop-down list, choose Disabled, click the Apply button, and then click OK to close the dialog box.**

9. **Close the Services window, close the Administrative Tools window, and restart your computer.**

There, you've done it. The Windows Zero Configuration utility is disabled. If your laptop has integrated Wi-Fi, be sure to turn off the built-in wireless radio. (See "Eliminating conflict between integrated wireless and wireless adapters" later in this chapter.) Otherwise you're ready to install your adapter.

If you have an integrated wireless card and you're only using a separate wireless adapter for situations in which you need greater power, then you may want to use the WZC to make connections with the integrated card. If this is the case, you need to re-enable the WZC (only when you're using the integrated card). To do so, first return to the Wireless Zero Configuration Properties dialog box as you did in the preceding steps and choose Automatic from the Startup Type drop-down list. Click Apply before you click OK to close the dialog box. Then, in the Services dialog box, make sure Wireless Zero Configuration is selected, and click Start the Service at upper left.

Eliminating conflict between integrated wireless and wireless adapters

If you've got built-in Wi-Fi *and* you install a high-power adapter to use in a low-signal-strength area, your computer may get confused about which Wi-Fi radio to use. To avoid this potential problem, turn off the integrated card.

To turn off the radio, most laptops have simple methods such as a button, function key, or utility. (Check your user's manual to find out which, if any, you have.) My laptop has two of those options: I can use the utility by right-clicking my wireless-radio icon in the tray and choosing to turn the WLAN off. Or I can press the button in the center of my laptop keyboard. Either way, the indicator light goes out, letting me know the built-in radio is off.

If you don't have any of these options available to you, fear not; a simple solution is available. If your manual shows no button, key, or utility for dis-abling a built-in wireless radio, just follow these instructions:

1. **Choose Start⇨Control Panel⇨Switch to Classic View.**

   The Classic View Control Panel opens.

2. **Double-click the Network Connections icon.**

   The Network Connections window opens and you see an icon indicating the type and status of each network connection.

3. **Right-click the Wireless Network Connection icon.**

   A menu box opens.

4. **Click Disable.**

5. **Click OK to close the Network Connections window.**

Your built-in wireless solution is now disabled. To re-enable the radio, you can follow the same steps that disabled it, clicking Enable in Step 4.

Installing a Wireless Adapter (Laptop)

With all the complicated and confusing things connected with computers, it's nice to know that installing an adapter is so easy. In fact, the entire process will likely take you less than 20 minutes.

Before you begin, here are just a few bits of information you need to know:

✔ Whereas a USB plug will only go into the USB port one way, it *is* possible to put a PC card into the PCMCIA slot incorrectly. Generally speaking, the PC card will go into the slot with the flashy product logo facing up and the dull, boring-looking information label facing down. If the card has little status-indicator lights, those have to face up.

Inserting the card the right way is important. If the card's upside down, and if you pushed really hard, you could mangle the way those 68 little holes in the end of the card fit into the 68 little pins inside the slot, damaging both the card and the laptop.

✔ To keep static electricity from damaging the adapter, avoid opening any protective packaging until just before you insert a PC card or USB plug into your laptop.

✔ In some cases (as with the SMC2532W-B card and most USB adapters), you need to install the drivers (tiny programs that handle communication between the hardware device and the program or operating system using it) *before* inserting the card or plug into the appropriate orifice. In other cases (as with the Buffalo WLI-CB-G54A), you can insert the card first. Make sure you know the order of events before you proceed with installing a card or USB adapter; the instructions that came with your card should steer you straight.

With so many different adapters on the market it's just not practical to give you the exact installation instructions for each and every one. Fortunately, no matter which adapter you've selected, the methods of installation are very similar. That's true whether it's a PC card adapter or a USB adapter. So, what follows are the exact instructions for installing the Buffalo Technology WLI-CB-G54A adapter. Even if you've got a different adapter, the steps will be very similar.

Installing the drivers

Chances are quite good that the box containing your adapter card also contains an *installation guide* (that is, instructions) and a CD that contains the hardware drivers and configuration utility. You've already read the instructions;

the adapter card is still nestled inside its protective wrap, and the installation CD is at hand. You're ready to begin the installation. Following are the steps, in excruciating detail, for installing the adapter, drivers, and configuration utility for the Buffalo WLI-CB-G54A.

Before handling your adapter card, make sure you discharge any static electricity by touching an object made of electrically conductive metal.

1. **Power up your laptop, and then unwrap your adapter card and insert it into the PCMCIA slot.**

   The Found New Hardware wizard, shown in Figure 4-3, opens automatically. (If, for some reason, it doesn't, remove the card, restart your laptop, and reinsert the card.) The *Install software automatically* radio button is selected by default.

Figure 4-3:
The wizard appears when you add your new hardware.

2. **Insert the CD included with your adapter and close the drive bay to move to the next step in the wizard. If the wizard doesn't automatically change screens, click Next.**

   The driver menu screen opens.

3. **Select the most recent driver version as indicated by the highest version number (see Figure 4-4).**

   A warning may appear, indicating that the driver isn't digitally signed. You can safely ignore it.

   If all version numbers are the same, use the driver listed at the top; this should be the default driver.

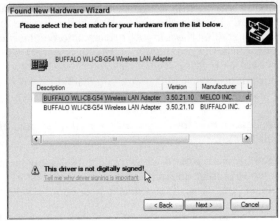

Figure 4-4:
Select the
correct
driver from
the list.

4. **Click Next.**

   A warning window, indicating that the driver hasn't passed Windows Logo testing, may appear and attempt to scare you half to death. This same warning screen may appear if you're installing the SMC2532W-B adapter card or any of several other cards from various manufacturers.

5. **Live dangerously (no, not really) and click Continue Anyway.**

   The Flying Files screen opens, indicating the software is being installed. As is the case with the installation of most software, Windows also sets a system *restore point* (which saves your settings as they are before you install something new). That way, if the installation goes awry, you can usually return your system to the way it was. When the files have finished their flight, the final screen opens.

6. **Click Finished.**

   The drivers are now installed. The next step is to run your adapter's connection utility, if it has one. Though I discuss WZC (the Windows XP utility), earlier in this chapter, the utility that comes with an adapter usually works better. The next section has all the details.

Running the adapter's connection utility

If you're going to use your adapter's connection utility, you need to install it after installing the drivers. The following steps use the Buffalo connection utility as an example of how this works:

1. **Click Start⇨Run.**

2. **In the Open field, type the following and then click OK (see Figure 4-5).**

   `D:\Setup.exe`

   The `D:\` indicates that the program to be executed can be found on a CD in the CD drive. Your CD drive might be assigned a letter other than `D` so be sure to check.

Figure 4-5:
Running
the setup
command.

The AirNavigator configuration utility opens.

3. **Select the Install Buffalo Client Manager radio button and click OK, as shown in Figure 4-6.**

Figure 4-6:
I choose to
install the
Client
Manager,
which is this
card's
connection
utility.

The Client Manager Installer opens, prompting you to close other applications before continuing.

4. **Click Next to open the EULA screen. Read the information (or at least pretend to) and if you find nothing objectionable, click I Agree.**

   A screen indicating where the files are to be installed opens. You're given the option of choosing another location — but since you're too smart to make that mistake, you simply . . .

5. **Click Next, as shown in Figure 4-7.**

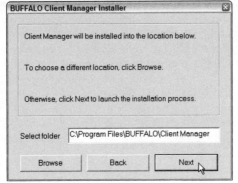

Figure 4-7:
Install the
files in the
default
location.

Installation commences; the final screen, indicating completion, opens.

6. Click OK.

You're done! You're ready to get connected, and I cover this issue in Chapter 6.

The PCMCIA slot allows *hot swapping*, meaning a PC card can be removed and re-inserted without powering down the laptop. This isn't always true for devices — including adapters — connected via a USB port.

Installing a Wireless Adapter (PDA)

With the multitude of PDA and Pocket PC devices available, not to mention the adapters, I can't possibly address every one separately. Fortunately, as with laptops, installation of adapters (though not completely universal) is remarkably similar for Palm OS and Windows Mobile OS — as is the method of installation, whether for SDIO wireless or Compact Flash adapters.

Okay, installing an adapter (or any other item requiring software or drivers) isn't quite as straightforward on a handheld as it is on a laptop — but it isn't overly complex. The only real difference is that any software must be loaded onto a PC and (via cradle or cable) synced with the handheld device.

It's worth repeating: Leave your adapter card in its wrapping, protected from static electricity, until you're ready to actually install it in your device.

Setting up the PDA or Pocket PC

The first step in loading the drivers and configuration utility on your handheld is to connect it, by sync cable or cradle, to your PC. Of course, before you do that, the ActiveSync (Pocket PC) or HotSync (Palm OS) software (whichever is appropriate) has to be installed on the PC. Then, with your PDA connected to your PC, make sure they're both powered up. What follows is the step-by-step process for installing a Linksys WCF54G Compact Flash wireless adapter card in a Pocket PC.

Don't insert the adapter card into your handheld until *after* you complete the installation of both the drivers and the configuration utility.

1. **Open the CD/DVD optical drive bay on your PC and insert the CD included with the adapter card.**

2. **Close the drive bay.**

    The CD starts automatically and the Installation wizard welcome screen opens, showing its menu.

3. **Click Install.**

    The End User's License Agreement (EULA) opens. By continuing, you accept the terms of the license. I haven't found any reason to object to any of its tenets, but if, after reading it, you find something you can't live with, you can click Cancel and exit the installation wizard.

4. **Click Next.**

    The Add/Remove Programs window opens.

5. **When asked if you want to install in the default application install directory, click Yes.**

    The Add/Remove Programs window remains open; an installation-progress status bar opens. Don't click the Cancel button. When the installation is complete, a notice opens, asking you to check your PDA screen to see whether any additional steps are necessary.

6. **Click OK.**

    The Congratulations screen opens.

7. **Click Exit.**

    You're now done using the PC and you can focus on your Pocket PC where you see the *Installation complete* screen.

8. **Click OK (on the *Installation complete* screen) and then disconnect your handheld from the PC.**

    The Pocket PC's Start screen appears.

9. **Insert the adapter card into the Pocket PC.**

10. **If it's not already selected, select *Use server-assigned IP address* and click OK.**

    That's pretty much it. The little wireless-network icon appears and you're ready to connect to a network via a hotspot. I tell you more about connecting to hotspots in Chapter 6.

Updating drivers and firmware

Every so often the manufacturers of wireless equipment — including wireless adapters — update or upgrade the software drivers and internal firmware (programmed operating instructions stored within a hardware device). It's a good idea to check the manufacturer's Web site on a regular basis to see if they've made something available for your adapter.

Firmware doesn't seem to get upgraded as often as the drivers but, especially in the case of USB adapters, it does happen. So, how often should you check the manufacturer's Web site? If you check the site once every three months, that's plenty. (Okay, if you never check for updates or upgrades, the world won't come to a screeching halt — but you might miss out on getting a bit better performance from your wireless equipment.)

In some cases, you may have to uninstall your currently loaded drivers and connection utility before you install updated or upgraded drivers. (This probably won't be the case if you're upgrading firmware.)

Attaching an External Antenna

For the most part — with the exception of an outdoor directional antenna — attaching an external antenna is pretty straightforward. There are, however, a few things worth mentioning, especially if you're planning to mount an external antenna outside your vehicle. If you're also including an amplifier, even then you won't need a working knowledge of rocket science — but planning and common sense save wear and tear on nerves.

Depending on whether you're setting up an outdoor omnidirectional antenna or an indoor antenna (whether directional or omnidirectional), you have different circumstances that influence your planned setup and installation. For example, if you have an outdoor directional antenna, consider what location will enable you to rotate it 360 degrees; with an omnidirectional antenna, you don't need to worry about that, because of the way the antenna works (see Chapter 3 for details).

No matter the type of antenna you intend to use — indoor or outdoor, directional or omnidirectional — here are a couple of universal rules:

- **Obstacle avoidance:** This rule of thumb applies especially to the folks who pull a high trailer such as a van or reefer. If that's you, then mount your antenna as far forward of the trailer as possible. Whether you're operating a semi pulling a high trailer or an RV pulling a snowmobile trailer, be sure to mount or place your antenna in an obstacle-free area.

Glass, fiberglass, and FRP (Fiberglass-Reinforced Plastic), while not completely transparent to a Wi-Fi radio signal, don't create a serious obstacle (like metal does). You can, for example, mount your antenna behind a fiberglass wind deflector without worrying that it will deflect your Wi-Fi signal as well as wind.

✔ **Mount your antenna as high as possible.** With or without a high trailer, if you can get your antenna up in the air, you have fewer obstacles to the line-of-sight to the access point's antenna. If you're pulling a high trailer and you can mount the antenna far forward — with the tip of the antenna reaching up to within a foot or so of the trailer top — then the trailer itself becomes much less of a potential obstacle.

Setting up an outdoor omnidirectional antenna

If you've ever mounted a CB antenna, then you know that it doesn't have to be the most challenging thing you've ever done. To plan your installation, you just find the best place to mount your antenna, determine where the coax will terminate, and make a plan for running coaxial cable between those two points. Rather than attempt to give you a step-by-step guide for installing an antenna, I've offered some general guidelines here to help you make a clean installation that operates efficiently.

Choosing your antenna location

With obstacle avoidance in mind, your first consideration is locating the antenna as close as possible to the area where you most often use your computer. If drilling holes in the exterior of your vehicle is acceptable in your situation, then you can probably mount your antenna relatively close to that area. If not, then a rail or mirror mount may be the ticket; then, no matter where you do your computing, the location of the rail or mirror you use as a mount will determine the antenna location.

If you're planning to drill holes in the exterior wall or roof, be certain that the mount is securely fastened — and well sealed with gaskets and sealant. (If neither surface is plastic or FRP, use a polysulfide sealant; otherwise use silicone.) And take a minute and see if there are any nearby entry points, like vents, that you might use for cable entry.

Finally, you don't want to minimize the value of a neat and aesthetically pleasing installation. For example, if you can mount the antenna so that a cabinet or shelving hides any ingress of hardware, that little bit of extra effort will go a long way in making the job look more professional. If you can use existing wire and cable entry points for the coax, that's even better.

Planning the coaxial cable path

Once you've determined where to mount your antenna, the next step is to lay out your cabling plan. You want to know:

✔ **How much cable is needed:** You don't want any excess cable because even the very best cable loses some signal strength over its length. You also don't want to coil any cable, because that creates another electromagnetic field that might easily create interference.

✔ **What kind of cable is needed:** There are two types of low-loss cable that are both effective and affordable:

- **LMR-400:** Used as primary antenna cable. The *attenuation* (loss of signal strength over distance) is approximately 6.69dB per 100 feet, so approximately .67dB is lost every 10 feet.

- **LMR-100:** Used as a pigtail connecting the computer to the main antenna cable. (*Pigtails* are short cables used to connect, for example, a device with connector A to a cable using connector B. The pigtail would have, say, a female A at one end and a male B at the other end.) The attenuation is approximately 39.363dB per 100 feet — a signal-strength loss of 1.6dB over a 4-foot length.

A typical coaxial-cable installation includes several feet of LMR-400 (larger RVs may use as much as 40 feet), with 3 or 4 feet of LMR-100 as a pigtail, to connect the laptop to the main (LMR-400) coaxial cable.

✔ **How the cable is to be secured:** Cable clamps are readily available at hardware stores such as Lowe's, Ace, or Home Depot. I'm a big fan of the clean and neat installation of cable, but just because it's covered up doesn't mean you don't need to secure it the best way you can.

In the next phase of creating your plan, you need to mark where antenna cable will run, mark the places where holes might have to be drilled, and make measurements. Here are the basic steps I follow:

1. **Gather the necessary tools: a tape measure, a pencil, masking tape, and a quarter-inch rope or cord.**

   The perfect cord to use in planning coaxial cable runs — because it's cheap and readily available — is clothesline. It usually comes in 50-foot lengths and you can use masking tape to hold it in place.

2. **To figure out the amount of cable that's needed, I use clothesline cord as a stand-in for the coaxial cable and tape the cord in place.**

   This approach makes it easier to plan for any corners or obstacles to be negotiated; I can try several different paths to decide which works best.

LMR-400 coaxial cable has a *minimum bend radius* of 2 inches, as shown in Figure 4-8; don't bend it tighter than that or you'll crimp and damage it. When negotiating a corner with this cable, be certain that the arc of the bend falls within 2 inches. LMR-100 cable is much more flexible, with a minimum bend radius of .25 inch.

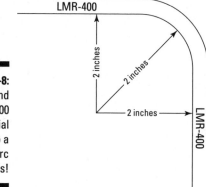

Figure 4-8:
Don't bend
LMR-400
coaxial
cable into a
tighter arc
than this!

Remember that you always want to use the shortest possible length of cable that's practical. That doesn't mean you have to cut diagonal paths from one place to another, but if you can easily and neatly use an angle between the antenna and termination point, go for it.

3. **I mark where to place the cable clamps by putting a piece of masking tape where the clamp will go, and placing my marks *on the tape* (not on the metal or upholstery).**

By using any existing screw holes — say, those for the mounting screws for panels, shelves, or cabinets — you can secure plastic cable clamps without making any *other* holes. Even if you have to replace the existing screw with a slightly longer one, it makes for a neater job.

4. **After you determine the path, take down your cord and measure it to find out how much cable you need for your antenna. Make sure you leave marks where the clamps will go.**

5. **I find it easiest to install the cable clamps, one at a time, as I'm running the cable. You can also slide 'em down the cable so they're stacked and ready to use.**

Making the connection

Once you've figured out where you're going to mount your antenna and the path the coaxial cable will take from the antenna to the termination point, it's time to make connections. Generally speaking, the antenna you purchase includes several feet of coaxial cable — and, on occasion, a pigtail. These ready-made cables come complete with the appropriate connectors.

If you need a longer or shorter cable, several online outlets offer custom-made cables, or you can purchase the cable and connectors separately and fabricate your own (or you might have an electronics-geek shop in town make a cable for you). In any case, make sure your connectors are compatible. Table 4-1 lists the most common types of connectors. You can have a look at these connectors (both male and female versions) in Figure 4-9.

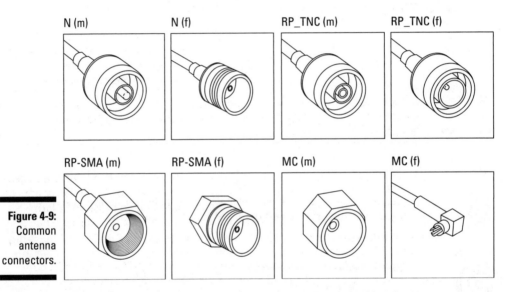

Figure 4-9: Common antenna connectors.

Table 4-1	Antenna Coax Cable Connectors	
Connector	*Description*	*Common Uses*
Type N connectors	5/8" in diameter with 24 threads per inch (tpi) Unified Extra Fine (UNEF).	These connectors are commonly used to join antenna cable to an outdoor-mount antenna. Appropriate for use on several types of coaxial cable, including LMR-400 and LMR-100.

Connector	Description	Common Uses
RP-TNC connectors	7/16" in diameter with 28 tpi UNEF. (The RP stands for Reverse Polarity.)	These connectors are commonly used to connect coaxial cable to both indoor and outdoor antennas. Can be used on LMR-400, LMR-100, LMR-195, and WBC-195 cables.
SMA and RP-SMA connectors	¼" in diameter with 32 tpi Unified Standard (UNS).	Most often used on indoor antennas and wireless adapter cards but also used on outdoor mounted marine antennas. Like RP-TNC connectors, they work with a wide variety of cable sizes.
MC, MMCX and RP-MC or RP-MMCX	These connectors snap into place rather than screwing on.	Used almost exclusively on wireless adapter cards.

Reverse Polarity connectors switch the dielectrics and contacts between genders. For example, a Reverse Polarity Male connector has a male body but the dielectric and contact are female. Don't try to mate a Reverse Polarity connector and adapter with a standard coaxial connector; doing so will damage the connectors.

If your antenna cable or pigtail terminates in an N, RP-TNC or RP-SMA connector, you can use a short *adapter pigtail* to make the connection to your adapter card. These cables are available from several sources.

All these connector types have available bullet-type adapters. These are used (for example) to join two N-type male connectors. In all cases, even though attenuation is minimal (usually between .15dB and .25dB per connector), use as few connectors or adapters as you possibly can to do the job.

For more information regarding coaxial cable and connectors and adapters I've found the following Web sites to be most helpful:

- ✔ **RadioLabs.com:** www.radiolabs.com
- ✔ **WarDrivingWorld.com:** www.wardrivingworld.com
- ✔ **HD Communications:** www.wirelessnetworkproducts.com
- ✔ **HyperLink Technologies:** www.hyperlinktech.com

Setting up an outdoor directional antenna

A directional antenna must be free to rotate 360 degrees around its vertical axis; you can probably imagine some of the difficulties in fabricating a mounting system. Most directional antennas include hardware (usually U-bolts, bar clamps, and nuts) designed to allow the mounting of the antenna to a pole. By using the included pole-mounting hardware to attach the antenna to a short piece of pipe, you've created half of the mount.

The second half of this high-tech (yeah, right) mount consists of another short piece of pipe with an inside diameter that's equal to — or ever so slightly larger than — the outside diameter of the pipe to which you've mounted your antenna. This second piece of pipe is what you affix, by whatever method you deem appropriate, to the body of your vehicle. The first pipe cleverly slides into the second pipe, leaving the directional antenna free to rotate in any direction, as shown in Figure 4-10.

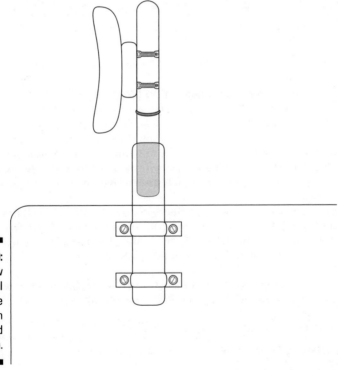

Figure 4-10:
This is how the mount I describe might look in its finished form.

If you fabricate and install such a mount, keep a few things in mind:

- ✔ Make sure that your antenna is free to rotate through a full 360 degrees without any interference and without being blocked by any obstructions.

- ✔ Once the antenna has been aimed toward the signal source, you need a way to secure the antenna in that position. There are several ways to do the job, ranging from a friction clamp to wedges made from Popsicle sticks to duct tape.

- ✔ You can use thick-walled (at least 1/16th inch) PVC pipe for both portions of your fancy homemade antenna-mounting device.

Once you've fabricated your mounting device, you need to run antenna cable. For the most part, you can follow the guidelines set out in the previous section — with the understanding that you have to be able to connect and disconnect your antenna quickly and easily from the main antenna cable.

I recommend attaching a short length of LMR-400 cable to your antenna that has a male type-N connector on the dangling end. That way, with a female type-N connector on the main portion of the antenna cable, you can easily connect or disconnect your antenna without disturbing the more permanently installed main antenna cable.

Setting up an indoor antenna

I could seriously impress myself if I could come up with some tantalizing high-tech secrets for setting up an indoor antenna — but there's just not much to it. You attach it to your adapter card and it works. There are only three things you need to consider, and I know, given the chance, that you (and possibly Fritz, my stuffed frog) would figure them out with no input from me.

Now that Fritz has heard his name mentioned, he's listening, so I have to be careful when I tell you (I don't want him getting a swelled head), that he *is* smarter than the average frog, stuffed or otherwise. For example, I know for sure that, after very little deliberation, Fritz would

- ✔ **Place the antenna as high as possible:** Yep, it doesn't matter whether it's an outdoor or indoor antenna; you want to get it up in the air.

- ✔ **Avoid obstructions:** Since wood and metal obstruct Wi-Fi radio signals and glass is almost interference-free, it makes sense to place the antenna as close to a window, or windows, as is practical.

✔ **Use a "protection" or adapter pigtail:** It's possible that the antenna you choose will utilize a connector other than the MMCX connection incorporated in the SMC2532W-B Wi-Fi card or the MC connector found on the Buffalo WLI-CB-G54A card. You can adapt the antenna to the card by using a pigtail with the appropriate connecters at either end. (See "Making the connection," earlier in this chapter.)

Putting an External Amplifier in the Mix

I've found it really handy to amplify my wireless signal when I'm hauling over-dimensional freight (you know — WIDE LOAD stuff). It's hard enough to find adequate parking when I'm hauling freight that fits nicely on the trailer, but hauling something wide or long cuts down my choices and usually leaves me looking for my hiking boots and canteen for the trek to the truck stop to get a shower and a meal. (It feels like that, anyway.)

When parking that far from the facilities, it often seems that the wireless signal strength lacks gusto. In those situations, if you have an amplifier in conjunction with a high-gain antenna, you're still in business. Here's where the sections entitled "Setting up an outdoor omnidirectional antenna" and "Setting up an outdoor directional antenna" come in especially handy: The same guidelines for installing the antenna, as well as for planning and installing the coaxial antenna cable, apply to an amplifier — with only one additional consideration: leave the coax a bit longer. Here's why . . .

When installing an external amplifier, always leave the terminating end of the coax about eight to ten inches longer than you otherwise might. That way, if you need to bend the cable to connect it to the amplifier, you can do it gently. The amplifier can then be easily incorporated into the system.

Providing power is the only real problem I've encountered when installing an amplifier, whether for intermittent or constant use. The amplifiers included in most kits include a power cord designed to provide 12 volts of DC power to the device. In most instances, this cord is long enough to reach the power source it's designed to access — but sometimes you might find that the placement you've chosen for your amplifier is a bit too far from the plug.

Resist the urge to alter the power cord provided with your amplifier. You'll likely void your amplifier's warranty and you might damage the transformer. Rather than try to splice extra lengths of wire into the cord, you're better off if you install a compatible plug close to the location of the amplifier. If you feel that you absolutely, positively, *must* lengthen or otherwise alter the cord, call the manufacturer before you do so. See whether they can make up a custom cord or provide you with an alternative solution.

I've been told by people I trust that the coaxial cable between an amplifier and an antenna must be a minimum of 18 inches long. I personally recommend doubling that minimum so any bends in the cable will be gentle.

Installing for intermittent use

The primary reason for installing an amplifier that you only use intermittently is purely one of neighborly consideration. Providing you followed my advice about extending your range in Chapter 3, your system, including an amplifier, won't exceed the FCC power-output regulations. Even so, when you find yourself parked three feet from another hotspot user, it's possible that your high-output setup might cause interference problems for your neighbors.

By mounting the amplifier near the termination point of your coax, you can simply disconnect your antenna cable and pigtail from the amplifier and connect the pigtail directly to the antenna cable, bypassing the amplifier. This arrangement gives you the benefit of a high-gain antenna without creating an interference problem for your neighbors every time you use Wi-Fi.

Be sure that your amplifier is powered down *before* you disconnect the coaxial cables. Failing to do so might damage the amplifier.

Installing for constant use

A permanent, constant-use installation differs from an intermittent installation only in the options available to you for slightly increasing the efficiency of your amplifier and antenna. By locating your amplifier close to your antenna, you can limit attenuation to a level that's nearly immeasurable. If you're using LMR-400 coaxial cable (as I've suggested) and your cable run is, say, 20 feet, then your signal-strength loss is approximately 1.34dB. This is by no means excessive — but you can reduce loss to less than .25dB if you place your amplifier 3 feet from the antenna.

Because you don't need to connect and disconnect from the amplifier, there's no reason to locate it near the area you'll most likely use your computer and you're free to mount it anywhere that's convenient. You might even, in this type of installation, be able to mount your amplifier in an area that's both nearer the antenna and closer to the power source.

If a constant-use installation is something you're considering, you might also want to make sure you have an alternate method of connecting with hotspots just in case you do run across a situation in which your amplifier is causing problems for your neighbors.

Part II
Surfing the Net Unplugged

The 5th Wave   By Rich Tennant

"Ironically, he went out there looking for a 'hot spot'."

In this part . . .

I cover the meat and potatoes of Wi-Fi — connecting to the Internet at a Wi-Fi hotspot. Here's where you find out about the directories and devices you can employ to help you find a hotspot, locate the best signal at that hotspot, and make your connection to the Internet. Okay, none of this is all that complex or complicated — but (as my sock-puppet savants have so often expressed) complications *can* arise. So, in Chapter 6, you find out how to troubleshoot some of the problems you can encounter when connecting at a hotspot. In addition, because sending e-mail from hotspots can sometimes be a source of frustration, I describe some means and methods of e-mailing from hotspots that make it at least as reliable as the Pony Express (and a lot more secure).

Chapter 5

Spotting Hotspots

. . . .

. . . .

*B*ecause public wireless networks (better known as *hotspots*) have limited broadcast ranges, you can't just park anywhere and expect to connect to the Internet via Wi-Fi. You might, however, be surprised at the number of places besides truck stops making wireless Internet access available to you. The trick is in finding those places when you're traveling through unfamiliar areas.

In this chapter, I tell you about my favorite methods of finding hotspots that might be hospitable to large vehicles.

Checking Wireless Directories

I'm big on directories. I've got about three truck stop and diesel fuel directories; I've got a couple of truck service directories; I've got two tire service directories, and I've even got a few phone directories that I carry around with me. For the most part, though, a lot of the information printed in these books is also available on the Net. For example, www.dieselboss.com has several excellent online directories available, including a comprehensive truck stop directory — which I've been using with greater frequency because it's updated often.

When it comes to finding hotspots, you also have several online choices. Online directories make perfect sense because the number of hotspots in the U.S., Canada, and around the world is growing so fast that a printed directory would be obsolete before it ever made it to the shelves. A few of the available online directories are

✔ **JiWire.com:** The JiWire search engine and database powers several directories besides their own. The best among them are

• *Wi-Fi Zone Finder:* Not long ago, the Wi-Fi Alliance partnered with JiWire to provide a directory of hotspots that are Wi-Fi Certified (meaning that, because all the equipment used by the hotspot is Wi-Fi Certified, your Wi-Fi Certified equipment is guaranteed to be compatible). It can be found at `http://wi-fi.jiwire.com`.

- *PC World Hotspot Finder:* Along with the hotspot locator powered by JiWire, PC World lists links to articles relevant to Wi-Fi users. Topics covered include buying guides and how-to articles. You can find it at `http://pcworld.jiwire.com`.

- *USA Today Tech wireless center:* Here you can find links to current news and articles pertaining specifically to wireless technology along with the JiWire hotspot locator. The page is found at `http://usatoday.jiwire.com`.

In true geek fashion, the word *JiWire* is a kind of acronym invented by the owners of this Web business. They couldn't find a verb meaning "to connect devices wirelessly," so they invented this one, which means, "joining invisible wires." This is my favorite online directory because it's more than just a directory service. JiWire offers a ton of advice and articles ranging from new product reviews to a Wi-Fi user guide and a discussion forum.

- ✔ **WiFi411.com:** This site isn't as versatile and doesn't offer as many services as JiWire.com, but I still use it quite a bit, because within the results, a lot of useful information is included, such as the number of access points and the wireless standard that the hotspot uses.

- ✔ **Wi-FiHotSpotList.com:** Billing itself as "The Definitive Wi-Fi HotSpot Directory," this site is an offshoot of Wi-FiPlanet.com. I don't know if they're the definitive directory or not, but I do know that a wealth of wireless information is tucked within the pages of Wi-FiPlanet.com.

- ✔ **VZ Local Search:** Although this site isn't technically a directory, I've found VZ Local Search to be a very useful traveling tool. This site, at `www.vzlocal.com`, focuses on finding highlights and attractions, including hotspots, in various localities.

- ✔ **The Wi-Fi-FreeSpot Directory:** There are more free access hotspots than you can shake a stick at, and this directory, which is part of the JiWire Network and found at `www.wififreespot.com`, focuses exclusively on them. It also provides some information and guidelines regarding etiquette and use of these free hotspots.

Getting the most out of online directories

Most of the directories use filters so that, by setting some parameters, you can narrow your search in ways that are likely to return results that fit your particular situation. The amount of filtering available varies from one directory to another, but in most cases, the better you get at using these tools, the better your search results are.

For example, at JiWire, the advanced search feature includes a filter that includes cafes and campgrounds as well as RV parks and travel centers. By specifying the type of business or venue you're searching for, you can narrow your search in such a way that the results should correspond nicely with your needs.

When you're using the filters provided within these directories, keep in mind that you don't want to totally ignore businesses like a coffeehouse or bookstore that might be located near an area easily accessible to an RV or truck. I've been able to connect, on occasion, with a coffeehouse or motel hotspot located near a truck stop that had no wireless access, and once, when staying in a motel that offered no access, I was able to connect to the hotspot provided by a neighboring RV park.

As good as these directories are, they're absolutely not perfection in motion. With the number of hotspots opening up each day, it's not likely that all of them will be listed in any one directory. Online directories also rely on information provided to them by either the proprietors or users of the business or venue making the hotspot available. Most of them take great pains to verify that the information they provide is accurate, but if, for example, a coffeehouse goes out of business or an RV park ceases to offer Wi-Fi to its customers and no one bothers to inform the directories, it might be quite some time before it's removed.

Putting a directory on your device

So, here you are with "Nowhere" lurking on the horizon, and you're wondering where you can find a nearby hotspot. Obviously, using an online directory when you're looking for a place to connect seems a bit silly. Fortunately, the good folks at JiWire have anticipated this very problem. In early 2004, JiWire unveiled a downloadable hotspot directory that can be updated whenever the user is online. In May of 2005, however, the free directory was rolled into a hotspot security utility known as SpotLock. The directory is still free, and you can download SpotLock and choose to use the directory free of charge. You can't, however, choose to download the directory only. I cover the full SpotLock security utility in Chapter 10, and you can find complete instructions for downloading and using it there.

Using Wireless Network Detectors

With or without a hotspot directory, online or otherwise, it's sometimes nice to be able to detect the presence of a wireless signal. You might, for example, want to connect to a particular hotspot, but you wonder if you're too far from the signal source to make the connection. You could get out your laptop, boot it up, and find out whether you've got a good signal where you're at — but an easier solution is to use a Wi-Fi network detector.

Network detectors, sometimes referred to as Wi-Fi *sniffers,* are usually fairly small units — some are designed to fit on a key chain. Before you rush out to buy one, know that owning one of these devices is indicative of potential membership in that group commonly referred to as geeks. I put a piece of duct tape over the Star Trek insignia on my shirt when I use one so that some doubt about my geek status remains.

Shopping for a Wi-Fi detector

Several manufacturers of wireless products include one or more Wi-Fi detectors in their line of offerings, and at least one company's primary product is a highly acclaimed wireless network detector. But the field isn't filled with a wide choice of products. In some ways, that's good because you don't have a confusing array of devices to choose from, but in other ways, it's not so good because there's not so much competition-driven innovation.

When you're shopping for a wireless detector, consider these things:

- **Accuracy of network detection:** This might seem too obvious to be listed, but not all detectors can detect the presence of a wireless network with a high level of accuracy. Some inaccurate detectors indicate the presence of a network when, in fact, a microwave oven or cordless phone is the only thing present. In other cases, it's not that the detector indicates the presence of a nonexistent network, but rather that they fail to recognize the existence of one or more networks in a given area.

- **Signal strength indication:** Most detectors offer only a few lights to indicate relative signal strength but at least one of them uses a bar graph displayed on an LCD screen.

- **Additional features:** With only the first two features, you have a good idea as to the presence and relative strength of a signal, but consider these things as well:

  - *SSID (Service Set Identifier):* The SSID is merely the name of the network. If you're trying to connect with the Flying J hotspot while you're in an adjacent parking lot, it's good to know whether your detector is picking up the Flying J signal or that of a nearby home or business wireless network.

  - *Security status:* Because you're looking for open networks, it's nice to know whether the networks being detected are open or secure. By the way, just because a network is open doesn't mean the owner intends it to be open to the public. I talk more about this issue in Chapter 6.

- *Channel:* This feature tells you how much interference there might be when connecting with a nearby hotspot. If several other networks are in the area and on the same channel you might have a bit more interference than if the channels of the nearby networks are spaced apart.

The device you choose to purchase, if indeed you want one of these gadgets, depends largely on the amount of information you want to gather. The following list illustrates a few of the choices you have:

- ✔ **Intego WiFi Locator** (www.intego.com): This keychain-type device looks a bit like those remote door-lock devices everybody seems to have. (I guess if I ever replace my '68 Ford pickup, I'll get one.) With only a button and four LEDs, this device doesn't give you a whole lot of info.

- ✔ **Smith Micro QuickLink Wi-Fi Seeker** (www.smithmicro.com): This one looks exactly like the Intego WiFi Locater, and if you look at the specs for both, those also match; they even cost almost exactly the same.

- ✔ **Kensington WiFi Finder Plus** (http://us.kensington.com/html/5703.html): This is another key chain device with a string of LED signal strength indicators. This one uses five lights and also includes a Bluetooth detector.

- ✔ **Canary Digital Hotspotter** (www.canarywireless.com/hs10.html): The Digital Hotspotter is a bit bigger than keychain devices but offers more information. With this device you can find out not only the presence and strength of the signal, but also name, channel, and security status.

Another group of Wi-Fi detectors does double duty as wireless adapters. As adapters, the ones I highlight are all USB-powered; as detectors, they use a Li-ion battery and can be used independently of your laptop. Here are three:

- ✔ **Linksys WUSBF54G:** SSID, signal strength, channel, and security status are displayed on the LCD screen in the order of strength. The device can also be configured so that only "open" 802.11b and g networks are detected. See www.linksys.com.

- ✔ **TRENDnet TEW-509UB:** You can customize hotspot searches to find networks by SSID, signal strength, or security, and the Li-ion battery is recharged when connected to the USB port. Find more at www.trendnet.com.

- ✔ **ZyXEL AG-225H:** Offering the ability to scroll through the available networks, this detector indicates, on its LCD screen, information including SSID, signal strength, and channel. Besides 802.11b and g networks, the AG-225H detects 802.11a networks, too. You can find details at www.us.zyxel.com.

Sniffing out a signal

To use a wireless network detector, you need to have mastered the art of pushing buttons. My wife tells me I'm an expert button-pusher, and I suspect that every truck driver on the face of the earth is also quite well qualified. (I'm sure this trait applies equally for those pushing an RV down the road.)

With the two keychain detectors, you just push the button, and if a hotspot or wireless network is detected, the LEDs light up, indicating relative signal strength. By turning a total of 360 degrees, 90 degrees at a time, you can get a good idea of the direction in which the detected signal is originating.

With each push of the button, these devices detect a single network. If you're in an area where more than one hotspot is present, you might have to push the button several times — and face a different direction with each push of the button — to find the strongest signal. You'd think that the strongest one would be detected first, but for some reason, that's not always the case. The Canary Digital Hotspotter, like the keychain detectors, also picks up just one hotspot at a time, so you need to push the button a few times to be sure you exhaust the potential list of hotspot candidates. When you push the button, the display indicates that the device is looking for networks, and if one is discovered, it displays information pertaining to it. If you push the button again, it scans for hotspots again. If a new wireless signal is detected, the information for that network is displayed, or if no other network is detected, the information for the first one is displayed. If no networks are present, the display gives that indication.

The detector-adapter combo units work in a similar fashion but, since they detect all the available networks with one push of the button, you only need to push buttons as you make each 90-degree turn.

Putting Network Detection Software to Work

Whatever connection management utility you happen to use, whether it's WZC, JiWire, or the utility included with your wireless adapter, it includes some form of active-scanning, network detection software. Also available are several stand-alone software applications designed to provide as much information as possible concerning the available networks in a given area.

Active scanning network detection software sends out probe requests on every channel that the wireless radio transceiver is configured to use. Most cards in North America are configured for Channels 1 through 11. (A few cards use Channel 6 only. If that's the only channel your card is configured for, that's the only channel that the probe request goes out on.) If any hotspots are detected in the area, the AP (access point) sends a probe response in answer to the request.

By installing one of these active scanning utilities on your laptop, you can get quite a bit of valuable information. Among other things, you can use it to help you accurately aim a directional antenna. With the installation of a network detection application, you can turn a PDA into a highly effective wireless network detector. Among the large number of available program applications are the following:

- **NetStumbler:** I think I can say, without fear of contradiction, that this is the most popular of the publicly available wireless network detection software applications.

- **MiniStumbler:** Designed to be used on Pocket PCs, the application is both effective and easy to use.

- **WiFiFoFum:** The name alone is reason enough to make mention of this application written for use on a Pocket PC.

Both 'Stumbler software programs are, according to the author, Marius Milner, "beggarware." Although they're offered free of cost, if you use one and like it, you can (as a person of honor) leave a donation to help defray costs and provide a bit of remuneration for the author's efforts. *Beggarware* also means the software has no warranty — so if it doesn't work, it doesn't work, and you can't expect a whole lot of technical support.

'Stumbler software isn't extensively tested for hardware compatibility; although it's compatible with most integrated wireless solutions and adapter cards, it might not work with yours. If it doesn't, just delete the program from your system — it won't cause any problems either way. I've tried it out with a few different adapter cards, as well as integrated wireless, and it's worked well in each case. But as they say on TV, your results might vary.

WiFiFoFum seems to be no more extensively tested, and it's compatible with the Windows Mobile 2003 platforms only. However, Aspecto Software (the group that developed WiFiFoFum) is continually working on newer versions, so I expect it to be compatible with Windows Mobile 5.0 as well. As far as which combination of Pocket PC devices and wireless solutions it works with — built-in, CF, or SDIO — all I can say is: Give it a try. The cool, radar-like display is worth the effort to download and install it.

Adding NetStumbler to a laptop

Open your browser, if it isn't already open, and navigate your way to the NetStumbler download page at www.netstumbler.com/downloads.

1. **Click the NetStumbler Installer link.**

   The Download Manager window opens.

2. **Click Save, and save the file to your desktop.**

3. **When the download is complete, close the dialog box and close any other currently running program applications.**

4. **Double-click the NetStumbler Installer icon.**

   A security warning might appear, asking whether you know the software is safe. It is.

5. **Click Run.**

   The NetStumbler setup wizard begins with the EULA. Read through it and, providing you don't find anything objectionable within it . . .

6. **Click I Agree.**

   The Network Stumbler Setup dialog box opens, allowing you to choose the components you want to install.

7. **From the Select the Type of Install drop-down list, choose the type of installation you want, as shown in Figure 5-1, and click Next.**

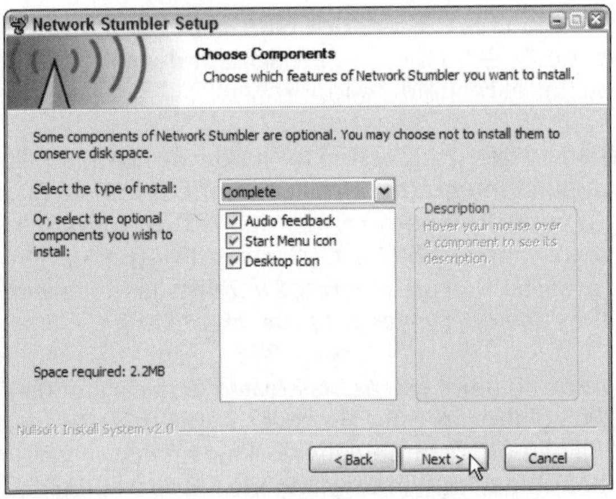

Figure 5-1:
I choose
Complete
to install
everything.

8. **Although you're given the opportunity to choose the location in which to install the files, I recommend you simply click Install to maintain the default installation location.**

   After the installation is complete, click Close.

   The NetStumbler Help menu opens to the release notes, as shown in Figure 5-2. It's a quick read, so go ahead and give it a gander.

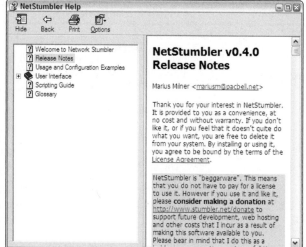

Configuring NetStumbler

Double-click the NetStumbler antenna icon on your desktop to launch the utility. The first screen you see might be empty and gray. That's okay. The amount of configuration you need to do depends on your situation. Familiarize yourself with a few of the items available on the two toolbars.

A lot of the available options are geared toward users who engage in the geek sport of *wardriving*. You might have seen this term — which, according to legend, was coined by Marius Milner — referenced in various places on the Internet. The term is derived from the 1983 movie, *WarGames*, in which David Lightman, played by Matthew Broderick, breaks into a Department of Defense computer by using a technique called *wardialing*. These days, *wardrivers* cruise around town in their geekmobiles, packing laptops loaded with active and passive scanning-detection software and some strange-looking antennas, searching out open wireless networks — otherwise known as *nodes*. Because the legality of this activity is in doubt, and because you probably won't be cruising through quiet neighborhoods in your truck or RV looking for open home networks you can hack into, I don't dwell on those features of NetStumbler.

Take a look at Tables 5-1 and 5-2 for a brief description of a few of the pertinent features.

Table 5-1	Status Bar Items
Item	*Description*
File	From here you can open a new or saved session, save a session, and close out a session.
View	Customize the way your 'Stumbler session window appears. The last menu choice, Options, allows you to set session parameters.
Device	Lists the wireless radios, the type of driver used, and allows you to choose the one currently used.
Window	Allows you to manipulate the way the session window is rendered and the way information is displayed.
Help	Brings up the Help menu.

Table 5-2	Toolbar Items
Icon	*Description*
New	Opens a new 'Stumbler session.
Open	Opens a saved 'Stumbler session.
Disk	Saves a session.
Arrow	Starts or stops scanning during a session.
Gears	Starts or stops Automatic Card Reconfiguration for scanning. WZC is disabled and the card is set for Any SSID.
Speaker	Enables or disables the Signal to Noise Ratio MIDI tone.
Options	Opens the Options menu to set session parameters.
Large Icons	Displays large icons in List mode only.
Small Icons	Displays small icons in either List or Detail mode.
List	Displays Active APs in a list with no information details.
Details	Displays Active APs including detailed information.

The first thing you want to do after starting NetStumbler is set some session parameters:

1. **Click Options, and click the General tab. Set the scan speed to fast, as shown in Figure 5-3.**

   This increases the frequency of the scans, which, in turn, increases the accuracy of the updates. It also makes it easier to use the available information to aim a directional antenna.

Figure 5-3:
Speed up
the scan
speed.

2. **Still working with the Options dialog box, click the MIDI tab, and select the Enable MIDI Output of SNR check box.**

   When you enable this feature, NetStumbler gives an audible indication of each AP's signal strength. The higher the tone, the stronger the signal. The other choices alter the tone sound and pitch, and you can fiddle with them until you've found a sufficiently annoying sound.

3. **Click Apply, and then click OK.**

   The Options dialog box closes, and the settings are applied.

Finding a network

When you first launch NetStumbler on your laptop, your screen is a lifeless gray. To find a network, follow these steps:

1. **Click the New icon to start a new session and open a new session display window.**

   You should notice, in the right pane of the window, a number of APs within your view. If, at the bottom of the NetStumbler window, you see the words No APs active, you're either in an area without any wireless networks, or NetStumbler isn't using the correct device.

2. **Click the Device menu, and if you see a check mark by a wireless card other than the one you're using, select it, as shown in Figure 5-5.**

   For example, NetStumbler by default wants to use my integrated wireless card, but because I'm using my Buffalo WLI-CB-G54A adapter, I need to select that card instead.

3. **In the pane on the right, you see the wireless networks available, as shown in Figure 5-4.**

   NetStumbler uses different colors for the active AP icons to indicate the strength of the signal. Green indicates a strong signal that you, very likely, can connect with. Red, as you might have guessed, is a signal that isn't a good connection candidate. Yellow indicates a marginal, maybe-yes-and-maybe-no signal, and gray indicates a signal that's barely detectable. If you see a small lock icon within the signal strength icon, that's an indication that the detected network is secured and unavailable for public connection. Hotspots, because they're open to the public, won't be secured.

Figure 5-4:
Two networks are in range of my card: Flying J and what appears to be a secured home network named Skydiver.

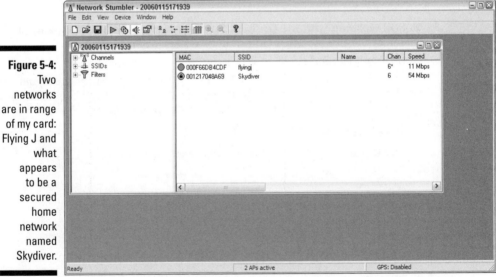

Using 'Stumbler to aim your antenna

Okay, you're ready to use NetStumbler to help you aim your directional. Focus your attention, now, on the left pane of the session window and follow these steps:

1. **Click the + (plus sign) next to the SSID heading to expand the information tree.**

2. **Now click the + (plus sign) next to the SSID name you're intending to connect with to further expand the information tree and display the hotspot MAC address.**

3. **Click the MAC address.**

   This changes the right pane into a graphic signal strength display. The green portion of the display represents the strength of the signal, and the red portion, on the bottom, indicates the noise level. Not every card displays the noise level.

4. **By slowly — very slowly — turning your antenna, you notice that the graph indicates a rise or fall of signal strength.**

   Because you enabled the sound feature, you should also hear tone pitch getting higher or lower.

5. **Once you've found the best direction to point your antenna, don't forget to move it up and down through the vertical axis to further increase the accuracy of your aim.**

   When the tone and the graph have reached their highest points, your antenna is optimally aimed.

In Figure 5-5, you can see that as I move my antenna, pointing it more accurately toward the signal source, the graph begins to move upward until I go past the optimal aim. As I begin to move back, the graph again spikes. You might also notice that after I connect the antenna, a whole bunch more APs appear. It might be noted that the Buffalo connection utility indicates the presence of only two APs, while the JiWire connection utility sees the same available networks that NetStumbler does.

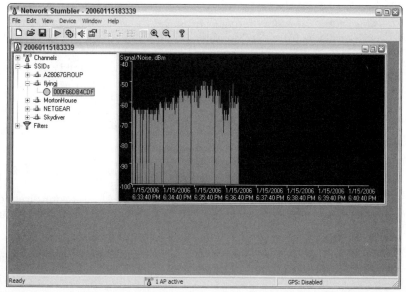

Figure 5-5:
The graph
helps you
aim a
directional
antenna.

Some other cool features are, if you're not wardriving, just toys. The main one I'm thinking of is the GPS function that can put a latitude and longitude with each location. Another handy feature lets you perform a WHOIS inquiry on the IP address of the AP, which might help to determine whether it's a legitimate hotspot. Just right-click the MAC address shown in the right pane to start the search. In addition, applications such as StumbVerter, by Sonar Security, that can take that information and import it to a mapping utility like MapPoint.

Adding MiniStumbler to your PDA

If you have a PDA, you can install MiniStumber on your computer, following the same steps for installing NetStumber, outlined earlier in this chapter. After the installation is completed, you can choose to open the Readme file. I suggest doing so, but if you'd rather do so later, you can access it from the Help menu. When a reminder to check your Pocket PC opens, click OK. You can now connect your Pocket PC to your computer via cable or cradle. Your sync software starts automatically, and the files upload to the handheld.

That's pretty much the size of it, and you're ready to give MiniStumbler a go.

The menus, icons, and features of MiniStumbler, although not as extensive, are very similar to NetStumbler. Each of the items and icons that correspond with those found on NetStumbler offers the same functionality. That means that you can configure MiniStumbler and use it in much the same way as you would NetStumbler, with a couple of exceptions. First, MiniStumbler doesn't support the MIDI tone, and second, it has no graphic display of the signal strength and noise.

Most of the information that you can get from the NetStumbler right pane is also available from MiniStumbler, but in order to see it, you have to scroll a bit more. MiniStumbler also uses the same intuitive colors to indicate signal strength and the same lock icon to indicate a secured network.

GPS functionality in MiniStumbler is also very similar to that of NetStumbler, and like in NetStumbler, right-clicking the MAC address opens a menu allowing you to perform a WHOIS inquiry on displayed IP addresses.

Chapter 6

Using Truck – and RV – Friendly Hotspots

*B*ack in the dark ages of mobile computing (those dismal days when dialup was dominant), an open phone jack was all an establishment needed to be considered-friendly. To a certain extent, that's still true — but because connecting to the Internet from the comfort of your rolling home is so convenient, many people avoid venues that don't offer Wi-Fi in addition to dialup. But how (considering the proliferation of providers) do you make an informed decision regarding which Wi-Fi service to sign up with — and whether to make a long- or short-term commitment to that provider?

In this chapter, I help you make some decisions by delving into the details of your available choices. I give you an idea of what you can expect the first time you pull into a truck stop or RV park in hopes of using a wireless Internet connection. I also help you make that connection — and offer tips on troubleshooting a few common problems. Because sending e-mail is sometimes an issue at hotspots, I spend some time investigating the problems surrounding it, and offer some solutions.

Evaluating Your Choices

I don't remember a technology that's caught on and spread as rapidly as Wi-Fi. I'm sure there've been hundreds of rapidly spreading technologies,

and that you can remember several, but I don't. I'm sure of one thing —
because of the rapid spread of Wi-Fi, no one has a monopoly on the wireless
Internet access market. As a matter of fact, while some dominant players
have emerged, literally thousands of Wi-Fi providers offer services ranging
from free wireless Internet access at their own business to nationwide or
international wireless Internet services. The latter are known as wireless
Internet service providers (WISPs).

Filling in the middle ground are vast numbers of companies and enterprises
engaging in the business of setting up hotspots custom tailored to their customers' needs. Often, these companies specialize in specific venues such as
truck stops and travel centers, RV parks and campgrounds, hotels and motels,
or restaurants and cafes. Most of these make an attempt to set up a network of
hotspots at similar locations so that folks who frequent these similar venues
can purchase a monthly Wi-Fi subscription and plan their stops accordingly.

Although long-term commitments at reduced rates are attractive — you can
whittle the cost from $4 to $10 per day to $1 to $2 per day — the caveat to
commitment is one of accessibility. If you, for whatever reason, don't find
yourself frequenting the same RV park or truck stop chain most days, the discount doesn't make the commitment worthwhile. Of course, influencing your
choice is part of the provider's plan. If you have a compelling reason to — such
as access to a pool, a good buffet, or Wi-Fi — you might bypass the mom-and-
pop park or truck stop so you can enjoy the amenity you seek. Some might
feel their freedom and spontaneity slipping away, while others might find a
new feeling of comfort in familiar surroundings and service.

Because of quality-of-service issues, I still recommend a try-before-you-buy
trial period. By that, I mean: Use the service at a few locations to find out
whether you're happy with the quality and ease of use. In addition to that,
make an effort to evaluate your habits before you enter a long-term commitment. Here are a few things to consider:

- ✔ **Regular routes:** Whether you travel by truck or RV, do you usually maintain a regular route? If you do, it's possible, even likely, that your stops
  are also fairly regular. If you find that you already stop at the same chain
  most of the time, a long-term commitment might be in order.

- ✔ **Mandated fuel stops:** With skyrocketing fuel costs, many trucking companies strive to control costs by making deals with fuel providers and
  insisting that drivers buy fuel at specific locations. If these locations also
  offer Wi-Fi, again, a long-term commitment might be worthwhile.

- ✔ **Long stays:** This pertains more to RVers than truckers. If you stay at a
  park for an extended period of time, signing up for a single week or month
  would seem to make sense — even though a multi-month or annual subscription might not be wise.

Truck stops and travel centers

A few years ago, I first found out that the Broadway Flying J in Tacoma, Washington, had become — at least, as far as I know — the first truck stop to offer a wireless Internet connection to its customers. I was ecstatic — never mind the fact that I have never been able to find a parking place anywhere near this truck stop, let alone in the parking lot.

Even though I knew I'd never use a Wi-Fi connection there, I was equally sure that it was just a matter of time before Wi-Fi spread across the country and became widely available at truck stops where I *could* park. And I was right. Before I knew it, truck stop after truck stop was becoming a hotspot. The early drawback was, however, that a few start-up WISPs bit the dust shortly after signing up a bunch of long-term customers. Others, though, (like Flying J and TA TravelCenters) became WISPs themselves or (like Pilot, Petro, and Love's) partnered with companies that demonstrated a level of stability and business sense that mirrored their own.

These days, a majority of truck stops and travel centers — both chains and independents — make wireless Internet connections available to those who find food and refuge in their restaurants and parking lots. Because of the number of independents and small chains offering Wi-Fi, a complete and comprehensive list is not forthcoming but what follows is a pretty good list of the major players.

- ✔ **Flying J Travel Plazas:** I have to list them first. They were the first to offer Wi-Fi, and they might well be the most widely available hotspot operator catering to truckers and RV enthusiasts. Besides offering Wi-Fi at their travel centers, they also have hotspots set up at various extended areas.

- ✔ **TA TravelCenters:** Offering what they call TA SpeedZone WiFi Hotspots at more than 150 of their travel centers, TA has to rank near the top of any truck stop hotspot list.

- ✔ **Pilot Travel Centers:** Pilot (like many others desiring to offer Wi-Fi to their customers) went through some hotspot growing pains, but now, with SiriCOMM, they've partnered with a very stable WISP.

- ✔ **Love's Travel Stops:** I include them just below Pilot because (like Pilot) they suffered through similar Wi-Fi woes, and now, (like Pilot) they've partnered with SiriCOMM as their wireless Internet access provider.

- ✔ **IdleAire Technologies:** IdleAire is an attractive choice because they're not a chain-specific service. You're as likely to find them located at a Pilot or Petro as you are to find them at a Love's or TA. Wi-Fi is only one small portion of what this company offers at truck stops equipped with their award-winning Advanced Truckstop Electrification (ATE) system.

> IdleAire, undergoing a rapid expansion, is popping up all over the place at truck stops and travel plazas.
>
> ✔ **Bosselman Travel Centers:** Although they're not a large, nationwide, chain, Bosselman is among the very few truck stops to offer free Wi-Fi at their locations in Nebraska, Kansas, and Iowa.

When you compare the plans and services, Bosselman Travel Centers offers the simplest of all the plans as I write this book — it's free. After that, although none of the plans are complicated, they do vary somewhat in cost, as you can see in Table 6-1.

Table 6-1	Wi-Fi Rates at Truck Stops and Travel Centers				
Provider	**Hourly**	**Daily**	**Monthly**	**Annually**	**Reward Cards**
Flying J	N/A	$4.95	$19.95*	$199.95	N/A
TA	$1.49	$4.49	$19.99	$149.99	Yes
SiriCOMM	N/A	$6.95	$21.99	$189.95	N/A
IdleAire (Sales tax may apply)	$1.25	$2.95	$19.95	$ 69.95	N/A
Bosselman's	Free	Free	Free	Free	N/A

*The monthly rate at Flying J, if you're not paying by an automatically billed credit card, is $24.95

An annual or even month-by-month commitment to Flying J, TA, SiriCOMM, or IdleAire is cheaper than similar subscriptions from most other national providers, particularly those common in coffee shops such as Starbucks. One of the few services that come close to competing with truck-stop and travel-center monthly rates is Boingo Wireless, which charges $21.95 a month, but some of their hotspot locations tack on an extra usage fee.

You should know, however, that even if you have an IdleAire Wi-Fi subscription, the cost of using the full IdleAire facilities isn't reduced. (But I did put that bug in someone's ear.)

Another area of interest, at least to truckers, is Wi-Fi at the weigh station. SiriCOMM is the primary WISP providing hotspots at PrePass weigh stations around the country. I'm not one that really enjoys hanging out at the scale house but — sometimes voluntarily and sometimes not — I have spent a night or three relaxing in the soft glow of the Scales Open sign. Doing so with wireless Internet access makes the stay much more enjoyable.

RV parks and campgrounds

Following hot on the heels of the wildfire-like spread of Wi-Fi availability in truck stops and travel plazas is the rapid proliferation of wireless Internet access at RV parks and campgrounds. Ranging from mom-and-pop parks installing a single wireless router that campers can access only if they're visiting the office to major deployments utilizing multiple access points, bridges, or antennas that cover every campsite, your choices are both varied and inconsistent.

Besides quality of service inconsistencies, the question of cost is equally varied and inconsistent. The RV park and campground operators seem to be separated into three camps of similar size. Yes, I did intend the pun. Anyway, some park and campground operators view wireless Internet access as an amenity to be included in the space rental cost, believing that "free" Internet access draws customers and promotes loyalty. At the other end of the spectrum, another group of operators apparently views Wi-Fi as a luxury — and charges accordingly. In between these two camps is a group offering wireless Internet access at a reasonable and competitive cost.

Many of the parks and campgrounds offering Wi-Fi partner with a WISP or a hotspot installation and management company that specializes in park or campground installations. These partnerships can be structured in several ways, but usually, customer and technical support, as well as any billing, is handled by the WISP or management company, not the park. In most cases, these installations are custom tailored to the park or campground, taking all the variables into consideration.

One of the major issues surrounding RV park and campground Wi-Fi installations is that of *signal coverage*. Because trees, buildings, hills, and even other RVs often clutter the line of sight between you and the access point, make sure that you ask — when you're renting your site — if the Wi-Fi coverage extends to the area you're being assigned.

Many of the providers, because of the way they set up their partnerships, offer fee-based access only one day or week at a time. Others, with set fee structures, offer daily, monthly, and annual subscriptions. A few of the major RV-park and campground Wi-Fi providers include

- ✔ **TengoInternet:** Wi-Fi charges vary from one RV park to another, and because of that, Tengo doesn't offer portable subscription plans. Users must sign up for service onsite, and most TengoInternet hotspot locations also offer prepaid cards.

- ✔ **Nomad Internet:** By providing a wide-ranging menu of installation levels and services, a venue owner can choose the installation that best meets its customers needs. The park operator can also choose whether to include the cost in the camping fee or charge separately. Only on-site signup is available.

✔ **RVwifi:** With partnership and roaming agreements, a subscription to RVwifi gets you access in many venues other than RV parks and campgrounds. Monthly subscriptions with an annual commitment also include dialup service. You can sign up onsite or on the Web at www.rvwifi.com.

✔ **Boingo Wireless:** Although they don't specialize in setting up RV parks or campgrounds, a subscription to Boingo garners wireless Internet access at over 200 RV parks and campgrounds as well as hundreds of other venues. You can sign up for Boingo, and download their free Wi-Fi-connection utility, at one of their hotspot locations or on the Web at www.boingo.com.

✔ **Coach Connect:** Offering daily, monthly, and seasonal (six-month) subscriptions, you can sign up at a hotspot location only. Coach Connect doesn't yet have a huge network of hotspots, but they're working on it. They also provide wireless Internet access at all the rest areas in the state of Texas. You can get more info at www.coachconnect.net.

✔ **Hotspotzz Network:** With hundreds of venues — most of them RV parks and campgrounds — you can choose a monthly subscription that includes both dialup and wireless Internet access, or Wi-Fi only. Hotspotzz is the WISP for most of the KOA Kampgrounds. You can get more information and sign up online at www.hotspotzz.com.

✔ **KOA Konnect:** If you usually "kamp" the KOA way, this might be the best deal on wheels. Most — not all, but most — of the hotspots provided by Hotspotzz and the KOA Konnect package also include dialup. You can get more information or sign up online at www.koakonnect.com/preportal/index.asp.

✔ **LinkSpot Networks:** They do it right. I've never had a problem getting connected at an RV park set up by LinkSpot. They offer hourly, daily, weekly, and monthly subscriptions. You can sign up on-site, or online at www.linkspot.com.

I can't come close to providing an exhaustive list of those WISPs servicing RV parks and campgrounds. Consult several online resources like Web sites and hotspot directories for more information. (I talk about directories in Chapter 5.) A few Web sites that I find both entertaining and helpful include

✔ **RV.net:** This site has more information than you could, if you were so inclined, shake a stick at. Check it out at www.rv.net.

✔ **RVtravel.com:** This site offers information, resources, and a pretty good forum. Point your browser toward www.rvtravel.com.

> ✔ **Trailer Life Directory:** This is the online home of the printed directory and offers information for those new to the life and those who could write a book. They've got, at least in my opinion, one of the best RV forums on the Web. You can find them at www.tldirectory.com/index.cfm.

Hotels, motels, and cafés

Although hotels, motels, and cafes might be frequented more often by airborne business travelers than RVers and truckers, they can, nonetheless, be handy places to get online while traveling the highway. These days just about every local specialty coffeehouse or bagel shop has a wireless hotspot, and many hotels and motels (and even a fast food restaurant or two), are serving up Wi-Fi.

Connecting at rest areas

Is using wireless services at rest areas a trend? I don't really know, but three states — Texas, Michigan and Iowa — offer wireless Internet access in their rest areas (or, as the Texans call them, safety rest areas). Each state, not surprisingly, has a different take on the concept of providing wireless Internet access to the traveling public.

In Iowa, you can log on to the World Wide Web wire-free, for free, at all but one rest area. You can't surf free of charge for long — 30 minutes is the limit — but that's long enough to download your e-mail; then you can head off to the next one and send your replies.

The Texas solution is far different. Cruise into any rest stop in Texas — choose from over a hundred of them — and you can get two hours of free wireless Internet access.

In order to log on to the hotspots provided in Texas rest areas, you need to enter credit card information to establish your account. Your card won't be charged for the first two hours, and at the end of that period, you're given the option of continuing the service; if you say yes, the WISP — which is Coach Connect — charges the cost to your card. Coast Connect, working under the name Road Connect, is also in the process of providing Wi-Fi services in the rest areas of Washington, Oregon, California, and Kansas.

Lastly, Michigan contracted with SBC (now AT&T) as their hotspot provider, so, if you're an AT&T Wi-Fi subscriber, you can get online under your current subscription. Otherwise, for $7.95 per day, you can get wireless Internet access through the MiWiFi program at three rest areas — the New Buffalo Welcome Center, Coldwater Welcome Center, and Clarkston Rest Area — as well as at several Michigan state parks.

For more information concerning rest area Wi-Fi, you can browse to the following Web addresses:

✔ **Iowa rest areas:** www.ispotaccess.com

✔ **Texas safety rest areas:** www.roadconnect.net

✔ **Michigan rest area information:** www.michigan.gov/wifi

When wireless Internet access is offered in a hotel or motel, it's usually an amenity included in the price of the room, but ask before you book the reservation. Cafés, restaurants, and coffeehouses, on the other hand, generally offer access in partnership with a provider that charges for the service. McDonald's, for example, in partnership with Wayport, is offering a nationwide plan in which, for as little as $5.00 per month, you can get Wi-Fi with your Big Mac.

Cost of access without a monthly subscription to one of the providers' plans specializing in the hospitality industry can vary between $6 to $10 per day. A few — very few — of the WISPs specializing in these venues offer service by the hour. Because a stay at a hotel or motel is the exception rather than the rule for those with homes on wheels and because only a few coffeehouses and bake shops offer truck and RV parking, a long-term commitment to any of their Wi-Fi providers is unlikely to make much sense.

Making the Connection

Getting logged on to a hotspot, no matter the provider or what the venue might be, involves very similar steps. If you're making the connection for the first time, you need the following items:

- ✔ **Wi-Fi-enabled device:** You need either a laptop or palmtop with an integrated wireless card or wireless adapter installed and working.

- ✔ **Connection utility:** You can use the WZC (which stands for Wireless Zero Configuration) utility in Windows XP, the utility that comes with your adapter, or a separate utility like JiWire SpotLock. (I tell you more about this in the "Using connection management software" section later in this chapter.)

- ✔ **Credit card:** To establish and pay for your new wireless account, you're asked to provide a credit card for nearly all but the free hotspots. Some providers do, however, offer prepaid Wi-Fi cards — much like prepaid phone cards — which include an account and personal identification number that you can use instead of a credit card.

Using the WZC utility to connect

If you have these items in hand, you're ready to get online. So boot up your laptop and follow these steps:

1. **If it doesn't open automatically, start the WZC.**

   To start the wireless zero configuration utility, I usually choose Start➪ Control Panel➪Network and Internet Connections➪Network Connections and right-click the connection for the wireless client. In the context

menu that opens, click View Available Wireless Networks, as shown in
Figure 6-1.

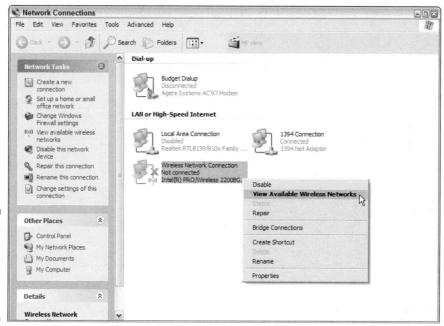

Or, you can right-click the WZC computer icon in your system tray and
choose View Available Wireless Networks. Assuming you're in range of
the hotspot, you see the SSID (the network or hotspot name) indicating
the strength and availability of the network.

Most providers use the same SSID at every hotspot they service. The
Flying J SSID, for example, is `flyingj` and the Coach Connect SSID is
`coach`. When you connect to one of these networks for the first time,
you create a new profile that is saved by the WZC or alternate connection utility. (See, later in this chapter, the "Using connection management software" section for more information.)

2. **Select the SSID of the appropriate hotspot, and click Connect.**

   After a few internal computer gymnastics, you're now connected to the
   hotspot but you're not yet connected to the Internet.

3. **Now you can close or minimize the connection window, shown in
   Figure 6-2, and open your browser.**

   Before you move on to the "Setting up an account" section, read the last
   two paragraphs of this section.

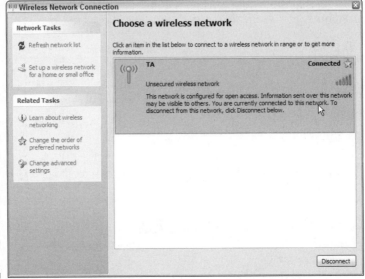

Figure 6-2:
As you can
see, the
signal
strength is
quite good,
and I'm now
connected.

When you're making a new connection, no matter the utility you're using, it's important, for security reasons that I cover in Chapter 10, to configure your connection so that you don't make an automatic connection to an available network. Whenever you're making a connection, especially for the first time, your connection management utility either assumes you want to make this connection automatically, as in the case of the WZC, or offers the option of saving a connection profile that connects automatically or prompts you to connect.

In Chapter 10, where I discus disallowing automatic connections, I tell you how to configure the WZC to show the SSID rather than automatically connect and, in the next section, I tell you how to configure a utility like JiWire SpotLock so that automatic connections are avoided.

Using connection management software

If you've skipped to this section, I assume you've installed (and want to use) either the connection management utility that comes with your wireless adapter or a utility like JiWire SpotLock. I happen to like JiWire SpotLock because of its security features (more about this in Chapter 10 where I also discuss using a Virtual Private Network, or VPN) but the choice is yours. Either way, you should have already disabled the WZC, as I discuss in Chapter 4 (if not, turn to that chapter for directions and do so).

If you're using the JiWire SpotLock connection utility to connect to an unsecured hotspot, for example, here's how you connect:

1. **Open the utility window, select and highlight the appropriate SSID, and click Connect.**

   Once the new connection's made, several Connection Wizard screens open, allowing you to create a hotspot connection profile.

2. **In the first dialog box, select the Use My Own VPN or No Security option. Click Next.**

   Even if you subscribe to the JiWire SpotLock service, as I do, you want to select this option. (It's not necessary to enter your username and password here unless you're giving the SpotLock service a trial run.)

3. **In this, the second dialog box, even though it seems counterintuitive, select the Use No Security option radio button. Click Next.**

   After you've completed these steps, set up (or logged on to) your hotspot account, and connected to the Internet, you can then start either your own VPN or the JiWire SpotLock VPN service. I tell you how to start SpotLock in "Getting logged on" later in this chapter.

4. **Unless you have Internet Explorer set to connect exclusively through a corporate VPN proxy server, you can ignore this Internet Explorer Proxy Settings dialog box. Click Next.**

   If, however, you've configured IE to connect through a VPN proxy server you can put a check mark in this box when you're using JiWire SpotLock rather than your VPN.

5. **When the Application Launch Settings dialog box appears, click Next.**

   You can use this feature to start applications that don't require an Internet connection, but because no Internet connection is established until after you're logged onto the network, it's best to avoid starting, for example, a browser or e-mail client upon connection to the hotspot.

6. **When the Save Network Profile dialog box appears, select the Save, But Prompt Me to Connect option, and you're done configuring the connection profile. Click Finish.**

With that chore out of the way, you can close or minimize your connection management utility. If this is the first time you've connected to this hotspot, you need to set up an account; if you've been here before, log on.

Open your browser and you can move on to the next section.

Setting up an account

Depending on what hotspot you're logging on to, the order of events when setting up a new account varies. Most of them require the same kind of information, but they all have their own unique way of getting it. You can count on providing your name, complete address, phone number, and e-mail address. It's likely that this is the first information you're asked to provide.

After you provide the requested information to set up an account, what you do next depends on the hotspot. At some point, you're asked to provide your credit card information or your prepaid card number and PIN, and you're also asked to set up a username and password.

When you're signing up for service at a Flying J, for example, they offer you the option of letting them choose, at random, a username and password. This is a handy feature that helps ensure that no one else shares, or is likely to guess, your account ID, but if you choose this option, make sure you write the information down. These randomly generated IDs aren't easy to remember.

If you need to contact either customer or technical support for the hotspot you're using (for any reason), you must have your username and password available so that support staff can identify you in their system.

Getting logged on

After all the information is gathered, and you've verified it, you see somewhere on the screen a button or link that says something like <u>Sign me up!</u> or <u>Create account.</u> Click it, and — depending on the hotspot you're logging on to — you see one of the following: a welcome screen directing you to click a link to be connected to the Internet, a welcome screen indicating that you *are* connected to the Internet, or a logon screen.

At Flying J, for example, after the account's set up, you're asked to log on. Then a dialog box appears, giving you the opportunity to get on the Internet or manage your account. This dialog box normally appears after every log on so that, in case you have a monthly or annual account you need to access, you can do so easily and securely. When you choose to get online, you then see an activation screen, followed by a "connected" screen. From here, you can start your VPN service.

When you're connected to the Internet, most hotspots serve up a secure screen indicating that you're connected to the Internet. If you use a corporate VPN or a public VPN like SpotLock, you can now start the service. (I tell you about VPNs in Chapter 10.)

After you've made the connection, enabling SpotLock security is easy. If the utility's not currently open, right-click the JiWire icon and click JiWire SpotLock at the top of the menu. The utility opens. Click the Secure tab, and assuming your username is already entered in the JiWire ID field, enter your password. Click Activate. Once the VPN is established you notice, in the upper right corner, that security is assigned to JiWire SpotLock and a gold lock icon is exhibited. To discontinue the SpotLock VPN, simply enter your username and password, and click Deactivate, as shown in Figure 6-3.

Figure 6-3: I'm feeling well protected from intruders now!

Being a good neighbor

Whenever you're using a hotspot, you're sharing a network with several other users. Each hotspot has — depending on the type of Internet connection in use — a limited amount of bandwidth available. If everyone sharing the bandwidth decides to download music or video files or e-mail a bunch of large picture files to friends and family all at the same time, the connection becomes as slow as molasses for everyone. If you plan on downloading a lot of music or video, you might want to consider doing so from your home or office to avoid using massive bandwidth at the hotspot.

If you need to e-mail large files, consider doing so later in the evening when the bandwidth won't be filled with so many users. If e-mailing large files is something you do on a regular basis, you might want to consider using a software application like SendLater by 4Team Corporation. You can find out more about it at `http://sendlater.4team.biz`.

Troubleshooting Your Connection

I've spent most of my life living in states where, in the winter, the temperature dips well below zero, and the frozen ground is covered with snow and ice. In the '80s, after having purchased a new home, I figured I should get a dog to go with it. Cisco was a good companion, but he acquired the annoying (and sometimes dangerous) habit of chewing on electrical wires. I'd fixed several, and one frosty Sunday morning when I woke to a rapidly falling inside temperature of 42 degrees, I figured the furnace wiring had been Cisco's latest victim.

Looking high and low, I failed to find any wires that had been mistaken as chew toys, so not wanting the indoor temperature to match the subzero outdoor temp, I called the gas company for emergency service. The guy showed up promptly, and in about two seconds, the furnace was humming along, warming my abode. I paid him double for the Sunday service call, and vowed I'd never again call for help until I'd checked to see *if the switch was on*.

Sometimes troubleshooting is that simple. Sometimes it's not. After spending some time discussing with help desk and support staff supervisors their most common problems and the solutions to them, I've come up with this troubleshooting guide. After you complete each task, make an attempt to establish a connection with the hotspot. If you're successful then, great, you're done; if not then go on to the next task. If you get to the end and you still can't make a connection then, finally, call the support staff. Make sure you tell them what you've already done so you don't have to repeat steps.

Identifying global issues

Several situations, either alone or in some combination, can cause difficulties for hotspot users. You can overcome some of them easily and immediately. On the other hand, solving some of these issues requires a little more effort and time. A few of the common issues facing hotspot users are the following:

✔ **Weak wireless cards or adapters:** I talk about adapting your laptop or PDA for wireless in Chapter 3. Although manufacturers have made many improvements, some internally integrated cards and many standard wireless adapters lack the power and antenna sensitivity to make a solid connection when you're parked in an RV site or truck stop lot. Seriously consider using a high-power adapter even if you have an integrated wireless solution. A few other related issues are

- *Mixing USB standards:* For example, if you have a USB 1.1 port on your laptop, connecting a USB 2.0 adapter will slow things down. If you're using a USB adapter, make every effort to match the standards.

- *Using outdated drivers:* Check for driver updates as soon as you install your adapter. The setup CD that came with the adapter might not be the most recent release. Other times, a driver problem is due to the initial installation, so if you're having problems, try uninstalling and reinstalling the adapter. You might have to use System Restore to reset your laptop to a time prior to the first installation of your card and drivers.

- *Trying a different adapter:* If the adapter you're using doesn't seem to be getting the job done, try a different type or brand. I don't know why this works, but sometimes, it does. An adapter that works great in one laptop sometimes just doesn't cut it in another one, even if they're the same brand and model.

✔ **Line of sight:** There might be nothing you can do about this. If you're in the last available RV site or truck stop parking slot, what can you do? Well, if you're using an external antenna (see Chapter 3), try moving the antenna around a bit. Sometimes you only need to move it a foot or two one way or another.

✔ **Operating system:** Windows XP is far superior to all the previous Windows iterations when it comes to using hotspots. Consider upgrading if you're having repeated problems related to early Windows systems.

✔ **Proxy servers:** If you use a corporate VPN or a private VPN service like JiWire (more about this in Chapter 10), be sure to disable it until a connection to the Internet is established.

✔ **Firewall settings:** This is especially relevant if you've just installed a new firewall. If you're using a firewall other than the one included in Windows XP, make sure you disable the Windows firewall. You might also need to disable the firewall to establish a connection to the Internet. After the connection is made, you can once again enable the firewall See Chapter 10 for more information.

Checking the simple stuff

I imagine you already have a good idea that the first thing you need to do is check the following:

✔ **Be sure everything's turned on:** It sounds simplistic, but before you call for support, make sure that your wireless adapter is connected. If it's a

PC card, push it in to be sure it's making a good connection, and if it's a USB adapter, make sure it's plugged in. If you use an integrated wireless card, be sure it's on.

✔ **Check your Wi-Fi card status:** To make sure your wireless card is working properly — whether it's integrated, PC card, or USB — follow these steps:

1. **Choose Start➪Control Panel➪Performance and Maintenance➪ System.**

   The System Properties dialog box opens.

2. **Click the Hardware tab, and click the Device Manager button.**

   The Device Manager window opens.

3. **In the Network Adapters area of the Device Manager window, find your wireless solution, and right-click it. If the device shows a red X through the icon, click Enable. If the device icon appears normal, click Properties, as shown in Figure 6-4.**

   The device's Properties dialog box opens.

4. **Click the General tab, and in the Device Status area, you see whether the device is working properly or not.**

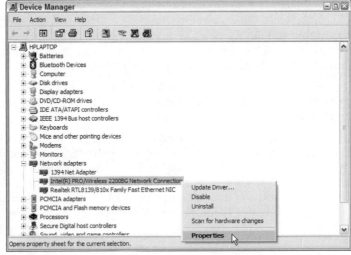

Figure 6-4:
Find your wireless solution in the Device Manager window.

If your device isn't working properly, you can choose to fire up the trouble-shooter, but personally, I recommend you call the manufacturer's support staff.

Okay, you know everything's turned on so, if everything checks out, and you don't need to make any adjustments or changes, you can move on to other troubleshooting tasks. If you did find anything amiss, make your adjustments accordingly.

Releasing and renewing your IP address

I suppose it's possible that, even though I advised you in Chapter 3 to install Windows XP, you're still using Windows 98, SE, or ME. If that's the case, I have it on good authority that one of the most common of all problems stems from issues surrounding Dynamic Host Configuration Protocol (DHCP). DHCP, among other things, allows a new computer to be added to a network without assigning it a unique IP address. Your laptop might be stuck on stupid.

To repair this problem in Windows 98, SE or ME, choose Start⇨Run and type winipcfg in the Open text entry field. Click OK. The IP Configuration dialog box opens. Make sure your wireless device appears in the window. If it doesn't, select it from the drop-down menu. Click Release and, after the little hourglass icon changes back into a cursor arrow, click Renew. You see the IP address change and, again, after the hourglass turns into a cursor arrow, click OK.

If you're now able to make the connection, remember this solution because, with these older operating systems, this problem apparently occurs quite frequently.

Getting the "Page cannot be displayed" message

You say the page won't display, and you can't log on? You're connected to the network, but not to the Net? And you restart your browser, but the browser's still stuck? Is that what's troubling you, Bunky? Don't give up the ship; I've got a possible solution.

With the annoying message appearing in your browser, follow these steps:

1. **In Internet Explorer, click Tools⇨Internet Options.**

   The Internet Options dialog box opens.

   If you use a browser other than Internet Explorer, you can accomplish this same task through the Control Panel. Choose Start⇨Control Panel⇨ Network and Internet Connections⇨Internet Options.

2. **Click the Connections tab, shown in Figure 6-5.**

Figure 6-5:
Click the
Connections
tab.

3. **Click the LAN Settings button.**

   The Local Area Network (LAN) Settings dialog box opens, as shown in Figure 6-6.

4. **Select the Automatically Detect Settings check box. Click OK in both the open dialog boxes.**

5. **Restart the browser.**

Figure 6-6:
The LAN
Settings
dialog box.

A couple of other issues to consider are

  ✔ **Browser caching:** If your browser has cached the last page you visited online, it might be trying to present that page. Try refreshing the browser a couple of times and restarting it.

✔ **Recently used dialup:** If you've recently used a dialup connection, be sure to select the Never Dial a Connection radio button in the Internet Options (Connections tab) dialog box.

✔ **Proxy settings:** In the Local Access Network (LAN) Settings dialog box, be sure that the Use a Proxy Server for Your LAN check box is deselected.

Configuring TCP/IP to use DNS

Say what? Fortunately, you don't need to understand acronyms such as TCP/IP and DNS to perform the task — and I'm not sure I can explain it anyway. So I won't try. I'll just give you instructions for doing it. There aren't any tell-tale symptoms or error messages indicating a problem; it's just another step in the process of elimination. If you're using Windows XP (or Windows 2000), follow these steps:

1. **Choose Start⇨Control Panel⇨Network and Internet Connections⇨ Network Connections.**

   The Network Connections window opens.

2. **Right-click your connection, and click Properties. (Refer to Figure 6-7.)**

   The Wireless Network Connection Properties dialog box opens.

3. **Click the General tab.**

   Scroll down in the This Connection Uses the Following Items list.

4. **Select the Internet Protocol (TCP/IP) check box if it doesn't have a check mark in it.**

5. **Click Internet Protocol (TCP/IP) to highlight it, as shown in Figure 6-7.**

Figure 6-7:
Make sure a check mark appears in the Internet Protocol (TCP/IP) box.

6. **Click the Properties button.**

   The Internet Protocol (TCP/IP) Properties dialog box opens.

7. **Click the General tab.**

8. **Select the radio buttons to the left of Obtain an IP Address Automatically and Obtain DNS Server Address Automatically if they're not yet selected.**

9. **Click OK to close the Wireless Network Connection Properties dialog box. Reboot your computer.**

Eliminating conflicts

If you've tried the previous troubleshooting tips and still can't connect to a hotspot, there could be a conflict between the wireless zero configuration utility and another connection management utility installed on your laptop. This conflict can occur if you haven't disabled the WZC. (I tell you how to disable the WZC in Chapter 4.)

First, check to make sure that the WZC is disabled. If it's not, disable it, and attempt to make your connection. If that works, great — you're done. If it doesn't work, you need to be sure that no possibility of conflict exists. To do so, you need to exit (if you're using JiWire) or uninstall (if you're using the utility that came with your adapter) any connection configuration or management utility and enable the WZC.

Even if you're not using the connection configuration or management utility that came with your wireless adapter, if it's installed, it can still cause a conflict.

Follow these steps to uninstall any connection utilities currently installed on your laptop. (If you later want to reinstall them, you'll need the setup disks that came with your cards.)

1. **Choose Start⇨Control Panel⇨Add or Remove Programs.**

   The Add or Remove Program dialog box opens.

2. **Scroll through the list to find the appropriate program, and click it.**

   The information box is highlighted.

3. **Click Change/Remove.**

   If the wizard opens, follow the prompts. Otherwise, after the program has completed the uninstall process, you can close the window and restart your laptop.

At this point, any conflict that might have existed has been eliminated — but if the WZC doesn't resume its network-configuration duty, take the following steps:

1. **Enable the WZC by following the steps outlined in Chapter 4.**

2. **Set the WZC to Use Windows to Configure My Wireless Network Settings by completing the steps shown here:**

    a. *Choose Start➪Control Panel➪Network and Internet Connections➪Network Connections.*

    The Network Connections window opens.

    b. *Right-click your connection, and click Properties. (Refer to Figure 6-1.)*

    The Wireless Network Connection Properties dialog box opens.

    c. *Click the Wireless Networks tab.*

    d. *Make sure a check mark appears in the Use Windows to Configure My Wireless Network Settings check box.*

You can now make another attempt to establish a connection to the hotspot. If you're successful and you were previously using a utility other than JiWire, reinstallation of that utility is ill advised. However, if you were using JiWire, you should call their support staff — especially if you'd like to use the SpotLock VPN.

If you've gone through this entire troubleshooting section and you still can't make a connection, it's time to call for help. Some help desk personnel go through a scripted list, so you might end up repeating some of these troubleshooting tasks. Others, like Flying J Communications, actually listen to you, so tell the person you're speaking with the steps you've already taken so that they can focus on other potential solutions.

Using E-Mail at a Hotspot

When I bought my first laptop to take on the road with me, I didn't know what all I'd do with it, but sending e-mail was of primary importance. In fact, it was the only thing that I knew, for sure, that I wanted to use a laptop for. Unfortunately, even when I used a dialup service, sending e-mail successfully was a hit-or-miss proposition. I finally hooked up with a prepaid dialup ISP that solved the problem, but it was frustrating until I did.

Similarly frustrating situations can occur when you're using a hotspot. Although I've encountered no problems when using any of the major truck stop hotspots,

I have had a problem or two in hotels, coffeehouses, and RV parks. To make matters even more confusing, these problems don't always have the same root cause, and therefore, the solutions can differ.

Receiving e-mail, for the most part, isn't a problem at a hotspot. *Sending* e-mail is what, on occasion, can be a little bit more than frustrating. The primary, although not exclusive, reason is spam. Not the gourmet delight made by the fine folks in Austin, Minnesota, but rather, the irritating advertisements and solicitations that seem to constantly and repeatedly fill everyone's e-mail inbox. What does spam have to do with your inability to send e-mail from a hotspot location? Well, some of the methods those ISPs, WISPs, and hotspot operators use in an attempt to battle spam make it difficult for everyone to send e-mail.

Exploring your options

Fortunately, if you find yourself at a hotspot battling spam by blocking outgoing e-mail, you're not without options. I'm not particularly crazy about all of them. But there are perfectly viable solutions to the problem of sending e-mail, from hotspots that block it, that work every time and others that have to be tailor-made to each situation. Some of your options are to

- ✔ **Use Web mail:** Most ISPs offer a Web-based mail client that bypasses all the restrictions because you're connecting via the Web. You can also use a free Web mail service like Yahoo!, Hotmail, or Gmail.

- ✔ **Use a VPN:** By using a corporate VPN or a private VPN service like JiWire SpotLock, you bypass all attempts a hotspot might make to block, redirect, intercept, or place restrictions on sending e-mail from their location. Because the e-mail's being forwarded, your ISP's server isn't involved either.

- ✔ **Use e-mail forwarding:** Several Web-based companies, like SMTP.com and mail2web.com, offer relatively inexpensive e-mail forwarding services. You might have to do some reconfiguration of your e-mail client, but after it's done, you should experience no other problems sending e-mail — the one possible exception being a WISP that requires using their server to send e-mail. See the next item.

- ✔ **Reconfigure your e-mail client:** This works only if the WISP requires you to use their server. In that case, you can change your SMTP server name to that of the WISP you're using. (Later, in the "Configuring an e-mail client" section, I show you how to do that in Outlook Express.)

Because I use JiWire's SpotLock service, I don't have any problems sending e-mail, but there could be a problem in receiving a reply. JiWire forwards e-mail from their proxy server so, even though it's unlikely anyone will notice it, the original From address gets changed to *username@jiwire-member.com*. The Reply address is the user's normal e-mail address, though, so, providing that the recipient just uses the Reply button on their e-mail client, the reply goes directly to the original sender. Most mail forwarding services, because you're only using their SMTP server, won't change your From address.

Comparing a few free Web mail services

I use Web-based e-mail accounts when I don't want my primary e-mail address to be publicly available. For example, anytime I signed up to post to a forum or want to have some information e-mailed to me, I use a Hotmail address (www.hotmail.com). But until recently, I haven't been too high on the idea of using Web-based e-mail.

With serious competition from Google's Gmail (http://gmail.google.com), both Yahoo! (www.yahoo.com) and Hotmail have made some improvements, although the improvements to Hotmail seem to have skipped over their free e-mail service and are available only in paid versions. In Table 6-2, I give you a quick comparison of the major features for these three services.

Table 6-2			Web Mail Services
Service	*Cost*	*Storage*	*Features & Comments*
Gmail	Free — with contextual ads.	2.5GB+	Comes with POP3 access (so you can use Outlook Express or other e-mail clients), spam filtering, virus protection, and E-mail Received notifications.
			Drafts are auto-saved so that you don't lose a half-written e-mail if you lose your connection.
			Personalized home page shows new messages.
			Allows 10MB attachments.
Yahoo!	Free — with graphical ads.	1GB	Offers spam filtering, virus protection, E-mail Received notifications, and allows 10MB attachments.

(continued)

Table 6-2 *(continued)*

Service	Cost	Storage	Features & Comments
Yahoo!	$19.99 annually — with no ads.	2GB	Provides POP3 access (so you can use Outlook Express or other e-mail clients), spam filtering, virus protection, and no ads at the bottom of sent e-mails.
			You can send large (20MB) attachments.
			You can also create e-mail aliases to avoid getting spam at your main e-mail address.
Hotmail	Free — with graphical ads.	250MB	Comes with junk mail filtering, virus protection, and E-mail Received notifications.
			Allows 10MB attachments.
Hotmail	$19.95 annually — with no ads.	2GB	Offers POP3 access (so you can use Outlook Express or other e-mail client), junk mail filtering, virus protection, and no ads at the bottom of sent e-mails.
			You can send large (20MB) attachments.

Besides the three biggies that I compare in Table 6-2, consider these other contenders:

- ✔ **FastMail:** Like Yahoo! and Hotmail, you can expect to see ads with the free version but in nowhere near the same amount. They offer only 10MB of storage space, however, with their free accounts. The paid versions they offer have plenty of features, and the Web interface gets rave reviews. Find out more at www.fastmail.fm.

- ✔ **AIM Mail:** 2GB of storage and, at least as far as the experts are concerned, very good spam filtering are two reasons you might want to look into AOL's free AIM Mail service. You can find them on the Web at http://mail.aim.com.

- ✔ **Inbox.com:** With a name like that, at the very least, you should give them a look. They offer 2GB of storage. and you can use their search function to find any e-mails you might have misplaced. Not surprisingly their Web address is www.inbox.com.

Configuring an e-mail client

Even if you're going to use a Web-based mail service, you can, in some cases, also use a desktop e-mail client like Microsoft Outlook Express or Mozilla Thunderbird. Before you set about the task of configuring your client, you need to gather just a bit of information. All this information is readily available from your ISP, WISP, or e-mail provider. Just ask them for e-mail client configuration information. Here's some advice on collecting that information:

- ✔ **Username or account name:** Your ISP assigns you an account or username. In some cases, your entire e-mail address serves as your account name or username.

- ✔ **Password:** This is the password you use to access your e-mail account.

- ✔ **Incoming server:** Usually, the name of the incoming server is something like `mail.`*`myisp`*`.com` or `pop.`*`myisp`*`.com`, but whatever it is, your ISP can provide it to you.

- ✔ **SMTP server:** Again, most likely it's something similar to `smtp.`*`myisp`*`.com`.

- ✔ **Mail ports:** You need to know the mail, or POP, and SMTP ports your ISP listens on. Usually, it's port 25, but as in the case of Gmail or SMTP.com, it can be different.

- ✔ **Secure Password Authentication:** You also need to find out whether your ISP requires a secure password authentication log on. This requirement is becoming very common.

Because you can configure Gmail for POP3 access, I'll show you how to configure Outlook Express to download and send e-mail through your Gmail account.

Gmail uses an SMTP port other than the troublesome port 25 that hotspots are fond of redirecting or blocking altogether. Because of that, and because it's free, it's a great candidate for use as your main e-mail provider while traveling.

The first thing you need to do is configure Gmail to use Post Office Protocol (POP). To do so follow these steps:

1. **From any Gmail page, click Settings.**

   The Mail Settings window opens.

2. **Click the Forwarding and POP tab.**

   The Forwarding and POP configuration window opens.

3. **In the POP Download area, select either Enable POP for All Mail or Enable POP Only for Mail That Arrives from Now On.**

   If you choose to Enable POP for All Mail, you can download any or all the mail currently in your Gmail account to your e-mail client. Otherwise, you can download only new mail.

4. **From the drop-down list, decide what action Gmail should take When Messages Are Accessed with POP.**

5. **Click the Save Changes button.**

Now you can configure your desktop e-mail client. I show you, as an example, how to configure Outlook Express.

1. **After opening Outlook Express, choose Tools⇨Accounts.**

   The Internet Accounts dialog box opens.

2. **Click the Mail tab, and select Add⇨Mail.**

   The Internet Connection Wizard opens.

3. **Type the name you want displayed to e-mail recipients in the text field, and click Next.**

4. **Enter your complete e-mail address in the text field. Click Next.**

5. **Make sure that POP3 is selected in the My Incoming Mail Server Is A drop-down list at the top of the dialog box. Type** pop.gmail.com **in the Incoming Mail Server text field, and then type** smtp.gmail.com **in the Outgoing Mail Server text field. (See Figure 6-8.) Click Next.**

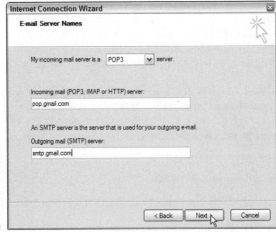

Figure 6-8:
Entering the server names.

6. **Enter your Account name and Password in the proper text fields. Be sure that the Remember Password check box is enabled.**

   In the case of Gmail, the account name is your full e-mail address. Other e-mail accounts might require only your username.

7. **Click Next, and then click Finish.**

   But you're not quite finished yet.

8. **In the Internet Accounts dialog box, which has remained open, click the Gmail account to highlight it, and click Properties.**

   The Pop.gmail.com Properties dialog box opens.

9. **Click the Servers tab. Put a check mark in the check box next to My Server Requires Authentication, as shown in Figure 6-9.**

Figure 6-9: The Properties dialog box for my e-mail account.

10. **Click the Advanced tab. In the Server Port Numbers area, type 465 in the Outgoing Mail (SMTP) text box. In the Incoming Mail (POP3) text box, type 995. Be sure that both check boxes for This Server Requires a Secure Connection (SSL) are enabled, as shown in Figure 6-10.**

   Not every e-mail server, either incoming or outgoing, requires authentication, so be sure to check with your ISP, WISP, or e-mail service to confirm. Most SMTP servers use port 25, and for this reason, most e-mail clients default to port 25. You'll have to check to find out on which port your server listens.

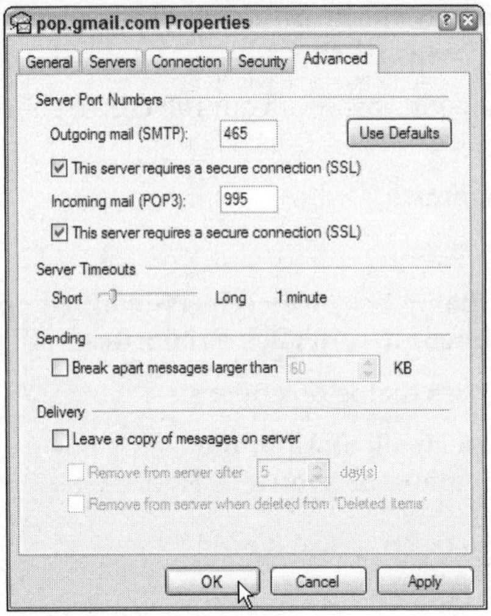

Figure 6-10:
Adjusting
settings
on the
Advanced
tab.

11. **Click OK.**

12. **Click Close.**

If you need to alter the SMTP settings to conform to the requirements of a particular hotspot, do it from the account Properties dialog box. Simply highlight the account under the Mail tab, click Properties, click the Servers tab, and make the appropriate changes to the Outgoing mail (SMTP) field. Be sure to double-check that you're using the proper incoming and outgoing ports as well.

Part III
Bridging the Wireless Gap

The 5th Wave   By Rich Tennant

"So, what kind of roaming capabilities does this thing have?"

In this part . . .

I cover a few of the methods you might want to employ to connect to the Internet when, during your travels, Wi-Fi just isn't available. Here, for example, you find out about cellular data services (Chapter 7), using dialup as a backup (Chapter 8), and satellite Internet systems (Chapter 9). After perusing this part, you might even decide that a satellite or cellular Internet connection would be perfect as your primary means of making a connection. The sock puppets (being big RV aficionados) are very excited by the prospect of setting up a satellite Internet system — and you might be equally excited by the prospect of using a cellular data service to get connected without the need for a hotspot.

Chapter 7

Cellular Data Services: Can You Connect Me Now?

· ·

In This Chapter

▶ Getting the right gear

▶ Selecting a service

▶ Configuring a data card

▶ Configuring a cellphone as a modem

▶ Extending your range

▶ Expanding access to a cellular signal

· ·

My first foray into the world of wireless Internet connectivity involved using my cellphone connected to a PC card modem with a dialup a connection. This worked, but it was painfully slow — much slower than a regular dialup connection. And, on top of that, I was burning up cellphone antennas at an alarming rate.

There have been, since that time, remarkable strides forward in cellular data technology, and now by using a cell data card, you can get a connection for your laptop that rivals speeds seen at Wi-Fi hotspots. Even using a cellphone as a modem, tethered by cable or Bluetooth to your laptop or PDA (I explain all this within the chapter), can be considerably quicker and less threatening to the life of the phone than standard dialup.

In this chapter, I help you explore the cellular possibilities and decide, first of all, whether you want to use a cell data card or cellphone to connect your computer to the Internet. And secondly, I help you choose a carrier that fits your needs. With all those details behind you, I get down to the nitty gritty and tell you how to set up your connections.

Choosing Your Tools

Every so often while traveling around the country, I pick up my cellphone in some remote location, and to my amazement, find that I have a signal. Sometimes it's pretty weak — nonetheless, there it is. But, as anyone with a cellphone and a will to wander will no doubt tell you, sometimes the signal-free zones are just as baffling.

In general, though, it seems that having a good strong signal is far more common than not, and that's what makes the idea of using this technology for Internet access so attractive. If you find yourself considering the cellular option, one of your first choices is between using a cell data card or cellphone for connecting your computer to the Internet. Consider the following when making your decision:

- **Cell data card:** The simplest way to use a cellular service is with a data card, but it can also be the most expensive. A few general attributes of the data card are:

    - *Fast:* The highest-speed cellular services, offering speeds rivaling 802.11b, favor the use of a dedicated data card.

    - *Simple:* Setup is almost exactly the same as a PC card wireless adapter: Slide the data card into a PCMCIA slot, install the software, and you're surfin' the Net before you know it.

    - *Expensive:* Data cards are far more expensive than wireless PC card adapters, and of course, you still need to have a cellphone to make calls.

- **High-speed cellphone:** Because you probably already own a cellphone, this might seem like the easiest choice. But first, the phone must be data capable, and second, your carrier must support data transmission for your phone. A few attributes tell the story; data-capable phones are

    - *Fast:* 3G (third generation) cellphones support high-speed technology. If you choose to use a cellphone, you should strongly consider upgrading your phone to take advantage of the maximum speeds offered by your cellular provider.

    - *Complex:* Although there are some fairly easy ways to set up your cellphone for Internet access, it's still more complex than installing a data card.

    - *Inexpensive:* This is true especially if you already own a cellphone that's data capable. Even if you don't, though, it's likely to be cheaper to get a new cellphone through your cellular provider than it is to purchase a data card.

Which will it be — data card or cellphone?

I've been spoiled by the speed of wireless broadband Internet access. The excitement and anticipation of watching a Web page slowly manifest itself on my display screen has been replaced by the wonder of browsing through the World Wide Web as easily as I might thumb through a well-worn book. Recently, cellular technology has begun to offer speeds rivaling those available at hotspots, and even when the high-speed networks are out of range, you can usually connect to a network that's at least as fast as dialup — usually quite a bit faster.

But which method of accessing those networks best meets your needs? Should you set your cellphone up as a modem and use it to access the high-speed networks, or should you purchase a dedicated cellular data card designed specifically for that purpose? Well, you're the only one who can answer that question, but consider these things when you're trying to make the choice:

✔ **Cost:** The high-speed data plans favoring the use of a data card — offered by Sprint, Cingular, Verizon and others — sets you back about $60 to $80 per month in addition to the cost of the data card. You can, though, pay little or nothing extra if you choose to use a high-speed cellphone and accept a slower, but better than dialup, connection speed.

✔ **Commitment:** If you use your cellphone for your connection, it's possible, even likely, that no other contractual agreement is required, but if you choose to use a data card, a separate contractual commitment is a necessity.

✔ **Consistency:** The speeds achieved can vary wildly. Both cellphones and data cards are capable of accessing the high-speed networks, so if you're in, for example, an urban area where high-speed offerings are available, you might experience Wi-Fi–like surfing. But at the edges of urbanity or in rural America, the speed you'll see is anybody's guess. If you choose to use a cellphone but not the high-speed service, you can expect to see speeds between 40 Kbps and 144 Kbps.

It seems to me that using a cellphone to make an Internet connection might be best for the occasional surfing session but probably not something on which you'd want to rely exclusively. On the other hand, even though sixty to eighty bucks a month is nothing to sneeze at (you could sign up for two or more annual truck stop Wi-Fi subscriptions for that price), it might be possible to use a data card and plan as your primary means of Internet access and bridge *that* gap with the occasional Wi-Fi connection.

Choosing a carrier

In the contest to get your business, the first round of eliminations has been taken care of for you because the pool of providers from which you can choose is limited to those servicing the area you call home. After the identification of potential players, you can take the following into consideration:

- ✔ **Coverage:** Most of the national carriers provide, on their Web sites, a link to coverage maps. At the Sprint Web site, you can even see a cell tower map. If your available choices include Verizon, Sprint, Cingular, Alltel, or T-Mobile, you should find adequate coverage available. If you limit your travels to a particular region, though, you might find a regional carrier to be the preferable choice.

- ✔ **Customer service:** One way to judge this is by asking a few neighbors and colleagues about their personal experiences with any carrier you're considering. You should also get a feel for a carrier's responsiveness when you're shopping for a service. If they're unresponsive when they're trying to get your business, how much more unresponsive might they be when you're under contract to them and having problems?

- ✔ **Data capabilities:** Even though the major and most of the minor cellular providers have switched to digital voice transmission, not every carrier provides digital data transmission. Make sure any carrier you're considering offers digital data transmission.

- ✔ **Data plans:** A few carriers charge by the kilobit, some have limited-use plans, some offer flat-rate, unlimited-use plans, and some offer all three. (I talk more about data plans a little later in the chapter in the "Sorting through the services" section.)

You're going to be stuck with whatever carrier you choose for an extended period of time, so take a little time to do some shopping around. Ask some questions and demand decent answers. There's nothing more frustrating than dealing with a communications company that refuses to communicate.

Comparing speeds and standards

To begin with, there are two basic cellular technologies: global system for mobile (better known as GSM) and code division multiple access (CDMA). GSM and CDMA work just great for voice transmission, but because data's a different duck, other technology enhancements were necessary to allow for a decent Internet connection. Some carriers, like Verizon and Sprint, have based their systems on the CDMA technology whereas others, like Cingular and T-Mobile, use GSM. Tables 7-1 and 7-2 should help to sort the enhancement standards.

Table 7-1	GSM Data Standard Enhancements	
Standard	*Full Name*	*Speed*
GPRS	General Packet Radio Service	56 Kbps
EDGE	Enhanced Data rate for GSM Evolution	56 Kbps – 144 Kbps
UTMS	Universal Mobile Telecommunication System	144 Kbps – 384 Kbps
HSDPA	High-Speed Downa Packet Access	1.8 Mbps

Table 7-2	CDMA Data Standard Enhancements	
Standard	*Full Name*	*Speed*
CDMA	Code Division Multiple Access	14.4 Kbps
1xRTT	Single carrier radio transmission technology	56 Kbps – 144 Kbps
Ev-DO	Evolution-Data Only (Optimized)	144 Kbps – 2.4 Mbps
Ev-DO Rev A	Evolution-Data Only Revision A	Up to 3.1 Mbps

Ev-DO, UTMS, and HSDPA are available only in select urban areas. If, for example, you've signed up with Verizon for their BroadbandAccess package and you leave the Ev-DO area, the speed you can achieve falls back to the 1xRTT standard.

Sorting through the services

Because it sometimes seems that cellular providers change plans and offerings more often than the wind changes direction, it can make comparisons somewhat difficult. After you've whittled your list of cellular contenders into a short list, you can begin to home in on your final choice by asking a few questions:

- ✔ **Do I need a data plan?** Most of the high-speed services are contracted and billed separate from voice plans, but some of the slower-speed networks might be available without a separate data plan. Verizon, for example, allows you to access its slower NationalAccess network using a cellphone as a modem at no extra cost.

- ✔ **Do I need a data card?** Even though Ev-DO– and EDGE–enabled cellphones are available, some of the providers don't offer the high-speed services unless you have a data card.

✔ **Will I be charged extra for roaming?** Many of the providers offer several levels of service, and some of those plans include the possibility of being charged a roaming fee. Find out how much any roaming charges are.

✔ **Are data plans available to business customers only?** A few of the providers make their data plans available, primarily, to business customers. Although this might not impact cost, it might affect your contractual commitment.

✔ **Do you have phone connection hardware available?** Having hardware available is an indication that using a cellphone as a modem is well supported. Not having it, however, isn't necessarily a negative indicator, and several vendors sell complete kits and individual data cables.

✔ **Do you have phone connection software available?** Most of the data cards, especially when purchased through the provider, come with a connection management utility that helps in managing connection profiles for both cellular and Wi-Fi. Ask if this software is also available for use with your cellphone modem.

Many of the cellular carriers offer lower-cost data plans that limit the amount you can download from the Internet. If your use falls within these bounds, you can save a few bucks, but charges can get expensive in a hurry if you go over your limits. Just to give you an idea, the average Web page runs anywhere from 30K to 75K. Some are a little smaller, and some are much larger. But, for example, if you've got a 5MB plan, you'd probably be able to browse somewhere in the neighborhood of 100 Web pages, and maybe get a bit of e-mail, before you run out of allotment.

Connecting with a Cell Data Card

The attraction, for me, to using a cell data card rather than a cellphone for making an Internet connection is the simplicity — possibly because of the similarity to using a hotspot. In fact, it might be simpler. All the cellular providers offering service through a data card also offer a connection management utility, similar to the WZC or JiWire utility, and you don't have to be anywhere near a hotspot to use it.

My primary complaints are speed and cost. The high-speed services are limited to urban areas, and I usually find myself, at best, near the edges of the coverage. Because of this, I'm often relegated to the slower-speed services which, although generally faster than dialup, are much slower than I can get at a hotspot. But that's just me. I don't like paying for something I'm rarely able to use. I do it sometimes; I just don't like it.

However, you might find yourself, more often than not, with a decent cellular signal and not a truck– or RV–friendly hotspot in sight. In that case, even though the speeds might barely hover above those of dialup, a data card and plan could be the perfect solution.

Making the hardware choice

Shopping for a data card, such as the one shown in Figure 7-1, isn't much different than shopping for a cellphone. For example, it's entirely possible to purchase a cellular data card from your local CompuMart or online discount retailer, but as is the case with cellphones, these cards are frequently available from the cellular provider at a deep discount when you sign a long-term contract.

If you choose to purchase your card from a source other than your cellular provider, you must still be certain that the card you purchase is compatible with your chosen carrier and the standard they support. Table 7-3 notes what cards are compatible with various, popular carriers.

Table 7-3	Carrier Compatibility	
Cellular Provider	**Supported Standard**	**Compatible Data Cards**
Verizon	CDMA, 1xRTT, Ev-DO	Sierra Wireless AirCard 580 Sierra Wireless AirCard 595 Kyocera Passport KPC650 Novatel Merlin V620 Audiovox PC5740
Alltel	CDMA, 1xRTT, Ev-DO	Kyocera Passport KPC650 Audiovox PC5740
Sprint	1xRTT, Ev-DO	Novatel Merlin S620 Sierra Wireless AirCard 580 Sierra Wireless AirCard 595 Audiovox PC5740
Cingular	GPRS, EDGE, UTMS, HSDPA	Sierra Wireless AirCard 860 Novatel Merlin U730
T-Mobile	GPRS, EDGE, HSDPA	Sony Ericsson GC89

Figure 7-1: The Kyocera Passport KP650 cellular data card comes equipped with a sensitive adjustable antenna that folds neatly away when not needed.

For more information regarding data cards compatible with Sprint and Verizon services along with some Ev-DO-specific tips, advice, and information, I've found the Web site EVDOinfo.com to be invaluable. As a matter of fact, if you purchase your data card through their sister site, Booster-Antenna.com, they'll supplement the support you receive from your carrier. They can be found by pointing your browser to www.evdoinfo.com.

I strongly suggest that you avoid purchasing a used data card. If the card was originally purchased through a cellular provider, it's almost certain to be programmed specifically, and exclusively, for that carrier. Beyond that, if it is a Sprint card or you want to use Sprint service, you should be aware that their frequency is incompatible with those of other carriers.

A few of the cellular data cards, like the Sony Ericsson GC89, are capable of switching between both cellular and Wi-Fi networks — so you can use the card with your phone or to connect at a hotspot. If this is important to you, be sure you ask about it prior to purchasing the card.

Recently, laptops that include integrated cellular data cards as well as integrated Wi-Fi cards have appeared on the market, but I don't recommend them. To use the built-in data card, you need to contract for the services, and unlike Wi-Fi, your choice of service is limited to a single cellular carrier. For example, if you purchase a Sony Vaio VGN-T350 equipped with a GPRS/EDGE card, you need to sign up with Cingular for service. Although having a data card integrated into a laptop is more than a little convenient, I don't like the idea of being stuck with the same cellular carrier for as long as my laptop should last (my first one lasted 8 years). Also, you can't swap out integrated cards for newer technology, so if the integrated card can't access a new feature, you won't be able to access that feature for the life of your laptop.

Setting up a data card

You install a data card in almost exactly the same way you install a wireless adapter, with one major difference: activation. All cellphones and data cards carry an Electronic Serial Number (ESN). Whenever you access the network, the ESN is automatically transmitted so the cellular provider can confirm validity.

When you buy a data card and set up your account, the cellular provider takes note of the ESN and adds it to its database so that your card is recognized. During the software installation process (see the "Configuring the card" section later in this chapter), the activation is complete when the number is detected, transmitted, and recognized for the first time.

Installing the drivers and management utility

When you make your purchase, along with the card you get a CD that includes the necessary card drivers and a connection management utility. Although the installation methods vary somewhat from one card to another, three basic steps seem to be universal. With the CD in hand, you're ready to begin this grueling process.

1. **Insert CD.**

   The CD starts automatically, and the installation wizard opens.

2. **Follow the prompts.**

   This varies from one card to another, but for the most part, you simply need to read and agree to terms and click Next a few times.

3. **Click Finish.**

   At this point, with the device drivers and connection management utility successfully installed, you're ready to configure the card (but not quite ready to put it into the PCMCIA slot).

Configuring the card

Verizon's VZAccess Manager is a bit more complex to configure than the others — maybe because it's such a useful utility — but the process is still somewhat similar across the board.

Some of the connection management utilities, such as Verizon's VZAccess Manager, Sprint's Power Vision Connection Manager, and the Cingular Communication Manager, can also handle managing 802.11 wireless connections. If you use a PC card or USB wireless adapter, make sure you've got it handy during the configuration of your connection management utility.

At some point, in almost every configuration process, you're asked if you want to check for updates. Because an update check is a good idea, I highly recommend that you maintain an Internet connection throughout configuration.

Follow these steps to configure your Verizon data card with VZAccess:

1. **Choose Start⇨All Programs⇨VZAccess Manager.**

   The setup wizard opens with the Welcome screen.

2. **Click Check for Updates. If any are available, you can install them now.**

3. **Click Next.**

   The Wi-Fi/WWAN Detection dialog box opens.

4. **You can select the Detect both Wi-Fi option or the WWAN or Detect WWAN Device Only (1xEV-DO/1xRTT/CDMA) option, depending on your preferences. If you've chosen the latter, click Next; if you've chosen the former, follow these steps:**

   a. *Insert your Wi-Fi adapter.*

      Note: You don't need to do this if your wireless device is built in.

   b. *Click Next.*

      After the device is detected, the WWAN Device Detection dialog box opens.

   c. *Remove your Wi-Fi adapter.*

5. **Click Next to open the Connectivity Options dialog box.**

6. **Select PC Card, and click Next to open the Find Wireless Device dialog box.**

7. **Insert your data card into the PCMCIA slot.**

   Windows recognizes it as a new device, and the Found New Hardware Wizard launches.

8. **Follow the prompts. If a Hardware Installation warning appears, click Continue Anyway.**

9. **After the wizard completes the installation, click Next.**

10. **Enable the Run VZAccess Manager at Startup check box if you desire it, and click Finish.**

At this point, your card has been detected and is now configured for use. But one last item, the Venturi compression client (which helps make your connection more efficient), remains to be installed. Upon completing the configuration process, the Venturi installation wizard automatically launches. Just follow the prompts through to completion, and you're ready to connect!

Every once in a while, software that helps a card access the Web, such as the Venturi compression software, comes into conflict with a program application or Web page. If most Web pages display normally but there's that one page that won't load, try temporarily disabling the software. To do this, right-click the software's icon in the system tray and choose Open. For Venturi, you then click the Off button under Venturi Mode to disable Venturi and (assuming this solves the problem) click it again to return it to Auto.

If you happen to be downloading a compressed file, usually denoted by a .zip extension, you should temporarily disable the Venturi, or any other, compression client. Compressing a compressed file can actually increase the time required for the download.

Logging on

Ready to use your data card? Here's a rough idea of what you can expect, again using Verizon's VZAccess Manager as an example:

1. **Double-click the VZAccess Manager icon to open the utility.**

   The Connect window opens and the available connection possibilities are clearly displayed.

2. **To log on, click your preferred connection, and after the Connect to WWAN or Connect to WLAN button's displayed, click that button.**

   With a connection established, the Connect to button changes to a Disconnect button. If you want to change your connection type, you need to disconnect and then go through the connection process again.

Connecting with Your Cellphone

For a long, long time my cab was a phone-free zone that provided refuge from the busy outside world. All well and good, but every time I wanted or needed to talk to someone, I had to get off the highway and make a time-consuming stop so I could make the call. Now, with voice recognition and hands-free technology, I can carry on a long-distance conversation as easily as I can talk to a passenger. And, on top of that, I can also use a cellphone to connect my laptop to the Internet. (No, not while I'm driving.)

If you want to use your cellphone to access the Internet, you need the following:

- ✔ **Data-capable cellphone:** Contact your cellular provider and ask whether your phone is compatible for use with their data plans. This information might also be available on your carrier's Web site.

- ✔ **Data plan:** Most carriers require that you sign up for a data plan if you're going to use your phone as a modem. But check before you buy.

✔ **Method of connection:** To configure your cellphone for use as a modem, you need to tether it to your computer. There are three ways to do this:

- *Cable:* This is by far the easiest and most widely accepted method of tethering your phone to your computer. Verizon, T-Mobile, and Alltel offer connection kits that include a USB cable and a CD loaded with the necessary drivers and connection management utility. For those carriers not offering their own kits, you can easily find cable and driver kits available from several sources. (See the next section for more information.)

- *Bluetooth:* This wireless technology is most often used as a cable replacement. Some phones, however, even though they're Bluetooth equipped, can't be tethered to a computer via Bluetooth wireless. Check with your cellular provider to determine whether you can use this feature. Your computer, of course, also needs Bluetooth capability.

- *Infrared:* Otherwise known as IrDA, this is possibly the least attractive tethering method. IrDA's range is only about three feet, and you must maintain an absolutely unobstructed line of sight between the phone and the computer's IrDA sensor.

You also need answers to a few pertinent questions that I've outlined, earlier in this chapter, in the "Sorting through the services" section. With acceptable answers to these questions, you're ready to set up your cellphone as a modem.

Making the connection via data cable

I just absolutely love being wire free, but at least when it comes to tethering a cellphone to a computer, I prefer to use a data cable. That could be because, first, my phone's not equipped with either Bluetooth or IrDA capabilities, and second, my carrier doesn't allow Bluetooth tethering anyway. With only one method remaining, I've prudently declared it my favorite.

Gathering the gear

Choose from one of two ways to go about setting up your cellphone as a modem using a cable as the tethering device. In both instances, you need two essential items:

✔ **Data cable:** The cable, depending on your phone, is either a USB or serial cable. Cables are available from several sources, including online retailers, cellphone manufacturers, and cellular providers.

✔ **Device drivers:** You can download most drivers from the Web, get them from the CD included when you purchase your cable, or get them from the CD that's included with a complete kit.

You can find most cables sold individually or bundled in a complete kit that includes the necessary drivers and, usually, a connection management utility that might also offer features allowing you to sync your phone with your laptop. Initially, I just bought a cable and downloaded the drivers. But I like these kits — primarily because, at the time, no other method of downloading the pictures I'd taken with my camera phone was available.

If you're a real do-it-yourself kind of person — meaning you're interested in purchasing only the cable, you might try these sources:

- ✔ **CellPhoneMall.Net:** This is where I purchased the cable for my phone, and as a bonus, I was also able to download the drivers, making it possible to set my phone up as a modem. You can find them on the Web at www.cellphonemall.net. Scroll down to and click the Data Cable link. The page that opens lists hundreds of cellphones with corresponding cables and also provides a link for downloading the necessary drivers.

- ✔ **CellularFactory.com:** It's not immediately apparent where the data cables can be found, but if you scroll to the bottom of the page, you can find a link for your make of phone. Using that, you can find all the accessories available at the Cellular Factory for your phone. They're found at www.cellularfactory.com, and it's highly likely that a CD including drivers and maybe a few new ring tones is included.

Your other choice is to purchase a data kit that includes the proper cable, device drivers, and very often, a connection management utility of some kind. Chances are pretty good that your cellphone manufacturer has available — somewhere on their Web site — a data kit for your phone, but a few other possible sources for these goodies are:

- ✔ **Verizon:** Their connection kits (which are phone specific) are offered under the Mobile Office moniker. They include a USB cable as well as a couple of CDs for use in setting up the phone as a modem and installing the VZAccess Manager. Finding the kits (or anything) on the Verizon Web site can be challenging, to say the least. Here's a link to the Mobile Office page that worked recently (www.verizonwireless.com/b2c/mobileoptions/mobileoffice/mobileoffice1.jsp); if it's moved, give them a call.

- ✔ **T-Mobile:** In the Accessories area of their Web site (www.t-mobile.com), find your phone, click the link, and a page with your phone's available accessories opens. Scroll to the Data section, and if your phone is supported, the kit is listed here. Most of these kits offered by T-Mobile are also available from the manufacturer.

- ✔ **DataPilot:** The DataPilot Individual Kit includes a data cable and CD you can use in setting up your cellphone as a modem. A lot of other handy cellphone management features are included as well. You can find DataPilot at www.datapilot.com.

✔ **FutureDial:** FutureDial doesn't offer a kit, but from them, you can buy a data cable and their SnapDialer software. If you're contracted to Sprint, Verizon, Cingular, or T-Mobile and you're using a data-capable phone, there's a good chance that this combination will get you connected to the Internet in a snap. FutureDial's found on the Web at `www.futuredial.com/Default.aspx`.

Other cellular providers, besides Verizon, might offer solutions to help you get your cellphone set up as a modem. For example, from Cingular you can purchase a data cable and download their Communication Manager, which will, during installation and in collaboration with the Found New Hardware Wizard, enable you to set up your phone for use as a modem. For more information, check out their Phones as Modems Web page at `www.cingular.com/sbusiness/phonemodem`.

Configuring your connection with a kit

If you're using a complete kit or a third-party software solution, such as Verizon's Mobile Office or FutureDial's SnapDialer, the necessary drivers are installed from an included CD. During the software installation, the wizard also takes you through the process of setting up and configuring your modem. You might still, however, find you need to fill in a few blanks with information specific to your cellular provider. In some cases the authentication process is, more or less, taken care of, but in other cases, you might need to enter information such as:

✔ **Phone number:** These aren't your usual phone numbers, so check with your carrier for the proper string. Sprint, for example, might use #777 and Cingular might require *99#, *99***1#, or a variation on that theme.

✔ **Username or ID:** Check with your service provider for this information. It might vary depending on the type of service for which you've contracted.

✔ **Password:** Make sure you find out from your carrier whether the password is case sensitive. Cingular, for one, requires the use of all capital letters.

The installation and configuration process using VZAccess Manager is very similar to that of a data card (see "Setting up a data card" earlier in this chapter) except that you're connecting to either a serial or USB device. After being prompted to insert the data cable into the appropriate port, turn on your phone, and the Windows Found New Hardware Wizard launches. Follow the prompts, enter any required information, and when you're finished, your cellphone is configured on your computer as a modem.

Your new connection is also set up, but you probably need to adjust the modem port speed. So jog on over to the "Configuring port speed" section later in this chapter for instructions.

Configuring a DIY connection with Windows

You can also choose the complete do-it-yourself (DIY) method of configuring your cellphone as a modem and set up your own connection through Windows XP. In this case, you've purchased a data cable compatible with your phone and, of course, you've either found, and downloaded, the necessary device drivers or you've been fortunate enough to have them included on a CD with your cable.

If you download drivers from the Web, chances are good that they're formatted in a `.zip` folder that includes drivers for several operating systems. I find it easiest to create a new folder in My Documents named Drivers and extract the drivers to that folder. In that way, I can find them easily when I need to use them to set up the modem.

The steps involved in setting up your phone as a modem and establishing a new connection are as follows:

1. **Power up your cellphone, and connect the cable to your phone.**

2. **Connect the cable to your computer using whichever port, USB or serial, is appropriate.**

   The Found New Hardware Wizard springs to life and appears before your eyes.

3. **Select Install From A List Or Specific Location (Advanced) and click Next.**

4. **In the dialog box shown in Figure 7-2, do one of the following, depending on where your drivers are located:**

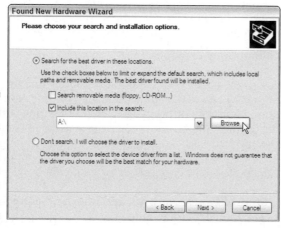

Figure 7-2: Select an option, depending on where your drivers are located.

If you have a CD containing the drivers, select the Search Removable Media check box, and click Next to proceed to Step 5.

If you've downloaded drivers, select the Include This Location In The Search check box and click Browse. When the Browse For Folder dialog box opens (Figure 7-3), scroll to the location to which you extracted the drivers, select the appropriate driver, and click OK. Back in the Found New Hardware Wizard, click Next to proceed to Step 5.

Figure 7-3:
Browse for drivers you downloaded to your computer.

5. **The chances are almost 100% that a warning from Microsoft, recommending that you abandon any further attempts to install this software, now appears. Smugly and confidently ignore the warning; click Continue Anyway.**

   The installation status bar, complete with flying folders, opens — and when it's finished, it closes. Your computer's still intact, and it appears as though the warning was a bit overstated.

6. **Click Finish. Still nothing explodes.**

At this point, Windows recognizes your cellphone as a fully functional modem. The final step is to create the connection, and for this, you need some information from your cellular provider. (See "Configuring your connection with a kit" earlier in this chapter for the minimum list of information you need to obtain.)

Follow these steps to create a new connection for your cellphone modem:

1. **Choose Start⇨Control Panel⇨Network and Internet Connections⇨Set up or change your Internet connection.**

   The Internet Properties dialog box opens.

2. **Click the Connections tab, and click Setup.**

   The New Connection Wizard welcome screen opens.

3. **Click Next to open the Network Connection Type dialog box.**

4. **Select Connect to the Internet, and click Next.**

5. **Select Set Up My Connection Manually, and click Next.**

6. **Select Connect Using A Dial-Up Modem, and click Next.**

   The Select a Device dialog box opens. If you've got an integrated modem or you've previously installed a PC card modem, it's listed here along with your cellphone modem.

7. **Deselect any other modems, select your cellphone modem, and click Next.**

8. **Enter the name of your cellular carrier or choose any other name for the connection that you might like, and click Next.**

9. **Enter the phone number, provided to you by your cellular provider, which must be dialed to connect to the cellular network, and click Next.**

10. **Enter the User name and Password provided to you by your cellular provider. You also want to deselect the check box labeled Use This Account Name And Password When Anyone Connects To The Internet From This Computer, as well as the Make This The Default Internet Connection check box.**

11. **Click Next.**

    And that's it! Well, almost. Before you click Dial, you should check your modem port speeds; they might need to be adjusted. You can find out how to do that in the following section ("Configuring port speed"), and after that's done, you're ready to dial.

The first time I set up my modem and connection, the connection didn't work. If this happens to you, try rebooting your phone. To do so, leave the cable connected between your phone and computer, power down the phone, count slowly to 20, and restart it. According to the support staffer that got me up and running, this step resets the SIM card.

Configuring port speed

At this point, you might need to configure your port speeds. Often the modem's set up at 112 Kbps, but if you plan to use a high-speed network, you have a definite need to increase port speed. To do so, follow these steps:

1. **Choose Start⇨Control Panel⇨Network and Internet Connections⇨ Network Connections.**

   The Network Connections screen opens.

2. **Right-click the icon for your cellphone connection and select Properties.**

   The Properties dialog box opens.

3. **Select the General tab, and under the description of your modem, click Configure.**

   The Modem Configuration dialog box opens.

4. **From the Maximum Speed (bps) drop-down menu, select the appropriate speed.**

   Recommended settings for the following standards are as follows:

   • *GPRS or CDMA standard:* 230400 bps

   • *EDGE or 1xRTT standard:* 460800 bps

   • *UTMS, HSDPA, or Ev-DO standard:* 921600 bps

You don't need to set the port settings every time you go from one network to another. If, for example, you occasionally make an Ev-DO connection but most often use a 1xRTT connection, your configuration should be set to accommodate the high-speed network. (I introduce standards in "Comparing speeds and standards" earlier in this chapter.)

5. **Click OK to establish the settings, and close the dialog boxes.**

   At this point you're ready to open the connection manager and log on to the network.

Making the connection with Bluetooth

The most convenient of all possible tethering methods is Bluetooth — that is, if your phone has the capability, if your computer has the capability, and if your cellular provider allows it. Of those three conditions, only one — the computer lacking Bluetooth capability — is easily remedied.

Vast numbers of Bluetooth adapters — easy remedies for computers lacking this capability — are available from a wide variety of vendors, but if your phone lacks Bluetooth, the only remedy is to replace the phone. And if your carrier disallows Bluetooth tethering, you can either purchase controlling interest in the company or switch providers — whichever you find easiest and most expedient.

Assuming, however, that Bluetooth tethering is a possibility, you might want to consider setting it up. Because this method of tethering requires no wired connection, it's extremely convenient. You can, if you choose, leave your phone in a coat pocket or sitting on a shelf or hanging from the mirror. What could be better?

What's Bluetooth?

Bluetooth: A condition resulting from the ingestion of far too many blueberry pies. Well, not really. But it is a strange name for a technology, don't you think? Of course, there's a good story behind it.

This wireless technology, with its developmental roots in Scandinavia, resulted from the co-operation and collaboration of several multinational companies, and its purpose is to unite various peripheral devices — like phones, keyboards, and computers — in seamless, wireless, communication. The development group decided to name the new technology *Bluetooth*

because it's a Scandinavian name synonymous with unification and collaboration.

The term comes from Harald Blatand, the King of Denmark from 940 to 985 A.D., and Bluetooth's symbol is a combination of the runic characters of King Harald Blatand's initials. Good King Harald, whose last name can be translated in English as *Bluetooth,* was responsible for uniting Denmark, Norway, and Sweden. I'd like to say it was united in peace, but unfortunately, King Harald's reign came to an end (not coincidentally) at the same moment he lost his life in battle.

Adapting a laptop or PDA for Bluetooth

It seems that no matter what technology might be missing from your laptop or PDA there's a method of adapting it for use. Such is the case with Bluetooth. If you need to enable Bluetooth for your PDA, for example, you can easily find, whichever is appropriate, a CF or SDIO adapter. Likewise, if your laptop lacks the capability, you can find a USB– or PCMCIA–powered Bluetooth adapter.

Bluetooth, like Wi-Fi, complies with various standards, ranging from v1.0 to v2.0, and like Wi-Fi, these standards are backward compatible. Bluetooth 1.1 and 1.2 specify a transfer rate of 723Kbps — which is plenty fast enough for all but the fastest of connections — while Bluetooth 2.0 is capable of speeds as high as 2.1Mbps. Besides these standards, however, Bluetooth also exists in three power classes, outlined in Table 7-4.

Table 7-4	Bluetooth Power Class and Range	
Power Class	*Maximum Output*	*Maximum Range*
Class 1	100mW	330 feet
Class 2	2.5mW	33 feet
Class 3	1mW	3 feet

As you can see from Table 7-4, it's probably a good idea to shop for a Class 1 or Class 2 adapter. A few of the available adapter choices include:

- ✔ **Socket Bluetooth SDIO Connection Kit:** Manufactured by Socket and available from many online and bricks-and-mortar discount retailers, this is a Class 2, Bluetooth v1.1 adapter.

- ✔ **Bluetooth PDA and PC Adapter Combo Card:** Manufactured by Belkin, this card can be used in a PDA's CF slot or in a PC's PCMCIA slot, making it very versatile. The adapter conforms to Bluetooth v1.1 and has a range of 33 feet.

- ✔ **HBTC1 Bluetooth USB Class 1 Wireless Adapter:** Manufactured by Hawking Technology, this USB adapter is widely available online and otherwise. The adapter conforms to Bluetooth v1.1 and, because it's a Class 1 adapter, has a range of 330 feet.

- ✔ **Targus USB Bluetooth Adapter:** Conforming to the Bluetooth v1.1 standard, this Class 2 adapter is manufactured by Targus and available from their Web site and discount retailers.

Bluetooth adapters come packaged with an installation CD that includes the necessary drivers. When you install the drivers and your adapter, be sure that Bluetooth support (My Bluetooth Places) is set up in Windows.

Configuring the connection

If you're using, for example, the Cingular Communication Manager, you can employ the connection utility to tether your Bluetooth device. If not, you can set it up in Windows as follows:

1. **Make your phone discoverable.**

   This just means that it's broadcasting a Bluetooth signal. Every phone menu differs greatly; consult your manual to find out how to access your Bluetooth configuration menu, where you find an option to make the phone discoverable.

2. **On your laptop, choose Start➪All Programs➪My Bluetooth Places.**

   The My Bluetooth Places window opens.

3. **Click View Devices in Range.**

   After a few moments, an icon representing your phone appears.

4. **Right-click the icon.**

   A dialog menu opens.

5. **Select Pair Device.**

The Bluetooth PIN Code Request dialog box opens.

6. **Enter a PIN code, and click OK.**

   You have to enter this same PIN into the phone as well. For this reason, use only numbers in your PIN — no letters.

7. **Redirect your attention now to your phone, where three questions await you: Accept, Add to Paired, and Decline.**

   - *Accept:* Pairs your computer with the phone, but the phone isn't paired with the computer.

   - *Add to Paired:* Pairs both devices with each other. I strongly suggest, for the sake of convenience, that you choose this option.

   - *Decline:* Neither device is paired, and you've just wasted a couple minutes.

8. **Assuming you've chosen to pair both devices, enter the PIN code into the phone.**

9. **On your laptop, once again, right-click the icon representing your phone. From the menu, select Discover Available Services.**

   Several icons, including Dial-up Networking, appear.

10. **Right-click the Dial-up Networking icon, and select Connect Dial-up Networking.**

    The Connect Bluetooth Connections dialog box opens.

11. **Enter your user name, password, and the number to dial.**

    You need to get this information from your cellular provider because it varies from one cellular provider to another.

12. **Choose Save This User Name And Password For Me Only.**

13. **Click Dial.**

You might need to configure your port speeds. (See "Configuring port speeds," earlier in this chapter, for the details.)

Logging on

If you're using the connection management utility provided by your cellular provider, there's no difference between using a Bluetooth tethered phone or any other supported device. If, on the other hand, you want to connect with Windows, choose Start⇨Connect to⇨Show all connections. With the Network Connections window open, right-click the icon related to your Bluetooth tethered phone, and choose Connect.

Combining Wi-Fi and Cellular

So here you are, traveling the highways and byways of this great nation with your whole crew. But everyone has his or her own computer and wants to be online at the same time. For everybody to be connected to a high-speed cellular service, at $60 to $80 per month *per person*, your fortune will soon be transferred from your bank to that of your cellular provider.

There is, however, a light on the horizon. Two companies have come up with devices designed to share a single, cellular connection. In much the same way that an access point at a hotspot broadcasts a single Internet connection, you can use the Junxion Box (manufactured by Junxion) or the Kyocera KR1 Mobile Router to expand the access of a single, cellular, Internet connection by broadcasting that connection as a Wi-Fi signal. (See Figure 7-4.)

Using a single, high-speed, cellular data account, you can connect several computers simultaneously to the Internet. Neither of these devices could be fairly described as "inexpensive," but because the connection can be shared among several users, you could recoup the initial cost in a matter of months, depending on how many users share the connection.

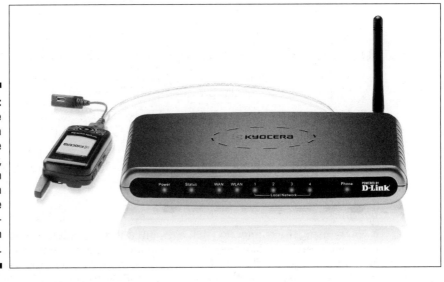

Figure 7-4:
The Kyocera KR1 Mobile Router, shown using a cellphone as connection medium.

Although the devices are similar, they do have a couple of important differences, as you can see in Table 7-5.

Table 7-5	Kyocera KR1 versus Junxion Box		
Device	*Cellular Standards*	*Wi-Fi Standard*	*Supported Connection Devices*
Kyocera KR1	1xRTT and Ev-DO	802.11g	Data cards and cellphones
Junxion Box	1xRTT, Ev-DO, GPRS, EDGE, and HSDPA	802.11b	Data cards only

As you can see by examining Table 7-5, the Junxion Box is limited to using data cards, but offers the ability and versatility to connect with all the national high-speed cellular providers (not, obviously, simultaneously). On the other hand, the Kyocera KR1 is limited to either Sprint or Verizon, but costs less than half that of the Junxion Box. The Kyocera KR1 also offers the option of using a cellphone tethered by a USB cable, rather than a data card, to establish the connection between the router and cellular network.

Both of these devices provide the option of using either Wi-Fi or Ethernet to make the connection between your computer and the router. The Kyocera KR1 has four Ethernet ports, whereas the Junxion Box has two.

Boosting Your Signal

By using an external antenna — either with or without an amplifier — you can increase your ability to connect to a distant cell tower, but as is the case with Wi-Fi adapters, not every data card comes equipped with an external antenna connection port. What's interesting, though, is that the amplifiers and antennas are compatible with both GSM and CDMA technologies. You can use these signal-boosting devices, for example, with a Kyocera KPC650 using Verizon's Ev-DO service or a Sierra Wireless AirCard 860 tied to Cingular's EDGE or HSDPA networks. A few things to keep in mind include:

✔ **Indoor versus outdoor antennas:** An outdoor, magnetic-mount antenna uses the roof as a ground plane, and therefore, can't be used inside a vehicle. If you're looking for one of the best indoor antennas available, I recommend you begin your search at www.booster-antenna.com.

✔ **Amplifiers:** An amplifier used in conjunction with an antenna can pull in signals that an antenna alone might not even detect. Some amplifiers, however, (because of the technology used) might boost your signal, but they do so by using considerable amounts of bandwidth. Currently, one amplifier, the Cyfre CA819 (sold under both the Inteligain and Shakespeare banners), has proven in test after test to boost the signal without hogging the network. In fact, it's the only amplifier approved by all U.S. cellular providers.

Finding Additional Information

Over the course of time, I've found a few Web sites that have provided me with consistently valuable information.

- ✔ **HowardForums:** Found at www.howardforums.com, this Web site is filled with information related to cellphones, data cards, signal boosting, and a whole lot more.

- ✔ **EVDOinfo.com:** I rarely come across a Web site with this much relevant information. Before you make any Ev-DO related purchases, you should visit www.evdoinfo.com.

- ✔ **Maximum Signal:** If you're shopping for an amplifier or an outdoor cellular antenna, this is the first place to look. You can find excellent products, excellent service, and honest advice at www.maximumsignal.com.

Chapter 8

Reattaching the Wired Tether

As much as I like and enjoy wireless Internet access, it's an unfortunate fact of life that Wi-Fi isn't everywhere. At times, the only way you can connect to the Internet is to turn back the clock. Yes, I'm talking about connecting wires to your computer. I don't like it any more than you do — but sometimes, if you want to get connected to the Internet, a wired connection is necessary.

So why am I telling you about this? Mainly because there are a few differences between using a wired connection while traveling and using one at home. For example, if you've been using a local ISP for your connection at home, most likely you'll need to make a toll call to get connected from your home on wheels.

In this chapter, I help you prepare to make the occasional wired connection. I also tell you about ways to avoid long-distance connections — and about an innovative way to make a wireless connection via dialup.

Preparing for Travel

After so many venues set up hotspots and joined the Wi-Fi revolution, I thought that I'd be able to throw my 20-foot phone cord in the trash. I couldn't have been more wrong. Granted, most of the time I can take advantage of a wire-free connection, but at times — especially if I'm spending a day or two in an out-of-the-way motel room — my only hope of getting online is by making a wired connection.

Because this is true — and because I believe it'll remain true for quite some time — I continue to carry the necessary gear for getting connected the old-fashioned way. Among the items I find necessary and useful are

- ✔ **Retractable phone cord:** When my laptop's wired to the wall, I don't like to sit *under* the motel desk. So I always carry a 20-foot phone cord. It doesn't have to be retractable, but retractable is nice.

- ✔ **Retractable Ethernet cable:** For the most part, you won't find retractable Ethernet cords in lengths much longer than eight feet. If you need more length, you'll have to carry it the old-fashioned way.

I use the Model PA205U retractable phone cord from Targus (www.targus.com/us), which also sells a variety of computer travel gear. You can also find retractable phone cords and Ethernet cables at CableOrganizer.com (http://cableorganizer.com/retractable), Cables To Go (www.cablestogo.com), and Belkin (www.belkin.com). Belkin's 7-in-1 Retractable Cable Pack is the Swiss Army Knife of cable organizers.

- ✔ **Modem:** Chances are good (especially if your laptop's less than a few years old) that you've got a built-in modem, but if not, you can purchase a PC-card modem that looks very much like a PC-card Wi-Fi adapter.

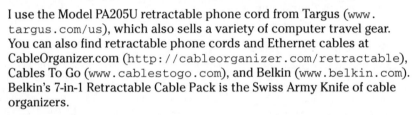

- ✔ **Modem saver:** Your phone modem's designed to handle a low-voltage analog signal. Many hotels and motels, however — because of their PBX switching needs — use a digital line. This can fry your modem like a cheap steak. Even worse, if you're using a laptop with an integrated modem, you can put your entire computer at risk because the internal modem's plugged into the motherboard. To alleviate the problem, look for a phone equipped with a data port in your hotel room. By using the data port rather than plugging your phone line directly into the wall plug, you can avoid any potential damage. If you don't have the option of using a data port, you can employ a *digital line converter*. These are handy items, but they're also pretty expensive.

Of course, even the lack of a data port doesn't necessarily mean the line's unsuitable for use with your modem. But how do you know for sure? Elementary, my dear reader — you simply use a *digital line tester*. TeleAdapt, for example, manufactures the TeleTester Pro (NF) that can, by detecting a high-amperage line, help you avoid damaging your modem. If the line's suitable for use, it'll indicate that, too. See www.teleadapt.com.

Delving into Dialup

Back in days of old, when dialup was dominant, I remember being thrilled to hear those familiar sounds indicating my modem was making a connection.

Now they're an indication that I'm stuck somewhere that Wi-Fi hasn't found. Still, it's nice to know that the dialup ISPs are alive and kicking — because at least occasionally, they're the only game in town.

The biggest dialup-related issue for me has always been whether to use a national subscription ISP or a prepaid service. ISPs such as EarthLink and AOL offer a lot of bells and whistles to go along with their dialup access, but now that I'm primarily accessing the Internet from wireless hotspots, I don't know that I really want to pay a subscription fee for dialup, too.

When I first joined the ranks of laptop-toting truckers, I ventured forth, believing that my trusty AOL account would provide me with a connection anywhere I went. For the most part, that assumption was true — but I hadn't considered the fact that I'd frequently be in areas lacking local access numbers. In those cases, I was forced to pay ten cents a minute to use the toll-free access number. All well and good — I could surf the Net, but I was paying that extra fee on top of my already-hefty monthly subscription rate.

Six bucks an hour plus $24 a month is quite a bit to pay for a dialup Internet connection, but being a newcomer, I didn't know I had other choices. Part of the problem, at the time, was that AOL hadn't yet built the large inventory of local access numbers it now offers. While the national subscription ISPs have increased the likelihood of being able to make a local call, the possibility of being forced to use the expensive toll-free number still lurks.

The alternative to a monthly dialup subscription plan — especially one that simply serves as a backup to Wi-Fi — is to use one of the many prepaid ISPs. The advantages are many, but you need to know about a couple of issues, such as a lack of (or limited) e-mail service, before you buy. Table 8-1 offers a quick comparison of several services.

Table 8-1	Subscription versus Prepaid Dialup Service		
ISP	*Cost*	*E-mail?*	*Other Services*
PeoplePC	$10.95 per month	Yes (4)	High-speed dialup free for one year; virus blocker included in monthly rate.
NetZero	$9.95 per month	Yes (1)	$6.95 per month for the first year. High-speed dialup at extra cost.
AOL	$23.90 per month	Yes (7)	High-speed dialup, 24/7 free tech support, e-mail virus protection included in cost. Includes $0.10-per-minute toll-free access number.

(continued)

Table 8-1 *(continued)*

ISP	Cost	E-mail?	Other Services
Budget Dialup	$0.60 per hour	Yes (1)	Free 24/7 tech support and Web accelerator. Provides $3.60-per-hour toll-free access when local numbers are not available.
MaGlobe	$0.54 per hour	Yes (1)	High-speed dialup on toll-free number. Offers $2.49-per-hour toll-free access and e-mail tech support.
BAMnet	$0.60 per hour	No	Free tech support from 9:00 a.m. – 9:00 p.m. (EST). Purchased time never expires. Provides $3.90-per-hour toll-free access number.

I've tried most of the prepaid services, and although they're remarkably similar, I've noticed a few differences — some subtle and some not so subtle. All the services, for example, require you to purchase a set amount of time up front (hence the term *prepaid*), but the minimum amount ranges from a low of $5.95, offered by Budget Dialup, to a high of $20 at BAMnet.

Some prepaid services, such as BAMnet, also offer a reduced rate for larger initial and recharge purchases — and while access minutes have a shelf-life of one year at Budget Dialup and MaGlobe, they never expire at BAMnet. Note, however, that if you purchase additional time prior to the expiration date, all time is renewed and no access time expires.

Both Budget Dialup and MaGlobe employ the use of an auto-dialer, much like the one AOL uses, while BAMnet uses the connection configuration software built into Windows. Budget Dialup also offers the option of choosing a manual setup if you don't want to use the auto-dialer. Why you wouldn't want to use it is beyond me, though.

The biggest — and, for me, the most significant — difference is in tech support. I haven't experienced a problem with MaGlobe, but at least to me, it doesn't seem as if e-mail tech support is going to be much help if you're experiencing problems getting online. I much prefer being able to speak with a human. Even a person who barely speaks English is better than being stuck with e-mail tech support *when you can't send e-mail.*

If you're interested in visiting the prepaid ISP Web sites, you can find them by pointing your browser toward these URLs:

- ✔ **Budget Dialup:** www.budgetdialup.com
- ✔ **MaGlobe:** www.maglobe.com
- ✔ **BAMnet:** www.bamnet.com

After you set up your connection (an installer wizard typically guides you through the process), the dialer can pop up every time you boot your laptop or close out a wireless connection. To keep it out of your way, in Internet Explorer, choose Tools➪Options and click the Connections tab. Select your connection from the Dial-up and Virtual Private Connections list box, and select the Never Dial a Connection radio button. When you need to use dialup, just double-click the dialup icon on your desktop and the dialer opens.

As you travel around using the software that comes with your connection, you simply need to select the local access number for wherever you are, and set the dialer to dial a 9 if your hotel or motel requires it to get an outside line.

Dialup Unplugged (Kind Of)

Other than the fact that it's considerably slower than a wireless broadband connection, I don't find dialup all that inconvenient, except for one thing: I just hate the phone line dangling from my laptop. I don't know how many times — especially before I began using a laptop with an internal modem — I've stepped on the cord and caused damage.

For that reason, I'm always on the lookout for a way to use a dialup connection without actually connecting a wire to my laptop — and I've found a few. For example, in the previous chapter, I talk about using your cellphone as a modem. There are also other, easier ways to get a wire-free dialup Internet connection.

Comparing wireless dialup modems

One of the indications that dialup will never die has to be the fact that products continue to be manufactured catering to the technology. With the world going gaga over Wi-Fi, a few folks have come up with dialup modems that use various technologies allowing for a wireless connection between your computer and the modem.

Getting down to brass tacks, the only real difference between these devices and a wireless access point is that the Internet connection is dialup rather than broadband. You can choose from at least four different methods of making the wireless connection between your computer and the modem being used:

- **Infrared:** Almost every computer has an infrared sensor located in the screen, but if by some chance yours doesn't, you can buy a USB-powered infrared adapter.

- **Bluetooth:** This wireless technology, though it hasn't yet seemed to realize its potential, has begun to be widely used to eliminate cabling between computers and peripheral devices. The range is less than the 802.11 standards, but when you're using it in a motel room, how far does it need to reach?

- **900 MHz wireless:** This is the same frequency used by many cordless phones — and though I know of only one device using this technology, it's worth a look.

- **802.11:** Again, I know of only one device using Wi-Fi to bridge the gap between your computer and a dialup connection, which is kind of puzzling because a large number of the people who want to use wireless dialup modems already have, in all likelihood, computers capable of making an 802.11 connection.

Bluetooth modems

The largest group — therefore the largest selection — of wireless dialup modems utilizes Bluetooth technology. If you don't have a built-in Bluetooth transceiver, you'll need to use an adapter. Many modems include a USB adapter; for those that don't, the manufacturer might sell one separately.

Among the group of Bluetooth wireless modems are the following:

- **EXP wireless Bluetooth 56K modem:** Manufactured by EXP, this modem functions under the V.90 standard and utilizes the older V1.1 standard, which is more than sufficient for dialup, but also uses a long-range Class 1 radio transceiver. It comes bundled with a 110v power cord and a USB Bluetooth adapter. This modem's available from EXP at `www.expnet.com/expweb.nsf` as well as other online retailers.

- **Socket Cordless 56K modem:** This V.90-standard Bluetooth modem can be used with the supplied AC power cord or battery; using the power cord charges the battery simultaneously. A connection-management wizard is included in the software, and the modem is compatible with both tone and pulse dialing. It's available from Socket Communications at `www.socketcom.com`, as well as several online discount retailers.

> ✔ **Zoom Model 4300 Bluetooth modem:** A Bluetooth Class 1 radio trans-
> ceiver provides a range of up to 300 feet, and the V1.1 standard easily
> surpasses the requirements of a 56K V.90 modem. The Model 4300 uses
> encryption to secure the wireless transmission; it's available from Zoom
> at www.zoom.com as well as discount retailers.

Infrared modems

Whereas a Class 1 Bluetooth transceiver is capable of communicating at distances in excess of 300 feet, an infrared (IrDA) modem is limited to distances
of somewhere around 3 feet. This limitation makes IrDA a much less attractive technology for use in a hotel or motel room. Most IrDA modems, as a
matter of fact, are probably purchased by PDA owners who desire a dialup
connection for their handhelds.

There have never been a lot of IrDA modems manufactured; the Pegasus III,
from 3JTech, is the only one I know of that's still being built. It's available
from www.3jtech.com and online discount retailers. You might also find a
Psion Travel Modem during your Internet travels — it's supported, but it's no
longer built by Psion.

Wireless modems

The two wireless modems I'm aware of take two completely different
approaches to achieving a wireless connection between modem and computer. The Nebo Wireless Link, for example, transmits and receives a 900MHz
radio signal between the base unit and a remote device that's plugged into
both a USB port on your computer and the modem port on your computer.

The Nebo Wireless Link also has an innovative security feature — making it,
possibly, more secure than 802.11-based devices. This security feature chooses
from more than 260,000 digital security codes and assigns one to the base
and remote unit. Base and remote units operate as a pair, communicating
securely. If you're interested in the Nebo Wireless Link, you can find it available from the manufacturer at www.nebowireless.com.

On the other hand, the WiFlyer, by AlwaysOn Wireless, employs the 802.11b
standard, making it possible to conveniently connect in the same way you
would at any hotspot. The WiFlyer is especially handy for couples wanting to
share an Internet connection: Because it's acting as a wireless access point,
you can set up your own local-access network.

Security, which is always a concern with a wireless connection, includes encryption, MAC address filtering, and other wireless-security protocols. Another
feature of the WiFlyer is its ability to make use of both a dialup and broadband connection. Turning your motel room into a wireless hotspot has never

been so easy. The WiFlyer is available from AlwaysOn at www.alwayson wireless.com as well as a few other online retailers.

Using the WiFlyer

Never have I come across a computer-related device that was as easy to set up and use as the WiFlyer. You might not believe this, but from the time the WiFlyer first arrived at my door to the time I was connected to the Internet, fewer than ten minutes passed. As a matter of fact, it took just under seven minutes. And some of that time, maybe even most of the time, I spent slicing through the tape on the well-packed box.

Configuring WiFlyer for dialup

If it only takes a few minutes to connect to the Internet, there's not (obviously) a whole lot involved in configuring the WiFlyer. When you open the box, you see a three-step guide to getting connected, and with just a couple of nuances, that's about it. The most detailed description of configuration follows:

1. **Connect the cords.**

   After you connect the phone line and the power cord, you see the first LED light indicating that all is well to this point.

   Don't connect the phone cord directly to a digital line.

2. **On your laptop, open your connection-management utility (WZC, JiWire, or other), look for the SSID** wiflyer, **and connect to that network.**

   See Chapter 6 for more information about connecting to a wireless network.

3. **Boot your browser.**

   Your browser should boot automatically, but if it doesn't, open it. Prior to opening your browser, make certain that your e-mail client (Outlook Express, Thunderbird, and so on) is closed. The WiFlyer dialup-configuration page opens automatically.

   If, for some unknown reason, the WiFlyer configuration page fails to open automatically, type **http://192.168.7.77** into the address window of your browser, and press Enter. (See Figure 8-1.) The configuration screen can be reached only by entering **http://192.168.7.77** into the address field of your browser. Save this page into your favorites so you can access it easily.

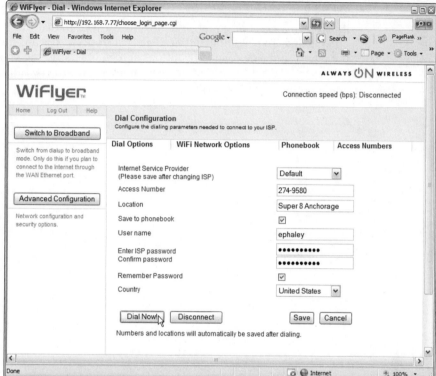

Figure 8-1:
WiFlyer
dialup
options,
at your
service.

4. **Select your ISP from the Internet Service Provider drop-down list.**

   If you use one of the ISPs listed in the drop-down list, select it and click
   Save. If you're using any other ISP, such as Budget Dialup, just maintain
   the Default setting on the menu.

5. **Enter an access number.**

   If you selected one of the ISPs listed in the drop-down list, the Access
   Numbers button is activated — and, if you click that button, you can
   choose an access number from the list that opens. Otherwise, use an
   access number provided by your ISP. If, for example, your ISP is Budget
   Dialup, you're bypassing the autodialer — but you still need to open it
   and select an access number.

6. **Enter your username and password.**

   If you're an AOL customer, your username is your screen name.
   Otherwise, it's the name and password you used when you signed up for
   service with your ISP.

7. Set dialing rules.

If you're in a hotel or motel, you most likely need to dial 8 or 9 to get an outside line. To accomplish this, click Dial Options (toward the top of the page), and when the Dial Options screen opens, as shown in Figure 8-2, select and set the necessary parameters. Save the settings and the configuration window reopens.

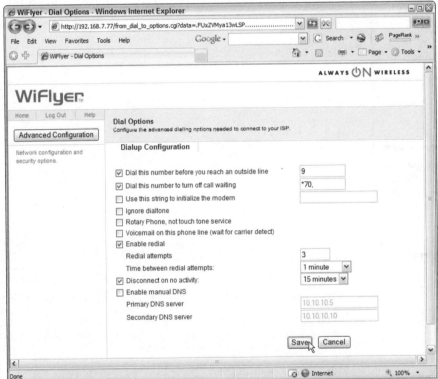

Figure 8-2:
Set your
dialing
options.

8. Click Save, and then click Dial Now!

A really handy feature of the WiFlyer is the Quick Connect button located just above the LED indicator lights. Rather than return to the configuration screen to disconnect, you can simply press the Quick Connect button. In a similar fashion, the next time you want to connect to the Internet, if you're accessing the same number, you can simply press the Quick Connect button. You can do this while you're booting your computer, and by the time it's up and running, your dialup connection is established as well.

Configuring the WiFlyer for broadband

If you find yourself in a hotel or motel room offering a broadband Internet connection, you can use the WiFlyer to set up a high-speed wireless connection with no more effort than was required to configure for dialup. You will, however, need to know whether you're using a cable or DSL connection, and you should be able to get that information from the hotel or motel staff. You should also ask if you need to know about any other issues prior to making a connection.

The first three steps are the same for both dialup and broadband. With the configuration screen open, follow these steps:

1. **Click the Switch to Broadband button.**

   A dialog box opens, asking whether you're sure you want to switch. You can think about it for a second or two.

2. **Click Yes.**

   The Broadband Configuration screen opens.

3. **Choose the Static, DHCP, or PPPoE mode, whichever is appropriate, for your connection.**

   This is where information from the staff comes in. If you need a static IP address, the motel staff will give you the necessary information. If the connection requires PPPoE (Point-to-Point Protocol over Ethernet), they'll give you a username, password, and authentication method. And, if it's DHCP (Dynamic Host Configuration Protocol) — meaning that they most likely employ a cable connection or you're connecting to their LAN (local-access network — nothing more than two or more computers networked together) — no other information is required. DHCP is the most common setting.

4. **Click Save. You might need to reboot the WiFlyer device, and after you do so, the Broadband Configuration screen reopens.**

5. **Click Connect if the button's active (if it's not, you're connected).**

Configuring security

A hotspot, by its very nature, is an open, unsecured WLAN (wireless local-area network; an access point, and one or more wirelessly connected computers). With the WiFlyer, you create your own WLAN, but because you might not want the general public joining your network, you can choose to close it by enabling a few security features. The nice thing about setting up WiFlyer security is that no matter where you go and regardless of whether you're using a dialup or broadband connection, the settings remain the same.

You can choose to use just one or all of the several levels of security available to you. In order to secure your connection, follow these steps:

1. **Open the Configuration page (dialup or broadband), and click the Advanced Configuration button. In the menu on the left side of the Advanced Configuration page, choose Security to open the Security page.**

   From the Security page, you can choose from four different security measures.

2. **If you want to enable password protection, put a check mark in the box and then enter and confirm a password.**

   Enabling the requirement for a password is the most basic of security features. It probably won't keep a determined hacker from joining your network, but it should keep the guy in the next room from barging into your network.

3. **To enable Wired Equivalent Privacy (WEP), click the Wireless Security link to open the Wireless Security and Encryption Settings page. When you're done defining your WEP settings, click Save and reboot the WiFlyer.**

   If you choose to use this feature — and I recommend that you do — you need to configure the following WEP settings (see Figure 8-3):

   a. *Put a check mark in the Enable WEP check box.*

   b. *Choose whether you want 64-bit or 128-bit encryption from the dropdown list.*

   I recommend 128-bit encryption, but it's up to you.

   c. *Choose your encryption keys.*

   You don't have to enter a key for all four fields, but I recommend it. 64-bit hexadecimal keys must be 10-hex-digits long, and 128-bit keys must be 26-hex bits long.

   A *hex-digit* is one of 16 letters or numbers, either 0-9 or A-F. Hexadecimal is a base-16 system in which all the bytes can be represented by using a combination of two hexadecimal numbers.

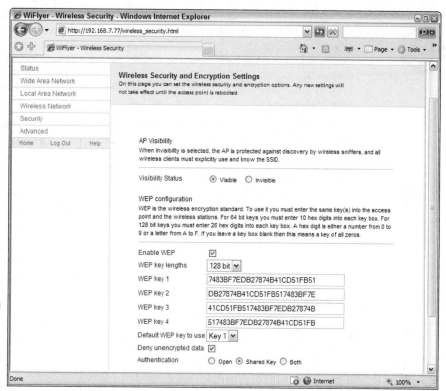

Figure 8-3:
Setting
encryption
settings.

Be sure to make note of the keys you've used, and put the note somewhere that you can easily find. This is the only way, once set, to access the WiFlyer; you can imagine the importance of being able to locate it.

d. *Make certain a check mark appears in the box next to* Deny unencrypted data.

e. *Choose Open or Shared Key authentication.*

I prefer Shared Key just because it puts another layer between me and everyone else.

I've had problems getting wireless devices to connect with invisible access points, so I recommend you maintain a visible one. Others can see your SSID on their Available Networks screen, but you can (if you choose) change the SSID they see. From the Advanced Configuration page, choose Wireless Networks, and when the page opens, simply change the name and click Save. You can also change the channel from this page if you've noticed any interference from other wireless devices.

4. **If you want to enable MAC Address filtering, choose, from the Security page, Wireless Address Filtering, enable it by placing a check mark in the box, and enter the MAC address of each computer allowed to join your network into one of the 16 text-entry fields.**

   By choosing to filter Media Access Control (MAC) addresses, you limit the computers able to access your network to only those you've placed on the Allowed Access page. To find the MAC address for a computer running Windows XP, follow these steps:

   a. *Choose Start⇨Run, type* **cmd** *into the text field, and click Open.*

      The Command Prompt screen opens.

   b. *Type* **ipconfig/all**, *and then press Enter.*

      The Physical Address, which is the MAC address for your wireless device, is shown. It's something like 00-15-28-68-BC.

WiFlyer help-desk personnel have recommended to me that *either* MAC Address filtering or WEP be used, but not both. Your WiFlyer won't explode should you choose to use both, but it's probably unnecessary and it could slightly slow your connection speed, especially if you include a lot of "allowed" MAC addresses.

5. **If you like, you can enable the port Filtering Firewall by choosing this option from the Security page and entering the pertinent parameters in the text entry fields.**

   Port filtering stops certain applications from sending traffic through the access point. I've never had occasion to use this feature and the MAC address filter rules take precedence over this firewall. Primary users of this firewall will be businesses with intranets that allow access to the Internet but want to stop certain activities (such as instant messaging).

Chapter 9

Sky-High Wi-Fi

*O*n October 4, 1957, one of my best friends celebrated a birthday while the Soviet Union sent Sputnik into space. Since that time, those celebrated birthdays have (sadly) come to an end. But satellites, now numbering in the thousands, continue to be blasted beyond the bounds of Earth. Many of these orbiting marvels of engineering are communications satellites that make it possible to speak with anyone in the world, watch television broadcasts, and (more recently) access the Internet from nearly any location in the world.

To me, having grown up in a small Oregon town that had a single television and radio station, the idea that you can park in the middle of nowhere and access both the World Wide Web *and* satellite television broadcasts — all at the same time — is nothing short of incredible. If you've got a clear view of the southern sky, you can have Internet access whether you're at the MGM Grand or the Grand Canyon. This convenience doesn't come cheap, but if you absolutely *must* be connected, it's an option to consider.

In this chapter, I give you an idea of the options available to you should you decide that Internet-via-satellite is something you want to explore. For example, with a look at several satellite-Internet system manufacturers (and more than one configuration), I help you sift through the possibilities. I also offer pointers on finding a reputable dealer (whichever configuration you might choose) and on getting the most out of your system.

Surfing with a Satellite: The Basics

With a satellite setup, you can surf in the desert, mountains, plains, and prairies. Just about anyplace you can drive to can become a connected campsite if you use Very Small Aperture Terminal (VSAT) satellite dishes to connect with communication satellites in geosynchronous orbit.

How do satellite connections work?

If you connect to the Internet via satellite, you connect to a network system comprised of several components, including the following:

- **Network Operation Center (NOC):** The NOC has a hardwired connection to the Internet backbone, usually T1 or better, and maintains a constant connection to the satellite(s). Every VSAT system making access to satellites handled by the NOC can be monitored for usage.

- **Outdoor Unit:** This is basically your satellite dish and all the components attached to it, as shown in Figure 9-1.

  - **Reflector dish:** The largest and most recognizable part of the system, the dish gathers the signal from the satellite and reflects it toward the feedhorn (when receiving), or gathers the signal from the feedhorn and reflects it to the satellite (when transmitting).

  - **Feedhorn:** The *feedhorn*, suspended in front of the dish on the Feedhorn Arm, focuses the signal that the dish reflects to it and feeds that signal to the Low Noise Block (LNB).

  - **LNB:** This component amplifies the satellite signal it receives from the feedhorn, translates it, and sends it on to the modem. If the feedhorn is integrated into the LNB, it's referred to as an *LNBF.*

  - **Transmit amplifier:** Mounted, most often, on the bottom of the feedhorn arm, this amplifier increases the transmission signal from the modem to (depending on your system) 1 or 2 watts.

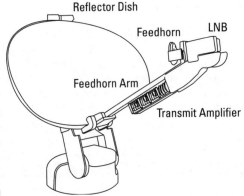

Figure 9-1:
The parts of a typical outdoor unit.

✔ **Indoor unit:** Also known as the IDU, this is the part of any VSAT system that remains inside the coach. The components making up the IDU may include the following:

- **Controller:** If the system auto-deployed and is self-pointing, a controller raises, lowers, and aims the dish. Newer controllers are fully integrated; the pointing software isn't loaded on a separate computer.

- **Modem:** As with any other connection to the Internet, you need a modem to convert the satellite signal into a data stream that your computer can understand.

- **Wireless router:** Connecting a wireless router to the modem turns your vehicle into a self-contained hotspot, enabling you to stow all the system components in a cabinet.

✔ **Satellite:** The satellite acts as a middleman, as shown in Figure 9-2. It receives and transmits radio signals from both the NOC and the VSAT dish mounted on or near your vehicle. Each satellite contains several transponders for sending and receiving data. When you subscribe to a satellite Internet provider, your account is tied to a specific transponder.

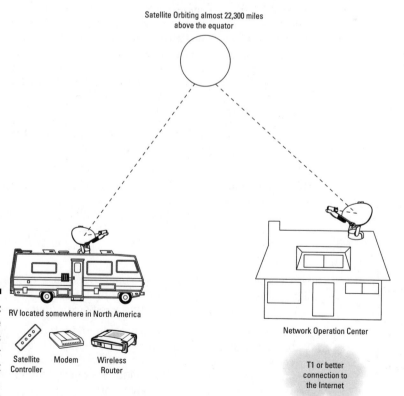

Satellite Orbiting almost 22,300 miles above the equator

RV located somewhere in North America

Satellite Controller   Modem   Wireless Router

Network Operation Center

T1 or better connection to the Internet

Figure 9-2: The satellite connects you to your Internet provider.

Maintaining a clear line of sight is one of the most important factors in getting a VSAT system to receive a strong signal from the satellite. Trees with leaves — even power lines (because of electrical interference) — can be effective barriers to effective communication with the satellite.

The limiting factors

Each transponder on a satellite has a limited bandwidth. This limitation results in two attributes that, although not exclusive to those accessing the Internet via satellite, are common to all satellite ISPs:

- ✔ **The download data-transfer rate is higher than the upload speed.** For most people who access the Internet to surf the Web and e-mail friends and family, this attribute means (for example) that Web pages download and open quickly. Those who need to upload large files, however, should expect some slowdown. For most basic satellite plans, you get an upload speed of about 128 Kpbs and a download speed ranging from 500 to 1000 Kpbs.

- ✔ **A Fair Access Policy (FAP) controls how much bandwidth you can use.** The purpose of a FAP is to ensure that everyone has equal access to the satellite and that nobody is using more than their fair share of the available bandwidth. Most ISPs monitor how much uploading and downloading is going on (in terms of data-transfer amounts measured in megabytes) on a running average. If a subscriber exceeds preset limits, their service is limited by slowing their data-transfer speeds until they're back within set tolerances. Some satellite aficionados who suffer such a slowdown refer to it as *being Fapped*.

When you sign up for a service subscription, be sure you entirely understand the FAP under which you'll be operating. There are two components common to all FAPs:

- • **Upload/download threshold:** This varies among providers and may also be subscription plan specific, meaning if you pay a higher monthly rate your threshold increases. Typically the upload threshold is much lower than the download threshold; if you e-mail a lot of large files, upload Web pages, or send program files to a server, you might run afoul of the FAP.

  If you simply browse the Web or e-mail friends and family, it's unlikely you'll ever find FAP an issue but, if you download a lot of music, video, or software you could easily experience a slowdown.

- • **Recovery rate:** In general, if you're Fapped, your data-transfer rate falls to a level that approximates that of dialup service until you've recovered enough bandwidth to be allowed full-speed surfing. Depending on your plan and provider, recovery could take anywhere from a few hours to a day or more.

The FAP is especially important to those who may be operating a business while traveling the country in their RVs. Most satellite ISPs offer plans, at a higher cost, that accommodate larger upload/download thresholds — and also (generally) allow higher data-transfer rates.

If you regularly use a virtual private network (VPN), you may want to opt for a public (that is, static) IP address. A more stable connection can be made if you've got a static IP address than may be possible with a dynamic IP address. I talk more about employing a VPN in Chapter 10.

Surveying the Known Universe of Options

Well, I doubt I can cover the entire universe of choices, but I can point out a few of the brighter stars. If you're contemplating the use of satellite communication as your method of accessing the Internet you should take the following into consideration while shopping:

- **VSAT reflector dish:** Although satellite Internet systems may seem similar, there are some differences. Among them are the following:

  - **Manually deployed dish:** Choosing this type of equipment decreases your cost but increases the time it takes getting set up for Internet access. Because it can be positioned 50 to 100 feet from your coach, however, it's also very versatile.

  - **Automatically deployed dish:** These systems are more expensive, but convenience comes at a cost. Boot your laptop, punch a couple of buttons, and voila´ — you're connected to the Net. This requires a controller that not only raises and lowers the dish, but also aims it and acquires the satellite signal. (Cool.)

  - **Dish diameter:** The most common dish diameter is .74 meters. If you require service near the edge of a satellite footprint, desire faster transfer speeds, or want to use a 2-watt rather than a 1-watt transmitter, you may find it appropriate (albeit more expensive) to opt for a .95-, .98- or 1.2-meter dish.

- **Cost:** All these companies offer monthly plans at varying rates; as might be expected, higher transfer speeds result in a higher cost. FAP is another cost factor; it pays to become familiar with its limitations. (For more about FAP, see the earlier section, "The limiting factors.")

- **Coverage:** Usually a number of satellites in geosynchronous orbit can provide Internet access. Each satellite, because of its position in the southern sky, has a somewhat different coverage footprint. Before signing a contract, you should be certain that the company you're considering provides coverage in the area you most often frequent.

✔ **Commitment:** Depending on the ISP providing the satellite service you can expect to see minimum contractual commitments ranging in length from 1 year to 18 months. In some cases, a longer contract results in lower monthly costs; in *all* cases, a stiff penalty may be assessed if the contract is terminated before the commitment is completed. I know of only one company, StarBand, than offers a month-to-month plan.

Manually deployed systems

A long, long time ago, during my first ski trip at Homewood Mountain Resort (overlooking lovely Lake Tahoe), I was taking the T-bar back to the top of the treacherous bunny hill when I noticed a fellow and his young son side-stepping their way up the slope. When I asked him why they were walking up the mountain when the resort was fully equipped with a number of well-maintained lifts, he chastened me with the reply: "There's more to skiing than just going down the mountain!" Indeed.

If, by chance, you feel that there should be more to surfing the Net than simply sipping a cup of coffee while your dish deploys itself and acquires a signal — or you just want to save a few thousand bucks — then you might be interested in a manually deployed VSAT dish sitting atop a tripod.

At this time, the StarBand Manual-Flyer is the only manually deployed mobile system that's officially sanctioned, but a few other companies do offer HughesNet-based tripod systems. HughesNet doesn't support or sanction these systems — technically, they operate outside the strict scope of their rules — but so far HughesNet hasn't moved to stop anyone from using one of these systems. Among those offering manually deployed systems are

✔ **StarBand:** The Manual-Flyer system includes a VSAT dish, mounting tripod, modem, set-up tools, and connection cable. The dealer from which you buy the system provides a training program that certifies you as a StarBand Certified Installer. The Web site: www.starband.com.

✔ **Dustyfoot.com:** Offering a HughesNet system including, among other items, the VSAT dish, tripod, modem, cable, and dish pointing tools. You get a manual and instructional DVD with the system; Dustyfoot.com provides technical assistance with every complete tripod system. Not surprisingly, their Web address is www.dustyfoot.com.

✔ **Maxwell Satellite:** Their system (also HughesNet-based) is known as the PortaSat. It includes the reflector-dish assembly, tripod, modem, and cable (in both 25- and 35-foot lengths). A 60-page instruction manual and customer-support Web site are also provided. They're located on the Web at www.maxwellsatellite.com.

✔ **Mobile Internet:** A VSAT dish, tripod mount, modem, pointing tools, and instructional video are included, along with a two-hour phone consultation to help with initial setup. They also offer an instructional and informative e-book on their Web site at `www.mobileinternet.bz`.

One point in favor of manually deployed systems is that they can, in most cases, be used to provide Internet access at home as well as on the road. This is important if you're not a full-time traveler since monthly charges may continue whether or not you use the satellite service.

Auto-deployed VSAT systems

When you search for a mobile satellite Internet-access solution, you find several companies clamoring for your business. In some respects, these companies are very similar — some may seem virtually the same at first glance. That's because several of them are *value-added resellers* (VARs) for HughesNet (formerly DirecWay).

A HughesNet VAR manufactures or assembles the mobile VSAT unit and/or controller — but instead of contracting with a satellite owner for their own transponder(s), they resell the satellite Internet access provided by HughesNet. Technically, that makes the VAR an ISP — but the satellite modem, in these cases, is the product of HughesNet.

Included among the HughesNet VARs are

✔ **MotoSAT:** DataStorm VSAT systems, manufactured by MotoSAT, might very well be the most recognizable of satellite systems. You've probably seen them, for years, on top of vans, RVs, and (occasionally) even trucks. They're found on the Web at `www.motosat.com`.

✔ **Ground Control:** As manufacturers of the Magellan MSS VSAT system they offer dishes in both .74 and .95 meter sizes. You can find their Web site by pointing your browser to `www.groundcontrol.com`.

✔ **DataTech:** The newest member of the HughesNet VAR club is DataTech and their offering is known as the DirecStar. You can get more information by visiting their Web site at `www.direcstar.com`.

The DataStorm, Magellan MSS and DirecStar aren't the only fish in the sea. For example, the iNetVu dish (by C-Com Satellite Systems, Inc.) is the platform on which StarBand builds its StarBand Auto-Pointing Flyer VSAT system. Here are a couple more major companies offering self-pointing units:

✔ **StarBand:** With transponder leases on Telstar 7, StarBand provides service throughout the contiguous 48 states, but service (with some conditions) may also be available in parts of Canada and Alaska. StarBand is located on the Web at www.starband.com.

✔ **RaySat:** The SpeedRay 3000, a phased array low-profile antenna rather than a dish antenna, is offered by RaySat. This unit, shown in Figure 9-3, is only a few inches high — and its innovative design lets you use it while the vehicle is in motion (more information at www.raysat.com).

Figure 9-3: The SpeedRay 3000 (shown here mounted on an SUV) can also be mounted on a truck or RV.

Focusing on the SpeedRay 3000

As winner of the prestigious "Best of Show" award, the shining star of the 2006 Consumer Electronic Show was the RaySat SpeedRay 3000. As with other self-pointing satellite antennas, it uses GPS to position its antenna — but (unlike traditional reflector dish satellite antennas) the SpeedRay 3000 employs phased-array panels. The antenna array's design allows the panels to turn freely within the housing, making the SpeedRay 3000 a low-profile unit that can maintain the antenna's orientation toward the Southern sky. That helps it maintain its connection to satellites, even while the vehicle it's attached to cruises merrily along the highway. As with reflector-dish antennas, it can also receive television broadcasts and remain connected to the Internet simultaneously.

Deciding which system suits you

While the greatest determining factors when assessing the available options are likely to be cost and convenience, they probably aren't your only considerations. When making comparisons, you may want to include the following items in your decision-making process:

✔ **Manually deployed:** You may notice that, while I refer to automatic systems as self-pointing, I don't call these systems manual-pointing. That's because pointing is only one step in the total dish-deployment process. If you're considering a manually deployed system, the following are some of the attributes you might want to keep in mind:

- **Storage:** Aside from the equipment shared by both manually deployed and self-pointing systems (such as a modem and wireless router), you'll also need to find storage space for the cabling, dish assembly, and tripod.

- **Dish location:** This can be both a positive and negative attribute. On the one hand, a manually deployed dish might be moved about the site and placed in a location unobstructed by trees or outbuildings. On the other hand, because the dish is only a few feet off the ground, nearby coaches might be more likely to block it.

- **Convenience:** If you don't move your coach very often, this may not be much of an issue. If you move more than once a week, however, you could quickly tire of unpacking, setting up, and pointing your dish every time you set up your site. And deployment makes up only two thirds of the issue. When you're ready to leave, you've got to pack it up and stow it away.

- **Cost:** Sure, the initial cost is considerably lower than that of a self-pointing system. In addition to the initial savings, you may also incur (depending on your plan and provider) lower monthly fees, and your maintenance costs are nearly nonexistent. For a basic plan, expect to pay $1,500 to $3,000 for your system, as well as $60 to $70 per month for an Internet service plan.

- **Complexity:** I'm not really sure these systems *are* simpler. GPS capability and pointing hardware are built into automatic systems, but for manual deployment some other tools come in really handy — for example, a GPS device, an accurate compass, and an electronic pointing tool such as a BirDog or Outdoor Pointing Interface (OPI) meter. At least if any of that equipment breaks, you won't have to tear into your system to fix or replace it.

When you begin to comparison-shop for a manually deployed system, give careful consideration to the equipment included in the system — especially the pointing equipment — and the training, documentation, and support available with the purchase of a system.

✔ **Self-pointing:** Of course, self-pointing is only one attribute of a roof-mounted VSAT system. Among the other characteristics you may want to consider are the following:

- **Storage:** Since the dish folds and stows neatly on the roof, the only storage required is a small, well-ventilated area in which to locate the modem, controller, and wireless router.

- **Dish location:** Since the dish is mounted on a coach roof, its elevation is well above the ground but maybe not above the trees. If you like to park in the shade, this could pose a problem.

- **Convenience:** While those with manually deployed systems are spending time unpacking and setting up, those with self-pointing systems are going about other business (or just relaxing), while the dish deploys and acquires a signal. What could be easier?

- **Cost:** Convenience comes at a cost; if you're prone to sticker-shock, you may want your spouse to write the check. But you've also got to consider what your time and effort are worth. For a basic auto-deployed system, the equipment costs from $4,000 to $7,000, plus $600 to $1,200 for the installation fee. Monthly Internet service plans cost from $50 to $80 per month. Your call.

- **Complexity:** Okay, self-pointing units are complex; besides the built-in electronics, a maze of gears, motors, and control boards takes the place of the manual labor. That complexity might mean more maintenance-related issues, but these units have been in use for quite some time, and have proven reliable.

Because of potential differences in installation and system costs from one dealership to another, it definitely pays to do some shopping. In the process of interviewing dealers you should also question them concerning their Internet service plan costs. Among the questions you might want to ask, no matter whether you're considering a manually deployed or self-pointing system, concerning Internet service plans include the following:

✔ **Can I reduce monthly costs with a longer contractual commitment?** While this isn't always a possibility some providers, like StarBand, offer lower costs with a longer commitment.

✔ **How much more will it cost me to get a faster connection?** All providers offer multiple mobile service plans that feature extra-cost enhancements to the basic plan.

✔ **What's your FAP?** This varies from one plan to another and it varies from one ISP to another. Be sure you understand the policy — and that it's something you can easily live with. In most cases, it's possible to increase the threshold by paying a higher monthly service fee.

✔ **Can I stop and start service?** If you're on the road full time, you may not need to suspend service temporarily. But if you spend half the year at home and half on the road, an option like this can be important.

✔ **If temporary service suspensions are allowed is there any reinstatement fee?** If they're willing to give you a service suspension, you should probably expect to pay a modest fee for reinstatement.

✔ **Can I switch satellites for better coverage?** If your satellite ISP is only using one satellite, then okay, this won't be an option. But if they employ several satellites in their network, it's worth looking into.

Going the DIY Route

There's a certain satisfaction that seems to go hand-in-hand with any do-it-yourself project. It's something that's hard to describe and something that those who don't do DIY may find themselves at a loss to understand. Not much doubt, however, about one reason that Martha Stewart and Bob Vila are such popular figures: They remind us that it's possible to accomplish a task, on our own, when others may have to seek professional help.

I think self-reliance is one of the primary attractions to manually deployed VSAT systems. The feeling of freedom that comes with self-sufficiency is difficult to quantify. Of course, saving a bundle of cash is entirely quantifiable — and being able to move a dish 50 to 100 feet away from a coach comfortably parked in the shade is more than just attractive. It's delightful. In fact, if you spend much time in tree-rich environments like state and national parks, a tripod-mounted system may be the only solution that has any chance at all of getting a clear view of the southern sky.

Becoming a certified installer

Since a satellite in geostationary orbit measures just a few feet in diameter and sits almost 22,300 miles above the equator, you can imagine accurately aiming a satellite dish at it requires more than a compass and a plastic protractor. Because the equipment used in satellite-signal acquisition isn't sold at your local discount hardware store — and a high degree of aiming accuracy is required — it stands to reason that at least a limited level of training might be required to set up a satellite dish used for Internet access.

Both HughesNet and StarBand require that anyone installing a satellite dish system, mobile or otherwise, be certified. The certification itself isn't technically required by the FCC — but FCC regulations regarding installation of any satellite Internet dish must be complied with, so both providers require installers to pass a certification test that demonstrates a general competence and understanding regarding those regulations.

Understanding the rules and regulations, however, doesn't mean that a person also possesses the knowledge and ability to accurately aim a satellite dish so that a signal can be acquired without creating interference. According to those who sell the Dustyfoot, Mobile Internet, and Maxwell Satellite systems and use HughesNet satellite service, you don't have to become a certified installer just to become proficient in the technique of deploying and aiming a satellite dish. Hundreds of happy customers tend to support those assertions.

Dustyfoot provides an excellent manual (clear and easily understandable), Mobile Internet offers a video and phone consultation to get you up and running, and Maxwell Satellite provides a clear, well-written 60-page user's manual. For an additional charge, Maxwell Satellite also provides hands-on training if you're in their area. All these vendors say that, with practice, a mobile tripod-mounted VSAT system can be set up in half an hour or less, and that certification is unnecessary.

Alas, doing things this way bends — at the very least — the rules and requirements laid out by HughesNet. You can, however, choose to become a HughesNet-certified installer by enrolling in (for example) one of the training classes offered by Ground Control. These training classes last three days and currently cost $799; some tools, at additional cost, may also be required. For more information about becoming a certified installer, you can e-mail Ground Control at `training@groundcontrol.com`.

Being a trained and certified HughesNet installer won't necessarily mean that you're operating completely within the spirit of the HughesNet customer agreement — unless you also sign up for a mobile, rather than residential, service plan. A *mobile plan* allows for constant dish relocation; the *residential plan* stipulates that a user may relocate only one time per year. To date, HughesNet has taken no action to discourage those who decide to apply a creative interpretation of the agreement — but they could.

With StarBand offering the only officially sanctioned tripod based mobile VSAT system currently available; all users of the Manual-Flyer are required to be certified installers. When you purchase the StarBand Manual-Flyer from one of their dealers you're given hands-on training to learn the finer points of setting up and aiming your VSAT dish. The training is normally completed in a single afternoon; when you're comfortable with your new skills, you can take the free certification test. If you pass, StarBand issues your certification.

There's something to be said in favor of personal, hands-on training and official certification — even if the process (as seems to be the case under the StarBand system) is somewhat informal. Another point in favor of using the StarBand Manual-Flyer with one of the StarBand Mobile Internet service plans is that everything you're doing is unquestionably ethical. You're paying for the service you're getting, you've complied with all the requirements of the ISP, and moving your system from one site to another is entirely sanctioned and supported.

Purchasing the pieces

Okay, you're ready to buy the gear, but I can just hear those DIY gears turning in your head. You're thinking that you might be able to buy a bunch of stuff from an auction site or three and put your own system together. Well, you might find it possible — but I wouldn't recommend it. A whole herd of people have invested a considerable amount of time and effort to create complete systems so you don't have to scrounge the Web in search of every component. Take advantage of their expertise and purchase your system directly from them or from one of their dealers.

If you're leaning toward Dustyfoot, Mobile Internet, or Maxwell Satellite manually deployed VSAT systems, then finding a dealer requires little more than a visit to a Web site. StarBand Manual-Flyer dealers, on the other hand, might be a little bit more difficult to come by. Because StarBand requires Manual-Flyer dealers to provide hands-on training to those who purchase their systems they've limited the number of StarBand dealers authorized to sell the system to those dealers also qualified to provide the training. Authorized dealers include the following:

✔ **Orbital Enterprises:** One of the first StarBand dealers in the nation to offer the Manual-Flyer for sale, this proprietor was also responsible (at least in part) for convincing StarBand to offer a fully supported, sanctioned, tripod-mounted mobile VSAT system. Several optional system configurations are available; it's well worth your time to visit their Web site at `www.orbitalenterprises.net/mobile.html`.

✔ **RV Networking:** A visit to their information-packed Web site can't help but be beneficial. Perusing a few pages reveals that these folks don't just sell these products; they really use them, enjoy them, and believe in their usefulness. You can find them on the Web at `www.rvnetworking.com`.

✔ **Roving Internet:** Located in Castle Rock, CO, this dealer is responsible for designing the off-set reflector dish mounting bracket that allows the dish and feedhorn arm assembly to be attached to a tripod while maintaining balance. The Web address is `www.rovinginternet.com`.

All three of these StarBand Manual-Flyer dealers are members of the Satellite Mobility Support Network. If you're considering the StarBand system, no matter your location, your time won't be wasted if you contact any one of them. They may be able to arrange meeting you at a convenient location, or make other suitable arrangements. You can also visit the StarBand Web site and purchase the Manual-Flyer from them directly, or find a nearby dealer by using their dealer-locator page. Just submit your Zip code and the resulting page displays the dealer(s) closest to you. (*Note:* Not every dealer displayed offers the Manual-Flyer; you may have to call a couple before you find one.)

Aiming your dish without screaming

At one time, while setting up a site, it was difficult to discern the difference between couples having a knock-down drag-out argument from those simply deploying a dish. One person would be outside aiming the dish; the other would be inside yelling back the signal strength indicated on the laptop. For couples with no two-way wireless radios, screaming was how they zeroed in.

Fortunately, you don't have to rely on lung capacity to find out whether your dish is perfectly positioned. Several devices are available to help make the job a bit easier — and some combination is generally included with any of the manually deployed systems. If your dealer doesn't include one of them as standard equipment, you might find they offer the device as an option (or you can obtain one from another vendor). They are as follows:

✔ **Outdoor Pointing Interface:** The OPI, connected to the RX (receive) cable, monitors signal strength without the need to have a computer (running appropriate software) connected to the other end of the cable. The OPI was developed by DirecWay and is available from Dustyfoot, Mobile Internet, and Maxwell Satellite mobile VSAT systems.

✔ **Digisat Meter:** Operating in much the same way as the OPI, this meter is often made available to those purchasing StarBand Manual-Flyer systems. It's also available from several online retailers.

✔ **BirDog Meter:** Considerably more expensive than the OPI or Digisat meters, the BirDog satellite signal finder is compatible with all the mobile VSAT systems. It mounts and operates in much the same way as the OPI and Digisat meters, but provides far more information. Several dealers offer this meter with their systems as standard or optional equipment; if yours doesn't, you can still find it readily available from online retailers. The BirDog Web site is www.birdog.tv.

✔ **Align-a-Site:** This device is different from all the other meters. It doesn't measure signal strength but, rather, helps you find a clear line-of-sight view of the satellite. By using the Align-a-Site with the optional dish mount you won't even have to level out your tripod. If there's a hole through the leaves you'll be able to find it with an Align-a-Site device. Several of the dealers offer the Align-a-Site with their systems and it's available from the manufacturer at www.alignasite.com.

Whenever you set up and aim your satellite dish a couple of the readings that you get from your pointing instruments indicate your cross-polarization and co-polarization. These two readings, important because you're both receiving and transmitting a signal, are an indication of how well your dish is aimed. If you're aim is off by a little bit you could be causing interference for other satellite users. Any interference caused by a user can result in action being taken by the FCC against the satellite provider. For this reason, StarBand requires all Manual-Flyer users to call their Consumer VSAT Automated Commissioning System (CVACS) with their cross-pol and co-pol numbers.

Calling CVACS can be inconvenient — maybe impossible — if you're in an area outside cellular coverage. In these instances, since you should already be online, it may be possible to send an e-mail to your dealer with the needed information and ask them make the call to CVACS.

Getting a Self-Pointing VSAT Installed

Okay, do-it-yourself projects are great, but there's something to be said for ease and convenience. If dragging the dish out of storage and setting it up each and every time you move doesn't sound much like "convenient" Internet access, then you might be in the market for a VSAT system that's permanently mounted on the roof of your coach. That said, I also understand that even if you don't jump for joy at the thought of manually deploying your dish on a regular basis, you may still enjoy DIY projects — and even consider installing your own self-pointing VSAT satellite Internet system.

Well, don't consider that for too long; it'll cut into the time you have available for finding a qualified dealership with competent installation technicians. It's absolutely necessary to have this job done by a professional installer. Of course, you could decide to become a dealer or installation technician your-self (I figure the marketplace is far from saturated), but if you don't want to go that route, you'll want to ferret out a good dealership.

Finding a dealer

MotoSAT, Ground Control and StarBand — the primary players in the self-pointing-VSAT-system game — all maintain a large network of dealerships and installers. If you choose, you can opt to purchase your system from them directly — and have their technicians install it at their location. Without hyperbole, I can say with confidence that your choice of dealership and installation technician makes the difference between enjoying your investment and spending your days in search of elusive support.

While going directly to the source may be convenient for some, most find themselves looking for a local dealer. You can begin your search for a reputable dealer by visiting the corporate Web sites (where links to their dealer networks are provided), or you can search sources such as the Yellow Pages and World Wide Web. Another method of locating a reputable dealer is to visit online RV-related forums. Here are some you might want to visit:

- ✔ **DataStorm Users Forum:** As you might guess by the name this forum's focused primarily on those who either use or are interested in using units manufactured by either MotoSAT or Ground Control but there's also quite a number of folks posting that use other systems. Quite a few dealers and installers of high reputation post regularly to the forum and, believe it or not, so do the President of MotoSAT and the Chairman of Ground Control. Think you might get your questions answered here? Yeah, me too; they're easily found by pointing your browser toward www.datastormusers.com.

- ✔ **StarBand Users Forum:** Although the traffic here isn't quite as heavy as it might be in other forums, still it's a good source of information. You have to pay $15 to join the forum group — but (especially if you're considering the purchase of a StarBand unit) the cost is minimal, considering the amount of information available to you. They're located on the Web at www.starbandusers.com.

- ✔ **RV.Net Open Roads Forum:** This forum is focused on the RV life more generally but there is a well attended forum that deals with technology and includes quite a lot of information regarding satellite Internet. Their Web address is www.rv.net/forum/index.cfm.

Some of the most highly skilled, eminently qualified dealers and installation technicians who specialize in self-pointing VSAT systems are themselves hooked on the RV lifestyle. These "roving dealers" may well be in an area near you — or may be able to schedule their travels to intersect with yours at a given time. One such dealer, a frequent contributor to the DataStorm Users forum, is Bill Adams of Internet Anywhere; his Web site address is www.internetanywhere.us.

Getting support

The primary providers of satellite Internet seek to insulate their network-operations personnel from the day-to-day drudgery of responding to customer questions and problems. To meet these goals, they require their network of VARs to handle the bulk of general support issues — and the VARs seek to insulate themselves as well, relying on their VAR dealer networks to be the first line of response for support-related issues.

For this reason, it's even more important to be certain that the dealer you choose is both competent and responsive. Both MotoSAT and Ground Control (for example) offer well-staffed and responsive support systems, but if you encounter difficulty, your first, best chance at getting up and running is likely to come from the dealer that installed your system.

Another method of getting support-related questions answered is to visit one of the user forums I discuss in the previous section, "Finding a dealer."

Receiving TV, Too

Okay, a reflector dish designed to receive satellite TV can't be used to provide Internet access as well. But if you have a reflector dish designed to provide Internet access, it can also receive satellite TV. Among the items necessary, in addition to those used for Internet access, to receive simultaneous TV broadcasts are the following:

- ✔ **Satellite TV LNBF:** The signal received from a satellite designed to provide TV broadcasts is somewhat different than that of a signal carrying data.

- ✔ **Mounting bracket:** A combined mounting-bracket-and-LNBF is known as a *bird-on-a-wire* (*BOW*). This bracket is attached to the feedhorn arm; the LNBF is attached to the bracket. *Universal* mounting brackets allow easy adjustment of the LNBF to access any available television satellite; *dedicated* brackets are set to access one satellite in particular.

- ✔ **Satellite TV receiver:** Also known as an Integrated Receiver Decoder (IRD), connected to both the LNBF and TV by coaxial cable; the IRD decodes the signal received from the satellite and provides it to the set.

- ✔ **Satellite TV subscription:** A separate subscription to DISH Network or DirecTV, whichever may be appropriate, is necessary.

The BOW is mounted on the feedhorn arm in a way that offsets the television LNBF a few degrees east or west of center, as shown in Figure 9-4. The reason for this offset position is that the satellites used for TV and Internet reside at different locations in the southern sky. Since the reflector dish is pointed directly at the satellite providing the Internet service, it follows that the satellite providing the television signal will be positioned a few degrees to the east or west of that satellite.

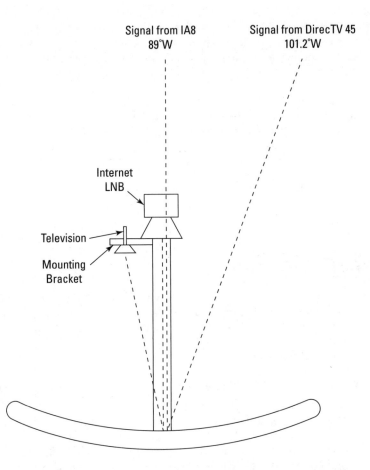

Signal from IA8
89°W

Signal from DirecTV 45
101.2°W

Internet
LNB

Television

Mounting
Bracket

Figure 9-4:
In this
drawing,
you can see
that the
television
LNBF is
offset a few
degrees.

Clearly, the satellite you want to use for receiving television broadcasts should be relatively close to the satellite you're assigned to for Internet access. So if you use a HughesNet satellite for Internet access, you'll probably have to subscribe to DirecTV and let them know to which HughesNet Internet satellite you're assigned. Likewise, if you're a StarBand subscriber, a DISH Network EchoStar satellite may be most compatible.

You can install the BOW, adding access to a television satellite, at any time. You don't have to install a BOW as part of your initial installation, but you may want to run the necessary TV cabling then anyway. It saves you hassle if you decide to add the BOW at a later date.

Part IV
Securing Your Information

The 5th Wave By Rich Tennant

"I can be reached at home on my cell phone. I can be reached on the road with my pager and PDA. Soon I'll be reachable on a plane with e-mail. I'm beginning to think identity theft wouldn't be such a bad idea for a while."

In this part . . .

I address the biggest concern most folks have surrounding wireless Internet connections: Security. (Even those normally fun-loving sock puppets get serious about security.) The three chapters included in this part help you understand the potential threats you face as well as the actions you can take to thwart the bad guys who seem determined to abscond with your information, money, and peace of mind. After reading Chapter 10, you'll know about the tools the bad guys use to invade your privacy — and you'll be armed with tools of your own to keep the invaders at bay. Chapters 11 and 12 go a little deeper; after reading them, you'll know how to encrypt your data and how to take control of a computer at your home or office while you're away from them both. You'll also know why you might want to take those actions — and if you want to keep that to yourself, you'll be able to.

Chapter 10

Taking Common-Sense Steps to Security

As wonderful as wireless Internet access is, it's not without its problems, and, at least in my humble opinion, the issue of security is the biggest one of them all. Whenever you log on to a hotspot, no matter where that hotspot is and no matter who operates it, your data and personal information is open to attack. I'm not trying to scare you here; I'm just imploring you to be aware that a potential threat exists.

When I log on to my wireless network at home, my data is protected because I use several security measures that block the public from joining the network. My data, just like at a hotspot, goes flying through the air and my computers are all connected via the network, but only those authorized to join the network have any possibility of accessing either the data I'm sending or the data stored on my computers. Hotspots, because they're open to the public, can't employ any of these security features.

In this chapter, I give you peace of mind — first, by helping you spot the potential threats to your online security and second, by showing you ways that you can stop information and identity thieves in their tracks. For example, I tell you about several methods in use by information and identity thieves to steal your data, and I give you specific ways to foil those attempts.

Identifying Security Threats

Several years ago, back in the days before widespread cellphone use, a lot of people used to carry around prepaid phone cards for making long-distance phone calls from payphones. Often, by carefully observing a person using one of these cards and entering the card and PIN numbers on the (easily visible) payphone keypad, a thief could steal those numbers. As an added bonus, if the card owner was recharging the card with a credit card, the thief might also steal the credit card number.

People went to great lengths, after they were aware of the potential threat, to cover up their calling and credit card numbers and hide their fingers when dialing. A very similar problem now exists in public hotspots all over the country. When you're signing on to a network, especially for the first time, thieves and scoundrels of all sorts might be able to get your credit card number, your username, your password, your home address, your phone number, and all sorts of personal information. And they can get this information just by looking over your shoulder, watching your fingers on the keyboard, or scanning your bright and beautiful display screen.

Besides the above-captioned (and, admittedly, low-tech-but-effective) method of gathering valuable information, today's thieves have developed several somewhat-higher-tech ways of procuring your personal information. The methods most commonly used include the following:

- ✔ **Using trickery:** For years, con artists of every stripe have been tricking people into handing over large sums of money, and these days, information is money. I tell you more about a few of the methods used to steal your info and ways to protect yourself from them in the "Beware of Geeks Bearing Grifts" section of this chapter.

- ✔ **Stealing your computer:** If you're a thief, what could be easier than just stealing the entire computer. I tell you about ways to avoid getting your laptop stolen — and how to protect your data even if it is stolen — in the "Protecting Your Data" section of this chapter.

- ✔ **Hacking into your laptop:** By exploiting open or unlocked doors into your computer, some thieves enter and steal your data out from under your nose. I tell you about ways to lock your doors in the "Blocking the Bad Guys with a Firewall" section.

- ✔ **Intercepting wireless transmissions:** Your information's flying through the air and, with the greatest of ease, it can be intercepted. Under the heading "Employing a Virtual Private Network," I tell you about services that help you establish a securely encrypted tunnel through which your info can travel safely.

Beware of Geeks Bearing Grifts

The first time I heard the term *grift* or *grifter* was in the 1990 movie, *The Grifters,* starring Anjelica Huston, John Cusack, and Annette Bening. It's a movie I enjoyed, even though the principal characters were all con artists — and, to the best of my recollection, all died horrible deaths.

A *grift* is a con and a *grifter* is a con artist. The fact that the grifters in the movie all died horrific deaths hasn't seemed to deter many from engaging in this activity. All too many cons are perpetrated on the Web-browsing public today. Some of them trick you, usually by e-mail, into volunteering personal and financial information by masquerading as legitimate institutions; these scams are commonly referred to as *phishing.* Others trick you into accepting program applications, commonly known as *spyware,* which allow grifters to gather information about you or redirect you to a fraudulent — but legitimate-looking — Web site where, they hope, you enter personal information. Variations of this grift are now referred to as *pharming.*

Avoiding the evil twin

Often referred to as a *rogue hotspot,* the phishing scam (or maybe it's pharming, I'm not sure) known as *the evil twin* is run exclusively on hotspot users. I've never experienced it at a truck stop or travel plaza, but I'm sure it's been tried more than a few times. The purpose of this grift is to gain access to usernames, passwords, and in some cases, credit card numbers.

Here's the way it works. A Wi-Fi hacker sits in the parking lot at a hotspot, or even somewhere inside the facilities, and by mimicking the SSID, poses as a legitimate hotspot. This person may even attempt to jam the actual hotspot signal as well. When an unsuspecting patron logs on to the phony network, the hacker serves up a sign-in page on which the user voluntarily and unwittingly hands over her username and password — or, if the grifter's really lucky, a credit card number.

The hackers (depending on how far they're willing to go) may even allow a connection to the Internet where they're in a position not only to intercept unencrypted traffic, but also to access any files open to sharing. (I talk about file sharing later in this chapter, in "Closing the file-sharing door.")

Why do they call it phishing?

Back in the '70s, a guy by the name of John Draper — using the alias Captain Crunch — invented a device known as the *blue box*. The blue box emitted a series of specially-pitched tones, allowing the Captain to hack into telephone systems. Captain Crunch, being very clever, called this illegal activity *phone phreaking*. Many consider Captain Crunch to be the original hacker.

In the mid-'90s, a group of Internet grifters began using e-mail lures to fraudulently obtain the passwords and usernames of AOL subscribers by tricking them into believing the e-mails were sent by AOL. When the unsuspecting *phish* took the bait by following the links in the e-mails, he was directed to phony Web sites that gathered personal information. Because the hackers were using e-mail lures, they compared their activity to fishing, and because these grifters idolized Captain Crunch, they paid homage to the Captain by replacing the letter *f* in fishing with a *ph*.

To help you avoid these rogue hotspots, take these protective steps:

- ✔ **Don't allow automatic connections.** No matter what connection management tool you use, configure it so that an automatic connection to a hotspot isn't allowed. I show you how to do this in the "Disallowing automatic hotspot connections" section that follows.

- ✔ **Scrutinize the SSID list.** If you see, at any hotspot, more than one SSID that's the same, or even similar, do some investigation prior to making a connection. Ask a manager, for example, whether they're running multiple APs with the same or similar SSID. Not likely. I suppose it's possible they *could* be named the same, but it's pretty dubious.

- ✔ **Disallow ad-hoc connections.** If you're running Windows XP with Service Pack 2, the ad-hoc mode is already disabled, but it doesn't hurt to take things a little farther and allow connections to infrastructure networks only. I show you how to do this later in this chapter in "Setting the infrastructure-only mode."

- ✔ **Use a firewall.** Even though a firewall won't keep you from connecting to a rogue hotspot, it will help protect you in case a connection is inadvertently made. I tell you more about firewalls under the heading "Blocking the Bad Guys with a Firewall."

Disallowing automatic hotspot connections

Unfortunately, once you make an initial connection to a hotspot via the Wireless Zero Configuration utility, it then assumes (always a dangerous thing to do) that you *always* want to make an automatic connection to that network whenever its SSID is detected. To disallow automatic connections with the WZC, take the following steps:

1. **Choose Start⇨Control Panel, and double-click Network Connections (in the Classic view of Windows XP).**

   The Network Connection window opens.

2. **Right-click your connection, and click Properties, as shown in Figure 10-1.**

   The Wireless Network Connection Properties dialog box opens.

3. **Click the Wireless Networks tab, as shown in Figure 10-2.**

4. **In the Preferred Networks area, click the network in question to highlight it, and then click the Properties button.**

   This brings up the Properties dialog box for the selected network.

5. **Click the Connection tab, and clear the check mark for the Connect When This Network Is in Range option.**

6. **Click OK in all open dialog boxes.**

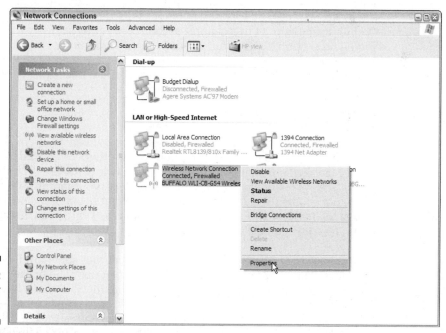

Figure 10-1:
Select your connection.

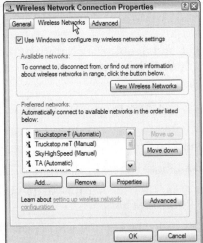

Figure 10-2:
The
Wireless
Network
Connection
Properties.

It's a bit easier to maintain an "ask before connecting" status with most other types of connection clients. For example, with the JiWire connection tool, you just choose the "Save, but Prompt Me to Connect" radio button the first time you make a connection to a new hotspot. (I discuss this utility a bit more in Chapter 6, and later in this chapter in the "Connecting securely through SpotLock" section.) With other connection utilities, such as the Buffalo connection client, you simply fail to save the profile. In most cases, you can choose to edit a saved profile so you're asked about making a connection to any hotspot.

Setting the infrastructure-only mode

When you're connecting to a hotspot, you want to make your connection to the hotspot's access point, and you don't want others to be able to connect to your laptop. Some hackers running the evil twin scam are set up as an ad hoc or peer-to-peer network. Also, in some cases, your laptop — especially if you're not running Windows XP with SP2 — might begin broadcasting the SSID of the network it was most recently connected with in an attempt to make an ad hoc connection with any nearby computers.

If this situation occurs, you're open to the threat that some low-life scoundrel is set up to listen for laptops begging for a connection. The hacker hears the connection cry, creates an ad-hoc network using the SSID that's being broadcast by your laptop, and makes the connection. This could be bad — especially if you haven't yet taken all, or most, of the security measures I've outlined in this chapter. Fortunately, there's an easy fix for this problem — just follow these steps:

1. **Choose Start⇨Control Panel, and double-click Network Connections (in the Classic view of Windows XP).**

   The Network Connection window opens.

2. **Right-click your connection, and click Properties.**

   The Wireless Network Connection Properties dialog box opens.

3. **Click the Wireless Networks tab (refer to Figure 10-2).**

4. **In the Preferred Networks area, click the Advanced button.**

   The Advanced dialog box opens, as shown in Figure 10-3.

5. **Select the Access Point (Infrastructure) Networks Only radio button.**

Figure 10-3:
The
Advanced
dialog box.

6. **Click the Close button in the Advanced dialog box, and click OK.**

Using a firewall also helps to eliminate this threat. I tell you about firewalls later in this chapter in "Blocking the Bad Guys with a Firewall."

Uncovering hidden extensions

Hidden extensions are another method that the unscrupulous use to trick us into installing a malicious program application on our PCs. One way they do this is by sending an e-mail or instant message with a photo or other attachment that has a benign file extension such as `.jpg`. What you don't know — because Windows, by default, shows only the first extension — is that the filename might actually be something like `photo.jpg.exe`, or `friendly-memo.txt.exe`. You open the attachment, and suddenly you're the victim of a virus that performs any number of unwanted — possibly dangerous — tasks. This trickery doesn't seem as prevalent today as it has been in the past — because, of course, you know to be wary of attachments that you're not expecting, even if they're from people you know, and to *never* open e-mails or attachments from people you don't know. But it's relatively easy to expose hidden extensions, so you might as well do so.

1. **Click Start⊃Control Panel, and (in the Classic view in Windows XP) double-click Folder Options.**

2. **Click the View tab.**

3. **Clear the check mark in the Hide Extensions for Known File Types check box, as shown in Figure 10-4.**

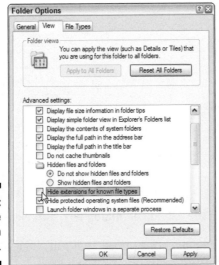

Figure 10-4: Show those hidden extensions.

4. **Click Apply.**

5. **Click OK.**

This eliminates a great deal of the problems, but a few extensions, such as .pif and .shc, might remain hidden. To display all extensions, all the time, you have to edit the Registry.

Going into the Registry and changing anything can cause catastrophic problems. So even though this Registry edit is really easy to do, the potential exists to make a slight error that would be irreversible. Directions for editing the Registry follow, with the disclaimer that you do this at your own peril.

Because a danger exists, before making any system or Registry change, be sure that you set a *system-restore point* so you can revert to the settings that existed prior to your fiddling with stuff — providing you haven't done anything so catastrophic that you're looking at the Blue Screen of Death. (In that case, a restore point can't help you — because you can't get to it.)

In order to create a system-restore point, choose Start⇨All Programs⇨ Accessories⇨System Tools⇨System Restore. With the System Restore window open, select Create a Restore Point, and click Next. Enter a name for your restore point — I usually name it something descriptive, like Registry Change — and click Create. The date is automatically added, and you can click Close. Now you've got a point to fall back on where you know everything worked.

Now you're ready to edit the Registry. Here goes:

1. **Choose Start⇨Run, and type** regedit **in the text box.**

2. **Click Open.**

    The Registry Editor opens.

3. **Choose Edit⇨Find.**

4. **Enter** NeverShowExt **in the text box, as shown in Figure 10-5.**

5. **Click Find Next.**

    The first occurrence of the phrase *NeverShowExt* is highlighted.

6. **Press the Delete key.**

    Answer in the affirmative when asked whether you're sure you want to delete the item — and leave your cursor in that position.

7. **Press F3 to search for the next occurrence, and repeat Steps 5 and 6 until the search is completed.**

8. **Close the Registry Editor, and you're done.**

From this moment forward, no one will be able to slip a file with a hidden extension under your nose. Now, if you see a file that has two extensions, such as `FunPhoto.jpg.exe` — especially if the last extension is `.exe` or `.pif` — you know that this file is best deleted.

Antivirus software, which I talk about later in this chapter in the "Vaccinating against viruses" section, often includes an e-mail scanning utility that may identify and eliminate e-mails carrying viruses under the cover of hidden extensions.

Protecting against drive-by spyware

After purchasing my first laptop — which was the first PC I'd ever owned — I just absolutely, positively, couldn't wait to get myself connected to the Internet. Being somewhat cheap, and believing that most salespeople will try to sell you lots of stuff you don't need, I didn't bother buying any of the anti-spyware or antivirus software offered to me — and walked confidently out the door, leaving a sea of shaking heads behind me. What a fool I was.

After browsing the Web for a few days, I started noticing that I had windows popping up all over the place whenever I opened my browser, and I was often directed to Web sites I hadn't asked to be directed to. After doing a little research, I found out that my browser had been hijacked, and I was the victim of one or more drive-by installations of spyware. Immediately, I downloaded an anti-spyware utility. After running it, I was stunned by the amount of junk that I'd picked up just by visiting Web sites. To protect yourself from these drive-by installs, you need to purposely install some anti-spyware and antivirus utilities. (I tell you more about antivirus software later in this chapter in "Vaccinating against viruses.")

Fortunately, there are great numbers of anti-spyware utilities available for download, and in fact, I now use more than one. Some spyware applications highjack your browser and redirect you to sites you never knew existed, or by monitoring your Web usage, serve up more and more ads. Others, known as *surveillance spyware,* can actually monitor and record every movement you make on the Web. Some surveillance-spyware applications log your keystrokes — and if you use VoIP (I tell you more about VoIP in Chapter 13), even your conversations are open to monitoring and recording. This problem, of course, isn't limited to those using hotspots, but I'd be remiss if I didn't mention a solution to such a widespread security threat.

Among my favorite anti-spyware programs, in no particular order, are

- **Ad-Aware SE Personal:** Produced by Lavasoft, this highly acclaimed utility is offered at the attractive price of *free*. The cynics among you will note that the free version doesn't do real-time scanning or perform automatic updates, but for something that's free, it does a whole lot of good stuff and does it pretty well. If you want the full-featured version you can always upgrade. It's available from Lavasoft at

  ```
  www.lavasoftusa.com/software/adaware
  ```

  To get the free version, go to that Web address and click the <u>Download.com</u> link on the top-right side of the page.

- **Spyware Doctor:** Another utility, produced by PC Tools Software, is highly thought of by reviewers in print and on the Web, but it's not free. (Although, it *is* reasonably priced.) This utility does a good job of protecting you from the most serious threats, such as key logging, and at around thirty bucks, it's definitely not overpriced. It's available at

  ```
  www.pctools.com/spyware-doctor
  ```

- **SpyBot Search & Destroy:** This is produced as freeware, which means that the developer would really appreciate it if you'd donate a few bucks to the cause, providing you like the utility. This is another well-thought-of application. It can be maddeningly slow, but it seems to do the job. It's available from Safer Networking at

  ```
  www.safer-networking.org/en/index.html
  ```

- **CounterSpy:** For about $20, this award-winning utility is available from Sunbelt Software. One of the biggest reasons you might want to consider CounterSpy is that they update their definitions through three different information sources, including Microsoft. It's available for download at

  ```
  www.sunbeltsoftware.com/counterspy.cfm
  ```

- **Windows Defender:** I haven't used this product, but Windows Defender (the second beta version of Windows AntiSpyware) has been remarkably well-reviewed by most of the major PC magazines, so you might want to give it a whirl. It's available at

  ```
  www.microsoft.com/athome/security/spyware/software/default.mspx
  ```

The foregoing isn't, by any stretch of the imagination, a complete and comprehensive list, but every one of the utilities has been well-reviewed and should make a good jumping off spot for you in your search for the perfect anti-spyware utility.

Not all anti-spyware utilities are what they claim to be. Some actually *install* their own spyware. If you choose to ignore those utilities I've listed and go out in search of a utility on your own, you might want to visit a Web site known as Spyware Warrior. Visit their Rogue/Suspect Anti-Spyware page, where they list many of these malicious programs. This site can be found at www.spywarewarrior.com, and they also offer other valuable information about spyware and anti-spyware.

Understanding EULAs

These are otherwise known as End User License Agreements. Whenever most folks in pursuit of a desired program, music, or video download see the EULA (End User License Agreement), they just click the I Agree button and continue on. Even though this won't cause you any problems most of the time, you should be aware that you might be agreeing — especially with some of the less scrupulous music-download sites — to download not only music but also some program applications that are spyware.

If the integrity of the site or company that you're downloading any type of file or program application from is in question, make sure you actually read the EULA (pronounced *YOO-la,* if you're wondering) before you continue the download. Even well-known sites include other marketing "resources" that can gobble up space and memory resources on your computer. So it's good to read any EULA.

If a EULA asks you to accept a program application as a condition of the file or program you desire, do a quick Web search to find out what it is and what others are saying about it before continuing. Or just play it safe and abort the download at the first hint of impropriety.

Protecting Your Data

By incorporating some of the measures previously mentioned, you've gone a long way toward protecting yourself from outside intrusion. But you're not done yet. A whole lot of your personal information resides in the files and folders stored on your laptop hard drive, and it needs to be protected too.

Locking up your laptop

This might seem a bit simplistic, but you just can't believe how many times, especially in coffeehouses, I've walked by an unoccupied table where someone has left a laptop sitting unguarded and unprotected. Usually it's booted up and a program or two has been opened — all a thief has to do is put it in standby mode, close the lid, and wander off with a nice laptop full of enough personal information to ruin the life of the person who just took a little too long in the restroom and trusted the patrons just a little bit too much.

 Fortunately, several manufacturers provide laptop locks that make it much more difficult for a thief to abscond with the valuables. Most of the newer laptops have a security slot into which a cable lock can be attached. They do vary quite a bit in price, but even if you can slow somebody down for a few minutes or make them more conspicuous, I think a lock is a no-brainer. Here's a fair representation of what's available:

- ✔ **Kensington:** This is possibly the most-recognized name in laptop-locking security, but they also manufacture a wide line of other products. My new laptop came equipped with a Kensington security slot, making lock installation a snap — literally. Kensington offers a wide range of locks, and they can be found on the Web by browsing to `http://us.kensington.com`.

- ✔ **LapLocker:** Manufactured by Think Products, this lock is more expensive than almost any other lock I've seen, but it includes more features than any other laptop locking mechanism I know of. To me, the biggest plus this lock offers is a table-top clamp, making it possible to secure your laptop to any desk or table. The lock also includes a lid lock that keeps the laptop open. A thief would be pretty conspicuous walking off with an open laptop. Their Web address is `www.laplocker.com`.

- ✔ **Defcon Notebook Lock:** Targus offers both keyed and combination locks similar in design to those made by Kensington. They also offer an alarm system equipped with a motion sensor that raises a clatter if your laptop is even moved. You can find them by browsing to `www.targus.com`.

Besides locking up your laptop, don't forget to secure your laptop case and any items you carry around in it. These items aren't as attractive to the average thief, but you never know what someone might deem worth stealing.

Password protecting your laptop

I don't know about you, but my whole identity in bits and pieces is stored on my laptop. Well, let's say that the unthinkable has happened, and I'm the victim of a clever thief. My laptop's long gone and not likely to be recovered. In this case, I definitely need to cancel credit cards, notify banks, move money, or any number of things I can't even imagine right now. I need time to do these things before somebody figures out how to get this information off my hard drive. This is where password protection can save the day.

I know that using passwords can be a hassle, but believe me, if you find your-self in a panic, trying to cancel accounts prior to becoming the proud pur-chaser of somebody else's Harley-Davidson motorcycle or a whole bunch of other stuff you'll never see, you'll be glad you went to the trouble to create strong passwords and put up with the hassle of actually using them.

The primary area where you need to use a password to protect your laptop is in the user accounts, which you see on the welcome screen. You want to be sure that, if anyone does get your laptop, they can't just log on to your laptop. If a password's required, you've slowed them considerably. If it's a highly effective password, you may have them blocked out for good.

You should also change the way users log on to the laptop. The default method is to log on from the welcome screen. All this requires is that a user choose their account and enter a password. By using the classic logon screen, users are also required to enter a username and then follow up with a password (provided you've logged off). It's likely that the thief stealing your laptop has little idea what your username might be. In order to switch your logon screen to the classic view, follow these steps:

1. **Choose Start⇨Control Panel⇨User Accounts⇨User Accounts. (Or double-click User Accounts if you use the Control Panel's classic view.)**

    The User Accounts dialog box opens.

2. **Under Pick a Task, click Change the Way Users Log On or Off.**

3. **Clear the check mark next to Use the Welcome Screen.**

    Both check marks disappear and the Use Fast User Switching option is grayed out.

4. **Click Apply Options, and close the User Accounts window.**

Okay, now you need to develop a password that's easy for you to remember and difficult for someone else to figure out.

Creating effective passwords

If a password's going to be effective, it needs to be something that's impossi-ble to guess. In other words, it needs to be more imaginative than u1eQ. Consider the following when working up a strong password:

- ✔ **Length:** By making your password at least eight to ten characters long, you considerably reduce the chances that anyone can ever hack it.

- ✔ **Character combination:** Use as many different characters as possible. If part of your password is a number, for example, hit the Shift key a couple times when entering those numbers, changing them to symbols.

✔ **Obvious choices:** Don't use your birthday, your name, your favorite team or player's name, your dog's name, your favorite TV character's name . . . you get the idea. As a matter of fact, you shouldn't even use a word that's in a dictionary, even if it's in a foreign dictionary. There exist several hackers' applications designed to break passwords that are based on dictionary words, even if they're spelled backwards or incorporate a number or two.

✔ **Memorable phrase:** I love the movie *Casablanca*. The popularly remembered phrase from that film is "Play it again, Sam," but what Rick actually said is "Play it, Sam. You played it for her; you can play it for me." By using the first letters of each word, I've got the password `PiSYpifhycpifm`. By substituting a couple of numbers and symbols for the letters, I could come up with the password: `P1$Ypifhycp!fm`.

The password I created using the infamous phrase uttered by Rick at the Café Americain meets all the criteria for a strong password: It's fourteen characters long, it uses a combination of letters (both uppercase and lowercase), it's not an obvious word, and it's not a word found in the dictionary. (But it's just an example — and now it's published in a book — so I'm sure I don't have to tell you not to use it for real.) When you've created a password of your own that you think is pretty good, you can check it out with available online password-checking tools. The Microsoft Web site, for example, offers one such tool at

`www.microsoft.com/athome/security/privacy/password_checker.mspx`

If the phrase you come up with is too short, just add a few easily remembered numbers and symbols. For example, if you want to use *Bond, James Bond* or *I'll be back*, you can add the last four digits of your social security number and the three symbols that correspond with your area code. If your social security number is 123-45-6789 and your area code is 425, the password might be `Ibb6789$@%`. Easy to remember and nearly impossible to crack.

Guarding your passwords

My memory being what it is, I'm always worried that I might forget a password, and that's why I suggest using a password based on a phrase you can easily remember. In general, it's a bad idea to keep your passwords anyplace other than in your head or in a locked safe. I know some people put them in password-protected files, but I don't recommend it.

A couple other things to keep in mind concerning passwords:

✔ **Don't give your password to anyone.** Especially if you're asked for your password in an e-mail. Some Internet scammers engage in the act of *phishing* for information via e-mail: They send you a legitimate-looking e-mail from your bank, credit card provider, eBay, or PayPal, asking for information such as your username and password. *Legitimate companies never ask for this information via e-mail.*

✔ **Don't use the same password for everything.** Use a different password for each account you log on to. If you just can't remember that many passwords, at least use three or four different ones and use your computer-logon password *only* for that purpose.

✔ **Don't use any Save Password options.** Internet Explorer (IE), Mozilla Firefox, and some Web sites ask whether you want to save your user-name and password. The *only* time to take advantage of this option is when you know for sure that unauthorized access to the site can *in no way* result in the user gaining any personal information about you. Obviously, any site from which you've ever purchased goods — or financial and related sites — are no place to take this risk.

Storing your passwords

You should *never* keep a list of passwords anywhere near your laptop or on your person. I don't recommend storing your passwords in a file on your laptop or PDA either, but there are a few utilities available that store pass-words under an encrypted lock. One such utility, developed by DataViz, is Passwords Plus. (See www.dataviz.com.) I've used this utility for almost a year now, after downloading a free "Lite" version of it early last year. The free version's not available anymore, but a free, 30-day trial version is.

Passwords Plus offers a lot of features, including the ability to generate extremely effective passwords, and requires that you remember only one master password to be used in gaining access to the utility. Versions are available for Windows, Mac, and Palm operating systems.

Closing the file-sharing door

It's possible — not likely, but possible — that while you're happily browsing the Web at a hotspot, a clever hacker could access your laptop via the Guest account. If this unlikely event were to occur, it's also possible that your files might be — due to something called Simple File Sharing — open to the person browsing your system. If you're running Windows XP Pro, closing this back door is as easy as following these steps:

1. **Choose Start⇨My Computer⇨Tools⇨Folder Options.**

   The Folder Options dialog box opens.

2. **Click the View tab.**

3. **Click Advanced Settings.**

4. **Clear the Simple File Sharing check box.**

5. **Click Apply, and click OK to close the Folder Options dialog box. You can then close My Computer.**

Using separate storage for sensitive info

If the worst case scenario occurs, in which your laptop is stolen or your hard drive fails, I assume that you have at least a few files on your hard drive that you'd really want. I have several types of files I'd like to be able to recover, including my music files, e-mail addresses, bookmarks to various Web sites, photos, program applications, and bank and tax files. You can back up your files to one of several types of external storage. Among the most popular are

✔ **Hard disk drive:** You can find good mobile units available in storage capacities ranging from 2GB to 60GB. Iomega is a leader in the field, but others make these drives as well, including Sony, Seagate, and IOGear. These drives often come with a utility to help you create your backups.

✔ **CD or DVD:** If your laptop has a CD-RW or DVD-RW drive, you can burn backed up information to one of these discs. CDs can store about 700MB and DVDs about 4.5GB.

The new Blu-ray technology will increase DVD storage capacity to as much as 27GB.

✔ **USB flash drive:** These little devices (about the size of a lighter) plug in to a USB port, and you can drag and drop files into them. Get a large one (a gigabyte or more) for storing your files. You'll use up that space faster than you think.

Another choice is to use an online service, but when you're using a hotspot, they're not so hot because you need to upload the files you're saving. Because hotspots limit the upload bandwidth, this could take quite a lot of time and slow down everyone using the hotspot.

If you burn files to CD or DVD, you can use your computer's CD burning utility for some files, but for a full computer backup, consider a third-party backup utility. If you're using CDs, DVDs, or a USB flash drive, look for a utility that saves files in a format that's easy to access, such as `.zip` files.

If (like me) you're running Windows XP Home Edition, the previous option isn't available, so the best you can do is to use the Make Private option in each folder's properties. For each folder you want to protect, perform the following steps:

1. **Right-click the folder.**

2. **Choose Properties.**

    The folder's Properties dialog box opens.

3. **Click the Sharing tab.**

4. **Select the Make this Folder Private check box.**

5. **Click Apply, and then click OK.**

If you're using a firewall, there's almost no chance that anyone can log on to your computer while you're using a hotspot without the firewall stopping the attack and notifying you of the attempt. I tell you more about firewalls later in this chapter, in the "Blocking the Bad Guys with a Firewall" section.

Vaccinating against viruses

Are you more likely to get a cold when the only people you interact with are your own family members, or when you spend your days mingling with large groups of strange people? Yeah, well, if your kids are in grade school, hanging out at home isn't safe either, but you get the point. Vaccinating your computer against viruses is important if you're using it only in your home or office, but *imperative* if you're taking your computer out to play in public.

Plenty of virus protection programs are available, so you won't have any trouble finding one that does the job. But purchasing and downloading a utility is only half the battle. You must also keep your utility up to date. Every antivirus utility worth its salt offers updates; some even offer to download the updates automatically. If you fail to update regularly and often, then your antivirus utility becomes obsolete and nearly useless in no time flat.

A few of the better-known and highly rated virus-protection programs also come bundled in complete Internet-security suites. Here's a short list of some top-notch antivirus programs available to you:

- **Trend Micro PC-cillin:** This highly rated antivirus product includes a personal firewall. This utility also monitors your wireless connection and notifies you if someone is making an attempt to connect to your PC. You can check out all the features and benefits by browsing to `www.trendmicro.com/en/home/us/personal.htm`.

- **AVG Anti-virus:** Developed by Grisoft, this well-reviewed utility is offered to private individuals (that's you and me) for the unbelievably low price of *free*. Being cheap, I use this utility, and at least in my opinion, it does a good job. If you need a utility for business or commercial use they also offer a reasonably priced utility that's full of features the IT guys find useful. You can find the free utility at `http://free.grisoft.com/doc/1`.

- **McAfee VirusScan:** McAfee is one of the best-known names in Internet security, and VirusScan is both an antivirus and an anti-spyware utility. The only drawback that I've seen is that it doesn't actively block the type of browser hijacking that either redirects you to unwanted and un-requested sites or serves up behaviorally targeted ads. McAfee also bundles this utility in a full Internet security suite that includes a firewall and spam blocker. You can find this utility at `www.mcafee.com/us`.

- **Norton AntiVirus:** Developed by Symantec, this highly regarded utility, which also includes anti-spyware capability, is available as a standalone product or in a full Internet security suite that includes a firewall. The antivirus utility blocks spam and checks outgoing e-mail for viruses as well. The Symantec Web site can be found at `www.symantec.com/index.htm`.

Note that, with most antivirus utilities, the purchase price is actually a subscription that must be renewed on a yearly basis. The reason: New and better viruses are being dreamed up daily, so your utility has to be updated regularly for the life of your laptop. Because the people who do this are trying to provide not only safety but an income for themselves and their families, they make the understandable request that they be paid for their efforts.

Using Built-in Security Features

"There is no need to sally forth, for it remains true that those things which make us human are, curiously enough, always close at hand. Resolve, then, that on this very ground, with small flags waving and tiny blasts of tiny trumpets, we shall meet the enemy, and not only may he be ours, he may be us."

— Walt Kelly

This quote is attributed to Walt Kelly, the author of the Pogo comic strip, and was eventually shortened to: "We have met the enemy and he is us." It describes to a tee the purpose of the built-in security features in Windows XP.

It's there to save us from an apathetic, oh-I'm-probably-fine attitude toward securing our systems from attack — and to save us from any seeming inability to avoid unsafe Internet-related activities. The XP features constantly remind us when security is lax. There aren't a lot of security features built in to Windows XP with SP2, but what *is* available is a whole bunch better than what was available in earlier Windows operating system iterations. The major features are

- ✔ **Firewall:** This is one of the biggest improvements made with SP2. It lacks a few features that, I think, are essential, but this one provides some protection from outside intrusion at least until you install a full-featured firewall.

- ✔ **Drive-by download blocking:** This works at least in Internet Explorer, and IE now blocks pop-ups, too. Well, no pop-up blocker squashes them all, but the IE browser included with SP2 does a darn good job — and you don't need to install another toolbar. Drive-by downloads are also foiled, and instead of automatically allowing a download, an information dialog box opens, giving you an option of continuing or cancelling. (Read more about this subject in the "Protecting against drive-by spyware" section earlier in this chapter.)

- ✔ **Unsafe attachment blocking:** This targets the primary way computers get infected with viruses, worms, and other bad stuff — that is, folks opening e-mail attachments from strangers. Some of these attachments may seem benign, and because they hide the .exe or .pif extension, people open them and get nasty computer colds. Outlook Express reduces this potential threat, and the security blanket is also thrown over Windows Messenger. (I talk about uncovering hidden extensions in the cleverly named "Uncovering hidden extensions" section earlier in this chapter.)

Using Windows Security Center

The centerpiece of the Windows XP with SP2 security enhancements is the Windows Security Center. Its primary purpose is to badger you into actually doing something about security-related issues, as well as to open avenues for defending yourself against attack. To open the Security Center, choose Start➪Control Panel➪Security Center (or, in some versions, Start➪Settings➪ Control Panel➪Security Center).

The Windows Security Center monitors three areas, as shown in Figure 10-6:

- ✔ **Firewall:** If you've got the Windows firewall enabled, the first status indicator is green. If the Windows firewall is disabled — or if a third-party firewall that's not recognized is installed — the indicator is red and you see a Recommendations button.

- ✔ **Automatic updates:** Windows automatically downloads and (if you so choose) installs important operating-system updates. If you have this feature enabled, the status indicator is green. If not, the indicator is red and the Recommendations button appears.

- ✔ **Virus protection:** Providing you have an antivirus utility recognized by Windows XP that's running and up-to-date, the status indicator is green. If it's a utility that isn't recognized, one that needs to be updated, or you don't have virus protection installed, the indicator is red, and — you guessed it — the Recommendations button appears.

When you click the Recommendations button, a dialog box corresponding to that feature opens, such as the one for firewalls shown in Figure 10-7. If you don't have a firewall, you can click the Enable Now button. But if you've installed a third-party firewall, such as ZoneAlarm or Norton, you want to disable the Windows firewall. Doing so may cause the Security Center to open a warning notice each time you boot your laptop. These warnings don't cause any problems, but because they're annoying, you want to let Windows know what's going on. Place a check mark in the box indicating that you have a firewall solution you'll monitor yourself. Click OK, and you notice that the firewall-status indicator changes to yellow.

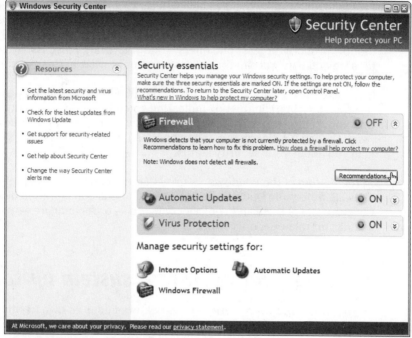

Figure 10-6:
The
Windows
Security
Center helps
you
safeguard
your laptop.

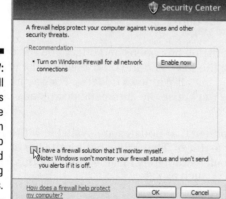

Figure 10-7:
Tell
Windows
you have
your own
firewall to
avoid
annoying
warnings.

If you don't have an antivirus utility installed, you can click the Virus
Protection Recommendations button. The two recommendations are
to Turn on Your Installed Antivirus Program or Get Another Antivirus

Program, followed by the clickable link <u>How?</u> If you click <u>How?</u>, a Web page opens and offers several antivirus software choices. Because you're a Microsoft XP user, these come with extended trial periods — mostly three months or more (at least one offers a one-year trial). I discuss virus software in more detail in "Vaccinating against viruses" earlier in this chapter.

If you already have an antivirus utility but Windows doesn't recognize it, place a check mark in the box indicating you have a virus protection solution that you'll monitor yourself. The status indication changes to yellow and (even though it's clearly not happy about it) the Security Center stops bugging you about your security status.

At the bottom of the Windows Security Center screen are links to the Windows Firewall, Automatic Updates, and Internet Options configuration dialog boxes. Click any one of them and you can configure — or reconfigure — your current settings for those security features.

Keeping your operating system up-to-date

I've put this Windows Security Center feature under its own heading because keeping your operating system updated is one of the most important things you can do to guarantee the continued health of your system. The easiest method of ensuring your operating system is kept up-to-date is to schedule automatic updates. To do this, follow these steps:

1. **Open the Windows Security Center, and click the Automatic Updates link at the bottom of the page.**

   The Automatic Updates dialog box opens and offers you the opportunity of scheduling the day of the week and the time at which the utility will check for, download, and install Windows updates. For any number of reasons, you may prefer to choose the automatic downloads but not the automatic installation.

   You may prefer to be notified that updates are available without enabling any automatic features. That's fine, but for the life of me, I can't imagine why anyone would completely disable or ignore this security tool.

2. **After you've made your selections, click Apply.**

3. **Click OK.**

   Your settings are updated to correspond with your wants and needs.

Another very similar automatic update, known as Microsoft Update, can be set up through the Windows Security Center, and is of interest to anyone who runs not only Windows XP, but also other Microsoft program applications (such as Microsoft Office). Once enabled, Microsoft Update operates in exactly the same way that Windows Update does. If you're running Microsoft programs released earlier than 2003, however, you should make sure you've got your installation CDs handy. That's because (at least the first time you perform updates) the wizard will probably ask for file locations.

Here's how to set up the Microsoft Updates:

1. **Click Start➪All Programs➪Windows Update.**

   The Windows Update welcome page opens in Internet Explorer.

2. **Select and click the Microsoft Update link and follow the prompts.**

   You might have to install an ActiveX plug-in, and you'll be asked to configure your updates as either Express or Custom.

It's always a good idea to point your browser periodically to either Windows or Microsoft Update to check for any updates you might want to download and install that aren't included in the Express configuration.

Blocking the Bad Guys with a Firewall

A firewall might be considered your first line of defense in Internet security. A lot of the issues I deal with in the previous sections can be made moot if you're using a good firewall. Firewalls do pretty much what the name indicates: They keep the danger outside a solid door of protection that's open only to those you invite in, and some firewalls keep the bad guys corralled so they can't do any damage.

Because a good firewall is the first line of defense when you're online, either at home or at a hotspot, you might be wondering why I bring it up so late in the chapter. Well, even though firewalls do a good job, they're not foolproof. If I told you about firewalls right away, you might rely entirely on a firewall — and fail to take any of the other security measures I tell you about. That would be a mistake; no matter how good your firewall is, it's possible that it might be breached. Not likely — but definitely possible.

So, you may be asking yourself: Because Windows XP has a firewall already installed, why would I want to go to the trouble of installing a different one? That's a fair question. The answer is that, even though the Windows Security Center does include a firewall, it lacks some features that other, third-party firewalls may include. Specifically, the Windows firewall doesn't block outbound traffic. You may not think that's a big deal, especially because you're concerned about intrusions, but in reality, it's a very big deal.

If, somehow — even after installing a firewall and virus protection, setting up anti-spyware, closing doors, and locking doors — you still manage to get a computer infection, your computer might be making outbound connections you know nothing about. A firewall that detects outbound traffic can corral that traffic, notify you that it's been blocked, and ask you whether you want to allow or disallow the traffic.

Of course, blocking inbound traffic is equally, if not more, important. The Windows firewall does a decent job of that, but again, some third-party firewall solutions are a bit better than the Windows firewall at this task, too.

Finding a firewall

Many Internet security suites bundle a firewall with their virus protection. In most cases, these firewalls do the job at least as well as the Windows firewall; because most of them also block outbound traffic, you could say they do the job better. If you decide you want virus protection and a firewall from two different companies, each offers a standalone firewall as well. (You can find a list of these companies in "Vaccinating against viruses," earlier in this chapter.)

Another developer, ZoneAlarm, offers a very good, standalone firewall in a basic, free version or a full-featured, paid version. I'm particularly enamored of the ZoneAlarm firewall. Probably because (as I said) I'm basically cheap and one of the versions is free, it's the first firewall I downloaded and used. It complements my free AVG virus protection quite nicely. ZoneAlarm is developed by ZoneLabs, and you can find it by pointing your browser toward www.zonealarm.com. Feel free to exercise your right to purchase the full-featured version, if you like — it's got some very useful bells and whistles.

Free utilities almost never include the full-featured capabilities that are available in the paid or subscription versions. If the free versions meet your needs (or if you've already got access to similar features through other programs or utilities), then by all means consider the free versions. If, however, you think you need features not included in the free versions, don't compromise your security just to save a few bucks. It can cost you in the end.

Setting up a personal firewall

Most firewalls, after they're downloaded and installed, take some time to set up and configure, because as you use different programs and utilities in conjunction with the Internet, you have to tell the firewall which activities to allow and which to disallow. This takes some time, but after it's done, everything begins to hum along quietly in the background; you can rest assured that after all your efforts, you've become a safer surfer.

If you download ZoneAlarm, for example, you have two ways you can config-
ure it so your programs can access the Internet. The easiest way is to let
ZoneAlarm ask you, each time a new program attempts to access the
Internet, whether you want to allow access for that program, as shown in
Figure 10-8.

Figure 10-8:
You can tell
ZoneAlarm
your
preferences
as you use
the Internet.

If the program is one, like Windows Messenger or Internet Explorer, that you
know requires constant Internet access, select the Remember this Setting
check box, and click Allow. That's all there is to it. From that time forward,
the program will have access to the Internet.

The other way to configure the firewall is by adding programs, one by one, to
the ZoneAlarm control panel. To accomplish this task, follow these steps:

1. **Open the ZoneAlarm control panel.**

2. **Select Program Control.**

3. **Click the Programs tab, shown in Figure 10-9.**

4. **Click the Add button at the bottom of the screen.**

   The Add Programs window opens, allowing you to choose a program
   application to add to the control panel. You can add only one program
   application at a time.

5. **Choose the program you want to add, and click Open.**

   You have to drill down to the executable file you want to add to the control panel. This might require you to go through two or three screens.
   After you've selected the proper file, it's added to the Control Panel and
   shows question marks to the right of it.

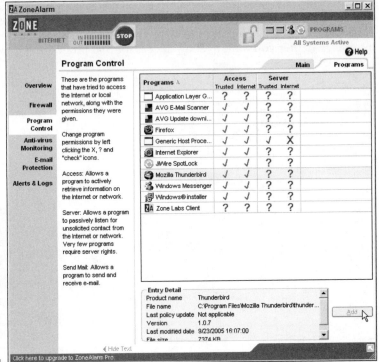

Figure 10-9:
Go to the
Programs
tab to tell
ZoneAlarm
what
programs
can access
the Internet.

6. **Back on the Programs tab, for the program you just added, click the question mark in the Internet column and click Allow, as shown in Figure 10-10.**

The first two question marks change to green check marks, indicating they're cleared for Internet access.

Only a few program applications need to be cleared as a server, so it's generally best to leave the two rightmost columns alone. Because question marks are showing in those columns, ZoneAlarm asks for your approval if an application requests access to the Internet as a server.

It takes a bit of time to get any firewall — especially one that monitors outbound traffic — configured to the point that it's not alerting you about one thing or another. But after you've configured the permissions for the bulk of the programs you normally use, you should be able to relax, confident that your laptop is well protected.

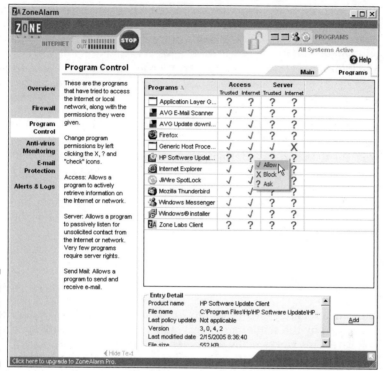

Figure 10-10:
Allow a
program to
access the
Internet.

 A firewall can sometimes cause unintended problems when you're attempting to make a connection at a hotspot. If you're having problems getting online, try disabling your firewall just until you establish the connection. If you — with the firewall disabled — make the connection, you should immediately enable your firewall and contact the firewall developer's support staff, telling them of the problem. It's probably a simple configuration issue that they can easily resolve.

Employing a Virtual Private Network

You might have heard or read the term *virtual private network* in various places. When I began reading about VPNs, they were usually mentioned in conjunction with business travelers trying to connect securely to their corporate network. It always sounded like a great way to stay safe if you were at a hotspot, but it wasn't (at least until recently) an option available to the general public.

When you're connected to the Internet at a hotspot, a lot of the data being transmitted to and from your computer is being broadcast in the clear. Not all of it, to be sure, but a good portion of it. With enough patience, the right equipment, and the right software, a hacker can intercept and read that data and information. You can be sure that if someone goes to those lengths, they're not likely to act in your best interests if they gather some valuable personal information.

If you're connected via the Internet to a secure Web site, whether from your home or a hotspot, the data being transmitted is secure from prying eyes. It's true, the data and the information are zipping through the air, but not as an open transmission. It's garbled and unintelligible because of encryption. You can know that you're on a secure Web site by the little gold lock icon that appears in the URL address window and in the lower right corner of your Web browser. Also, the first part of the Web address is https, which, by the way, stands for *HyperText Transfer Protocol, Secure.*

What's a VPN?

A *VPN* is a securely encrypted link for data traveling over the Internet. It's encrypted by the sender and decrypted by the receiver with specialized VPN software. This works really well when one end is a corporate network and the other end is a business traveler. And I hear you saying, *That's great if you're connecting to a company network over the Internet, but what if I just want to connect to the Internet? Even if I encrypt my outbound traffic, the Web site I'm connecting to won't be running any kind of decryption program.*

Well, you're right. But there's a way to take advantage of this technology, even if you just want to connect to the Internet. Several companies are now set up in such a way that you can connect to them under the protection of a VPN. With that secure connection between you and them, they (in turn) connect you to the Internet.

In geek-speak, you're *connecting securely,* via the Internet, to a proxy server that's connected to the Internet. When you make a request for a Web page, that request travels over an encrypted link to the proxy server. That server, acting on your behalf as a proxy, decrypts your request and resends it over a wired Internet connection to the Web server hosting the requested Web page. The Web server, by request, serves up the page, sends it to the proxy server that then encrypts the page, and resends it to your laptop. The VPN client on your laptop decrypts the page, and you can then view it on your screen.

As you might guess, this all takes a little bit more time than simply connecting to the Internet directly. The slowdown with 128-bit encryption is barely noticeable, but you might not want to use a connection like this for playing games. If, however, you're sending e-mails that include personal information or you're surfing the Net, a service like this can be invaluable.

Another benefit of using a VPN service is that you surf the Web more-or-less anonymously. Because the proxy server is making the actual request for the Web pages, the IP address read by the Web server is that of the proxy, not your laptop. Lest you believe that this would enable you (or others) to engage in mass spam-mailing or any other ethically questionable or downright illegal activity, you should be aware that the records of the company operating the proxy server are subject to subpoena by law enforcement agencies.

At least three companies I know of offer this type of service. They are

- ✔ **HotSpotVPN:** HotSpotVPN offers their service by subscription to a variety of users, including those using Palm or Pocket PC PDAs. They also — if you choose — block unwanted Internet ads and offer three levels of encryption. Their Web address is `www.hotspotvpn.com`.

- ✔ **PublicVPN.com:** Although this subscription service is easy to use and configure, they also offer extensive setup instructions on the Support page of their Web site. They can be found at (as you may have guessed) `www.publicvpn.com`.

- ✔ **JiWire:** Marketed under the name SpotLock, this service, along with its VPN, includes an Internet connection management utility and an easily updated hotspot directory. The VPN security feature is available by subscription, but the connection management utility and directory can be used free of charge. They're found at `www.jiwire.com`.

Examining SpotLock by JiWire

Because SpotLock is (at least right now) the lowest-priced of the choices — and because it includes features like the portable directory and connection-management utility, I've chosen to subscribe to this VPN. My laptop doesn't contain a whole lot of top-secret trucking documents that get e-mailed back and forth, and most of my other online activity is pretty boring and benign. Nonetheless, I do my banking, budgeting, and tax work online, and even though this is all done on secure Web sites, I just feel better knowing I'm doubly secure.

Some of the key features of SpotLock include the following:

- ✔ **Portable directory:** I talk a bit about this in Chapter 5, and I've had this feature installed for a long time. At one time, it was the primary product offered by JiWire, and it's how I was first introduced to them.

- ✔ **Connection-management utility:** I get into the nuts and bolts of this utility in Chapter 6. This utility is the only connection utility I've used that detects as many networks as NetStumbler does.

✔ **E-mail relay:** Some hotspots block e-mails that would normally go through your ISP's SMTP (Simple Mail Transfer Protocol) server. Under these circumstances, you can receive e-mail but you can't send it. SpotLock, like most VPN services, includes an e-mail transfer service that eliminates the problem.

✔ **VPN:** This is the primary service offered by SpotLock; it protects all the Internet traffic emanating from and destined for your laptop by placing it in a cryptographic tunnel.

Downloading and installing SpotLock

If you want to give SpotLock a try, JiWire offers a short, free trial. I say *short* because you get to connect through the VPN only three times before that option expires, and you're asked to make a decision. You can continue to use all the other features of SpotLock from that point forward, and should you decide to take advantage of the security feature, you can sign up at any time from the connection utility's Manage tab.

The download process could, in my opinion, be a bit more streamlined. But until they start taking my advice, you need to follow these steps:

1. **On the JiWire home page (**www.jiwire.com**), click the button labeled Secure.**

   You can choose to Buy Now! or Try it Free! I always try before I buy if given the choice, and that's what I suggest you do.

2. **Click Try it Free, and the logon/registration screen opens. Fill in the appropriate information, and click Create Account & Start Download.**

   The registration confirmation page opens, and once again, you're given the option to begin the download or get more information.

3. **Click Download.**

   A page opens that includes the Release Notes for the version you're trying to download and (again) giving you the opportunity to either buy the utility right away or accept a free trial.

4. **Click Try It For Free, and, finally, the download manager opens.**

5. **Choose Save to Disk, and with the download complete, you can open the Installation Wizard.**

6. **Close out any program applications you've got running, and shut down your antivirus software. Double-click the new icon with the caption SpotLock-Installer.**

   The Installation Wizard opens.

7. **Click Next.**

   The EULA window opens.

8. **Read the EULA; if you agree to the terms, select the radio button indicating that you're accepting the terms. Click Next.**

    The Customer Information window opens.

9. **Enter the appropriate information, and decide whether you want the installation to be available to all users or just you by selecting the corresponding radio button. Click Next.**

    The Destination Folder window opens, displaying the default destination folder. You can choose to change it if you so desire. In a word: Don't.

10. **Click Next.**

    What I like to call "The Hesitation Window" opens, giving you the option to go back and make changes. You don't want to do that.

11. **Click Install, and several installation status bar windows open and close during the process.**

    The final Installation Wizard window opens, indicating completion.

12. **If you don't want to start the program or don't want an icon on your desktop, deselect the radio buttons, and click Finish.**

    Assuming you leave the radio buttons alone, you now have a new icon appearing on your desktop, and the connection-management utility opens.

If any hotspots, or home or business wireless networks are in range, they appear in the Connect window. Any secured networks have a little blue key icon showing to the left of the SSID, and conversely, unsecured networks, like hotspots, simply indicate the SSID. Below the SSID, you see the signal strength, ranging from Very Low to Excellent.

Connecting securely through SpotLock

After you install SpotLock, you can use the following steps to connect and configure it:

1. **With the connection-management utility open, click the hotspot SSID you want to connect to, and then click Connect in the upper-right corner of the window.**

    Because this is the first time you've connected to this hotspot, the connection wizard opens.

2. **You can choose to use the SpotLock VPN security feature, or choose to use another VPN/ No Security.**

    On occasion, the use of a VPN proxy server makes it impossible to make the initial connection to a hotspot that requires you to use a logon page. To avoid this problem, I suggest that you choose, initially, to use no security. After the connection's made and you receive the You're Connected to the Internet screen, you can enable the SpotLock VPN feature by clicking the Secure tab on the connection manager, entering your username and password, and clicking Activate.

3. **After making your VPN selection, you have the opportunity to choose whether you want any applications to start immediately and whether you want to disable any Internet Explorer proxy settings.**

   I suggest that you don't start any other programs in conjunction with the connection-management utility, but it's your choice. You need to be concerned with the IE proxy server settings only if you have IE set to connect through a corporate VPN.

4. **When asked whether to allow an automatic connection, I suggest you save the settings you've made, but disallow the automatic connection.**

   See the "Disallowing automatic hotspot connections" section earlier in this chapter for details on the evils of automatic connections.

   The connection is now made and you're surfin' safe.

The JiWire connection utility automatically disables the Windows Zero Configuration utility. If, for whatever reason, you want to use the WZC, you have to right-click the little JiWire icon in the system tray and choose Exit. Then you have to enable WZC, following the steps outlined in Chapter 5.

Configuring the ZoneAlarm or Windows firewall for use with SpotLock

If you're using the ZoneAlarm firewall, then the first time you make a connection to a hotspot with SpotLock, a ZoneAlarm New Program security alert balloon appears — saying `jiwire-pluto.exe is trying to access the Internet`. Select the Remember this Setting check box, and click Allow. (Refer to Figure 10-8 for an example of the alert.)

After that, open the ZoneAlarm control panel, open the Program Control window, and check the following:

- ✔ **On the Main tab, be certain that the Program Control is set to Medium and the Automatic Lock is off.**

- ✔ **On the Programs tab, click the blue question marks in the Server column to the right of the** `jiwire-pluto.exe` **program, and choose Allow from the menu that appears. Do this under both the Trusted and Internet subheadings.**

Configuring the Windows firewall for use with SpotLock requires less effort because the Windows firewall doesn't block any outbound traffic. All that's required is quick mouse and cursor reflexes. When the Windows firewall alert balloon opens, all you have to do is Unblock the `jiwire-pluto.exe` program to enable communication between your laptop and the SpotLock servers.

If your mouse and cursor reflexes are a little slow on the draw — allowing the Alert balloon to disappear — all you need do is disconnect from the network and then reconnect. Doing this causes the security alert to reappear, giving you another shot at unblocking SpotLock.

Chapter 11

Encrypting Data

A recent FBI computer-crime survey found that 50 percent of respondents had been the victims of a laptop theft. That's an astounding number, even if you take into account that the survey was limited to companies and corporations with more than 5 employees and more than a million dollars in revenue. And the cost of these thefts isn't limited to the price of a replacement laptop. Not by a long shot.

Even though I'm not a corporate mogul, plenty of the data on my laptop has great value to me — and, were it to enter the public domain, could result in the loss of my identity, potentially putting me on the hook for debts I never incurred. What data do *you* have sitting on your laptop hard drive just waiting to be exploited by thieves?

In this chapter, I tell you a little about data encryption and help you set up a free data-encryption utility on your computer. I also tell you a bit about how to use it. For example, I show you how to set up an encrypted vault and how to send encrypted e-mail attachments. I spill the beans about a utility you can use to lock down programs, and I tell you how to encrypt files and folders with Windows XP Pro.

Examining Data Encryption

If you watch some of the popular television crime shows, you might think that encrypting data a waste of time — most crime-scene investigators, a couple of doctors in the Boston medical examiner's office, criminal investigators employed by the Navy, and the janitor at CTU can crack any encryption code in a few minutes, right? Well, like your mom used to tell you, don't believe everything you see on TV. Although it *is* possible to break encryption, no one can do it between a couple of commercials, and anyone who tries needs a supercomputer (or a giant network of PCs) and a lot of time.

For example, in a competition sponsored by RSA Security, a 64-bit encryption key was broken after almost 5 years, using tens of thousands of computers networked together. According to experts, cracking a 128-bit encryption key is 16 times harder. That doesn't mean, again, that it can't be done. But your average laptop thief just won't see the point in spending millions of dollars and years of time breaking the encryption on your laptop to get your checking account information.

The longer an encryption key is, the more bits it uses — and the more difficult it is to crack. A 128-bit encryption key, based on the AES, TEA, Blowfish, or IDEA algorithm, is considered "strong" encryption and it's around 300,000,000,000,000,000,000,000,000,000 times more complex than the 40-bit encryption used in the early days of Internet security. While TOP SECRET government documents are required to use 192- or 256-bit encryption, you should find 128-bit encryption to be more than sufficient for keeping your information safe from prying eyes.

Exploring the advantages

Aside from the fact that using encryption makes you feel like an international spy, you have more compelling reasons to consider using an encryption application to protect some of the files and folders you keep stored on your laptop. Some encryption programs even secure program applications, making it impossible, for example, to open your Web browser without a password.

If you carry personal information (either yours or others'), carry sensitive company documents, or discuss information that shouldn't be available to the public in e-mail, then using an encryption utility makes good sense. No one expects their laptop to be stolen, but it does happen. If it happens to you, it'd be nice to know that at least the information stored on your laptop won't be used to further victimize you or your associates.

Another key reason to use encryption is that viruses can't read or alter encrypted files, folders or program applications. Nor can Trojan Horses, spyware, curious co-workers, or those who are simply snooping.

Perusing the possibilities

Plenty of companies provide various encryption utilities that offer a wide range of features. Not every utility will, however, encrypt anything and everything. A few focus on encrypting e-mail, and a few focus on encrypting files and folders. And at least one focuses on password protecting your program applications, although it does encrypt files and folders, too.

The following utilities are among the most popular:

- ✔ **Folder Lock:** With this versatile program, you can choose three levels of protection and the interface is extremely easy to use and understand. You can choose to set security for individual files and folders, or you can place groups of them into a security vault. Folder Lock is produced by New Softwares and can be found by browsing to `www.newsoftwares. net/folderlock`.

- ✔ **PGP Desktop:** Available in both Home and Professional versions, depending on your needs, PGP Desktop allows the user to send encrypted e-mail that can't be read by anyone but the intended recipient. PGP also includes Self-Decrypting Archives that allow for the exchange of secure e-mail even if the recipient doesn't have PGP. They're found on the Web at `www.pgp.com`.

- ✔ **WinGuard Pro:** With the paid version of this utility (a free, limited-capability version is also available), you can password-protect the 30 built-in program applications or lock up programs of your own choosing. You can also encrypt files and folders, lockout Internet program downloads, lock your desktop, and set password timers to foil hackers. It's available from WGSoft at `www.winguardpro.com`.

- ✔ **TrueCrypt:** This program offers a choice of encryption algorithms and, like other utilities, allows for the creation of a virtual drive in which to keep encrypted volumes. With large container sizes available, you can install program applications into an encrypted container so a program can only run, or even be seen, when opened with the password key. This free utility is available for download at `www.truecrypt.org`.

- ✔ **Steganos Security Suite:** Using a 256-bit AES encryption key, this utility makes it safe to carry nuclear secrets alongside your personal information. Among the features and abilities the utility includes are a password generator/manager and a file shredder. A free trial is available from the developer at `www.steganos.com`.

- ✔ **Cryptainer LE:** A free encryption utility developed by Cypherix, which also offers several other premium encryption utilities, Cryptainer LE uses the 128-bit Blowfish algorithm to create 25MB vaults that files and folders can be dropped into. It also lets you create self-extracting, encrypted e-mail files that can be read by the recipient, without Cryptainer LE, providing they have the password. You can download it free from Cypherix at `www.cypherix.com`.

Some of the utilities offer 448-bit encryption (based on the Blowfish algorithm) or 256-bit encryption (based on one of several algorithms). You might wonder why anyone would need such a strong encryption cipher, but for those involved in, for example, the medical professions, entrusted with the responsibility to keep the personal information of their patients and clients safe from prying eyes, the extremely strong encryption provides the peace of mind that comes with knowing files and folders are completely safe.

Getting Started with Cryptainer LE

Most encryption programs use encrypted logical containers — *vaults* — to store files and folders on virtual drives, and they all do so in a similar fashion. For the purpose of illustrating how using these programs work, I decided to use Cryptainer LE, because it's free and easy to use. No matter what program you decide to use, the sections that follow can help you understand the value, and the ease, of encrypting files and e-mails.

And did I mention Cryptainer LE was free? I did, didn't I? Well, quite a few others are free, too, but if you accept a free trial for a premium utility and find that you like it, don't let a few dollars stand in the way of your security — most are less than $50 and all I've seen are less than $100.

Downloading and installing the program

Like so many other program applications, the installation of this program requires little more than an ability to click Next. After downloading Cryptainer LE from the Cypherix Web site and saving the installation file to your desktop, double-click the new icon on your desktop and the installation wizard opens. You don't really want to alter any of the default names and locations so, just accept the terms, keep clicking Next until you get to the Install prompt (click Install) and the last window, where you click Finish.

If you're still using Windows 98, SE, or ME you're instructed to restart your computer. Restarting isn't absolutely necessary in Windows 2000 or XP, but I recommend you do so anyway, before you open the utility and get started.

Setting up Cryptainer

Prior to creating your first encrypted vault, you need to create a password. Since Cryptainer supports passwords of up to 100 characters in length, and since the encryption is only as strong as the password, I suggest that you create an extremely strong password.

If you forget your password, your data will be unrecoverable. It's important to have a strong, crack-proof password but it needs to be something you can remember. For tips on creating strong passwords (that are also easy to remember), flip to Chapter 10.

Whereas most passwords will fall into the 8- to 14-character range, you should, with Cryptainer, use as near the full 100 character length as you possibly can. While using the first letters of a popular phrase with a few other characters thrown in works well for shorter passwords, you may want to employ a different strategy for creating a longer password to use with your encrypted files. Using a pass phrase is a great idea, but you must be certain that it's unique. You don't want to use a pass phrase that, once a couple of words are ascertained, will be immediately recognizable.

Encrypting Files

The first thing I wondered when I decided to give Cryptainer LE a try was, "What the heck should I encrypt?" Well, in case you're asking yourself this question, first and foremost you should encrypt anything and everything that you wouldn't want John Q. Public having clear and easy access to. A few of those items might include

- ✔ **Your saved e-mail:** Whenever I sign up for something on the Web, I seem to (inevitably) get an e-mail that includes, at a minimum, my username and password. Because I don't want to remember all that stuff, I save the e-mails. However, I save them to a couple of files stored in a Cryptainer vault instead of in Outlook Express or Thunderbird.

- ✔ **E-mail addresses:** Exporting and importing e-mail addresses is a bit of a hassle but, if you've got some addresses that it'd be best to keep confidential, it's quite possibly worth the effort.

- ✔ **Financial information:** I keep my budget and a lot of tax information on my laptop. It's not something I want just anybody to have access to.

- ✔ **Business-related information:** Most employers entrust employees with information they'd prefer not to make readily available to the public. If it's business-related, no matter how sensitive you think the information might be, treat it like the secret recipe to Bush's Baked Beans.

Creating an encrypted vault

Cryptainer LE creates a separate, removable (although, because it's a virtual drive, it's not physically removable) drive located on your hard drive. This drive acts like any other drive on your computer. When the Cryptainer LE utility is open, this drive is visible and when the utility's closed, or even minimized, the drive disappears. As long as the utility is open and the drive is visible, the files, folders or program applications stored on this drive will act, and can be acted upon, as though they were on your hard drive or any other removable drive.

Your first step in creating an encrypted container in which to store files and folders you want to keep completely safe is to open the Cryptainer utility. The first time you start Cryptainer LE, the program prompts you to start creating your vault. Specify the following in the Specify Cryptainer Volume Details dialog box (shown in Figure 11-1):

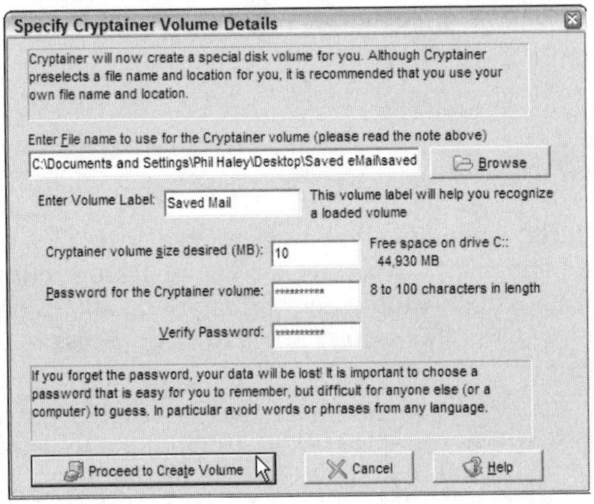

Figure 11-1:
Setting up a vault in Cryptainer begins with this dialog box.

✔ **The Cryptainer volume file name:** The default file name and location is `C:\WINDOWS\system32\cxl1705` but it's suggested that you come up with something on your own. It can be anything you like. You can either browse to use an existing path or you can create a new folder and file. For the purpose of this demonstration, I specify the file `saved mail` be created in `Saved e-mail` — and so the full path is

`C:\Documents and Settings\Phil Haley\Saved e-mail\ saved mail`

To create a new folder and specify the path, as I've done, follow these steps:

1. **Click Start⇨All Programs⇨Accessories⇨Windows Explorer.**

2. **Highlight the location at which you intend to create the new folder.**

   For example, if you highlight Desktop, the new folder will be created in the Desktop menu tree. (Of course, you *could* just right-click your desktop and create a new folder that way.)

3. **Click File⇨New⇨Folder, enter the name of your new folder, and click Enter.**

4. **Minimize the Explorer window; then, in the Cryptainer vault-creation wizard, click Browse.**

5. **Find your new folder and double-click it. In the text-entry field, type the desired name for your vault file and click Save.**

✔ **Volume name:** The default name is `Cryptainer`. It's suggested you change the name, so I call this volume `Saved Mail`.

✔ **Volume size:** The default size is 10MB but you can specify any size up to 25MB in Cryptainer LE. If you need a larger vault size than that, you need to upgrade to another Cryptainer product or choose one of the other encryption utilities that feature larger vault, or container, sizes.

✔ **Create a password:** Come up with a secure password that's as long as possible and enter it in the text-entry field.

✔ **Verify the password:** Type — *don't* copy and paste — the password in the verification field. The reason you don't want to paste it from the first field is that you may have made a typing error (it happens) — and if you paste an erroneous password into the re-entry field, you may never figure out the error, forever dooming the utility.

After you enter all the necessary information, click Proceed to Create Volume. A creation-progress bar opens, followed by a reminder to jot down the full path to your newly created file and a notice indicating the drive letter assigned to your new vault. It's a good idea to jot down the path, especially if it's a secondary vault. (Later in this chapter, in "Creating new vaults and other tricks," I tell you how to create secondary vaults.)

Moving your files into the vault

You can move files and folders into the Cryptainer vault in two ways. The primary method is to drag them from one location, like Windows Explorer, and drop them into the Cryptainer Vault. The second method is to create folders within the Cryptainer vault and save documents, like your e-mails, to those folders.

Now, you can't actually create folders within the normal Cryptainer view, but you can create new folders or files within the Explorer window that opens by clicking View in Explorer (on the Cryptainer toolbar). Then just click File➪New and choose to open a new folder (or to open a new document type). For my receipts and registrations, I created a couple of folders with the clever and highly imaginative names — `Receipts` and `Registrations`. I can now save e-mail receipts or registration confirmations directly to the appropriate folder. (I tell you how to do this in the next section.)

Dragging and dropping existing files and folders into Cryptainer is likely the most common way folks use this utility. You can, for example, open Windows Explorer and drag any folder into your vault. You can also, if you're using the View in Explorer option, move files and folders from one Explorer window to another, as shown in Figure 11-2. If you move a file or folder out of the vault, however, it's no longer protected by encryption.

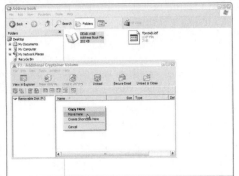

Figure 11-2:
I'm moving
my address
book files to
a Cryptainer
vault.

 If you right-click and drag a file or folder into your vault you can choose to move the file to that location. If, however, you left-click and drag the file you can only move a copy of the file or folder. Because the point of protecting files and folders with encryption is to keep them hidden, it's probably best to move, rather than copy, folders to the vault.

 Certain files, like those relating to program applications or system functions, should never be moved because moving them can prevent systems and programs from functioning. If you get a warning from Windows Explorer concerning access to certain folders, you should heed that warning. In general, if the folder contains items other than documents, music, photos, videos, Web pages, or other similar media, leave it where you found it.

Accessing your encrypted files

Working with files located on the Cryptainer LE virtual drive, once the utility and vault are opened, is exactly the same as working with files or folders located anyplace else on the hard drive. To open your secure vault, double-click the Cryptainer icon, enter your password in the text-entry field, and click OK. Your newly created vault opens and you're ready to work with it.

With the Cryptainer volume open (not minimized), I can also open Outlook Express and save a receipt or registration confirmation to one of the folders I created for that purpose. In order to save, for example, an e-mail receipt I just highlight the e-mail I want to move, click File➪Save As, and save the e-mail to the proper folder.

 Folders kept within a Cryptainer vault aren't viewable unless the utility is open and the vault is loaded. The first vault you create is the Primary volume and, when you open the utility it is, by default, loaded.

Working with an encrypted Address Book

You may be curious to know how you can store your address book in an encrypted volume rather than within, for example, Outlook Express. After creating a volume in which to store the addresses open Outlook Express, click Tools⇨Address Book, and the Address Book screen opens. Click File⇨Export⇨Address Book (WAB) and browse to the export location. Name the file and click Save. Your address book, at this point, is saved to your encrypted vault.

The address book also still exists in Outlook Express. If your goal is to hide this address book completely, you can now delete it, in its entirety, from Outlook Express. When you find yourself

in need of the address book you open the encrypted volume in which it resides, and import it. This is done in a fashion similar to the process used to export the address book.

Click Tools⇨Address Book. With the Address Book screen open click File⇨Import⇨Address Book (WAB) and browse to the address book's location. Click the address book name to highlight it and click Open. In the blink of an eye your address book's back in Outlook Express. If you make additions to it while you're using it, just export it back to the volume and overwrite the existing file. It's a bit of a hassle, yes, but taking these steps safeguards the e-mail addresses that others have entrusted to you.

Creating new vaults and other tricks

It's highly likely that you'll want to create more than one encrypted vault. And after you have files tucked away in these separate vaults, a few tips will help you navigate them more easily. Here's a quick list of the basic tasks you need to know:

- ✔ **Creating a new vault:** Open the Cryptainer utility and click Tools⇨ Additional Cryptainer Volumes⇨New Volume. The Specify Cryptainer Volume Details window opens and, just like you did with the original volume, you now specify the path, volume name, size and password.

  Since Cryptainer, for security purposes, doesn't keep a record of your volume names and locations it's important, especially if you have several, using various paths, that you keep a record of these names and locations.

  When you create a new volume, you can also create it on removable media or devices like CDs or Flash Drives by specifying that media in the vault location. Another option is to install Cryptainer LE on a removable drive so you can use it on more than one computer.

- ✔ **Accessing a secondary vault:** By default, the Primary volume, the only one that Cryptainer remembers the location of, is the one that loads upon opening the Cryptainer utility. Accessing your other vaults is done in a fashion very similar to that of creating them. Click Tools⇨Additional Cryptainer Volumes⇨Load a Volume and select the volume you want to work with. You can have as many as four volumes, or vaults, open at any one time.

✔ **Specifying a volume as the Primary Volume:** To do this, once the Cryptainer utility is opened, load the volume you want to be Primary and choose File⇨Make this the Primary Volume. From now on, unless you decide to make one of the other volumes Primary, this is the volume that will load when you open Cryptainer.

Shutting down Cryptainer LE

Before you close any Cryptainer volume, or close the utility, be sure you've saved any of the changes you might have made in any documents you had open and close those documents. If you've got more than one volume loaded, it's not necessary to close each one separately; just click Shutdown & Exit on the Primary Volume window. Cryptainer then unloads all the open volumes and shuts itself down safely.

Normally, any open Explorer windows will close when the Shutdown & Exit is performed but it's possible that you may have to close them out as well. If any file or folder is still in use, maybe in another program application, Cryptainer won't shut down but, instead, an error message appears. In that case just acknowledge the error, close the offending file or folder, and repeat the shutdown steps.

Sending Encrypted E-Mail or Attachments

With some e-mail-encryption programs, you may well have the ability or option to encrypt both the e-mail message itself and any attachments you might be sending.

If your correspondence needs to be secure and confidential, it might be best to create a message in a separate word processing application and send it as an encrypted attachment to a normal e-mail message. Although you can create self-extracting encrypted attachments that don't require the recipient to have a decryption utility, the message is usually bundled with an executable (.exe) file that enables the recipient to read the message, and antivirus programs almost always strip these .exe files. A better choice is to send an encrypted attachment, which does require a recipient to have a special utility but doesn't ring alarm bells in antivirus software. I figure, if the file needs to be secure, your recipient will likely understand and won't mind getting a simple utility.

Other encryption programs, especially any specializing in encrypted e-mail, might be a bit easier to use or offer more versatility than Cryptainer LE — but for sending encrypted file or folder attachments by e-mail, it does a pretty good job. This is accomplished quite easily, as you discover in the following steps:

1. **Open the Cryptainer utility in the usual manner and click Secure E-mail⇨Encrypt File to Send by E-mail.**

   The Encrypt File to Send by E-mail dialog box appears, as shown in Figure 11-3.

2. **Enter either the complete path to the file you want to encrypt or click the cute little file icon to begin browsing for the file. Once you find the file, double-click it.**

   The path to the file is entered in the field.

3. **Enter and verify the password needed to open the e-mail.**

   This password needs to be transmitted to the recipient in a separate e-mail or, preferably, by other means.

4. **If you have no way of transmitting the password to your intended recipient, you can, in the "hint" text box enter a hint or riddle to which they're sure to know the answer.**

5. **Choose whether to leave the original file alone or delete it following the encryption by selecting the appropriate radio button.**

6. **Click Encrypt File. Once the encryption is completed, click OK on the Pathway Information box.**

   Providing the encrypted file to be sent as an attachment doesn't reside in an encrypted vault, you can close the Cryptainer utility.

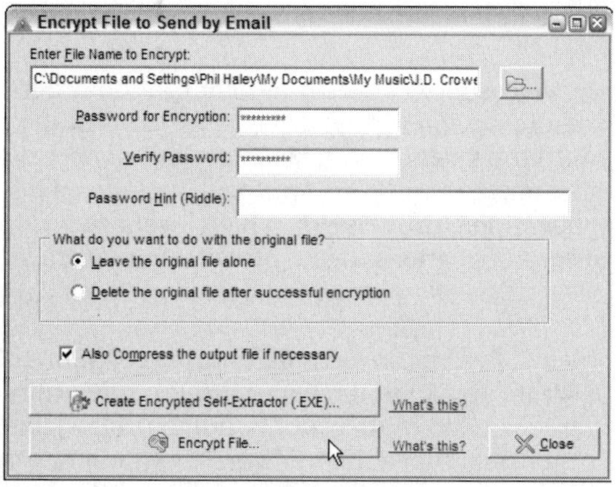

Figure 11-3:
Set your options for encrypting an e-mail attachment.

With the file encrypted, you can open your e-mail client and compose the message to which the file is meant to be attached. You can recognize the encrypted file, in case there's some confusion, by the `.sit` extension at the end of the filename.

After you send your encrypted message, you don't want your recipient to wonder, "How in the world am I supposed to open this?" This is one area in which all the Cryptainer utilities shine. Just remember that your recipient needs the following:

- ✔ **A utility:** Your recipient can download and install either the free Cryptainer LE utility or, if they have no need of that, the free DeCypherIT utility.

  DeCypherIT can be downloaded from the Cypherix Web site by visiting `www.cypherix.co.uk/decypherit.htm` and selecting the FREE Download button. DeCypherIT decrypts any e-mail created by any of the Cypherix software products.

- ✔ **The password:** Remember the password that you created to protect the file? You should relay this password to your intended recipient in some way other than an e-mail — whether you call, text message, or attach a note to an arrow.

Encrypting Program Applications

I really like the idea of locking up entire program applications so no one has any hope of accessing them. For example; I lock Internet Explorer. That way, even if my laptop's stolen, the thief has no hope of accessing my Favorites folders or browser history. Without that access, they can't possibly know where I do my banking — or with which Web sites I engage in other financial transactions.

With Cryptainer LE, as well as most of the other encryption programs that make use of volumes contained on virtual drives, you can install program applications directly into the vault — with some notable exceptions. The primary problems I've encountered with this approach include an inability to specify, with some applications, the drive on which I want the program installed, and, with other applications, being blocked from installing to a removable drive.

To resolve these problems, I've employed a different encryption utility that password protects program applications. WinGuard Pro, the utility I use for this purpose, offers a free version of their utility but, because I like the ability to specify programs other than those the free version supports, I purchased the fully functional premium utility. Using WinGuard Pro, I can lock up my Web browsers, e-mail clients, or, if I want, my entire desktop.

Installing WinGuard Pro

WinGuard Pro is available for download from the developer's Web site. Point your browser to `www.winguardpro.com/products.html` and click Download Now. No matter whether you want the free or premium version — and you might as well give the free version a try — the download includes both. If you want to upgrade later, you're given ample, and annoying, ways of doing so.

After the installation file is downloaded, you simply double-click the newest icon on your desktop and follow the prompts of the installation wizard. This is another wizard that requires little more from you than to click Next repeatedly, click Install and Finish once, and remain breathing.

Using WinGuard Pro

To lock down a program application, you must first open the WinGuard Pro utility. When you open it for the first time, you can use the password **LET-MEIN** and then, once open, click **Set Passwords** in the menu on the left so that you can reset the password. Make sure you use a strong password. (I offer tips on creating strong passwords in Chapter 10.) One password is used for all the items you intend to lock, and one password is used to open the configuration utility.

Once that task is done, you can choose to lock miscellaneous program applications, encrypt files and folders, or set Internet keyword restrictions using the Web Content Filter (which stops kids or adults from doing an Internet search using terms or phrases set by you). Prior to shutting down my laptop, I lock down both Outlook Express and Internet Explorer. Two separate actions are required to lock these programs. To lock down Internet Explorer, follow these steps:

1. **Right-click the WinGuard Pro lock icon in the system tray and select Configuration. Enter your password and click Continue.**

   The menu screen opens.

2. **Click Additional Locks.**

   The Configuration dialog box opens.

3. **Select the Additional Locks tab.**

4. **Under Internet Explorer, select the Lock Internet Explorer check box.**

   You notice that, by placing a check mark in the Lock Internet Explorer check box, that several other boxes are automatically checked, cutting off all avenues to access Internet Explorer. Figure 11-4 show how it looks.

5. **Click Apply.**

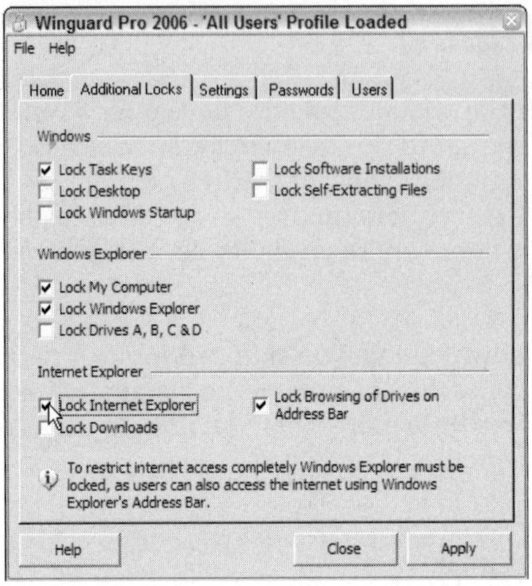

Figure 11-4:
Locking
down
Internet
Explorer.

With Internet Explorer locked, you can now lock Outlook Express from the same dialog box.

1. **Select the Home tab and click Lock a Program or Window.**

   The Lock an Item dialog box opens, as shown in Figure 11-5.

2. **From the menu find Outlook Express and put a check mark in the box on the left.**

   At this point you can either choose to lock additional programs or, with Internet Explorer and Outlook Express password protected, you can simply close out all the open boxes.

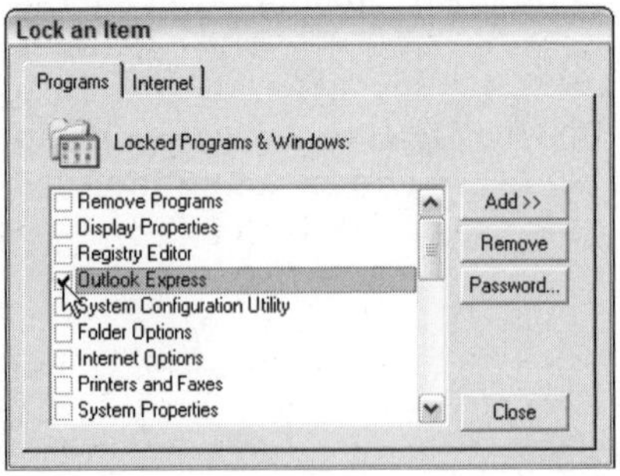

Figure 11-5:
Locking
Outlook
Express
from prying
eyes.

You can, with the premium edition, also lock down other programs and windows. I use Mozilla Firefox more than I use Internet Explorer. To lock down that, or any other program, from the Lock an Item dialog box, follow these steps:

1. **With the application in question open click Add⇨Refresh.**

2. **Click the program you want to lock, in the lower menu window that's now open, and click the Add button to the right of it.**

   This moves the program into the upper Locked Programs and Windows area, with a check mark next to it.

If you're locking a program like Firefox, it's important that the window you lock is the Home Page. That way, if someone other than you tries to open the program, it immediately locks down until the password is entered. You could also choose, if you desire, to lock windows that are doorways to financial institutions. Be aware that once you enter a password to open the program or window, you have to re-lock it when you shut down in order to keep it secure.

Using File Encryption in Windows XP Pro

If you're using Windows XP Professional, you have the ability to encrypt files and folders with what Windows calls the Encrypting File System (EFS). By using EFS, the encrypted files and folders are protected from being viewed or altered by malicious programs or unauthorized users. EFS uses a pair of encryption keys, a private key that's owned by the authorized account user, and a public key that's generally available.

When a file or folder is encrypted with EFS, a *file-encryption key* (FEK) is automatically generated. The FEK, along with an encryption algorithm, is used to create the encrypted file. The FEK is also encrypted and stored with the encrypted file. Access to the encrypted file is quick and easy because, as the creator, your user account holds the certificate verifying you as the owner of the private key that's used to decrypt the FEK which, in turn, is used to decrypt the file or folder.

Anyone accessing the user account under which files or folders were encrypted has access to those encrypted documents. For this reason it's important to set up a separate user account, accessed only from the logon screen, protected by a very strong password.

Setting up user accounts

It's a good idea, if you're going to use the EFS, to set up a separate account from which files and folders will be encrypted. To accomplish this worthy goal, follow these simple steps:

1. **Click Start➪Control Panel➪User Accounts.**

   The User Accounts screen opens.

2. **Select the Users tab and click Add.**

3. **Type a name for your new account in the text-entry field.**

   Unless your computer is a part of a client/server network you don't need to enter a domain name.

4. **Enter and confirm a strong password for the account. Click Next.**

   See Chapter 10 for details on creating strong passwords.

5. **Decide whether you want to grant the account administrative rights or limit the account. Click Finish.**

Encrypting folders and files

You can choose to encrypt individual files, but a better choice is to encrypt the entire folder and all its contents. As a matter of fact, you can, if you like, choose to encrypt the My Documents folder or, if you prefer, create a specific folder in which encrypted files and sub-folders will be stored. Any file or sub-folder subsequently created in, or moved to, the encrypted folder is automatically encrypted.

You can't encrypt a compressed folder or file. If you attempt to do so, the item will be encrypted but will no longer be compressed. One solution is to store the compressed folder or file in an encrypted vault (like those I tell you about earlier in the chapter), using Cryptainer LE.

To encrypt a folder and its contents, simply follow these steps:

1. **Right-click the folder you want to encrypt and click Properties.**

   The Properties dialog box opens.

2. **Select the General tab and click Advanced.**

   The Advanced Attributes dialog box opens.

3. **Select the Encrypt Contents To Secure Data check box. Click OK.**

4. Click OK to close the Advanced Attributes dialog box.

If the folder you're encrypting already contains files or sub-folders the Confirm Attribute Changes dialog box opens.

5. Select Apply changes to this folder, subfolders, and files and click OK.

EFS won't work without a recovery agent certificate, but a recovery agent account is designated by default, and the necessary certificate is generated automatically, if you don't do it manually. I talk more about this a bit later under the heading "Making sure you can access encrypted data."

Decrypting files and folders

Providing you're working from the user account in which the folder you want to work on was encrypted, file decryption happens automatically. This happens so quickly and seamlessly that you might wonder if the file was actually encrypted. If, however, you want to send the file to another person or move it to another user account, you want it decrypted. The process is pretty much the reverse of the one you followed to enable encryption. Here's how it works:

1. Right-click the folder you want to decrypt and click Properties.

The Properties dialog box opens.

2. Select the General tab and click Advanced.

The Advanced Attributes dialog box opens.

3. Deselect the Encrypt Contents To Secure Data check box. Click OK.

4. Click OK to close the Advanced Attributes dialog box.

If the folder you're decrypting contains files or sub-folders the Confirm Attribute Changes dialog box opens.

5. If you want to decrypt all the contents of the folder select Apply changes to this folder, subfolders, and files and click OK.

You can choose to decrypt only the folder but, if this is your choice, none of the files or sub-folders contained in the folder will be decrypted.

Making sure you can access encrypted data

One thing about the certificate authorizing use of the private key that decrypts the file-encryption key (which is then used to decrypt the folder you've encrypted): You have to keep it somewhere — and normally the certificate is stored in the same user account in which the folder was encrypted. If this user account (or the private key held within it) gets deleted or corrupted, the encrypted data becomes unrecoverable. What to do?

Sure, you can do a lot of complicated computer stuff and create what's known as a "designated recovery agent," but it's a whole lot easier simply to back up the certificate to a floppy disk or CD that you can use to recover the data if there's a problem. To back up the certificate, follow these steps:

1. **Click Start⇨Control Panel⇨Network and Internet Connections⇨Internet Options.**

    The Internet Properties dialog box opens.

2. **Select the Content tab. In the Certificates section, click Certificates.**

    The Certificates dialog box opens.

3. **Select the Personal tab.**

4. **In the Certificate Intended Purposes field, select one certificate at a time until you find Encrypting File System.**

    When you encrypted your first folder, this certificate was generated by default.

5. **Click Export.**

    The Certificate Export Wizard opens.

6. **Click Next.**

7. **Click Yes, export the private key.**

8. **Click Next.**

9. **Click Enable strong protection.**

10. **Click Next.**

11. **Enter your password.**

12. **Decide whether you want to save the key to another location on your hard drive, to a virtual Cryptainer drive, to a CD, or to a floppy disk — and specify your preferred destination.**

13. **Click Next.**

    Your private key is sent to the destination of your choosing. If you sent it to a CD or floppy disk, be sure to keep it in a safe place. You can breathe easy; if disaster strikes, you can still decrypt your data.

Chapter 12

Accessing Your Home PC Remotely

A whole bunch of folks, my little family included, own multiple computers. As a matter of fact, we've got more computers than we have people. Well, that is unless you count the cats. But, beyond chasing the mouse across the desk, sharpening their claws on towers, and sleeping on laptop lids, they hardly ever use computers. Even so, multiple computers mean that each one has a different primary purpose (even to the cats), and each one contains files, folders, and program applications unique to it.

When everybody's home, it's no big deal because I can either use the computer that's best suited for the job at hand, or because they're networked, I can grab the file or folder that I need from the computer that contains it, no matter which one I'm using. When traveling, though, that type of free access always seems as though it might be impossible to achieve. In truth, however, while it might be a little bit more difficult — because some pre-planning's involved — it's definitely not impossible or even all that complicated.

In this chapter, I give you the information and help you locate and use the tools necessary to access your home computer while traveling about the country. For example, I tell you specifically how to use the tools built into Windows XP Pro, and if you don't have a computer at home running that version of Windows or you have one that's not practical to use, I supply you with two alternative solutions. I also help you begin to identify ways in which using remote access can make your on-the-road computing experience easier and more secure.

Examining Remote Access

You might not have previously considered the possibility of using your home computer while on the road as though you were sitting right in front of it. Well, I'm here to tell you that, not only is it possible, but it's also really fairly easy to do. Currently, any one of the following methods makes it possible for you to access and control a computer that's sitting at home from anywhere in the world:

- **Windows Remote Desktop:** If the computer you want to access is running Windows XP Pro, you can access and control it from any computer running Windows 95 or better, providing that other qualifications are met.

- **Virtual network computing:** Several VNC solutions that operate in a fashion similar to that of the Windows Remote Desktop (and all based on the same basic program) are freely available.

- **Subscription services:** Probably the easiest method of accessing a PC from a remote location is to use a subscription service. At least one service offers a free but relatively basic plan, whereas most of the others charge between $10 and $20 per month for the service.

The computer that's being accessed remotely is commonly referred to as the *host, server,* or *target* PC. The computer making the connection — the one you're physically using — is most often referred to as the *client* or *local* PC.

Why would I want to do this?

By using one of the VPN subscription services that I talk about in Chapter 10, you can surf the Web and send e-mail within an encrypted tunnel. By using a remote desktop application or service, however, you can connect to a computer sitting in your own home or office, often through a securely encrypted tunnel, and operate it as though you were sitting right in front of it.

So . . . big deal; the question of why you'd want to add remote access to your bag of tools still remains. Well, one of the biggest reasons is that by making use of remote access, you can increase both security and utility. Among the other benefits are the following:

- **Program application access:** Not every computer has the same software installed. Any programs installed on the host, whether they're installed on the client or not, can be used. Some remote access subscription services even make it possible to use a PDA or Pocket PC to access a remote computer and use program applications that would be otherwise incompatible with the device.

✔ **Secure file access:** If you've ever wished that you could just get a look at that one file or folder stored on your home computer, you can appreciate the value of remote access.

✔ **Secure file storage:** Laptops and PDAs are prime targets for thieves. By using the host computer for file and folder storage, you eliminate any chance that a thief can access sensitive information.

✔ **Secure transactions:** You wouldn't even need to bookmark the Web sites of financial institutions with which you do business. Because you can initiate and complete all transactions on the host computer, your laptop (or client) wouldn't even have a browser history to make available to a would-be identity thief.

✔ **Remote printing:** Although not available with every remote solution, you can, in most cases, print from the host computer. In some cases, you might be able to print remotely and directly from the client.

The last two benefits I cite are the primary reasons I'm a big fan of remote access. I can do my banking, pay bills, manage investments, purchase goods and services, and leave no trace of these transactions on my laptop. Beyond that — because a printer is connected to my host computer — I can print permanent records of all these transactions that just sit safely waiting for me to return, when I can file them appropriately.

Almost anything you can do on your own computer can be done remotely. There are, however, some significant limitations almost entirely related to the fact that you can't physically touch the computer. You can't, for example, insert a CD, floppy disk, flash drive or USB plug into any of their corresponding drives or ports. You also will, most likely, need to leave the remote, or host, computer running because in most cases, you can't boot a computer from a remote location.

You might want to consider setting up your host PC so that it's *headless*. By that, I mean that after you've taken the steps necessary to set up and configure your host PC for remote control, you really don't need to have a monitor, keyboard, and mouse permanently attached to the tower. Only one client at a time can access the host desktop, but as long as that's not an issue, you might want to consider this option. The biggest advantages to doing this are related to cost (no monitor and peripherals to buy) and security (no one can see what you're doing) as well as space (the tower could go in a closet if you had power and an Internet connection).

Exploring the possibilities

Several methods of achieving access to a remote computer, using various technologies, are available to you. The cost of these services and utilities, as well as their versatility, varies from one to another. Depending on how you plan to use a remote access solution, any one of the following might fit the bill:

- ✔ **Remote Desktop Protocol:** Built into Windows XP Pro, the remote desktop capability can come in handy for many users, but it might not be appropriate for everyone because, even if it's installed on your home PC, you might still encounter the following road blocks:

  - • **IP address:** Most ISPs use dynamic IP addresses (a number that identifies your computer, but *dynamically,* so it changes) for home subscribers. If your IP address should change while you're on the road, it might be difficult or even impossible to locate your remote PC on the Internet. If, however, you can convince your ISP to assign a *static* IP address for your home (that is, an IP address that doesn't change), you can overcome this obstacle.

  - • **Router firewall:** If you have more than one computer at home, like me, you've likely networked them through a wireless or Ethernet (wired) router. Routers effectively block inbound traffic to your network by employing one or more firewall solutions. This problem is overcome by forwarding port 3389 to the host computer. (Most router manuals don't cover this but, if you call tech support, they can walk you through the steps required to accomplish the task.)

  - • **LAN:** Routers generally dynamically assign a local IP address to each PC included in the network. In order to forward port 3389 to the host computer, the router needs to know where to find it. If, after configuring port forwarding, the router changes the local IP address of the host, the router won't know where to forward the port. You might, after consulting your router's users' manual, be able to configure it to assign a static IP address to the host PC.

If you're new to the terminology of networking and are curious about how all this works, check out *Networking For Dummies* by Doug Lowe (Wiley).

- ✔ **RealVNC:** The VNC stands for *virtual network computing,* and this program application allows a home computer not equipped with Windows XP Pro to be accessed from a remote location in much the same way. Some of the same limitations found in the remote desktop feature of Windows XP Pro might apply to this utility as well. If you're interested in more information, you can visit their Web site at www.realvnc.com.

A handy program application called Hamachi makes it possible to circumvent all the roadblocks associated with both Windows Remote Desktop and any of the VNC applications. This little client can help you set up a virtual private network comprised of computers that might be spread across the planet. I tell you more about Hamachi in the next section.

✓ **GoToMyPC:** This subscription service accesses the host PC through a Web server, and then, when the connection's made, transfers the connection to the communication server for the remainder of the remote session. The data stream is encrypted using Secure Sockets Layer (SSL) technology. The service is a bit spendy at $20 per month, but it's the most feature-rich of the services. You can find them on the Web at www.gotomypc.com.

✓ **LogMeIn:** Like GoToMyPC, connections are made through secure servers, so you don't need to configure the host PC, router, or network. LogMeIn also offers a completely free version of its service. You don't get the same bells and whistles as you would with their paid service, but most folks find that it's a good place to start and the free is version more than sufficient. You can find them on the Web at https://secure.logmein.com.

Each one of these programs and services has points in its favor, so figure out what you want to accomplish with remote access and visit each of the Web sites to find out more about their offering. A few others you might want to check out include:

✓ **Laplink Everywhere:** www.laplinkmobile.com

✓ **I'm InTouch:** www.01com.com

✓ **TightVNC:** www.tightvnc.com

✓ **UltraVNC:** http://ultravnc.sourceforge.net

Using RealVNC

To show you how accessing your home PC might work, I chose RealVNC as an example application, simply because most of their executive staff is comprised of the original members of the research team who created their product. Who better to continue the development of a product than those responsible for its genesis?

RealVNC offers a free version of the software as well as Personal and Enterprise editions that are licensed for a fee. Both of the licensed versions offer quite a number of features, including encrypted connections, not available on the free versions. However, I use the free version because first, I'm kind of a cheapskate, and second, depending on what I'm doing, I can use either the JiWire SpotLock or Hamachi VPN to secure my hotspot connections anyway. (I tell you more about JiWire in Chapter 10.)

As a matter of fact, the Hamachi VPN is the little gem that enables me to securely and remotely access my home computers. Because I don't have a static IP address for my home and because I use a router that also dynamically assigns local IP addresses, I find it beyond my capability to configure my home network in such a way that I can connect with it remotely. I'm sure it could be done, but it's one of those "too many buttons, not enough brain" situations that I strive to avoid.

Hamachi allows me to set up a secure peer-to-peer local access network that exists on the Internet. (That is, it enables my two computers to talk to each other.) In this way, remote access occurs exactly as if I were at home making the remote connection within my wireless home network (or WLAN, if you prefer the technical term). The initial connection is made through the Hamachi mediation server in much the same way that I might connect to the Internet through the JiWire proxy server, but then it's handed off and all communication is directly between members of the network. Setting up this kind of a network connection completely eliminates all the issues that might block use of VNC or remote desktop applications.

The following components are all you need to set up a hassle-free, globally accessed LAN with remote access capability:

- ✔ **Hamachi VPN:** Install the free Hamachi client on each PC that you want to include in your network. Because the network is created over the Internet, you can include PCs at home, work, or anywhere.

- ✔ **RealVNC:** Install the RealVNC application on each of the computers that you want to control remotely. You can choose to install only the Server portion of the application on the host computer (the one you want to access remotely) and only the Viewer portion on the PC you use to access the host.

- ✔ **Broadband connection:** Although you can use dialup on one end of the connection between host and client PCs, it's likely to be maddeningly slow.

Yes, it's true; I tend to opt for the free versions of quite a few program applications. Most of the time, however, if the Web site solicits donations for software they offer freely, and if I've found their program useful, I contribute a few bucks. Because the RealVNC Web site accepts donations, you might consider showing your appreciation for their hard work with some hard cash.

Hamachi, at this time, is in beta development and available for use with only Windows XP or 2000 operating systems. I'm unsure as to whether the standard release will be compatible with any other operating system.

Setting up RealVNC

After downloading the RealVNC program application from their Web site (www.realvnc.com) and saving the executable to your desktop, you're ready to install it on each computer you'd like to access remotely. For the most part, this installation process is much like any other program application. But in a couple of instances, you must specify a configuration element. To install RealVNC, follow these instructions:

1. **Double-click the RealVNC setup icon on your desktop.**

   The VNC Setup Wizard opens.

2. **Click Next.**

   The License Agreement window opens.

3. **Select the radio button accepting the agreement if, after reading it, you choose to continue, and click Next.**

4. **With the Destination Location window open, ignore the option to change the installation location. Just click Next.**

   The Select Components dialog box opens, as shown in Figure 12-1.

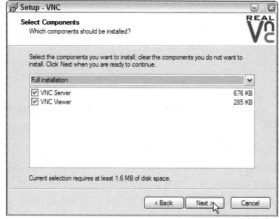

Figure 12-1:
Select components for the installation.

5. **Make your component selections, and click Next.**

   If you're setting up the host computer, you can choose to install the VNC Server only. If you're setting up the client PC (the one you'll use to remotely access the host), you can choose to install just the VNC Viewer. Doing a full installation on both computers is fine as well.

   After you proceed, the Start Menu Folder selection window opens.

6. **Maintain the default values, and click Next.**

7. **With the Additional Tasks dialog box open, you can choose whether to add icons. Make sure both boxes are checked under VNC Server Configuration. After making your selections, click Next.**

   The Ready to Install dialog box opens.

8. **Examine the information to see that everything is set up as you want, and click Install.**

   The VNC Server Properties dialog box opens, as shown in Figure 12-2.

Figure 12-2: Here, you begin setting up a password for remote access.

9. **Be sure the VNC Password Authentication radio button's selected, and click Configure.**

   The VNC Server Password dialog box opens.

10. **Enter and confirm the password you want to use for remote access. Click OK to close the dialog box, and click OK to close the Properties dialog box.**

    The Information dialog box opens.

11. **Click Next.**

    The final dialog box opens, indicating that you've completed the installation.

12. **Click Finish.**

You might need to configure your firewall to allow RealVNC to act as a server. If you're using ZoneAlarm, for example, you'll receive a Security Alert. I use ZoneAlarm as an example in Chapter 10, where I discuss using a firewall in more detail.

Setting up Hamachi

With RealVNC installed and configured on the computers you want to use as host and client, you're now ready to download and install the Hamachi VPN client. With the executable client downloaded from http://hamachi.cc and saved to your desktop, you're ready to begin the installation and configuration process:

1. **Double-click the Hamachi setup icon on your desktop.**

   The Hamachi Setup Wizard opens.

2. **Click Next.**

   The Hamachi agreement dialog box opens.

3. **Accept the agreement, if you find it acceptable and want to continue, and click Next.**

   The Hamachi Setup dialog box opens.

4. **Don't alter the default values for Installation Location or Start Menu Group, but do select the Automatically Start Hamachi When You Log In check box. Click Next.**

   You're ready to install the application.

5. **Click Install.**

   The installation progress window opens, displaying each element as it's installed.

6. **When all the elements have been installed, click Next.**

   The Hamachi Quick Guide opens, along with a strange-looking rectangular object, shown in Figure 12-3. The gray obelisk is the Hamachi client.

7. **Read the Welcome and Control information and click Next after you've familiarized yourself with the information contained in each dialog box.**

   The Hamachi Address information dialog box opens.

8. **Read the information, and click the Power button located at the lower left corner of the Hamachi client. (Refer to Figure 12-3.)**

   The Create An Account dialog box opens.

Figure 12-3:
The
Hamachi
client as
it first
appears.

9. **Choose a nickname, and click Create.**

10. **Once again, you have to configure your firewall to allow the Hamachi Client to access the Internet. If you're using ZoneAlarm, select the Remember this Setting check box, and click Allow.**

    After the Hamachi client resolves, the connection to your local IP address appears at the top of the obelisk along with your nickname.

11. **Click Next on the Hamachi Quick Guide dialog box.**

    The Hamachi Quick Guide dialog boxes that follow lead you through the process of joining a network. (After completing each task described in the guide, the Next button is enabled. Click it to move to the next dialog box and task description.)

12. **Click the Network icon on the Hamachi client, and select Join Existing Network from the dialog box.**

    The Join the Network dialog box opens.

13. **Enter** test **in the Network Name text box, and enter** secret **in the Network Password text box. Click Join.**

    You see that you've successfully joined the test network.

14. **Follow the prompts in the next couple of Hamachi Quick Guide dialog boxes to find out more about the network you've joined.**

15. **To leave the test network, right-click the network name and choose Leave Network from the menu. You can now close the Quick Guide.**

You need to set up the Hamachi client on each of the computers you want to include in your network. If you've got only one PC at home and one laptop you take with you on the road, your job is quick and easy. But if you've got several, you might want to get a cup of coffee. Heck, you might want to get one anyway. Yeah, I'll take one too; thanks for offering.

Configuring your network

Although not absolutely critical, I recommend configuring your Hamachi VPN from the host computer. That's because the PC used to create the network owns the network, and all the other PCs are just joiners. To begin the network-creation process, start by booting the host computer. If you followed the steps I laid out in the previous section, you know that, in Step 4, I had you configure the Hamachi client to start during boot up — so when the PC's ready to go, so is the client. With both the computer and Hamachi at the ready, follow these steps:

1. **Click the Network icon on the Hamachi client (it's the triangle-shaped one) and choose Create New Network from the menu.**

   The Create New Network dialog box opens.

2. **Type the name you want to assign to your new network in the Network Name text box.**

   I call my network `OTR Wireless For Dummies`.

3. **Create and enter the password to be used in the Network Password text box.**

4. **Click Create.**

Boy, that was tough! I'm all worn out. Don't worry, though, I won't rest until you've joined the network and accessed the host computer from a remote location (even if that's just another room), with your client PC. Get ready because this is almost as difficult as creating the network. Here are the steps:

1. **Boot the client PC (the one you want to use on the road to access and control the host).**

2. **Click the Network icon on the Hamachi client.**

3. **Choose Join the Network from the menu, and when the dialog box opens, enter the network name and password in the appropriate fields.**

4. **Click Join and — poof! — you're connected to the network, as shown in Figure 12-4.**

You can repeat this grueling exercise with every PC you want to include in the network, and then, maybe, take a little break. Next, I show you how to take control of the host PC from the remote client.

Figure 12-4:
Your network name appears after you join the network.

 Unless you choose to leave the network, you're connected to it each time you boot the client computer. If you enable file sharing for this network, you can access or move files from any of the computers you've included in your VPN, provided they're online. By connecting a printer (one that you don't mind leaving on at all times) to the host, you can print documents stored on the client PC.

 Hamachi uses a mediation server to make the connection between all the computers included in your VPN. After a connection's established among them all, the server hands everything off, and the network communication is direct between the peers. If, however, the Hamachi server is down when you boot your PC, you can't make the VPN connection. It doesn't happen often, but you should be aware that it can.

Controlling the host from a remote location

Okay, here's the fun part. For some unknown reason, having the ability to take over the desktop of a computer that's not in the same room or even the same state as I'm in and manipulate it like I'm sitting right in front of it makes me feel like I'm one of those highly trained and technically savvy computer geeks that all the best criminal investigators and counter-terrorism agents consult. I don't think I feel, or look, much like my two favorites, though, because they're named Abby and Chloe. Anyway, if you want to take remote control of your host PC, just take the following steps:

1. **Choose Start⇨All Programs⇨RealVNC⇨VNC Viewer 4⇨Run VNC Viewer.**

   The Connection Details dialog box opens, as shown in Figure 12-5.

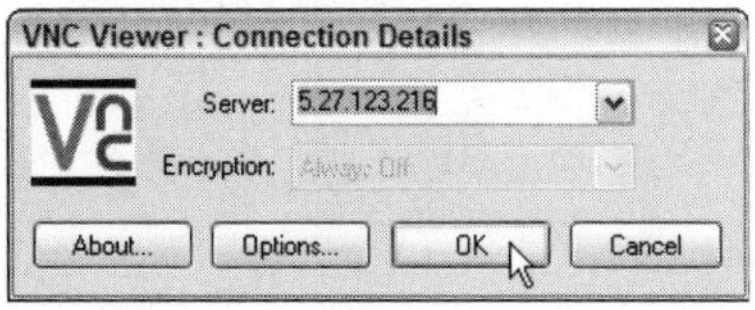

Figure 12-5:
The
Connection
Details
dialog box.

2. **Type the local IP address of the host computer, which you can find listed on the Hamachi client, into the Server text box, and click OK.**

   The Authentication dialog box opens.

3. **Enter your password, and click OK.**

I set up a network including one of my laptops and the laptop my wife uses for school, as shown in Figure 12-6. By making her laptop the host and owner of the network, I was then able to join the network with my laptop and take remote control of the host desktop. Pretty cool, eh? The wallpaper is a photo of Beeker, and it seems like my wife's got a lot of games on a laptop used for school, doesn't it?

As if by magic, the desktop of the host computer opens in a browser window right there in front of your eyes. By default, the VNC Viewer renders the desktop using only 64 colors, but you can, if you so choose, configure it for full-color renditions of the desktop. To do so, just click the Options button on the VNC Viewer Connection Details dialog box before making the connection.

You can also configure the elements that the server makes on the host computer. Just right-click the VNC Server icon in the system tray and select Options; with the Properties dialog box, select the Desktop tab and remove or disable elements as you choose by selecting the check box next to the appropriate description. You might want to reduce color renditions and eliminate things like wallpaper in order to reduce bandwidth usage. The more detail included, the greater the bandwidth being used, and vice versa.

Figure 12-6:
I set up
my wife's
computer as
the host.

Using Windows XP Pro Remote Desktop

If you have the option of using the Remote Desktop utility included with Windows XP Pro, you might want to make use of it rather than RealVNC or some other remote access solution. To circumvent potential roadblocks, I recommend that you set up a VPN with the Hamachi client as I describe in the previous section. With your VPN configured, you can then set up the Remote Desktop feature on your host computer.

Getting started

To use Remote Desktop, you need, at a minimum, the following:

- ✔ **Windows XP Pro:** The host computer (the one you're leaving at home) must have XP Pro installed as the operating system.

- ✔ **Remote Desktop client:** The client computer (the one you're taking on the road) doesn't need to be running XP Pro, but it does need to be running a Windows operating system. The client's pre-installed on both XP

Home and Pro, or if you're not using one of those, you can download `msrdpcli.exe` from Microsoft.

✔ **Name or IP address of host:** If you're making the connection to the host via, for example, the Hamachi VPN, you need the local IP address or the name of your PC. If you're fortunate enough to have a static IP address for the host PC, make a note of it.

If you're curious about the names of your computers, choose Start⇨ Control Panel⇨Performance and Maintenance⇨System and click the Computer Name tab in the System Properties dialog box. The name of your PC, along with any workgroup to which it might be assigned, is clearly listed on the screen.

Setting up the host PC

With the host computer up and running, just follow these steps to get it ready to accept remote control:

1. **Choose Start⇨Control Panel⇨Performance and Maintenance⇨System.**

   The System Properties dialog box opens.

2. **Click the Remote tab.**

3. **In the Remote Desktop area, select the check box labeled Allow Users To Connect Remotely To This Computer.**

4. **Click OK to enable the changes, and close the dialog box.**

The other issues you might have to deal with, depending on your situation, in configuring the host computer for remote access and control include the following:

✔ **Firewall:** If you're using ZoneAlarm, I recommend attempting to access the host computer from the client PC while you're still in the same room with them both. In that way, you can allow the connection to be made and make certain that ZoneAlarm remembers the setting. I discuss configuring ZoneAlarm in more detail in Chapter 10. If you're using the Windows Security Center firewall, you can follow these steps to configure it to allow the Remote Desktop utility to be used:

   1. **Choose Start⇨Control Panel⇨Security Center.**

      The Windows Security Center screen opens.

   2. **Click Windows Firewall.**

      The Windows Firewall dialog box opens.

> **3.** Clear the check mark in the box to the left of Don't Allow
> Exceptions and select the Exceptions tab.
>
> **4.** Be sure that a check mark appears to the left of Remote Desktop
> and click OK.

✔ **Port forwarding:** If your host computer is connected to a router, consult
the user's manual for port forwarding instructions and forward port
3389 to the host.

Preparing your client

If you've got Windows XP Pro or Windows XP Home edition on the client computer, then chances are good that you've got all you need. It's possible, however, that you might need to get your XP installation CD out from its hiding
place. With your CD in hand, insert it in the CD drive and, when the Welcome
screen opens, click Perform additional tasks⇨Setup Remote Desktop
Connection and follow the prompts.

If Windows XP isn't your operating system, then visit the following page and
download msrdpcli.exe:

```
http://www.microsoft.com/windowsxp/downloads/tools
           rdclientdl.mspx
```

Install the utility as usual, and you're all set.

Making the connection

With all the previous steps completed, you're ready to take control of the
world. Oh . . . sorry, sometimes I get carried away. I doubt it's even possible
to take control of a small unsuspecting country. You can take control of the
host computer, though, by following these steps:

1. **Choose Start⇨All Programs⇨Accessories⇨Communications⇨**
   Remote Desktop Connection.

   The Remote Desktop Connection dialog box opens.

2. **In the Computer text box, type the name or IP address, whichever**
   might be appropriate, and click Connect, as shown in Figure 12-7.

3. **With the Log On to Windows dialog box open, type your username**
   and password into the appropriate text fields.

4. **Click OK.**

Figure 12-7:
Connect
with Remote
Desktop.

There you go; you're looking at the host computer desktop, and for the most part, it works just like you're sitting right in front of it. When you're ready to end your remote session, just click Start and log off.

Getting Your Feet Wet with LogMeIn Free

LogMeIn Free is a subscription service that connects the client (local) PC with the host (target) PC over the Internet. Using LogMeIn Free in conjunction with either RealVNC or Remote Desktop is different from using the Hamachi VPN. Whereas the Hamachi mediation server initiates the connection and then hands it off, the LogMeIn server never severs itself from the network connection. Instead, the connection between the host and local computers is maintained and secured through the LogMeIn servers. Another difference is that you need to install LogMeIn Free on only the host computer.

It's just ridiculously easy to use and depending on your needs, LogMeIn Free might be all you require. In order to get the versatility afforded you by setting up a network with Hamachi and using RealVNC or Remote Desktop, you'd have to opt for the paid LogMeIn service rather that the free service, but believe me, for most people, LogMeIn Free is all you need.

Setting up LogMeIn on your host PC

You can install the LogMeIn software on as many computers as you like, but if you need only remote access and control of one (the host), that's the only one on which the software need be installed. Using the host computer, follow these steps:

1. **Open a Web browser, and visit the LogMeIn Web site** (`https://secure.logmein.com`). **Click the link to LogMeIn Free, and following the prompts, set up your account.**

2. **With that complete, you're given the opportunity to install either a free trial version of the LogMeIn Pro software or just the LogMeIn Free application. Decide which one you want to install.**

   It's up to you, but you might want to give the Pro version a whirl just so you know what it includes and whether or not you might be willing to pay $70 per year for the extra bells and whistles. If you find that ringing the bells and blowing the whistles is worth the bucks, you're all set; if not, you can simply opt for the free version and bounce merrily along your way.

   With that decision out of the way, you're now ready to install the software.

3. **Depending on your browser configuration, you might be given prompts to install a plug-in or two before continuing, and you might need to verify the digital signature or security certificate.**

   Install and verify as needed, making the choices that enable you to run the application.

4. **With the installation wizard open, follow the prompts to click Next or agree to the EULA until you get to the Computer Description window.**

   The Description window displays your computer name, and if you choose, you can change the name to something more descriptive or appropriate.

5. **When you click Next, the installation begins and the familiar green installation status bars start flashing away. Click Finish, and you're ready to go.**

LogMeIn requires that you use a username and password to make a remote connection. If you don't normally use them to log on to the target PC, then, during the application installation process, you'll be asked to create a Computer Access Code. (If you're not asked to create the Computer Access Code, you simply use your normal logon name and password.) You're going to need this information, so make sure you can either remember it easily or make a note of it that you store separately.

Configuring firewalls to allow remote access

If your host computer has a firewall installed, as it should, it'll block any attempt to connect with the host from the Internet. Further, if you're using ZoneAlarm, during the installation process, you notice that you must first allow LogMeIn to act as a server and allow the LogMeIn Desktop Application to access the trusted zone. If your host computer's running an OS other than Windows XP and using ZoneAlarm, you might also find that other application elements need to be allowed to act as a server, or access the Internet and trusted zones. It's best to put LogMeIn through its paces while you're actually sitting right in front of both the host and client computers. In that way, you'll be able to configure your particular firewall as it puts up roadblocks.

Accessing the host remotely

One interesting feature regarding LogMeIn is that you can access your home PC from almost any computer that has a Web browser and a connection to the Internet. (Although I don't recommend this, you could potentially use a public computer as the local PC connecting to the host.) To begin a remote session:

1. **Visit the LogMeIn Web site, and log on with the e-mail address and password you used to create your account.**

2. **Click the LogMeIn button.**

   The My Computers page opens, and you find your target PC listed.

3. **Click the icon, and the connection process begins.**

   If this is the first time you've attempted to begin a remote session, it's likely that a browser plug-in might need to be installed. If this is the case, depending on the browser you use, you're either prompted to install the plug-in or it's installed automatically. With that step out of the way, the connection process continues.

4. **When prompted, enter the Computer Access Code you created during the installation process or the username and password you normally employ to gain access to the target PC. Then click Login.**

   On the next page, decide whether you want to view the target PC desktop in either a new browser window or the current one. You can also choose to make display configuration changes or access the help resources.

5. **Make your choices, and click Go.**

   One more configuration window opens, giving you another opportunity to customize your connection.

6. **Make your selections, click Proceed and, before you know it the desktop of the target PC is displayed before your eyes, as shown in Figure 12-8.**

Figure 12-8:
Yes, my host computer wallpaper is a picture of penguins.

Part V
Taking Care of Business

The 5th Wave   By Rich Tennant

"He saw your laptop and wants to
know if he can check his Hotmail."

In this part . . .

The central theme is that by using a computer, a connection to the Internet, and a few programs and peripherals, you can make your over-the-road experience, in many ways, more profitable. For example, when you wander the world in your home on wheels, staying in touch with friends, family, and business associates gets expensive. So, in Chapter 13 you find out how to make money-saving calls using your computer and an Internet connection. Additionally, in Chapter 14, you find out about a few tools, ranging from GPS (that can help you avoid out-of-route related expenses) to software and online services, that help you use your time and talent more efficiently. (And, of course, time is money.)

Chapter 13

Talking Cheap with VoIP

. . . .

. . . .

A few years ago, while reading a popular magazine, I came across an article devoted to a new technological development that enabled some folks to make phone calls using the Internet, instead of wires, to carry the voice stream. After reading about this new technology called Voice over Internet Protocol (VoIP), I was instantly excited about the potential VoIP presented for easing and enhancing long-distance communication for the traveling public. (*Traveling public* meaning, at the time, me, but because I'm such a magnanimous guy, I now also include you.)

Since that time, VoIP has gone from being a cutting-edge technology used mainly by geeks to a mainstream technology used by everyone from geeks to grammas. And with more and better software and hardware choices, it's both proving and expanding on its potential as a valuable communication tool for travelers.

In this chapter, I help you decide whether VoIP might be a useful tool by first giving you a basic understanding of what VoIP is and also helping you set up a free but powerful VoIP solution. In between, I help you decide which VoIP provider might be best suited to your purposes and point out some of the hardware choices that can get you started and enhance your experience. I also try to point out a few of the problems you might face while using VoIP in a mobile environment.

Exploring VoIP

The importance of communication in trucking is rivaled only by that of diesel fuel. Most trucks today have satellite systems, and some companies also pay either part or all of a driver's cellphone bill. With these developments, communication between drivers and dispatch has improved to the point that land lines are the option of last resort. Communication between drivers and their family and friends, however, is a different subject.

When I was full time on the road, I was constantly irritated by the amount of money it cost me to stay in touch. Calling cards were usually the best bet, but I had to sit in a cramped phone booth or take up space in the restaurant while diners eavesdropped on my conversations. When I started using a cellphone, things got better because I could sit in the privacy of my truck, but I was still spending somewhere around ten cents a minute to talk, in addition to a phone bill at home. This situation was, essentially, mirrored by those in RVs.

And then along comes VoIP. Computer geeks had been using the computer for voice communication since the early– to mid–'90s, and some mainstream VoIP software products began to appear on the market by 1996. Using dialup for VoIP communication was a little bit cumbersome, and at least when I first became aware of it, you couldn't make calls to the public switched telephone network (PSTN) or Plain Old Telephone Service (POTS) phones. So VoIP, at that time, had limited utility. Not so today.

Understanding the basics

It's now quite possible, in many cases, to carry on a reasonable conversation over a dialup connection, and when conversing via broadband, the call quality's sometimes better than using a cellphone or POTS. Further, not only is it now possible to make VoIP calls originating from a computer and terminating at any type of phone (or vice versa), but it's also possible to make phone-to-phone calls carried over the Internet instead of PSTN.

Wi-Fi, though, presents a few problems that can sometimes adversely affect the quality of calls made using VoIP. For several reasons — some of them inherent in all Wi-Fi transmissions and some of them more likely to be present in a truck stop or RV park environment — Wi-Fi tends to drop or lose some packets that carry the phone conversation from one point to another. The result is *latency,* or speech that sounds clipped, which can make a conversation more difficult. But this doesn't happen all or even most of the time.

Even considering some of the problems, VoIP isn't impossible or overly irritating to use in a mobile environment. Further, the 802.11e wireless standard has been developed specifically to deal with quality of service issues facing voice and multimedia transmission over IP. (I introduce wireless standards in Chapter 2.) As more and more wireless equipment supporting this standard is deployed, the problems might become not just an exception, but downright rare.

Getting started

I originally became interested in VoIP service because I wanted to increase the amount of time I could spend talking with friends and family and reduce the amount of money I was spending to do so. At the time I began my investigation into the ways I could use VoIP on the road, most of the software programs were relatively inexpensive and although the person I was calling also needed to have the software installed on their computer, no fees beyond the initial purchase of the software and the cost of my Internet connection were necessary. That's not always the case any longer, but my original goal, cheap conversation, is still quite possible.

To start making use of this technology while traveling, you need the following:

✔ **VoIP service:** Although some services are targeted more toward the home user than the traveling public, several services truly cater to travelers. When searching for a service, you find two basic types:

- *Computer-based:* By installing software on your computer, you can, with an attachment or two, turn it into a phone. Because less hardware is needed, this is usually the preferred choice for truckers and RVers.

- *Converter-based:* With a broadband Internet connection at home, you can connect a VoIP converter, known as an Analog Telephone Adapter (ATA), to your modem and connect a traditional phone to the converter. In some cases, you can also connect the converter to a computer and make your calls that way. Converter-based systems are targeted toward residential and business customers.

✔ **Internet connection:** High-speed broadband connections are best, but several of the computer-based solutions support VoIP over a dialup connection as well. If you're at a hotspot that connects to the Internet via satellite or if you have a satellite Internet connection, making a VoIP call might be tedious, or even impossible, due to latency. (I discuss the latency that's inherent to satellite connections in Chapter 9.)

There can be no doubt that faster connections make for better call quality.

✔ **Compatible computer:** Unless you're using a converter-based VoIP solution, you need a computer. Most laptops are likely capable of making use of VoIP services, and several Pocket PCs and PDA devices can be used.

Recently, a few manufacturers — including NETGEAR, Linksys, and UTStarcom — have developed VoIP-based phones that look a whole lot like a cellphone. For example, check out the NETGEAR phone in Figure 13-1. These Wi-Fi phones are equipped with the hardware necessary to make a Wi-Fi connection and the software necessary to make VoIP calls. Currently, though, these phones have issues that make them difficult — or in some cases impossible — to use at most paid hotspots. I suspect, however, that most of these problems will be overcome in the near future.

Figure 13-1: This NETGEAR Skype WiFi Phone is pre-loaded with Skype software, making it possible to call other Skype users at no extra cost.

Selecting a Service

Not surprisingly, when you begin to search for VoIP services and software, you find quite a large menu of selections. Some offer converter-based solutions, some offer computer-based solutions, and some offer a combination of the two. As you consider which is best suited for your situation, consider the following:

✔ **Intended use:** Will you be using VoIP primarily or exclusively while traveling, or will you be combining the use of VoIP between both home and road? Further, what type of calls do you think you'll most often be making? Will they be . . . ?

- *Computer-to-computer:* If all, or even most, of your calls will both originate and terminate with computers, then a computer-based service and software is likely your best choice.

- *Computer-to-phone:* If the majority of calls originate from a computer and terminate with a traditional phone, computer-based service and software should be high on your list of potential choices.

- *Phone-to-computer:* Phone-to-computer calls, especially those between family members at home and those on the road, will probably benefit most from a service that offers a combination of both converter– and computer-based services.

- *Phone-to-phone:* These types of calls generally originate at home. If this is the type of call you most often make, a converter-based service might be best suited for you.

✔ **Incoming calls:** Several services support incoming calls, offering a personal phone number (sometimes referred to as Direct Inward Dialing, or DID), but don't expect to get this feature free of charge. If this feature is important to you, then you might also want to include the following related features:

- *Area code choice:* Most VoIP providers allow you to choose your own area code, making it cheap and easy for friends and family who might not have adopted VoIP for themselves to call you on the road. Some even allow you to have more than one incoming number.

- *Voicemail:* Because you can't be connected to Wi-Fi while you're driving, there are probably going to be instances when you miss incoming calls. Voicemail could come in handy.

- *Call forwarding:* If your absence will be extended, especially if extended absences are frequent, a call forwarding feature could be invaluable.

- *Caller ID:* Do you like it at home? You'll love it on the road.

- *Conference calling:* Sometimes three-way calling is the maximum number you can include in a conference call, but a few providers offer the ability to conference as many as 10 calls.

✔ **911 calling:** If you're considering replacing your traditional home phone with a converter-based service that also offers the use of a computer-based soft phone (a software utility that enables you to make and receive calls on your laptop) for traveling, you want to know whether 911 calling is a supported service.

Though you might be considering the use of VoIP at home, you might not be quite ready to trash your traditional phone service. Or maybe the VoIP service you'd like to use doesn't yet offer 911 calling. Either way, you might be able to get a VoIP converter that also supports POTS. That way, you can still use VoIP for long distance and maintain the ability to make emergency calls using the same handset. If that sounds good, make sure you ask about it when you're interviewing prospective providers.

✔ **Cost:** In some cases, you might be able to use VoIP absolutely free. As with many things that are free, though, some restrictions do apply. The calls, almost without exception, must be computer to computer, and both the call originator and recipient must use the same service or software. Almost everything that falls outside those parameters will result in a charge of some kind.

Comparing converter-based services

If one of the reasons you're considering VoIP is to reduce both your home and mobile phone bills, you might want to consider signing up with a service that provides an ATA for your home and a soft phone for the road. To be sure, you can achieve this worthy goal by setting up a computer-based system that can be used at home and away, but a converter-based service is likely to offer features and capabilities making the transition from traditional to Internet phone service almost seamless.

However, if you're thinking of trashing your traditional phone service, consider these issues:

- ✔ **E911:** Developed, initially, for use with cellphones, the E911 service as implemented by the VoIP providers' converter-based systems differs from the traditional phone 911 service in the following ways:

  - *Power outage:* During a power outage, you'll have no 911 availability. Of course, if all you've got in the house are cordless phones, then there's no difference.

  - *ISP problems:* If your Internet service is disrupted for any reason, you won't be making emergency calls. Or any calls at all, for that matter.

  - *Registration:* E911 is available in certain areas only, and even then, you need to register your address with the 911 call center. If you move, forget to register your new address, and call 911, they'll be on their way to your old house.

- ✔ **Broadband connection:** All of the converter-based services I'm aware of require the use of a high-speed broadband Internet connection.

- ✔ **Multiple providers:** If any problems crop up, you might find yourself in the middle while your broadband ISP blames the VoIP provider and the VoIP provider blames the ISP.

Converter-based VoIP service providers target their service toward business and residential customers. Because of this, and because of the requirements of E911 service, not every provider offers service throughout the U.S. That doesn't mean you can't take advantage of VoIP services, but it does mean that you might need to look more closely at a computer-based solution if you can't find a provider in your area.

Those offering VoIP services that might be compatible with your intended use include the following:

- **AT&T CallVantage:** When AT&T divested themselves of many core business components, they did keep the VoIP service. Makes you think, doesn't it? You can find them on the Web at `www.usa.att.com/callvantage/index.jsp`.

- **Vonage:** They might not be the oldest residential and business VoIP provider, but they're most definitely the most recognized. You can find them at `www.vonage.com`.

- **Packet8:** Offering several innovative features and options including broadband VideoPhone service, Packet8 has also partnered with CounterPath to offer an accompanying soft phone feature for use with a laptop. They're found at `www.packet8.net`.

- **BroadVoice:** Their unlimited plan includes service to the U.S., Canada, and 19 other countries. They also offer — either instead of or in addition to the ATA converter — a Wi-Fi phone for use at home. You can easily find them at `www.broadvoice.com`.

- **Anya VoIP:** This is one of the lowest-cost residential VoIP providers offering full-featured service. They're located on the Web at `www.anyavoip.com`.

- **iConnectHere:** The deltathree company offers both residential, converter-based service requiring a high-speed broadband connection as well as computer-based service that can get by fine on dialup. You can get more information at `www.iconnecthere.com`.

As you compare these services, be sure to check the cost per month, activation fees, the cost of an ATA converter, the cost of an extra phone number if you need one, and the availability of a soft phone.

Comparing computer-based services

Computer-based PC-to-PC and PC-to-phone services and software are, at least in my opinion, more appropriate for use in a mobile environment than their converter-based counterparts. Although most of the converter-based services offer a soft phone for use with your laptop, you might get fewer features on the road than you do at home. In addition, you pay a set monthly fee for your VoIP service, whereas many computer-based systems offer free calls between those using the same service or software.

For example, if you use a computer-based service, you might never incur a charge of any kind if you limit your VoIP use to calls made between yourself and your home or the homes of family and friends also subscribing to the same service. If you do make calls outside those bounds, in most cases, you pay for only the time you actually use. Does this then replace your home phone? Well, not if you want to maintain 911 services, but it can eliminate the cost for long-distance calls between all those subscribing to the service.

ATA converters that support computer-based services, like the VoSKY Internet Phone Wizard from Actiontec, designed to be used in conjunction with Skype, make it possible to more easily use these services in a home environment. You still don't get 911 capability, so you probably want to keep your traditional POTS line, but you won't have to be tethered to your computer to make VoIP calls from home. You can find this device by visiting the Actiontec Web site at www.actiontec.com.

Among the many established and upstart entities offering computer-based services and software are the following:

- ✔ **Skype:** After eBay purchased Skype for $2.6 billion, a lot of Skype users worried that elements of the service they'd come to know and love — like free Skype-to-Skype calls — would change. Founders Niklas Zennström and Janus Friis might be driving better cars or flying on private jets; but for the most part, the basics are the same, and the improvements are positive. You can find Skype on the Web at www.skype.com.

- ✔ **NetZeroVoice:** Offering free PC-to-PC calls between NetZeroVoice users, this service also offers a monthly subscription service that allows unlimited PC-to-PC, PC-to-phone, and (by assigning a personal phone number) phone-to-PC calling. Their Web address is www.netzerovoice.com.

- ✔ **Gizmo Project:** Developed by SIPphone, Gizmo Project (besides having a catchy name and a host of features) is working on an agreement with Google Talk that'll allow users of the two services to freely call each other. You can find them at www.gizmoproject.com.

- ✔ **CrystalVoice LIVE:** CrystalVoice software powers a portion of the NetZero Voice service as well as CrystalVoice LIVE. The biggest drawback to CrystalVoice LIVE is the inability to receive calls. They're worth checking out, though, by visiting www.crystalvoicelive.com.

- ✔ **FWD:** Otherwise known as Free World Dialup, this service was, initially, a PC-to-PC service requiring both parties to have the FWD client installed on their computer. Currently, they're implementing services to also include phone-to-PC and PC-to-phone capability. You can find them at www.freeworlddialup.com.

As you compare these services, ask how much each provider charges for user-to-user calls, PC-to-phone calls, phone-to-PC calls. You may also want to ask if a provider's service is compatible with dial-up and whether you can get voicemail.

Because of the low protocol overhead designed into both CrystalVoice LIVE and NetZeroVoice services, they're both well suited for those using Internet connections like satellite systems, in which latency and data transfer (FAP) limitations might be an issue. See Chapter 9 for more details on satellite connections.

Several WISPs, including Flying J Communications, are poised to begin offering a VoIP solution bundled with their Internet services. By tailoring a VoIP service to an existing or upgraded network, it might be possible (*might* being the operative word here) to reduce a few of the potential problems and irritations faced by those using VoIP in a truck stop parking lot.

Turning Your Laptop into a Phone

Using my laptop to make calls is just another one of those cool things that makes me feel like maybe I've entered the 21st century along with everyone else. Some of you who've grown up in the computer age might be a little less impressed, but for those among you who, like me, remember the words FOR-TRAN and COBOL or have ever wondered what happened to those little index cards with the rectangular holes punched in them, just carrying a computer around in a satchel is amazing. Using it as a phone is downright inspirational.

In order to begin making phone calls from your computer, you need a couple of items:

- ✔ **VoIP provider:** My suggestion, just to get you started, is that you choose a VoIP provider that offers free PC-to-PC calls between common users. You might also want to make calls from your PC to traditional phones, so the VoIP provider you choose should offer that option as well.

- ✔ **Phone hardware:** There are quite a number of possible choices for the hardware necessary, ranging from a simple microphone used in conjunction with your computer's built-in speakers to USB devices that allow you to connect a cordless phone to your laptop. Among your choices are the following:

  - *Headset:* I kind of like headsets. I got the one I own and use from RadioShack — it's similar to the multi-function, full-purpose Plantronics Audio 320 (shown in Figure 13-2). It consists of a pair of headphones, a swiveling microphone boom, and a pair of jacks for microphone and speaker on a long cord. It's ideal for VoIP, speech recognition, video conferencing, and voice recording.

  - *USB phone adapter:* Quite a number of manufacturers offer adapters, making it possible to connect a traditional phone to your computer. In some cases, providing the phone and VoIP providers support it, you can even get caller ID on the phone.

Figure 13-2:
I use a
headset like
this one.

Finding the hardware you need

So, where do you find the stuff you need? Well, several of the VoIP providers, like Skype and NetZeroVoice, also offer equipment and accessories to make your VoIP experience more enjoyable. Several other manufacturers offer an extensive menu of choices as well. Included among those you might want to visit are:

✔ **Actiontec:** The VoSKY product line's designed to be used with Skype service and includes a speakerphone known as the Chatterbox, the VoSKY Call Center, and the Internet Phone Wizard. They're located on the Web at www.actiontec.com.

✔ **PhoneConnector:** Offering an innovative USB-to-RJ-11 phone adapter bundled with software that recognizes your VoIP provider, PhoneConnector rings your cordless phone and can even display caller ID on compatible phones. You can find them by browsing to www.phoneconnector.com.

✔ **Plantronics:** Scroll down the menu on the left side of the page at www.plantronics.com and click the Computer link. The page that opens lists a variety of solutions and accessories. Plantronics is known for high-quality cellular headsets, and they bring that reputation to bear on products designed to enhance the VoIP experience.

✔ **AUVI Technologies:** Offering more stuff than you can shake a stick at, you can find them on the Web at www.auviusa.com.

✔ **RadioShack:** Finding headsets on their Web site can be a bit confusing, but if you just search for "computer headsets," you'll find them listed under the heading "Computers." It's easier to go to one of their bricks 'n mortar stores, but if you insist, you can find them on the Web at www.radioshack.com/home/index.jsp.

✔ **CrystalVoice LIVE:** Their online accessory store is filled with several items, like the Actiontec InternetPhoneWizard, specially designed to be used with CrystalVoice LIVE service and software. You can find them on the Web at `www.crystalvoicelive.com`.

Getting started with Skype

After you've found yourself a suitable headset or phone device, the next step in turning your laptop into a phone is to sign up with a service and download the software. I like Skype, so that's the service I use as an example as I explain how to set up service with a provider. Free Skype-to-Skype calls got me hooked, initially, but what's keeps me interested is their commitment to continuing quality. There's a lot of competition these days, and it seems like you hear about an upstart VoIP service every week. But Skype has been around for a while, still offers free and reasonably priced services, and is easy to use. In short, it's a good choice for getting your feet wet with VoIP, and you just might stick with Skype for the long haul.

Installing Skype software

Getting Skype is both free and easy:

1. **Visit the Skype Web site (`www.skype.com`), click Download on the toolbar, and then click the Windows link. On the page that appears, click the Get It Now! button.**

2. **Click Download, and save the file to disk.**

   The setup file is almost 10MB, so it takes a minute or three, even on a high-speed connection.

3. **Double-click the Skype setup icon.**

4. **If you use ZoneAlarm as your firewall, you're notified that Skype Setup is trying to access the Internet. Select Remember This Setting, and click Allow.**

   The Skype Setup Wizard opens.

5. **Select the language you want to use during the setup process, and click Next.**

   The EULA window opens.

6. **Accept the agreement, if in fact you do and want to continue, and click Next.**

   The Select Destination Location window opens.

7. **You don't want to alter the default location, so just click Next.**

   The Select Additional Tasks window opens.

8. **Select the Create a Desktop Icon check box and/or Start Skype When the Computer Starts, if you choose. Then click Next.**

   I prefer not to start Skype on boot-up, but if you're planning on receiving calls you might want Skype to start when the computer does.

   The installation status window opens followed by the final Wizard window.

9. **Click Finish.**

At this point, the software's installed, and you now need to configure your firewall to allow Skype access to the Internet. If you, like me, employ ZoneAlarm, the configuration requires little more than selecting Remember this Setting and clicking Allow when Prompted. In ZoneAlarm, you need to do this once when Skype desires access to the trusted zone and once when it requests access to the Internet. If you're using the Windows Firewall, follow these steps:

1. **Choose Start⇨Control Panel⇨Security Center⇨Windows Firewall.**

   The Windows Firewall dialog box opens.

2. **Be sure the box to the left of Don't allow exceptions is clear and click the Exceptions tab.**

3. **Skype should appear in the list under Programs and Services but, if it doesn't, click Add Program, select it from the Add a Program menu, and click OK.**

4. **Put a check mark in the box to the left of Skype and click OK.**

Configuring Skype

With the software installed and the firewall configured to allow Internet access, the Skype client is open, and you're now ready to configure Skype for use. The first step is to set up your Skype Account. Click the Don't Have A Skype Name? link and follow these steps:

1. **With the Create Account window open, enter the required information in the text entry fields, choose whether you want to be signed in when Skype starts, whether you want Skype to start when the computer starts, and indicate that you've read and agree to the terms of the EULA. Click Sign In.**

   The Help your friends find you window opens. (You might have to configure ZoneAlarm to allow Skype to act as a Server.)

2. **Enter the appropriate information in the text entry fields and click Next.**

   The Getting Started Wizard opens, the Skype client is updated with the provided information, and you see Skype Test Call under the contacts tab.

3. **In preparation to make a test call, connect your headset or phone device to the computer so you can both speak and hear.**

4. **Turn your attention to the Getting Started Wizard and click Start.**

5. **Following the instructions on page 1 of the Wizard click the green Call icon, as shown in Figure 13-3.**

   You're connected to the Skype Test recording.

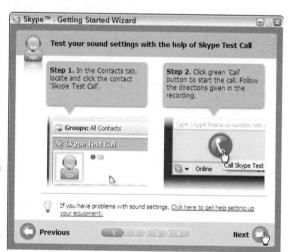

Figure 13-3: Click the green Call icon.

6. **Follow the instructions to test your call sound settings.**

7. **With the test call completed familiarize yourself with the remaining three Getting Started Wizard pages and, when you reach the final page, click Search Now.**

   (The Getting Started Wizard can be accessed at any time from the Help menu.)

   The Import Contacts wizard opens.

8. **Click Start.**

   The Checking Your Address Books page opens. You see a check box for each address book Skype finds.

9. **Select the address books you want to search and click Next.**

   Page two of the Checking your address books screen opens.

10. **Read the instructions and click Search.**

11. **Once the search is complete click Next.**

12. **Depending on the information gleaned from the search, you have the following options:**

    - If you find that you already know a few people using Skype, you're given the opportunity to Say Hello!

    - If not, or after you finish saying hello, you're then given the opportunity, by putting a check mark next to the e-mail address, to send a Join Skype e-mail invitation to selected contacts.

13. **With any hellos and invitations done, and after following all the prompts, the final page of the Import Contacts Wizard opens. Click Finish and you're nearly ready to begin making calls.**

Making and Receiving Calls

My primary purpose in setting up Skype was to make free phone calls to my wife. To achieve that goal I also had to install Skype on the computer she'd be using. With that done we were able to freely call one another whenever we were both online. That worked out pretty well and, with our recently added Actiontec Internet Phone Wizard, it's now even easier. Further, by inviting other friends and family members to install and use Skype we're all able to stay in touch for the cost of an Internet connection.

Calling another Skype user

Before you can call another Skype user you've got to find one. To do this you can follow these steps:

1. **Open the Skype client and click Add Contacts.**

   The Skype Add a Contact window opens.

2. **Type the Skype Name, full name or e-mail address of the contact you'd like to add in the text entry field, and click Search.**

   The contact information opens below the search parameters.

3. **Select the contact from the list and click Add Selected Contact.**

   The Say Hello! To... window opens, as shown in Figure 13-4.

4. **Click Options and choose whether or not to share information.**

5. **Click OK to send a greeting, closing the Say Hello! To... window, and click Close to close the Add a Contact window.**

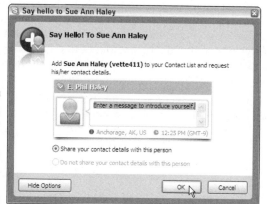

Figure 13-4: The Say Hello! window is where you begin a call.

With your new contact information added to the Skype client you can now make your call. If the party with whom you wish to speak is online the icon next to their name is green; if not, the icon's grey. If they're online all you have to do is select your contact and click the green Call icon. Their computer begins to ring and a little notification screen, indicating an incoming call, pops up. They answer the phone and you converse. Cool. By the way, to answer a call all you've got to do is click the green phone icon.

Calling anyone and everyone

Another reason for making VoIP calls is to reduce the costs incurred when calling those folks who're using traditional phone service. To do this with Skype, you must first sign up for SkypeOut and buy some credits. To do so simply visit the Web site, follow the SkypeOut link, and purchase a block of time.

Before you can purchase either SkypeOut or SkypeIn credits you need to verify your e-mail address. When you sign up for Skype they send you an e-mail asking for verification. You can choose to copy the verification code from this e-mail and enter it when prompted on the Web site or follow the verification link included in the e-mail.

With a few dollars worth of credit you're now ready to make a call. Here's how it works:

1. **You can either click the Call Phones icon or select the Dial tab to open the soft phone dial pad, shown in Figure 13-5.**

2. **Enter the number you want to call.**

   To call any number, no matter where it is, even if it's your next door neighbor, you must dial the complete number including the country code and area code. The country code for the U.S. is +1. To dial the plus sign on the Skype dial pad you need to click and hold the 0. After a second the plus sign appears near the bottom of the dial screen; you can then release the mouse button and continue selecting numbers.

Figure 13-5:
Dial the number you want to call.

3. **Click the green Call icon and the connection process begins.**

   After your call is over, the Add a Contact screen appears and you have the option to include this number with your other contacts. The number you dialed is already entered.

4. **If you choose to save the number as a contact, type a name in the text entry field and click Add Number.**

Note that the caller ID displayed on the other end of the call will be unfamiliar to the party you're calling. When I make SkypeOut calls, they're routed all over the country but most often, it seems, east coast area codes are displayed. At least, that's what most people tell me they see on their caller ID screen when I call.

Setting up Skype to receive calls

When you install Skype, you're ready to receive calls from other Skype users immediately. If, however, you want to receive calls from those using traditional phones you need to obtain a SkypeIn number. By following the SkypeIn links you eventually end up on the Get a SkypeIn Number page where you can choose the country for which you want a number. For most, choosing a number in the U.S. will be appropriate but, if, for example, you've got friends in Germany or Japan you could choose a number in one of those countries, which might make it a whole lot cheaper for them to call you.

Once you make your country selection, and I'll assume it's the U.S., you're given the opportunity to choose the area code you want to use. If you've got a lot of friends or family in a particular state, maybe one you don't live in, you can choose an area code that might enable them to call you without making a long-distance call. With your area code chosen, all you've got to do is select a number and pay for it. Skype, like some other VoIP providers, charges a quarterly or annual subscription fee instead of per-minute fees.

You can choose to have as many as ten different SkypeIn numbers, each in a different area code. Of course, you've got to pay for all of them so you might want to go easy at first.

Once you've paid the fees, and they've been credited to your account, your Skype client is updated and you can, because voicemail is free with a SkypeIn number, set up your voicemail message. A boring and sterile sounding message is loaded into your voicemail by default but you can easily personalize it by recording a new one. To accomplish this task follow these steps:

1. **Open the Skype client and click Tools⬩Voicemail.**

   The Options dialog box opens with the Call Forwarding & Voicemail page selected. Near the bottom of the window, you see three icons: a green Playback button, a red Record button, and a red Reset to Default button.

2. **Click the Playback button to hear the default message. You can choose to keep it in the event that you really like it; otherwise, click the Record button, in the center, and record a personalized message.**

3. **Click the Playback button to hear your recorded message.**

   If you hate it, you can record a different message, or if you prefer, you can reinstate the default message by selecting the Reset button.

4. **Select the Send Unanswered Calls to Skype Voicemail check box, as shown in Figure 13-6. Click Save.**

   You're now ready to receive calls, and when you're away, Skype voice-mail handles the messages. All you've got left to do is let people know how to reach you!

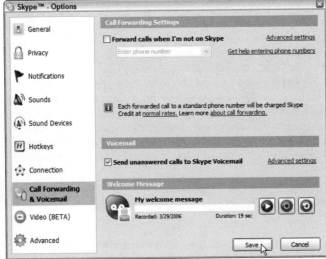

Figure 13-6: Set up your voicemail.

Chapter 14

Managing the Over-the-Road Office

*W*ith more and more husband-and-wife teams taking up the reins of a big rig, and with ever-growing numbers of families taking to the road in their RVs, it's become increasingly important to tend to all kinds of business while on the road. Fortunately, it's also become increasingly possible to do that because a wide spectrum of tasks, ranging from finding freight to paying bills, has become both easier and more efficient with hardware, software, and online solutions targeted toward the traveling public.

In this chapter, I tell you about a few tools that can help you save money and increase your income, as well as a few tools that can simplify and streamline your paperwork and record-keeping duties. For example, I tell you about navigational tools that can help you reduce both stress and expenses, and I also tell you how you can put your paperwork on your computer. In addition, I tell you about some tools that can help you keep track of where your money goes and one that can help you keep it from going places it shouldn't.

Setting Up Your Office

The age-old adage, "The job's not finished 'til the paperwork's done," still holds true. Whether you want to admit it, you do manage a mobile office. Each and every day, no matter whether you're trying to build a business, or like me, you're handling home finances and road-related chores, you engage in a variety of office-related duties. To help make those jobs easier, a wide variety of software and hardware tools has been developed. A few areas in which these tools of technology can assist you in managing the over-the-road office include:

- ✔ **Navigation:** When you live on the road, navigating is part of your day-to-day business. Adding GPS (global positioning system) to your toolbox can help minimize unnecessary miles, help you plan stops to get the most out of your road time, and generally reduce stress when you're trying to find your way.

- ✔ **Finance:** You can handle everything from banking to budgeting to taxes safely, securely, and quickly from the comfort of your rolling home. Other tools, like online load matching services, help you increase both income and efficiency.

- ✔ **Occupation:** If you're driving a truck, you've got state and federally mandated duties to perform, and in addition, with the cost of everything from diesel to doughnuts on the rise, it makes sense to use any tool available to stretch your dollar and avoid unnecessary expenditures. (I'm pretty sure doughnuts fall into that "unnecessary expenditures" category, but I'm not aware of any tool that'll help you avoid them.)

- ✔ **Organization:** The pursuit and administration of business almost always results in the generation of records and receipts. Managing this outpouring of paper is a job well suited to available software tools.

In addition to your tools, you need space. There can be no doubt; from condo to cab-over, Class A to camper, no matter the rig, no matter its configuration, if you're living on the road, space is at a premium. It's not generally necessary, however, to dedicate a specific area of your vehicle to office space. Often having been designed with an altogether different purpose in mind, mobile office space almost always does double duty. I use a folding laptop desk while sitting in the bunk, and you might have another entirely workable workspace solution.

Aside from a work area, though, there are a couple other reasons to give more than just a passing thought to the space you have available for office-related tasks:

- ✔ **Storage:** Depending on your ability — or inability, as the case might be — to throw things away, documents, records, and receipts have a tendency to fill all the available space. In an effort to tame the storage shrew, it can help to classify the types of items to be stored as well as the types of storage available. For example:

  - • *Indoor:* Along with documents or records that you need to update or access on a regular basis, store any electronic equipment indoors where the temperature's likely to be controlled.

  - • *Outdoor:* If you've got documents, records, or receipts that you just don't need to see for a while and the outdoor storage is weather-proof, there's no reason to use up your limited indoor space.

- *Digital:* Don't forget the option of digital storage. You can scan documents into memory, you can defer printing by storing documents in digital format, and you can sometimes even rely on remote digital storage.

✔ **Accessibility:** The advantage of a dedicated workspace is that all the tools are at hand and readily accessible. Even if you don't intend to dedicate a particular area as a workspace, you should make every effort to keep the tools and documents you most often use close by and easy to reach.

Navigating by Satellite

A few years ago, I was tooling along the highway in the company of a technically savvy trucker. We were both on our way to the same remote delivery destination, and neither of us was familiar with the area. The consignee had no phone onsite, so calling for directions was out of the question. However, the driver I was traveling with had added both GPS capability and mapping software to his computer. With his laptop voicing directions, we were able to navigate our way to the consignee's yard without a single misstep. On that day, I became a believer in the ability of GPS coupled with mapping software to reduce the level of both my stress and expense.

In the sections that follow, you find the ways in which you can add GPS to your office. I think you'll appreciate the extra fuel, the better use of time, and the reduced stress a GPS system can bring.

Ready-to-use GPS devices

If all the previously mentioned reasons or others of your own have convinced you that it's time to start using GPS navigation, you've got quite a wide range of choices available to you. Among the ready-to-use systems are the following:

✔ **Dedicated devices:** With one primary purpose, which is to provide accurate voice and visual guidance, these devices are fast becoming the choice of many. In general, dedicated GPS navigation devices provide the greatest available feature set, but prices, which are an indication of included features, can vary from somewhere around $400 to well over $2,000. Examples of these devices include the following:

- *TomTom GO 700:* Employing easily updatable TeleAtlas maps the GO 700 offers door-to-door, turn-by-turn navigation in a very easy to use, feature rich, package. More information about this and other TomTom navigation products is available at www.tomtom.com.

- *Garmin StreetPilot 2650:* Even if you're in an urban canyon, surrounded by satellite-blocking buildings, the SP 2650, using dead-reckoning, continues to provide accurate guidance. By adding the optional GTM 10 FM TMC receiver, you can also get real-time traffic updates. Garmin offers an extensive line of products with various feature packages at www.garmin.com.

- *Magellan RoadMate 760:* Giving you voice prompts that include both the distance to and the name of the upcoming street onto which you're about to turn is just one of many features included on the RM 760. Along with a large selection of GPS navigation products it's available at www.magellangps.com/en.

- *Lowrance iWay 350C:* Easily updatable maps combined with a choice of one 3D display option and two 2D display options are just a couple of features available with the iWay 350. Lowrance offers the iWay 350 and iWay 500 GPS mapping devices at www.lowrance.com.

✔ **Combination devices:** A few manufacturers are beginning to offer GPS navigational devices that also include a wide range of multimedia features. These devices often offer the option of integrating real-time traffic updates with alternate routing capability as well. Included among this group are the following:

- *Pioneer AVIC-N2:* Combining a blind-spot camera with a DVD player and an AM-FM/XM Satellite radio receiver, this unit can also interface with XM NavTraffic to help drivers avoid slowed and congested traffic. XM NavTraffic is available as a standalone subscription for $9.99 per month or in conjunction with a standard XM Radio subscription for an additional $3.99 per month. The AVIC-N2 is available at www.pioneerelectronics.com.

- *Garmin StreetPilot 7500:* Traffic, weather, and entertainment are all rolled into a single unit that also offers state-of-the-art GPS navigation. As with other XM NavTraffic devices, optional equipment and a subscription are required. You can get more information on this device from the Garmin Web site at www.garmin.com.

✔ **Handheld devices:** Audible voice prompting is one of the features I feel is essential to a GPS navigational device appropriate for use in an over-the-road environment. Many handheld devices seem to lack this feature, but several higher-cost PDAs combined with built-in navigation features often include voice prompts. A couple you might consider are:

- *Garmin iQue M4:* This handheld combines a fully functional PDA with a well-appointed GPS navigational device that provides turn-by-turn, voice-prompted directions. It's available at www.garmin.com.

- *Magellan Meridian:* The GPS Traveler Value Pack includes the Magellan Meridian Color GPS receiver and adds turn-by-turn guidance, audio prompts, and clear visual indicators to a well-reviewed handheld navigation device. Available from Magellan at www.magellangps.com/en.

Finding your way by phone

With GPS-based location technology now required to be incorporated in newer cellphones, several companies, including InfoSpace and MapQuest, are trying to take advantage of the capability by providing subscription services that offer, among other things, low-cost navigation information. InfoSpace Find It! is geared toward making its online directory accessible to cellphone users while enhancing current local information by providing driving directions to nearby attractions. MapQuest Navigator, on the other hand, seeks, according to their Web site, "to turn your phone into a full voice-guided, turn-by-turn, GPS navigation system." Other similar services, offering both point-to-point navigation and information relevant to a specific location pin-pointed by GPS, are sure to follow.

Easily upgradeable software is one of the most important features to look for when searching for any GPS navigation solution. New roads are built every year, and road construction, even though it never seems like it, does come to an end. Of course, when one project ends, another one usually begins, so as you can see, having the ability to update your software to include new addresses and construction information on a regular basis is a real benefit.

Adapting a laptop or PDA for GPS

Very few laptops — in fact I know of only one — and just a handful of PDAs come equipped with GPS capability. Fortunately, though, it's very easy and relatively inexpensive to add a GPS receiver to either device. For example, some GPS navigational systems cost well in excess of $2,000, but you can adapt a laptop or PDA for less than $200. And while one of the primary reasons to take this route is, undoubtedly, that of economics, you can, in some cases, end up with a navigational device that has an equal or better feature set than many standalone models.

A few of the GPS receivers and corresponding or bundled mapping software available include the following:

✔ **TomTom Navigator 5:** By employing a Bluetooth GPS receiver and Navigator 5 mapping software, this kit can turn your Bluetooth-enabled PDA into an effective and easy-to-use GPS device. In addition to its normal capabilities, it provides door-to-door, turn-by-turn, voice-prompted navigation. Available from TomTom at www.tomtom.com.

✔ **DeLorme:** Offering GPS solutions for a variety of applications, two of the best known GPS receiver and software bundles appropriate for over-the-road use are the following:

- *Earthmate GPS LT-20:* DeLorme Street Atlas mapping software is combined with this USB-powered GPS receiver that transforms your laptop into a navigational device that both gives and accepts voice prompts. Available from DeLorme at `www.delorme.com/earthmatelt20/default.asp`.

- *Earthmate Blue Logger GPS receiver:* This Bluetooth receiver can be used with DeLorme Street Atlas software, turning either your laptop or PDA into an efficient and effective GPS navigation system. Available from DeLorme at `www.delorme.com/bluelogger/default.asp`.

✔ **Garmin GPS 18:** The Garmin 18 GPS receiver, bundled with nRoute and City Select software, gives you turn-by-turn, voice-prompt directions that guide you safely to your destination. It's available from Garmin at `www.garmin.com`.

✔ **Microsoft Streets & Trips with GPS locator:** Free road construction updating is just one feature that makes this product worthy of a serious look. The package is available for both laptops and Pocket PCs, and if you've already got a GPS receiver, you can choose to purchase the mapping software by itself. You can get more information by visiting `www.microsoft.com/streets/default.mspx`.

✔ **ALK Technologies:** As developers of the popular PC*MILER mapping software used by many trucking and related transportation companies, ALK Technologies is uniquely positioned to provide GPS navigation solutions with trucking-specific features such as scale and truck stop locations. Two of their products geared toward truckers are:

- *CoPilot Truck/Laptop 4:* Routing options let you choose between the shortest or most practical. In addition, you can choose to avoid tolls or find routes compatible with HazMat shipments. The mapping software is available alone, in case you already have a GPS receiver, or bundled with a Bluetooth-connected or USB-powered GPS device.

- *CoPilot Truck/Mobile:* If you've got a Bluetooth-enabled Smartphone running Windows Mobile, you can add GPS navigational capability to it. Like the laptop software, it includes features important to truckers.

ALK Technologies also offers a variety of other navigational products that, although they might lack the trucking-specific information, might meet your needs if you'd like to turn your laptop or PDA into a GPS navigation tool. You can find them at `www.alk.com`.

Hardly any laptop screens and only a few PDA screens are easy to see in bright sunlight. If you're making use of one of these devices for navigation, voice prompts are a must, and I highly recommend the ability to accept voice commands.

Mounting your device for easy access

If you buy a standalone device designed specifically for GPS navigation, it's a good bet that it'll either come with some sort of mounting device or one will be available for purchase separately. As a matter of fact, a few require professional installation because the *dead-reckoning features,* which are used when satellites are blocked by buildings or mountains, might, in some cases, require a tie-in with the vehicle's speedometer and backup lights. If, however, you choose to adapt your laptop or PDA for use as a GPS navigator, you also want it securely mounted in your vehicle.

Looking for a laptop stand

Several laptop mounting solutions are available for those traveling in cars and SUVs, but far fewer are designed for use in a truck or RV. Key features that should be high on your list when you begin shopping for a laptop mounting system include

- **Shock resistance:** You could mount a laptop in your truck or RV by duct-taping it to the dash, but because vibration is the enemy of your hard disk drive — and because it'd look really tacky — I don't advise you to do so. Look for a mounting system that offers some method of absorbing shock.

- **Display support:** Because your display is fragile, and because it'll be open with the vehicle in motion while doing navigational duties, you want some method of securing the laptop lid.

- **No-drill installation:** If you're installing a mount in a company truck or you just don't want to drill holes in the floorboard, the no-drill installation option is well worth shopping for.

With these qualifying features in mind, you can begin your search for a suitable mounting system. A few of those available that should meet your requirements include the following:

- **RAM Mount:** They manufacture a wide variety of mounting systems, and included in their list of offerings are the RAM-VB-140-SW1 and the RAM-VB-151-SW1. Both of these mounts are designed to be installed without drilling, but if neither of these is compatible with your situation, they also offer a couple of universal vehicle mounts that, although they require minor drilling, might fill the bill. You can find them on the Web at `www.ram-mount.com`.

✔ **Jotto Desk:** If you've ever had the opportunity — or misfortune, as the case might be — to sit inside a police car, you might've seen a Jotto Desk laptop mount. And, yes, I've seen a few. But they also manufacture some sturdy systems designed for use by truckers and RVers. You can find out more by visiting www.jottodesk.us.

✔ **Trucker's Workstation:** Distributed by CyberTrucker.net (I love that name) this unit was designed and developed by a trucker, for truckers. It features dual cooling fans to help extend the life of your laptop as well as a sturdy backrest for your laptop lid. You can easily find them on the Web at www.cybertrucker.net.

✔ **AirDesk:** You won't be able to use this mounting system if you're passenger seat is usually occupied but, if not, it's worth a look by browsing to www.airdesks.com/cardesk.asp.

By locking your laptop to a securely installed laptop stand, you can reduce the likelihood that your laptop will be stolen if your vehicle is broken into. In Chapter 10, I mention a few laptop lock manufacturers. You might want to pay special attention to the LapLocker because it includes a feature that makes it possible to secure your laptop lid in the open position.

Picking a PDA mount

Because most PDAs incorporate solid-state technology in place of hard drives, vibration might be less of a factor when you begin searching for the perfect PDA mounting device; but duct tape isn't the answer here, either. When you begin your search, you find a variety of mounting devices available that fall, generally, into the following three categories:

✔ **Dash mounts:** Available in both permanent and semipermanent configurations, these mounting devices sometimes use Velcro or bolts to secure them to the dash.

✔ **Windshield mounts:** Attaching to the windshield through the use of suction cups, these types of mounts are well suited to travelers who might not want a more-permanent mounting device. Sometimes short mounting arms, however, can be a drawback when using this type of mount in a truck or RV.

✔ **Vent mounts:** Using a combination of clips and clutches, these mounts don't usually require any kind of permanent installation, making them a good choice for anyone desiring a dash mount but not wanting to risk damaging the dash in any way.

All three categories of PDA mounts can usually be found in both powered and unpowered configurations.

After you've decided the type of mount that most appeals to you or comes closest to meeting your requirements, you can begin shopping. When you do, you might include the following manufacturers in your search:

- ✔ **RAM Mount:** Offering a wide variety of mounts covering every category — including mounts specially designed for both handheld and dedicated GPS navigational devices — you can find them on the Web at www. ram-mount.com.

- ✔ **Arkon Resources:** They bill themselves as "The Mobile Mounting Specialists," and the description seems to be right on target. Whether you want to mount a PDA, GPS navigational device, or a cellphone in your vehicle, you should visit their Web site at www.arkon.com.

- ✔ **Bracketron:** Manufacturing the versatile, one size fits all, FreeWay PDA Mount, Bracketron can be found by pointing your browser toward www. bracketron.com.

Using Online Load Matching Services

In 1981, I briefly joined the ranks of owner-operators and got my first taste of finding freight while sitting in a truck stop far from home. I booked my first load by browsing through the broker's offices that were once located on the back lot of the Iowa 80 Truck Stop in Walcott, IA. Boy, has that place changed over the years! I spent the better part of that day wandering from office to office, and while the walk was good for me, my time wasn't exactly being used efficiently. Besides that, every time I left one office for another I ran the risk that I'd miss out on the perfect load.

I finally found a decent westbound load that day, but you could now, simply by browsing an Internet load board, accomplish in seconds what once took me hours. Not only that, but by posting your truck on one of these boards and taking advantage of alarms or alerts, you can take care of other business while waiting to be notified of one or more loads that meet your criteria.

Whenever you contract transportation with a broker or shipper for the first time, you need to provide pertinent information such as Motor Carrier number and proof of insurance, often naming the broker or trucking company as a certificate holder. Some allow you to fax or e-mail scanned documents, while others require that a third party, like your insurance broker or the carrier you're leased to, fax certificates or documents to them.

Comparing the contenders

With literally thousands of truck and freight brokerage companies dotting the landscape, and seemingly every trucking company in America employing at least one person engaged in brokering excess freight, it's not surprising that online load matching services have become increasingly popular. When you begin browsing the Web in search of freight, you find among those competing for your subscription dollar the following contenders:

- ✔ **The Internet Truckstop:** Their standard service, providing you meet certain qualifying criteria, is $25 per month and allows for unlimited searching and posting of trucks and loads. Other services, such as credit reports, are available at extra cost. If you decide to buy all the bells and whistles, this can be the most expensive of the load boards, but it's also got bells and whistles not offered anywhere else. You can find them on the Net at www.truckstop.com.

- ✔ **TruckersEdge:** Powered by DAT, one of many TransCore companies, the TruckersEdge service is tailored to owner-operators and small fleet owners. Their Owner Operator package is priced at $19.95 per month and offers a wide range of features beyond simple searches, including credit scores and accurate mileage and routing. Their Web address is www.truckersedge.net.

- ✔ **123Loadboard.com:** With a standard plan priced at $20 per month and a premium package priced at $30 per month, one of the primary reasons to take a look at 123Loadboard is their ten-day free trial. You can find them at www.123loadboard.com.

- ✔ **Getloaded.com:** Although all the load matching service Web sites are easy to navigate, especially after you've used them a few times, the Getloaded.com site is, possibly, the most user-friendly of them all. Signing up costs you $35 per month, but you can test-drive the service free for 30 days. They're located at www.getloaded.com.

Considering alternatives

I'm sure anybody who's ever spent more than a day driving a truck has heard of the C.H. Robinson company. For a long time, as a matter of fact, I couldn't figure out why one company I drove for wasted money paying the salary of our inbound dispatcher because all he ever did was tell me to call the nearby office of C.H. Robinson. Nevertheless, they did a pretty good job of getting us back home, and now, through their CHRWtrucks Web site, they offer a load matching service similar to those listed in the previous section. Of course, all the freight listed is brokered exclusively by C.H. Robinson.

To use the CHRWtrucks load matching boards, you must first register, and before you can register you need a CHR ID number, which is more informally known as a *T number.* You also need to provide your MC or ICC number, proof of insurance naming C.H. Robinson as a certificate holder, and a completed W-9 form. To get more information about using the CHRWtrucks Web site and load matching service — which, by the way, is free of charge — you can visit them at www.chrwtrucks.com.

Another interesting alternative, uShip, is one that might just catch on and change the way some freight, especially household goods, is moved in the information age. Following in the footsteps of eBay, those wishing to move a wide range of items from point A to point B put their shipping needs up for auction, and carriers bid for the business. As a matter of fact, quite a number of the items available for shipment have been won in an eBay auction in which the winner must arrange shipping.

One thing I've noticed is that a few of those putting shipments up for bid don't have much of a clue regarding current shipping costs or requirements. For example, one recent load(s) up for bid weighed more than 75,000 pounds, needed to be moved more than 2,500 miles, and the shipper was hoping to get it done for around $3,000. Still, it's an interesting concept and at least worth a look, especially if you find yourself with a little extra room on your trailer. You can find them on the Web at www.uship.com.

Trucking Simplified with Software

I entered the transportation industry on the cusp of the computer age. Paper and pencil, although not always used well, was used widely, and I carried a little ninety-nine cent notebook around with me to keep track of everything from phone numbers to daily expenses. The notebook I now carry cost in excess of $1,200, has a keyboard in place of a pencil, and can carry more information than can be written in ten-thousand notebooks. Especially the way I write. In addition, with the proper software installed, I can use it in ways I never dreamed possible in those days of yore.

Keeping your logbook on your laptop

Logbooks have never been my friend, and they're still not. Rather than get into a discussion that no one can win concerning the insight or ignorance, depending on your viewpoint, of the Political Action Committees that have left us with our current Hours of Service rules and regulations, I point you in the direction of a couple of software applications that can help to make the chore of maintaining a logbook a little bit easier. Surprisingly, these programs can also help pull some valuable information together that's usable in other areas.

REMEMBER

It's now legal in the U.S. and most of Canada to keep your logbook on your computer, providing that, first, you have a functioning printer capable of printing the current day's log if requested to do so, and second, you have the previous seven days' log pages printed out, signed, and available for inspection.

Among those offering logbook program applications are the following:

✔ **Drivers Daily Log (DDL):** Having been around since 1997, it's the granddaddy of logbook programs. This application has so many features and is so easy to use that I can't imagine trucking without it. You can download the Full program and try it free for 60 days. If you don't think you need all the bells and whistles, you can, when you buy the license, opt for the Lite version. DDL can be used "on the fly" between the U.S. and Canada as well. You can find them on the Web at www.driversdailylog.com.

As you can see in Figure 14-1 in my example log page from a fictitious trip driving a fictitious truck, this program tracks all sorts of information, including your duty status, miles, vehicle data, and hours. You also have the option to include a wide range of other pertinent data such as fuel, manifest, or trip information. If you do a good job of maintaining these records, you can, at the end of the month or quarter, generate a multitude of reports that provide you with a lot of information usable for a variety of purposes.

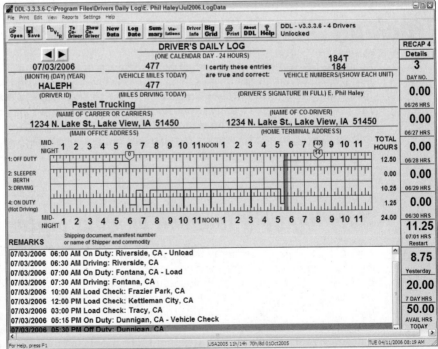

Figure 14-1:
DDL is incredibly handy for a trucker's mobile office.

✔ **Log Calculator:** Available from and developed by DieselBoss, the Log Calculator program requires that Microsoft Excel also be installed on your computer. The nice thing, though, providing that Excel is installed, is that it works on a PDA as well as on a laptop. The Log Calculator program is pretty basic and can't be used in Canada, but you can beef it up a bit by opting for their TruckerTracker program that includes some basic book-keeping features. More information's available at `www.dieselboss.com`.

Whether you decide to print pages on a daily basis, you might still find it necessary to carry a logbook maintained by hand. That's because not every company employs compatible log-auditing methods, so your company might not accept DDL-generated log pages. I'd suggest you download the trial copy, print out a few pages, and bring them to your safety department for approval. Several companies have found the DDL Classic log pages compatible with their programs, and further, DDL has developed several Print Modules that alter the Classic page in ways that make it compatible with various companies' log-auditing programs.

Keeping track of expenses

Failing to acknowledge expenses doesn't, unfortunately, make them go away. Quite the contrary. In fact, the more you know about where your money goes and why it goes there, the better chance you have of reducing over-the-road expenses. To that end, several software programs have been developed with the goal of helping truckers with their bookkeeping and accounting chores.

Bookkeeping is something you do so that you know where your money went, say, for tax purposes. *Accounting,* on the other hand, is the act of organizing and analyzing those records in order to make future spending and investment decisions like, for example, calculating the amount of money to be set aside out of each settlement to buy tires, pay for an upcoming overhaul, or invest in new equipment. Obviously, everyone (company drivers and owner-operators alike) needs to keep expense records. But more complex, and more expensive, accounting software is likely required only by owner-operators or those oper-ating small fleets.

Among those programs currently available, you might want to take a look at the following:

✔ **Truckers Helper:** Offers several software programs ranging from one tai-lored to the needs of a company driver to one suitable for use in a fleet operation. The Drivers Version and Owner Operator Version also include a log maintenance program that is easy to use and effective. They offer a 31-day free demo program, and I suggest that if this program strikes your fancy, you accept the demo offer.

You can either download the program, or if you prefer, opt for a two-CD package that includes the program and tutorials. This program can be relatively complex, so I strongly suggest taking advantage of the tutorials. You can get more information from their Web site at www. truckershelper.com.

✔ **HammerLane:** The applications they offer are probably more than any company driver could make use of, but those designed with the owner-operator, leased fleet, and full fleet in mind are worth a look. Their programs are designed to be *single-entry,* meaning that when you enter data in one area, it's automatically copied to all the other related records or reports. You can find them at www.hammerlane.com.

✔ **Easy Trucking Software:** Okay, trucking's not easy and no software program will alter that fact, but the two applications developed by Omni Communications are comprehensive, easy to use, and should help you get a handle on your expenses. The Profit Per Mile program module probably includes more features than a company driver needs, but most will be useful. Owner-operators can couple Profit Per Mile with Fuel Manager for a complete and powerful package. More information's available by visiting www.easytruckingsoftware.com.

Managing the Home Front

Before advances in computing and technology enabled me to stay well-connected while I was on the road, I found it difficult, if not impossible, to get my mail in a timely fashion and often found myself sending off payments for utilities, credit cards, and other obligations without always knowing for sure how much was due. Now, that's not such a bad thing because even when I didn't quite send enough, I rarely got charged a late fee. Other bad things, however, can and do happen. For example, I once dropped an envelope containing a utility payment into a mailbox near Kingman, Arizona, and went merrily along my way thinking all was well. It wasn't.

I'd forgotten to put a stamp on that bill and realized the problem only after I got home and had to light a candle to see. Fortunately, nothing was frozen solid and the local Light & Power Company was kind enough to not charge a reconnect fee.

Since I began taking care of household finances online, I no longer worry about making payments on time, and in most cases, I usually know exactly how much I owe. Among the ways personal finances can be tailored to an over-the-road lifestyle include:

✔ **Direct deposit:** Without a doubt, this is the foundation of over-the-road finance. If you've ever come home to a pile of paychecks or had to rely on others to make deposits for you, then you know the value of getting the check deposited automatically.

✔ **Online banking:** It's like having your local bank open for business 24-hours a day, seven days a week. Most banks offer full access to account information, and some include features such as transfers between accounts and bill payment services.

✔ **Online payments:** Whether you use an online bill-paying service offered by your bank or make use of the online payment options offered by your credit card company, home and auto loan providers, or utility companies, making payments online is one sure way to know your payments are always on time. Even though some services charge a monthly fee, it's probably less than it costs to buy stamps and checks.

✔ **Online tax preparation:** For a couple of years now, I've prepared and filed my taxes online. By keeping books on my laptop — meaning that I've got all I need close at hand — it takes me no more than a few hours to accomplish what previously took as much as a week at home. Not only that, but I can also do it on the road at my convenience.

You can find several services that can help you file your taxes online. Among your options are TurboTax (`www.turbotax.com`), H&R Block's TaxCut (`http://taxcut.com`), E-File Online (`www.e-fileonline.com`), TaxAct (`www.taxact.com`), and eSmart Tax (`www.esmarttax.com`).

✔ **Budgeting software:** I believe in budgeting; it helps me get a handle on my money and hang on to it. Several programs, such as Intuit's Quicken or Microsoft Money, can help you keep and track your budget on the road. The budgeting program that works for me is called Mvelopes. When I was growing up, lots of folks divided cash into envelopes: one for food, one for utilities, one for clothing, and so on. This system worked especially well for those whose pay varied from week to week, and because Mvelopes is based on this system, I think that's why it works so well for me. The Mvelopes budgeting system divides funds into the digital envelopes and is connected via the Internet to your banking and credit card institutions. Find out more at `www.mvelopes.com`. (And you can find the version I use by visiting Crown Financial Ministries at `www.crown.org`.)

✔ **Online investment management:** Whether you've got an IRA, a 401k, or individual stocks and bonds, almost every brokerage house offers full online account access. You can move money between funds, make trades, or take advantage of a host of other management features.

If you're concerned about conducting business that's related to finances online — especially while accessing the Internet at a public hotspot — you might want to use a VPN, which I cover in Chapter 10, or conduct transactions remotely through your home computer, which I explain in Chapter 12.

Printing Records

It's a fact of life. Even though we can digitize more information than has ever before been possible, it's still necessary to transfer some of that digital data to a piece of paper you can hold in your hand. That means, somewhere along the line, you need access to a printer. Because you can't rely on truck stops, motels, or RV parks to have a compatible printer available for your use, you're going to need to make other arrangements.

When you're attempting to make a decision regarding a method of meeting your printing needs, you find you've got roughly three options:

- ✔ **Mobile printing:** Fortunately, a few manufacturers have begun to build a variety of printers suitable for use in a mobile environment. Generally weighing in at less than 5 pounds and taking up less than one square foot of space, these printers are entirely suitable for over-the-road use.

- ✔ **Deferred printing:** You can choose to print documents at a later date by storing them in a file or folder on your hard drive or on a removable storage device, like a USB flash drive.

- ✔ **Remote printing:** By accessing your home computer remotely, it's entirely possible to print things at home while you're on the road. You can also perform tasks likely to produce documents in need of printing on the host PC and print from that computer.

You can find details about choosing a travel printer or deferring printing in the following sections. For details about remote printing, flip to Chapter 12.

Choosing a travel printer

If you must print while you're on the road — for example, if you need to print invoices or print logbook pages that you maintain on your computer — traveling with a printer might be your best or only choice. If that's the case, you need a printer that's small, sturdy, and reliable. When you begin shopping, you might want to consider looking for a printer that includes the following features:

- ✔ **Wireless connectivity:** Printing without wires is as handy as accessing the Internet wire-free. Some mobile printers offer optional 802.11b or 802.11g capability, while others use Bluetooth wireless technology. (For a refresher on wireless standards, see Chapter 2.)

- ✔ **Full-size paper:** Be aware that micro-printers often use A7 paper, which measures about 4 x 3 inches. That won't cut it for printing log pages. Make sure the printer you choose is capable of printing on 8½-x-11-inch paper.

- ✔ **Rechargeable battery:** While not absolutely necessary, it's nice to know you can print on battery power if you absolutely have to.

- ✔ **A/C adapter:** Chances are good you've got an inverter (to change DC power into AC power), but again, just in case you want to power the printer or recharge the battery using the cigarette lighter/power port, one of these cords can come in handy.

To help you start your search, here are a couple of printers currently available that include these features:

- **HP Deskjet 460wbt:** Featuring wireless Bluetooth connectivity, you can print to the 460wbt at a distance of up to 30 feet from your Bluetooth-capable computer. This printer also includes fold-up feeder and out-feed doors capable of handling 50 sheets at a time. You can get more information from the HP Web site at www.hp.com.

- **Canon Pixma iP90:** Designed primarily as a mobile photo printer (you can print photos directly from your camera, PDA, or cellphone), this mobile printer does a great job on documents as well. Bluetooth capabilities, as well as a rechargeable battery, are optional. If you visit www.usa.canon.com you can get more information.

If you often need to fax documents, as well as print them, consider using a scanner. By creating a scan, you can email the document as an attachement instead of spending money on fax fees and waiting in the line. (If you work with lots of documents that require signatures, make sure the scan is acceptable first.) A few mobile scanning devices, like the Strobe XP 300 or the One Touch 7300 (both manufactured by Visioneer) won't take up much room and will likely meet your needs. You can find out more about the Visioneer line of scanners by visiting www.visioneer.com.

Saving documents for future printing

Okay, so printing out your log pages isn't a big deal to you, and besides that, you don't really want to put a printer in your truck or RV. I can relate to that. But you still find that, on occasion, you want or need to print a receipt, record, or some other document. As long as you don't need to print it this very second, no matter whether it's a text document or Web page, you can choose to print it at a later date — when you get home or back to the office, most likely.

There are a couple of ways to do this but only one that I really recommend. For example, if you want to print a Web page, you can, even without a printer currently connected to your computer, just click the Print button on your browser and the page is put into the print queue. In theory, when you get access to a printer, you can bring up the queue and print everything it contains. The reality (at least in my experience) is that you sometimes just get an error message, and at that point, you're out of luck.

Under certain circumstances and with the proper supporting software, you can Print to File, but I'm not a fan of this method either. So, now that I've told you only what I'm against, you probably think I'm running for political office. Well, just to prove I have no political aspirations, I'll tell you that my preferred method of deferring a print job is to save the document or Web page to a file or folder.

I usually save Web pages indicating the receipt of my money in exchange for an item that I just can't live another minute without. I save these pages, and other documents, in a folder I've named Deferred Printing. To accomplish this easy task, all you need do is follow these simple steps:

1. **With the desired Web page open in the browser window of your choice, click File⇨Save as (in Internet Explorer) or File⇨Save Page As (in Firefox).**

   The Save Webpage (IE) or the Save As (Firefox) window opens.

2. **Select the proper folder from the Save In drop-down list.**

3. **Enter appropriate information in the File Name text field.**

4. **Click Save.**

When it comes time to print the file, again, there are a couple of ways to accomplish the task. I prefer to open the saved Web page by right-clicking the file, choosing Open With, and then choosing my Web browser from the list of programs that appears. With the file open, I then either choose File⇨Print or click the Print icon on the browser. By doing this, the page displays and prints as it would if you printed directly from the browser when the page first displayed.

I like to store files — whether they're documents or Web pages — that I'm going to print at a later time on removable storage rather than on my laptop. I talk about using separate storage for sensitive information in Chapter 10.

Part VI
Entertaining Electronics

The 5th Wave   By Rich Tennant

"Of course your current cell phone takes pictures, functions as a walkie talkie, and browses the Internet. But does it shoot silly string?"

In this part . . .

I focus on the central theme of my life: entertainment. Do I examine every possible form of electronic fun and games? Nope. It might take a book or two to do that; but I do cover a few of the things that make me and the sock puppets smile when it's time to put up our feet and kick back for a bit. In Chapter 15 you discover how Satellite Radio can enhance both your working and leisure time, and I help you decide which of the services and what equipment you might want to include in your bag of toys. And, in Chapter 16, you find out about ways you can use your computer and an Internet connection to bring music, movies, and books into your over-the-road abode. Downloading music and movies has gotten a lot of bad press in the past, but you can find out how to do so safely. I point out some fun alternatives, too.

Chapter 15

Extra-Terrestrial Radio

*F*or years, I, like you, have traveled the highways and byways of this great land listening to the radio. In fact, I've often told people, when asked what I did for a living, that I got paid to do so. I know a lot of folks prefer to listen to their own digitally or otherwise recorded music collection but, along with my Moldy Oldies, I've always liked to hear human voices read the news, perform silly skits in local commercials, and, of course, expel huge amounts of hot air on talk-radio stations. Radio helps me feel connected to the community of humanity.

Even so, I often lamented the lack of continuity, never knowing from one day to another whether I'd be able to hear a particular show or sporting event, and I can't possibly count the number of times a radio station I really enjoyed faded into the ether, forcing me to click seek or scan buttons in a frustrating attempt to find an acceptable replacement. When I began to see billboards advertising satellite radio, especially in areas where radio signals were as rare as rain, I knew this was something I had to explore.

In this chapter, I help you decide, first, whether you can justify the expense of satellite radio and, once you do, which satellite radio service offers the programming and features most attractive to you. Also, to help you decide which type and style radio might best meet your needs, I point out a few attributes of the many equipment choices you face. When you've made your choice, I help you configure your system. Lastly, I give you a bit of information regarding system and subscription activation.

Surveying the Satellite Radio Scene

The first thing you may notice when you begin to investigate satellite radio is that the list of service providers for those who live on the road is pretty short — even if you include Canada. There are, currently and exactly, two: XM and Sirius Satellite Radio.

Even though the list is short, don't think for a minute that making a choice between the two will be easy. Both offer plenty of attractive programming choices, both are competitively priced, and both are supported by multiple equipment manufacturers.

Making any comparison between Sirius and XM Satellite Radio is kind of like trying to compare Galas and Granny Smiths. They're both apples, but the one you're going to like best is a matter of taste and circumstance. So in the sections that follow, I first cover what both options have to offer and then discuss the ways in which their content is different. By the time you're done, I hope you have a good idea whether satellite radio is a good choice for you, and if so, which provider you'd like to choose.

What does satellite radio have to offer?

When I was a kid, I lived with my family in a small Oregon town that had exactly one television station. Because we were surrounded by signal-blocking mountains, cable was our only hope of getting a variety of choices. When cable finally came to town, I was stunned and surprised to hear people whine and complain about the cost. Apparently they felt that their constitutionally protected right to watch free TV was being infringed upon. Unfortunately for me, my dad led the complainers' choir.

Eventually though, when he could no longer stand the sound of *my* whining and complaining, my dad agreed to install cable and, after discovering a few features and entertainment options we never knew existed, he even bought a fancy TV with one of those newfangled, high-frequency remote controls. Since that time, I've rarely been without a cable TV subscription and barely blink when I write the check.

I guess I look at paying for radio pretty much the same way. When I began comparing satellite radio with free radio, I looked beyond the cost, trying to remember that one often gets what one pays for. Among the features and entertainment options that you won't find on free radio are the following:

✔ **Quality:** Digital satellite signals mean you get near-CD-quality sound without fade or static from sea to shining sea.

✔ **Variety:** I've heard the same songs so often, especially when listening to oldies stations, that I've almost forgotten anything else was ever recorded. With both XM and Sirius offering somewhere around 70 music channels along with several sports, news, talk, and specialty channels, you need never again be bored.

✔ **Unique content:** Where else can you hear All Elvis, All the Time? Or classic rock and country songs you haven't heard since high school? Not to mention personalities heard exclusively on satellite, channels devoted to truckers, and old-time radio dramas.

✔ **Ad-free:** For now, the only advertisements on the music channels are for other channels. Some find these service announcements annoying, but if a special event's coming up on a channel you might not otherwise listen to, how else are you supposed to know about it? Or what if a brand new channel's offered? Again; no way to know unless your channels announce it!

✔ **Graphic display:** If you've ever been frustrated by terrestrial DJs playing song after song without so much as a mention of titles or artists, you'll love graphic displays that give you not only title and artist info but also other interesting stuff like upcoming concert dates, sports scores, or stock tickers.

✔ **Continuity:** I happen to be an Indianapolis Colts fan. Without the NFL on Sirius, there'd be no chance that I could be sure of hearing every game. Likewise, if you're a big-time baseball fan, I know of no way to follow the home team, no matter where either you or the players are at, other than by subscribing to XM Radio.

So, cut to the chase — how much does it cost? Well, a subscription from Sirius or XM, in either one- or two-year increments, will cost you exactly the same. The price of a one-year subscription is $142.45, or $11.87 per month, and a two-year stint will run you $271.95, which works out to $11.33 per month. To put it in different terms: If you listened only while on the road, and you were on the road 250 days per year, your two-year subscription would cost you less than $0.55 per day. I spend more than that on soda pop and coffee.

Comparing content

Sirius and XM, in an effort to bring the best to their listeners, are constantly upgrading, altering, and adding to their content. That's a good thing, but it makes a side-by-side comparison nearly impossible. Not only that, but also simply comparing the available number of channels does little to differentiate between the two services. As with cable TV, the total number of choices is less important than the number of choices that are of interest to *you!*

For example, my vehicle always has been, and will forever remain, a Stern-free zone. Additionally, you couldn't find my interest in Eminem's *Shade 45* channel with a scanning electron microscope. But that doesn't mean I wouldn't consider Sirius as my satellite radio choice. Quite the contrary; when I survey the menu of choices offered by Sirius, including *Radio Margaritaville, The Roadhouse, Revolution,* unique talk channels, and the NFL, I find plenty of reasons to pony up the pesos for a subscription.

Likewise, I'm just about as excited by XM offerings *Raw, Fungus,* and *The Opie & Anthony Show* as I am about getting a Novocain-free root canal. Does that mean I'd scratch XM Radio from consideration? No way! XM offers far more than enough to get my business, including Major League Baseball and IndyCar Racing as well as *The Message, Hank's Place,* and *The Loft.* With so many channels and such varied content to choose from, I think almost anyone can find enough reason to support an XM subscription decision.

I guess I make it sound like I subscribe to both Sirius and XM, don't I? Well, don't think I haven't considered it, and should you choose to avoid choosing by subscribing to both, I wouldn't think you'd gone overboard. But, alas, my subscription choice will remain anonymous. I will tell you this: For me, the choice came down to a single channel offered by one and not the other. I'll leave it up to you to figure out whether I couldn't live without the Colts or the Twins.

Both XM and Sirius offer three-day trial periods during which you can listen online. The content streamed over the Internet includes all the music channels, but you won't hear most of the talk or news channels. Nonetheless, this can be a great way to help you decide to which service you'd prefer to subscribe. XM also offers, for $7.99 per month, an Internet-only subscription, and this online service offers a couple channels heard exclusively online. By the way, XM Radio Online recommends the use of a broadband connection (wired or Wi-Fi) and, further, if you normally connect to the Internet via satellite, because of latency, you might want to adopt a try-before-you-buy stance.

Setting up satellite radio

As you continue with your investigation, and if you find that satellite radio is something you want, there are four steps to follow in getting set up for service:

1. **Choose a provider.**

   Before you go shopping for radio gear, you must decide which satellite radio service best meets your needs, wants and desires. You don't need to subscribe quite yet, but because some of the equipment is designed specifically for use with one service or the other, you at least need to know which service you prefer.

2. **Gather the gear.**

   With the issue of satellite service settled, you're now faced with the task of determining the type of system you want. There are several manufacturers building systems and accessories ranging from high-tech built-in units with functions galore to portable units that can be accessorized beyond belief.

3. **Install your system.**

   Whether you choose to have the system installed professionally or you do it yourself, everything needs to be up and running prior to activating the service.

4. **Activate your service and equipment.**

   You can sign up for a subscription and activate your satellite radio equipment all at the same time. After you've paid for your subscription, the service provider you chose will send a signal from space that activates the tuner.

Evaluating Equipment

The importance of choosing the radio receiver that best meets your needs can't be emphasized enough. As a matter of fact, for some, the available choice of gear might be the deciding difference when choosing between Sirius and XM Satellite Radio. When you begin to shop around for radios, you find that the available equipment falls into four categories:

- ✔ **Head unit:** These in-dash units closely resemble most other terrestrial radios, and the high-end units usually include features like CD and MP3 playback. Satellite-ready head units require the use of a separate Sirius or XM radio tuner to enable access to the satellite radio signal. Some, however, do come equipped with a built-in XM or Sirius tuner.

- ✔ **Plug & Play:** These easily transportable satellite radios, when used in conjunction with separate connection kits, can be enjoyed in both rolling and stationary homes. Most Plug & Play units broadcast an FM signal to your vehicle's radio but some can be connected by cable.

- ✔ **Portable:** These units are similar to Plug & Play units, but depending on the unit and the service, they can also receive satellite radio signals without the necessity of a separate home or car kit, which makes them perfect for toting around town or a trip to the ballpark.

- ✔ **Home:** Pretty self-explanatory; you probably wouldn't take your home stereo with you on the road, and you probably wouldn't want to take a satellite radio system designed for the home with you, either.

Examining system configurations

Whether you decide to install a system built around an in-dash head unit or one that incorporates a Plug & Play or portable unit, you find somewhat different configurations. All systems, however, contain the following elements:

- ✔ **Antenna:** If you plan on using your satellite radio subscription in a vehicle, an external antenna is a requirement. Even though a portable radio has a built-in antenna, this antenna is nearly useless inside a vehicle or building. Antennas, because of the slightly different signals, are *service-specific,* meaning that an XM antenna picks up only XM signals, and a Sirius antenna can be used only with Sirius service.

- ✔ **Tuner:** Tuners are compatible with only one service provider. Satellite-ready radios, for example, can be used with either XM or Sirius services but require an external, service-specific, tuner. Plug & Play units are, essentially, service-specific tuners with control and display functions.

- ✔ **Input feed:** Satellite-ready head unit radios receive their input audio from the tuner through a cable that plugs into the back of the radio. Plug & Play units may use any one of several methods of feeding audio to a vehicle's FM radio, including direct cable or FM radio transmission. (I tell you more about audio input later in this chapter, in the section "Sending sound to the stereo.")

Satellite radio subscriptions, both XM and Sirius, are tethered to the tuner. If you choose to install a built-in head unit and tuner in your vehicle and later decide you'd like to have satellite radio in your home as well, you will, under most circumstances, need to get another subscription to go with your new home unit. Plug & Play and portable units can help eliminate the need for multiple subscriptions to the same service.

Another component necessary for use in systems built around Plug & Play or portable units is known as a *car kit.* Now, I know, you're interested in getting a satellite radio system installed in your truck or RV, not your car, but they don't call 'em truck kits or RV kits; they call 'em car kits. Anyway, most car kits come with everything you need, for use in whatever vehicle you choose, including the following:

- ✔ **Mounting bracket:** At the very least, an adhesive-backed bracket suitable for sticking on a flat surface should be included in the kit, but in many cases, an assortment of brackets may be included. (I talk more about mounting brackets in the section "Choosing a Plug & Play cradle mount," later in the chapter.)

- ✔ **Cradle:** The cradle, sometimes referred to as a docking station, provides connection points for the various cables as well as a secure place to park your Plug & Play or portable unit.

- ✔ **DC adapter:** The adapter provided is usually the typical power port or cigarette lighter type.

✓ **Input device:** Most car kits include an assortment of input devices ranging from FM modulators to auxiliary input cables. (I tell you a bit more about this subject later in the chapter, in the section "Sending sound to the stereo.")

✓ **Antenna and cable:** Most kits include about 20 feet of antenna cable as well as a magnetic antenna. I tell you more about installing antennas later in this chapter, under the clever section title "Installing the antenna."

Finding the right radio

One of the primary indicators that satellite radio is both the wave of the future and here to stay has to be the proliferation of radio receivers available for both services. Several manufacturers, betting that both Sirius and XM will survive and thrive, even build multiple units for each brand. When you begin shopping for radio equipment, you find the following among your choices:

✓ **Sirius Plug & Play models:** Several manufacturers offer Plug & Play units designed for use with Sirius service. Some include car kits, and some don't, so make sure you get all you need to install the unit in your vehicle. Among those offered, you find the following:

- **Sirius Sportster Replay:** Possibly the most popular of all Sirius radios, the Sportster Replay includes the Game Alert feature, which lets you know when your favorite teams are playing, and the Game Zone feature, which lists channels and scores. See Figure 15-1.

- **Clarion Calypso:** The Calypso features S-Seek, which saves the info for up to 20 songs and alerts you when a saved song is playing anywhere on Sirius. You can also search by category, channel, artist, or song title by using the included remote control.

- **JVC KT-SR3000:** This innovative unit is also sold packaged with a car kit under the designation KT-PK3000 and looks a little like a PDA. Including, among other features, a 6-line graphic display, S-Seek, Game Alert, Program Alert, and a 44-minute replay memory, this little unit packs a big punch.

✓ **XM Plug & Play models:** As with Sirius, a number of manufacturers have jumped on the XM bandwagon and provide a variety of units designed for use with XM Satellite Radio service. Among them are the following:

- **Delphi Roady XT:** Like many Plug & Play units, a built-in transmitter broadcasts the XM signal over any unused FM frequency on your vehicle's FM radio. TuneSelect alerts you when any one of 20 saved songs is played on any XM channel, and a stock ticker scrolls up to 20 stock symbols across the display.

- **Audiovox Xpress:** If your vehicle's stereo has an auxiliary input, you can use the line output to make a direct audio connection, or if not, the built-in transmitter will broadcast sound through your FM radio. TuneSelect and scrolling sports scores or stock ticker symbols are also included in this compact unit.

- **Delphi SKYFi2:** The Replay/Pause feature continuously records 30 minutes of the XM channel you're listening to, and the TuneSelect preview mode allows you to see what's playing on other channels. The built-in FM transmitter broadcasts the XM signal on any of several unused FM frequencies. You can see this model in Figure 15-2.

✔ **Head units:** When combined with a Sirius or XM tuner, these built-in vehicle stereo systems provide clear satellite radio entertainment as well as a multitude of other audio entertainment options. As with the Plug & Play radios, several models, including the following, are offered for sale:

- **Alpine CDA 9857:** Besides being satellite radio ready (requiring a Sirius or XM tuner) you can listen to terrestrial AM and FM radio or, with the optional tuner, HD Radio. You can also enjoy listening to commercial and homemade CDs, or by connecting the included cable, you can play and control your iPod.

Figure 15-1:
The Sirius Sportster Replay generally comes packaged with a car kit and remote control.

Figure 15-2:
The Delphi SKYFi2 is sold as a package that includes the car kit and is compatible with various Delphi Boombox accessories.

- **Sony MEX-1GP:** This unit incorporates almost too many audio choices. Along with AM, FM, HD (with optional tuner), and Satellite radio (with required tuner), you can listen to your choice of CDs or store, for replay, up to 1GB of WMA, MP3, or ATRAC3plus files in the included flash memory.

- **Pioneer DEH-P6800MP:** With the optional iPod adapter, you can plug in your iPod and listen to your whole music library, should you ever tire of listening to satellite radio. As with most of the satellite-radio ready receivers, you need to purchase a separate tuner and service subscription.

Another way to get satellite radio in your vehicle is to have it factory installed in your next new truck or RV. Both Sirius and XM have signed deals with various truck and RV manufacturers to offer service-specific equipment as an option at purchase, but some manufacturers, like Delphi, also offer satellite-ready radios, designed specifically for use in heavy-duty trucks, allowing the purchaser to install the service-specific tuner of his or her choice.

✔ **Portables:** Some of the most versatile products to come down the pike are portable satellite radios, but at least up to now, the only truly portable units are designed to be used with XM. Among your choices are the following:

Because of the ability to store and replay music, the Recording Industry Association of America (RIAA) has filed a lawsuit against XM Radio citing that, through the use of time-shifting or on-demand devices like the Inno, Helix and NeXus, XM has overstepped the bounds of its licensing agreements. As I write this book, chances are good that XM and the RIAA will hammer out an acceptable agreement making everybody happy but, until that time, you might want to put the Inno, or similar devices, on your "wish list" instead of your "buy now" list.

- **Pioneer Inno:** The Inno is roughly the size of a cellphone and has a built-in antenna that receives the XM signal almost anywhere. You'll need an optional kit for use in your vehicle, but the Inno comes with all the necessary gear to play it over your home stereo. The Inno can record up to 50 hours of programming, either one song at a time or in blocks, and up to half the memory (although not quite 25 hours) can be used to store MP3 or WMA files. As the 2006 "CNET Best of CES Peoples Voice" award winner, the Pioneer Inno is a truly innovative product.

- **Sirius S50 Portable:** The S50 isn't really a portable radio because it can receive the Sirius satellite signal only when it's docked in a home or vehicle cradle, but it can store up to 50 hours of Sirius programming and MP3 or WMA music files. By the way, Sirius has an agreement with the RIAA to make a per-unit royalty payment on each S50 sold so; no lawsuit.

XM Passport

One of the most interesting devices debuting at the 2006 Consumer Electronics Show (CES), because of its potential impact on the satellite radio industry as a whole, is the XM Passport. The low-cost Passport, which looks a little bit like an SD card, as shown in the following figure, can take the place of the bulky radio tuners needed to receive the XM Satellite Radio signal. The tiny tuner, to which the satellite radio subscription is tied, provides programming when inserted into a built-in port or when used in a docking device connected to the radio receiver. As more and more manufacturers make XM radio-ready devices available, including a Passport slot, the need for multiple satellite radio subscriptions will be, if not eliminated, greatly diminished.

The XM Passport, manufactured by Audiovox, is expected to be bundled with, among others, the Samsung Helix and Nexus, for use in conjunction with a docking station. You can expect to see several Passport compatible head units follow suit.

- **Samsung Helix:** Boasting a feature set almost identical to the Pioneer Inno, the Helix also includes a built-in rechargeable battery and a USB cable for uploading MP3s from your computer.

With so many equipment choices you may be wondering where you're going to find it all. Well, there are a number of retailers offering satellite radio equipment including Best Buy, Fry's Electronics, and Circuit City, but at least in my opinion, you can't go wrong by starting your search at Crutchfield. They offer a huge selection of products as well as installation, advice, and online tutorials covering a wide range of satellite radio-related issues. You can find them at www.crutchfield.com. Choose Car Satellite Radio from the Car Audio & Video drop-down menu and start your tour!

Setting Up a Satellite Radio System

Because every satellite radio system installation is different, any attempt to give you step by step installation directions will fall short of the mark. There are, however, a few issues that most, if not all, system installations have in common. Included among those considerations are the following:

- **Placement:** Depending on the type of system you're installing, you need to determine where you're going to place the antenna, tuner, cabling, or mounting device. If you're installing an in-dash radio, then, obviously, it gets installed in the dash; but if you're installing a Plug & Play unit, you have a number of placement options.

✔ **Mounting:** Most vehicle kits include a few different types of mounts, ranging from suction mounts for use on a windshield to vent mounts for use on the dash. It's also possible to purchase mounting brackets designed specifically for use in your truck or RV.

✔ **Connections:** Ranging from connecting the antenna to the tuner to connecting a Plug & Play radio to the vehicle's stereo, you must make a number of wired or even wireless connections.

✔ **Activation:** With everything installed and powered up, you can then activate your service and equipment.

Because everything needs to be installed before you can activate the service, and because after a device is installed it might be difficult to relocate if there are problems, I recommend that you make sure everything's going to work before you start drilling too many holes. You can do this by following these steps:

1. **Place the antenna approximately in the area that you expect to set it up more permanently, and then make a temporary connection to the radio tuner.**

2. **Provide temporary power to the radio tuner.**

   If you're installing a Plug & Play radio, you can use the power port plug. Otherwise, just run a couple of jumper wires: one for power and one to ground the device.

3. **If you have an XM radio, tune it to channel one, which is the XM Preview channel, and if you have a Sirius radio, check the signal strength meter on the screen.**

4. **Make adjustments, if needed, to the antenna location to fine-tune the signal, and when all is well, continue with the installation.**

Location, location, location

Yep, location is a key consideration in restaurants, real estate, and radio equipment, but for decidedly different reasons. Where you locate your radio, tuner, or antenna will be determined, to some extent, by circumstance, but in areas in which you can exert some control, you may want to keep the following in mind:

✔ **Cables:** If you're installing a head unit, tuner, and antenna, make sure you've got enough cable to reach easily between the antenna and tuner as well as the tuner and radio. If you're installing a vehicle kit for a Plug & Play or portable unit, you need sufficient cable to span the distance between the cradle and antenna.

✔ **Access:** If you're installing a vehicle kit for a Plug & Play or portable radio, you want to be sure you can reach the controls and easily read the display. It also needs to be in close proximity to the vehicle stereo system if you're using a cassette adapter or auxiliary input cable, and be sure it's within reach of the DC outlet (cigarette lighter) for power.

✔ **Interference:** You don't want the location of your radio, tuner, vehicle kit, or cables to interfere with the safe operation of your vehicle. Be sure that all items are safely secured, afford unobstructed use of all your vehicle controls, and don't block your vision in any way.

Installing the antenna

The most difficult part of installing an antenna is running the cable in such a way as to avoid making it easy for water to find its way inside. After that, the most difficulty is found when trying to run the cable in an unobtrusive way. You're on your own with those two issues, but hey, it's not like you've never done it before, right? There are, however, a couple other things to keep in mind when you begin looking for a place to install your antenna:

✔ **Obstructions:** I know people who've just stuck their antenna up on the dash and seem happy with the reception. Don't do that. The roof of any vehicle makes a great satellite-signal-blocking obstruction. For best results, the antenna should be placed outside the vehicle in an obstruction-free area.

✔ **Attachment:** Most of the antennas included with radios and tuners have a magnetic base, although a few use an adhesive-backed base. I like the magnetic-base antennas, but depending on your situation, you might need to find an antenna, like a bolt-on marine mount, that allows for an alternative method of attachment.

✔ **Mounting:** If you have a good metal roof on which to attach your magnetic-base antenna, you have no issues, but if you'd like to mount your antenna on a mirror, you might be scratching your head wondering how to do that. Well, scratch no more! A couple manufacturers make an innovative little metal bracket that attaches to your mirror, onto which you can set your magnetic or, if you insist, adhesive-backed satellite antenna. The two mounting brackets in question are

• **Pro.Fit:** This company makes a nice black, powder-coated, satellite antenna mount that attaches to the top bar of the mirror. For most folks, that should place the antenna in a relatively obstruction-free area. You can find Pro.Fit on the Web at `www.pro-fit-intl.com`.

- **Terk SRB-MM:** Very similar to the Pro.Fit model, the Terk antenna mount also attaches to the top bracket of the mirror and has a small opening near the front through which the antenna coax cable fits. The Terk SRB-MM can be purchased from several online retailers, including, who else, Crutchfield.

Having a satellite radio antenna sitting somewhere on your vehicle is like having a flashing neon sign telling thieves and criminals that you've got some expensive satellite radio gear sitting in your vehicle. Make sure you take proper precautions.

Choosing a Plug & Play cradle mount

Most car kits include at least one mounting bracket, and some include several. The most common types are

- ✔ **Universal brackets:** These are great for ease of use, but because anything meant to work everywhere results in compromise, you might not get the cleanest-looking installation with a universal mount. Among the group of universal mounts, you find the following methods of attachment:

  - **Adhesive:** Most car kits include an adhesive backed mounting bracket. These are great if you have a flat surface onto which you can stick the bracket, but if you ever need to remove the bracket, get ready for a fight. Additionally, if you do remove the bracket, a very sticky residue that's difficult to remove will be left behind.

  - **Suction cup:** These mounts, sometimes included with the kits and also available from other sources, are used to attach the mounting bracket to a windshield. If you choose this type of mounting bracket, be certain that your vision isn't obstructed in any way.

  - **Dash vent:** I've never been a big fan of dash-vent mounts because I'm not sure it's a great idea to blast heat on any electronic item that cost me more than twenty bucks. These brackets clip on the vent slats and are surprisingly secure, but vents aren't always located in places you'd like to have your radio.

- ✔ **Vehicle-specific brackets:** A couple companies offer brackets that are designed for use in specific vehicles. If you can find one for your truck or RV, these are usually preferable to almost any other option. They're easy to install, and because they're designed for your vehicle, they usually place the radio in the best possible location. A few places you can find these mounts include

  - **Crutchfield:** Offering a number of brackets designed for use in a wide variety of vehicles, you can find Crutchfield on the Web at www.crutchfield.com.

- **Arkon Resources:** Although they don't offer a line of vehicle-specific mounting brackets, they provide a viable alternative to those brackets bundled with typical car kits. You can find them on the Web at: www.arkon.com.

- **Satellite Radio Superstore:** There's one Satellite Radio Superstore targeted to XM users and another for Sirius subscribers. They offer a wide variety of mounting brackets as well as other satellite radio services and accessories. You can find them at the following addresses:

  ```
  http://www.xm-radio-satellite.com/
  http://www.sirius-radio-satellite.com/
  ```

- **Pro.Fit Int'l:** Pro.Fit manufactures quite a number of vehicle-specific mounting brackets for a variety of products, including satellite radio cradles and cellphones. The Web site is located at www.pro-fit-intl.com.

Sending sound to the stereo

Plug & Play satellite radios aren't really radios at all. In fact, they're primarily satellite radio tuners. Therefore, if you're using one of these units, you must have a way to send the sound to your vehicle's FM radio. Of course, that also means you need to have a regular radio installed in your vehicle, but you have one of those, don't you? I thought so. Anyway, you can use any of several methods to get your satellite radio audio to play on your terrestrial FM radio. Included among them are

- ✔ **Cassette adapter:** If your vehicle's radio is also a cassette tape player, you can use a cassette tape adapter to connect your satellite unit to the stereo. The cassette adapter looks like a standard cassette tape with a wire attached to it. Just stick the cassette into the slot, connect the wire to the cradle, and you're in business. I've heard and read conflicting reports concerning the audio quality obtained by using this connection method. Some love it, and some hate it; I'll let you decide for yourself.

- ✔ **FM modulator:** An FM modulator transmits the satellite audio feed to your radio by using FM radio frequencies. Because the FM frequency used by the modulator can't be used by any local stations, you may, during the course of the day, need to find open frequencies as you travel. Two types of modulators are currently in use, and they are as follows:

  - **Wireless:** Most Plug & Play units and some portable units include a wireless FM transmitter that broadcasts an FM signal that can be picked up by your FM radio antenna. In my opinion, this is the least desirable method of sending the signal to your radio, but I also recognize that it's the easiest.

- **Wired:** A wired modulator connects to the audio output port on your cradle and plugs into the antenna input port on your FM radio. So what do you do with the terrestrial radio antenna you've disconnected from your radio? Well, your FM modulator comes equipped with a female antenna plug into which you insert the standard antenna.

✔ **Direct input:** Making a direct connection, in a fashion similar to that used by satellite-ready in-dash radios, is the best option, but it's also an option that may not be available to you. If, however, your current stereo does include an auxiliary input port, you can run a cable with a mini-jack plug on one end and an RCA plug on the other from the cradle output to the stereo's input, or if need be, you can purchase an auxiliary input adapter from one of the following places:

  - **Crutchfield:** Crutchfield just keeps showing up, doesn't it? You can find this company's Web site, which hasn't changed since you began reading this chapter, by using this URL: www.crutchfield.com.

  - **Precision Interface Electronics:** Better known as PIE, this company makes a wide range of interface products for the audio installation industry. You can visit PIE on the Web at www.pie.net.

Activating the service

Getting your radio tuner activated isn't rocket science, but rocket science is, or at least was, involved. That's because activation occurs when your satellite radio service provider sends an *activation hit* to your particular unit from a satellite that's in geo-stationary orbit. To get your tuner activated, you need the following items:

✔ **ID number:** Sirius requires you to provide the System Identification Number (SID) or Electronic Serial Number (ESN), which can be found on the tuner under the bar code. XM radios use an 8-digit ID number that displays when you tune your radio to channel 0.

  If you have an XM radio, be aware that the ID numbers won't include the letters I, O, S, or F so as not to be confused with the numbers 1, 0, 5, or 4. I don't really think an F looks like a 4, but that's what they tell me.

✔ **Working radio:** Because the company is sending a signal to your radio telling it to unlock itself, your radio must be on and operating prior to activation. If you're signing up with XM, you need to tune your radio to channel 0; if you're signing up with Sirius, tune your radio to channel 184.

✔ **Credit card:** Yep, the company will take the money before it sends the signal. You also have to set up an account, so make sure you know to which address your credit card billing statement goes if you use more than one.

You can save a few bucks by choosing to activate the equipment online. Both XM and Sirius charge about $10 to activate online and about $15 to activate by calling customer service.

With both services, after you've set up your account and provided payment, an activation hit will be sent to your radio. This can, at times, take as long as 30 minutes, but in most cases, activation is completed within 15 minutes. With XM radio, for example, when you can hear channels 7, 9, 47, and 122, you know your activation is complete, but in both cases, you should simply be able to scroll through the channels and hear each one.

Chapter 16

Taking the Show on the Road

*O*kay, I hate to admit it, but I must; the primary purpose of my laptop is to keep me entertained. Yes, I use it for all kinds of business-related purposes, but if you really pressed me, you'd find out that I've focused a fair amount of my time and effort in the search for entertainment. And even though I justify electronic expenses with professional needs, I know, down deep, I travel with a laptop because I can do all sorts of fun things with it.

Of course, my electronic entertainment isn't limited to my laptop alone. Perish the thought. For example, I've got music downloaded onto my laptop and MP3 player; if I ever get around to it, I'll have it on my phone as well. As far as video entertainment goes, I've downloaded movies, rented DVDs, subscribed to satellite TV, and streamed TV over the Internet. In addition to that, I found a couple of great places to download digital books.

In this chapter, I take a brief look at just a few ways you can play with your electronic toys. For example, I tell you a little bit about the many ways you can bring a little music to your ears using the Internet and your computer. In case you're more of a visual person, I tell you about a few ways you can satisfy your need to watch movies, and if you're more in the mood for TV, I tell you how you can stream it from the Net and beam it from the sky. Finally, a word about books because you know, reading is a good thing, even if you let someone read to you.

Getting Music, Movies and More (Legally)

I think all moms sing to their kids, but my sister and I were especially fortunate — our mom sang with a concert-quality voice. As a matter of fact, the greatest *a cappella* rendition of "Silent Night" ever heard by man or beast might have occurred one winter evening, many moons ago, inside a tiny Southern Oregon church. When my mom finished the last note, no one moved, no one spoke, and the only sounds that could be heard were those of quiet weeping. She says — at 70-plus years of age, still teaching piano and voice — that she can no longer sing; but that's okay because whenever I hear "Silent Night," it's always sung by my mom, and strong men still cry.

It was from her, I'm sure, that I got my love of music. Now, understand that the only instrument I can play is the stereo, and I can't carry a tune in a tin bucket. But I definitely appreciate and enjoy the efforts of others more gifted. In addition to a love of music, I also gained from my mom an appreciation of movies that bordered on obsession.

When I first realized that not only were movie and music downloads available from the Internet, but that they also could be had at little or no cost, I was absolutely euphoric. That euphoria, however, quickly faded when I realized there were serious ethical issues involved with many sites set up for music and movie downloads. When you decide to download one of those items, there are a few things you want to keep in mind:

- ✔ **Ethics:** Even though Web sites have been shut down, laws have been passed, and people have been sued, it's still possible to find Web sites offering pirated music and movie downloads. No matter how you rationalize it, downloading an unauthorized copy of a song or a DVD is, at the very best, unethical.

- ✔ **Safety:** It doesn't happen as often as it used to, but it's still possible to run across a Web site offering spyware cleverly disguised as a harmless music or movie download. Additionally, some file-sharing programs can open your private information to public scrutiny.

For centuries it's been recognized as fact that an author or artist creating an original work, a publisher who creates authorized copies of the original, and individual owners of these copies all have certain rights. Although a few copyright laws existed in earlier eras, most agree that the precursor to modern copyright law was the Statute of Anne passed by British Parliament on April 10, 1710. Copyright law has continued to change and adapt since the Statute of Anne was adopted, but the basic need and purpose has remained the same: To protect the creator and the contracted publishers of artistic and intellectual work.

It doesn't take a moral or mental giant to determine that simply owning a copy of a work doesn't convey to the owner the right to create and distribute unlimited copies, regardless of whether the copies are sold or given freely. It's true that Fair Use and Access policies do allow an individual to create copies for personal use — and teachers or journalists can (in most cases) use copyrighted works for educational and informational purposes without the owner's explicit permission. However, any copies failing those tests exist outside the law.

If you want to remain on the right side of the law — and I'm sure you do — make sure you keep the following in mind:

✔ **Avoid sharing copyrighted files on peer-to-peer networks.** File-sharing programs like BitTorrent, LimeWire, Kazaa, and Morpheus can be used within online networks to share, among other things, music, movies, TV shows, games, and software. This type of trading, besides running afoul of copyright laws, can expose you to spyware and make private information on your laptop public, too, as I mentioned earlier in this chapter. So if you do decide to use these networks for the legitimate trading of files, know the risks.

✔ **Use common sense.** If a movie hasn't yet been released to DVD, why would it be available for download on the Internet? Only one answer: It's a pirated copy. Other clues to potentially illegal download sites include

- *Very low cost:* If your only cost is a $20 to $50 annual subscription fee, you can bet that a good portion — not all, but enough to cause concern — of the music, movies, games, or software available for download is pirated.

- *Lack of affiliations:* Most of the legal movie and music download sites proudly advertise their affiliation with legitimate entertainment creators, producers, and publishers.

- *Lack of accountability:* Some file-sharing sites tell you not to download — or offer for download — copyrighted material, but they take no responsibility for ensuring that the files available are legally obtained and offered. Quite the contrary — they tell you that you and you alone are responsible, and I'm sure they'll be happy to point the police in your direction should the opportunity arise.

Putting a Little Music in Your Laptop

Whenever I'm using my laptop for some mundane business task like maintaining my logbook, bookkeeping, or budgeting, I like to listen to a little music. It doesn't make the job any easier, or any more fun, but it does make it easier to take. Being a bit of a music junkie, I've got multiple options for listening to music, and I've got a few methods of putting music on my laptop, including the following:

- ✔ **Ripping from CD:** I'm not sure where the term *ripping* originated, but all it means is to extract (rip) the digital audio tracks from a CD and store them on your laptop (or, in some cases, iPods or other portable audio players) in a different format.

- ✔ **Downloading:** I buy a lot of songs from several Web vendors and download them to my hard drive. This way, if there's just one song from a particular CD that I want, that's all I've got to buy.

- ✔ **Streaming:** I subscribe to one music service that allows me to stream music. I don't own the copies, but who cares? I can listen as often as I want without filling up my hard drive. I also, on occasion, stream the audio from one of several radio stations.

Finding a media player

Before you can listen to music on your computer, you need to install a media player. Several are available, and even though some offer extra-cost Pro or Plus versions, most of them are free. If you've got Windows XP, chances are good you've already got the Windows Media Player, but there are a few others as well, including the following:

- ✔ **Winamp:** I like this player because I can listen to AOL Radio (which includes several XM Radio channels; see Chapter 15), and it's integrated with SHOUTcast radio and TV. Winamp also offers a Pro version that allows you to rip and burn CDs. It's available for download at www.winamp.com.

- ✔ **MediaMonkey:** Although this one boasts several attractive features, the thing I like best about the MediaMonkey media player is its ability to convert MP3s, OGG, FLAC, and WMA files into other formats. You can get more information and download the player by visiting www.media monkey.com.

- ✔ **Musicmatch Jukebox:** Now owned by Yahoo!, this media player — unlike so many others — concentrates on audio only. Because of that, I think it does an excellent job of both playing and managing music. You can find more information by visiting www.musicmatch.com.

- ✔ **RealPlayer:** With a menu of features too long to list, the RealPlayer is the media player I use most often. It has the ability to play both audio and video files in almost every format currently in use, and the optional Plus version can even help you transfer your record or cassette collection to your laptop or MP3 player. You can get a ton of information and download the player of your choice by visiting www.real.com.

✔ **iTunes:** It's free for the taking, but believe me, Apple figures to make a ton of money with this versatile little player. You can rip your own CDs into the library, but the iTunes store is always open. Besides music, you can buy TV shows and audiobooks. You can also browse the iTunes store for free and premium podcasts. More information about iTunes is available by visiting www.apple.com/itunes.

There's just no reason to limit yourself to one media player. Although I have only one premium player installed, I've got and use three others. I suggest you download a few of the basic players, give 'em a spin, and if you find one you really like, use that as your default player and delete the ones you don't use or need. You can find a comprehensive comparison of media players at http://en.wikipedia.org/wiki/Comparison_of_media_players.

Ripping CDs to your computer

Once you've got a media player or three downloaded and installed, you can begin to transfer your CD collection to your computer. Some of the media players, like Windows Media Player, RealPlayer, and iTunes, include CD-ripping capability with their basic players, whereas others include this feature only with their Pro or Plus versions. Personally, I use a completely separate program application known as Audiograbber for ripping CDs. (I tell you a little bit more about Audiograbber in Chapter 18.)

Using Windows Media Player as an example (because nearly everyone has it installed on their computers), follow these steps to rip a CD to your computer:

1. **Open the Windows Media Player application.**

2. **Right-click the Rip tab and choose Tools⇨Options.**

   The Options dialog box opens.

3. **Click the Rip Music tab, shown in Figure 16-1.**

   From this window, you can determine where music files are stored, what information will be included in the file names, and what format the files will be saved in, as well as what size and quality the files are.

   Windows Media Player, by default, uses the .wma format, but because it's almost universally recognized and compatible with most portable players, I prefer to rip into the MP3 format. MP3s are more bulky files, but by using the 256Kbps sampling speed, I get a reasonably sized file that sounds, at least in my opinion, better than the smaller WMA file.

4. **Make any changes or adjustments. Click Apply, and click OK.**

5. **Insert the CD you want to import to your computer.**

6. **Select the tracks you want to transfer, as shown in Figure 16-2, and click Rip Music.**

Figure 16-1:
Select
options
for ripping
a CD.

Figure 16-2:
You can
choose to
copy only
a few files
to your
computer.

Downloading music files

I've become addicted to downloading music — so much so that I've had to strictly limit the number of songs I allow myself to purchase for download each week. No, I'm not going to tell you — and by default, my wife — what that number is, but let it suffice to say that I'm currently spending less money on music each week than I used to spend on a single CD. And sometimes two whole weeks go by without a single musical purchase! I'm always so proud of myself when that happens.

I think downloading music is addictive because you can purchase one single song at a time. You don't have to buy a whole album, thereby getting at least a few songs you don't want, but before you know it, you've found 15 songs you can't live without for one more minute. At almost a buck a crack, that habit can get expensive in a hurry.

 Because downloading anything, including music, uses up a lot of bandwidth, I strongly suggest that you try to do all the downloading you can while you're at home. That way, you don't run afoul of any hotspot data transfer or usage limits, and you don't slow the Internet connection for everybody else.

I used to buy music from a lot of places, and now . . . only a couple. The reason for this is purely out of convenience. I tried a bunch of them, settled on two, and set up accounts so that I can just download the music, and my card's billed automatically. Included among those sites that I've tried are the following:

- **MSN Music:** They don't offer as many tracks as some of the other services, but they're definitely easy to use. Once you've set up an account, all you've got to do is browse and download. They bill your credit card once a month. You can find them online at `http://music.msn.com`.

- **Real Music Store:** Lots and lots of music, but at least for me, it's a little less convenient to use. You can access the music store only through RealPlayer, so if you want to shop here, you've got to install the media player. After that, you've got to set up an account. Once the account's set up, though, all you've got to do is find the songs you're looking for and click Buy.

- **iTunes Music Store:** Did Apple start the whole "legal music download" deal? I'm not really sure, but having been around since January of 2001, they're definitely among the oldest of the legal online music stores. The iTMS, as it's commonly known, can be accessed from the iTunes media player. Install the player, set up an account, and you're all set to spend money on music.

✔ **Napster:** The nice thing about Napster is that you can register with them, listen to a tune up to five times, and then either purchase it or subscribe to their service. (I tell you more about that in the next section.) It's well worth your time, I believe, to visit them at www.napster.com.

If you're downloading music with an eye toward transferring the music to an iPod, you should be aware that many of the music-download stores (such as Napster, Yahoo!, and MSN Music) use the WMA format, which is incompatible with the iPod. Music purchased from iTunes, as well as most of the CDs you rip — providing you rip to the MP3 or AAC format — *is* iPod-compatible. If you've got a portable player of a different brand, make sure you check to be sure it's compatible with the music you intend to download.

The format of music purchased from the Real Music Store is incompatible with almost every media player, but by using a conversion tool, you can change the format to WAV, MP3, or Ogg Vorbis. One such tool is included with the program application known as Audacity. I tell you a little bit about Audacity in Chapter 18.

Subscribing to a music service

Several sites have begun to offer music subscription services. Now, at first, I didn't think this was something I'd want to do, but after taking advantage of a few free trials, I can see how a subscription service could actually *save* me money. I mean, I buy music (sometimes, every week), and generally, I'd say I spend somewhere around $20 a month in doing so. Most of the subscription services, however, cost around $10 a month, and although you don't own the music, you get unlimited access to more than you could afford to buy for as long as your subscription's current.

Nearly all the music subscription services require the use of a proprietary media player or some other software application, and in some cases, as with Rhapsody, it's different from their standard player. This just means you might have to download another player to go along with your others, but it's a good reason to avoid purchasing a premium player until you've fully investigated your options.

Among those offering music-subscription services are the following:

✔ **Rhapsody:** To say that I like Rhapsody is a serious understatement. After having used it for a while, I'm considering scrapping all my other media players. I can save as much music as I want, I can transfer it to my MP3 player, and when I'm home, I can stream it to my stereo. The thing I like best, though, is the radio stations that I can build and program. I enter up to ten artists, and then Rhapsody streams music from them as well as artists in the same genre. It's amazing, and I can't get enough of it. I could go on and on about the service and the player, but because space is limited, you can instead find out more by visiting `www.real.com`.

✔ **AOL Music Now:** After purchasing Music Now from Circuit City, AOL intends to eliminate MusicNet@AOL (which was an extra-cost option available only to AOL customers) and switch those customers to the new service. MusicNow is open to the general public and because it's Web-based, can be used from any PC. The only thing I don't like is that the ability to transfer music to an MP3 player is an option available only for an additional fee. You can get more information from their Web site at `http://aol.musicnow.com`.

✔ **Musicmatch On Demand:** The AutoDJ feature in the Musicmatch media player works a little like the Rhapsody Custom Radio. You can build a playlist around a few artists, and by incorporating some user-set filters and On Demand, the playlist will be enhanced with artists and music that are compatible with your pre-set playlist. This feature really and truly adds to your enjoyment of music. If you pay for a year, this is one of the cheapest services. You can get more information by browsing to `www.musicmatch.com`.

✔ **Yahoo! Music Unlimited:** You would think, because Yahoo! already owns Musicmatch On Demand, that they wouldn't have started an entirely new service, but here it is. If you take the time to configure your preferences, YMU can make playlist suggestions you might not have thought of. And I'd have to say that the personal-preference-driven LAUNCHcast radio is a strong competitor to the Rhapsody Custom Radio. This service, like its On Demand sister, is only $4.99 per month if you pay for a year in advance. More information is easily found by navigating to `http://music.yahoo.com`.

✔ **Napster:** The cool thing about Napster is that you can really give it a workout before you finally decide whether to subscribe to the service. They let you play every song up to five times before requiring you to either subscribe or purchase the song. That's a good deal. On top of that, they've got a huge online community that provides playlists and suggestions; you can build custom radio stations like you can with Rhapsody, and Napster can be streamed to your stereo. As with AOL MusicNow, though, you have to pay an extra five bucks a month if you want to load music onto an MP3 player. It's worth a look, though, and you can get a glimpse by browsing to `www.napster.com`.

If you're planning on using free trial periods to evaluate the suitability of each one of these services, I strongly suggest that you evaluate only one at a time. If you miss the trial-cancellation date, you're on the hook for (at the very least) a full month. AOL, at 30 days, offers the longest trial period, while those of the Napster and the two Yahoo! services are only a week in duration. Give 'em each a good whirl, and choose carefully.

As with the music-download sites, none of the music from subscription sites can be transferred to an iPod. Make sure you check the FAQs for information concerning portable-player compatibility for each of the services.

Watching Movies on the Road

I purchased a wide-screen laptop specifically so I could watch movies on it. I'm sure I justified the extra expense by convincing myself that a wide-screen laptop would let me open and work on several windows at the same time, but really, it was just so I could use my laptop as a DVD viewer. Lots of people carry a DVD player with them for watching movies on their TV, but for me, I've found that my laptop works remarkably well. If you really want to, though, most laptops can be connected to a TV and used like a traditional DVD player; more about that a little later.

Currently, movies that can go mobile are found in the following formats:

- **VHS tapes:** It's difficult for me to turn my back on a technology that I once held so dearly, but alas, I must say, "Good night, good night! Parting is such sweet sorrow, that I shall say good night 'til it be morrow." (*Romeo and Juliet,* Act 2, Scene II) As we all know, "morrow" never comes, and the demise of tape isn't tragic.

- **DVD discs:** Other than their ridiculously high price, what's not to like? They don't take up much space, the playback quality is spectacular, and DVDs usually include some great bonus features.

- **Digital downloads:** Taking up space only on your hard drive, these are the ultimate in mobile movies, but because disk space is limited and downloading a large file can be a hassle, they're not without their issues.

Downloading pros and cons

Right now, if you want to legally download movies, you've only got a couple of choices:

- **Movielink:** According to their Web site, Movielink is "a joint venture of Metro-Goldwyn-Mayer Studios, Paramount Pictures, Sony Pictures Entertainment, Universal Studios and Warner Bros. Studios. Movielink draws its content offerings from the vast libraries of those studios as well as Walt Disney Pictures, Miramax, Artisan and others on a non-exclusive basis." Movielink's Web site URL is www.movielink.com.

✓ **CinemaNow:** Included among the companies affiliated with CinemaNow are 20th Century Fox, ABC News, Disney, Endemol, MGM, Miramax, NBC Universal, Sony, Sundance Channel, Warner Bros., and Lions Gate Entertainment. You can find CinemaNow on the Web at `www.cinema now.com`.

Both Movielink and CinemaNow offer movies for sale or rent, but while all are available for rent, only some are available for purchase. If you choose to rent a movie from either vendor, you find they share the following traits:

✓ **24-hour viewing:** Once you start watching a movie, you have 24 hours to finish watching it. The clock starts ticking as soon as you begin to watch it, and when 24 hours is up, the movie disappears from your hard drive.

  • **Pro:** The good thing about this is that once you're done watching the movie, even if it's not *Mission Impossible,* it self-destructs and no longer takes up space on your hard drive.

  • **Con:** The bad thing is that if you start watching the movie and something prevents you from finishing within the 24-hour period, you're probably going to have to pay another rental fee. It's possible, though, that you might not have to download the movie all over again.

✓ **30-day storage:** After you rent a movie, you've got 30 days in which to download and watch the movie.

  • **Pro:** You can download several movies before leaving on a trip, and they'll be ready to view when you are ready to watch.

  • **Con:** If you don't get around to watching or downloading the movie within the 30-day time period, you're out of luck.

✓ **Streaming:** If you want, you can start watching a movie shortly after you begin downloading — usually within a minute.

  • **Pro:** If you just can't wait to see the movie, you don't have to.

  • **Con:** Your 24-hour viewing period begins before you've even finished downloading the movie.

The 30-day storage period, due to licensing agreements that limit the length of time a movie can be offered for download, might be shorter than 30 days. Make sure, before you download a movie, that you know exactly how long the movie can be stored. Generally, if the storage period is, for whatever reason, shorter than 30 days, it's clearly and prominently stated in the preview area.

If you'd rather own the movies you download, you can, if you choose, purchase certain movies from either Movielink or CinemaNow. As with the rental movies, both services have certain common traits. Among them are the following:

- ✔ **Download window:** As with the rental downloads, you have 30 days from the date of purchase to download a movie, but if the movie's removed from the site due to licensing agreements before the 30 days is up and before you download it, you might be making calls to customer service in an effort to recover your funds. Good luck with that.

- ✔ **Large file size:** What can I say; movie files are huge, sometimes exceeding one gigabyte. It takes up to 90 minutes to download a movie, even on a fast connection, and if your hard-drive capacity is 40 gigabytes or less, you can fill it up in a hurry with movie files.

- ✔ **DVD-burning:** Although you can burn a purchased movie to DVD, the Windows Media Player format won't allow it to be played in a traditional DVD player.

I strongly urge you to avoid using a public hotspot for movie downloads. For one thing, some hotspot providers impose a data transfer limit, and if you exceed that limit before your movie download is completed, you could encounter some problems. Common courtesy, though, is the biggest reason to avoid downloading any large file at a public hotspot. Big files clog the bandwidth, and while you're downloading your movie, everyone else's connection is slowed to a crawl.

Renting instead of downloading

Even though I've downloaded a rental movie or three, I much prefer to watch DVDs. They don't take up space on my hard drive, and I don't have to spend an hour and a half downloading them from the Web. The thing is, I can watch most movies only once or twice. I've got my favorites that I can see over and over again and never tire of them, but for the most part, if I've seen it once I'm done with it.

In the old days, it used to be impossible to rent movies to take on the road because, by the time I got home and returned the movie, I'd end up paying more in late fees than the movie was worth. Enter: Netflix. Well, they entered the room way before I ever knew they existed, so, I guess, it's more like, Enter: Awareness of Netflix.

With Netflix, you pay a monthly subscription fee, choose a bunch of movies you want to watch, and depending on your subscription plan, they start sending them to you. When you're done with one, you send it back in the postage prepaid envelope that they provide, and they send the next one in line. It works out great if you get home every once in a while because you can drop the movies in the mail as you watch them, and by the time you get home, you've got new ones waiting for you.

If you hear about a movie currently showing in theaters that you'd like to see, but you're afraid you'll forget about it before it's released as a DVD, Netflix allows you to add it to your movie queue. When the DVD's finally released, it takes its turn in rotation.

Of course, Netflix isn't the only game in town. Included among the online movie rental sites are:

- **Netflix:** Yeah, I know, I already mentioned them, but I didn't tell you that you could find them on the Web at `www.netflix.com`.

- **Blockbuster:** If you don't think Netflix had a hand in the elimination of late fees at Blockbuster, you'd better think again. And because I'd put my credit card on the line for my oldest nephew's Blockbuster membership, no one was happier than me. Blockbuster's service and pricing are very similar to Netflix, but Blockbuster also rents games. You can find them on the Web by pointing your browser toward `www.blockbuster.com`.

- **CafeDVD:** They're a little more expensive than both Netflix and Blockbuster, but because their subscription plan's more flexible and because they offer a *lot* of movies that you just can't get from Netflix or Blockbuster, you might want to give them a close look. They also sell some DVDs at wholesale prices to subscribers. You can find out more about CafeDVD by visiting their Web site at `www.cafedvd.com`.

- **GreenCine:** Again, it's hard to compare them with the others because their subscription plans work out a little bit differently, but they're definitely competitive. GreenCine specializes in independent films, but they also carry current releases. Like CafeDVD, they have out of print DVDs available, and they also offer a Video On Demand service you might want to check out at `www.greencine.com/main`.

Using your laptop as a DVD player

Although you can simply watch movies on your laptop monitor, many people prefer to watch them on a larger TV screen. Providing that both your laptop and your TV share common connections or can be adapted, you should find it fairly easy and fairly inexpensive to plug your laptop into your TV and use it as a DVD player. Most laptops recently and currently available include either an S-Video or Super S-Video connection port. The S-Video port has four pin holes, while the Super S-Video port sports seven. Assuming your TV also has one of these connection ports, you should be able to make the connection. Even if your laptop, for example, has a seven-pin Super S-Video port and your TV has a four-pin S-Video port, you can find and buy a compatible connection cable. Rather than provide step-by-step setup instructions I point you to the best setup guide I've seen, which is found on the CinemaNow Web site at `www.cinemanow.com/PC-to-TV.aspx`. They provide a complete setup guide as well as links to Web sites that offer connection cables and adapters.

Streaming TV

Since Newton Minow, the Chairman of the FCC from 1961–1963, first uttered the words, in a speech to the National Association of Broadcasters on May 9, 1961, TV has often been referred to as a "vast wasteland." Whether that's true or not is up to you to decide. Personally, I really enjoy TV, and while not every episode ever produced has found my favor (or even most of them), there are a fair number that I really enjoy.

Most of the time, I prefer to watch TV while sitting sprawled in my comfy chair with my feet propped up on the ottoman. No truck I've ever driven has come equipped with such a setup, but I've still found watching TV from my home on wheels to be an enjoyable diversion. Recently, the "wasteland" has expanded to the Internet as several Web sites have begun to offer TV episodes and series that can be either downloaded or streamed.

Getting TV via the Internet

A lot of the TV available for viewing over the Internet has made me believe that, just maybe, TV is, after all, a vast wasteland. I'm sure there are some entertaining things said at school board meetings and state senate sessions, but I think I'd prefer something more like *Maverick* or *Monk*.

Fortunately, though, both *Monk* and *Maverick* — along with a whole bunch of other current and classic TV episodes — are offered by several sites, including:

- ✔ **iTunes:** According to their Web site, the iTunes Music Store offers select episodes and complete series from, among others, ABC, NBC, MTV, ESPN, Sci-Fi Channel, Comedy Central, Disney, Nickelodeon, and Showtime. You can buy one episode at a time, or in some cases, you can purchase a whole season. More information's available from their Web site at www.apple.com/itunes/videos.

- ✔ **In2TV:** This is where I found *Maverick,* along with old episodes of *Chico and the Man* and *The FBI* with Efrem Zimbalist, Jr. You can watch full-length episodes of old favorites at no cost, and should you choose, you can join their Hi-Q Video closed network and receive full-screen, DVD-quality videos of some classics. It's offered by AOL and you can find out more at http://television.aol.com/in2tv.

- ✔ **SHOUTcast:** Available with the Winamp media player, SHOUTcast is one of those offering a multitude of channels — some interesting and some just downright strange. The most popular stations, running both current and classic episodes, are those run by ESS. They're offered free, but because they limit the bandwidth available to nonpaying viewers, you might never find a time when their server's not full. If you pay a $5 monthly subscription fee, you're assured of access. You can find out more about SHOUTcast from the Winamp Web site and more about ESS from their Web site at www.ess.tv.

✔ **CNN Pipeline:** Offered as a subscription, Internet-only news service for $2.95 per month, you can choose from four different live feeds, browse broadcasts from earlier in the day, or choose on-demand videos. The Pipeline is downloaded from CNN and operates independently of your Web browser. You can get more information by visiting www.cnn.com/pipeline.

✔ **Trio Network:** I can't tell you much about this yet because, as I'm writing this, it's not yet a reality. About the same time cheers were going up in Times Square to signal the end of 2005 and celebrating the beginning of 2006, Bravo pulled Trio from cable and began working on bringing it, in total, to the Web as an Internet-only offering. You can find out more and sign up to be notified of its debut by visiting www.trioplus.tv/plus.

Slinging TV from home

One high-tech gadget that I haven't yet tried, even though it's been on the market for a while, is called the Slingbox, which you can see in the following figure. With this amazing little device connected to both your home TV and the Internet, you can actually watch your own TV from anywhere you've got an Internet connection. All you need at home is a TV source (like satellite, cable, or antenna) and an Ethernet connection to a router with a broadband Internet connection. Sling Media even offers a Powerline Ethernet Bridge that will connect your Slingbox to the router through your electrical wiring.

After you set up the necessary hardware at home, you just need to install the free SlingPlayer on your computer and connect to the Internet. If you've got TiVo or some other DVR, you can watch your recorded programming, watch live TV, or even program your DVR right over the Internet. Even if you're not sure whether this is something you're interested in, you should, at the very least, visit the Sling Media Web site at www.slingmedia.com.

SlingPlayer Mobile software also makes it possible to watch your home TV on a Pocket PC, cellphone, or smartphone using the Windows Mobile OS.

Scoping Out Satellite TV

Satellite TV, especially for those spending week after week on the road, is quite possibly the preferred TV viewing choice. Currently, you have two choices in a satellite TV provider:

✔ **DIRECTV:** Their Total Choice MOBILE package offers 155 channels of programming, including several XM Radio channels, for $41.99 per month. The DIRECTV Web site is located at www.directv.com, but I recommend you call customer service (at 888-777-2454) or visit a nearby dealer for more information.

✔ **DISH Network:** Just trying to figure out which of their plans would best suit your needs could take days. The DISH Network, offering a little more flexibility in the local programming available to those with wheels on their homes, allows you to choose up to two local network packages from Chicago, Atlanta, Denver, Los Angeles, or New York. You can find more information at www.dishnetwork.com.

Even though plenty of information is available from the DIRECTV and DISH Network Web sites, I suggest that you visit your local dealer for the best information. The Web sites and customer-service representatives you're likely to contact by phone have lots of information regarding home installations, but usually aren't quite so prepared to answer your questions regarding a mobile installation.

The three items necessary to secure service for a mobile system include the following:

✔ **Satellite antenna:** Those little dishes they used to sell in the truck stops are now best used as Frisbees, according to those in the know. You can find satellite TV antennas ranging in price from a couple hundred dollars to a couple thousand dollars, so shop around to find the antenna that best suits both your needs and desires.

✔ **Receiver:** Your best bet is to purchase your receiver from the dealer. You can find them on eBay and in the classifieds, but because there have been many new developments in the technology, you should shop the dealership before going elsewhere for the hardware. For example, both DISH Network and DIRECTV now offer DVR– and HD–capable equipment.

✔ **Service subscription:** Even though there are only a couple of providers, these providers offer plans galore. These plans and the channels available for mobile subscriptions vary from those available for home-based subscriptions, so make sure you carefully consider those choices that might be available to you.

As a mobile subscriber, you must provide proof to your chosen service provider that you meet certain criteria. Before either DISH Network or DIRECTV will accept your subscription application, you must provide a signed Declaration of Intent. In addition to that, if you're an RV owner, you need to provide a copy of your current state vehicle registration, and if you're an OTR trucker, you need to provide a copy of your CDL and a copy of your current state vehicle registration. (You can't use a satellite TV dish to get a satellite Internet connection, but you can use a satellite Internet dish to get both TV and the Internet. If you're interested, check out Chapter 9.)

Settling on a satellite antenna

One of the first considerations in setting up a satellite TV system is the satellite antenna. Because most satellite TV dealerships are set up, primarily, to install systems for homes, they might not be able to provide you with an antenna. Not to worry, you should be able to find an RV dealership in your area that sells and installs suitable satellite antennas. The two primary satellite TV antenna manufacturers are:

- ✔ **Winegard:** With satellite TV antennas ranging from the low-profile LP1000 that can maintain a satellite connection even with the vehicle in motion to the portable, ground-mounted RD-9046, chances are good that Winegard has an antenna that meets your needs. For the budget-conscious, you can check out the RM-DM46 or RM-DM61. You can find them on the Web at www.winegard.com.

- ✔ **KVH Industries:** Offering a serious selection of satellite antennas that can maintain communication while your vehicle is in motion, the KVH TracVision R6 and A5, as well as Series 2 and 3, provide enough versatility to meet anyone's needs. They're located on the Web at www.kvh.com.

Before you begin looking at the in-motion antennas, you should get ready for some sticker shock because these antennas, which are taking over the market, will, in all likelihood, set you back well over $1,000. As a matter of fact, the very cool-looking KVH TracVision A5, which is designed specifically for use with the DIRECTV Total Choice MOBILE Package, has a suggested retail price of $2,295.

Setting up the system

I'm a big-time do-it-yourself kind of guy. However, were I getting ready to install a satellite TV system in my truck or RV, I'd be on my way down to the local satellite shop. It's not that I don't think I couldn't get the job done, it's just that I like things installed in a neat, clean, and orderly fashion — and the chances are good that your local dealership either does a lot of mobile instal-lations or they can point you in the direction of someone who does. Experience counts.

Once you've got the system installed, it's time to get it commissioned. Your dealer can walk you through the process, and because the satellite antenna needs to be aimed with a fair amount of precision so that the activation signal can be sent to your receiver, this is another good reason to have the system installed by a professional.

Getting Bookish

For a long time, I've enjoyed books on tape, and even though the words "always" and "never" are seldom appropriate, I think I can safely say that I'm never found without a book to read. As a matter of fact, I usually have several just in case I finish one while I'm in a book-free zone. Recently, I found a few Web sites that offer digital books. A couple of them provide books in print, while the others offer audio books that can be downloaded to your computer. A few of the sites are

✔ **Audible.com:** Considering the cost of books on tape, this Web site offers downloadable digital books at bargain-basement prices. You don't have to subscribe to the service to buy books, but if you purchase even an annual subscription for less than $10, you can get an even bigger dis-count. Once you've downloaded the book, you can listen to it on your computer, burn it to CD, or transfer it to a portable player. For more information, go to www.audible.com.

Gaming on the go

Entire books are written about games and gaming, but not so much about games, game boxes and consoles that are being used in a mobile environment. That could be because, although live gaming over the Internet is great at home, it doesn't seem to translate into quite as much fun at hotspots. Xbox Live, for example, can be more than a little frustrating to play at a hotspot that, because it's using a VSAT connec-tion to the Internet, doesn't maintain an upload and download speed sufficient to support the games. In addition, the latency inherent with satellite Internet connections will absolutely wreak havoc with the gaming experience. Games designed to be played online, but with a computer rather than a game box or console, seem to be more playable, but latency and vari-ations in connection speed can cause a problem here as well. Your best bet for gaming-on-the-go is to bring your games with you and see if you can set up a local-area network (LAN) with some nearby gamers rather than taking it to the Net.

✔ **eBookwise:** Offering e-books specially formatted for use with the eBookwise-1150 e-book reader, they've got hundreds of books for sale, but they can be read only on the reader. You can get more information by visiting their Web site at www.ebookwise.com.

✔ **Project Gutenberg:** With over 18,000 free e-books available for download, this site is a bookworm's delight. Most of the books offered on the site are in the Public Domain (meaning the U.S. copyright has expired), so you won't find any recent bestsellers here — but for those among you who haven't read everything by Herman Melville, Jack London, or Sir Arthur Conan Doyle (to name a very few), it's well worth taking a look. The Web site address is www.gutenberg.org.

Part VII
The Part of Tens

The 5th Wave   By Rich Tennant

"Why can't you just bring your iPod like everyone else?"

In this part . . .

I'm not sure where or how the inclusion of The Part of Tens in every *For Dummies* book originated. Maybe it was inspired by the top ten lists of David Letterman who, like those good folks at Wiley Publishing, hails from Indianapolis, Indiana. Anyway, in Chapter 17, I tell you about at least ten accessories that can add to the life, utility, and your enjoyment, of your over-the-road electronic devices. In Chapter 18, you find out about ten good program applications that, besides being interesting and useful, won't cost you a dime.

Chapter 17

Ten Must-Have Travel Accessories

*O*nce, a long time ago, the owner of the company I drove for asked me to make a quick trip to Sioux City, Iowa — just to pick up a trailer from the Thermo King shop. Although it was my day off and my truck was being serviced, I agreed to go anyway. Wearing a T-shirt, cutoffs, and sandals, without any of my gear, I jumped into an empty truck and bobtailed to town. I figured I'd be home by three o'clock.

I was gone for ten days. Sometime around Day Two or Three, severely under-accessorized and singing along with the Beach Boys' version of "Sloop John B," I vowed that I'd never again go anywhere without all my stuff — 'cause stuff's important.

As I've grown older, the list of stuff I consider to be indispensable — the stuff I won't leave home without — has grown a bit beyond a bag of jeans and boxers. Included among those items are, of course, various accessories, electronic and otherwise, designed to make life on the road a little easier. Now, I know that a ton of toys can add to enjoyment on the road, but the more you've got, the more you've got to move. That's why, in this chapter, I include in my list of accessories — not only items that enhance your ability to use and enjoy your tools and toys, but an item or two that can help you keep things organized and get them packed away.

Toting Your Laptop in the Right Luggage

Everything you lug around with you requires luggage, yes it does, and I now have a selection of laptop bags ranging in condition from tattered to top-notch. After ripping my way through quite a number of inexpensive bags, I've come to the conclusion that, when shopping for laptop luggage, cheap is not the way to go. There are a bunch of really good bags on the market, and there are two that I know, for sure, I can recommend:

✔ **Kensington Contour Roller:** I always thought that wheels on luggage were for flight attendants and lazy businessmen. I no longer hold that antiquated view — now that I'm somewhat of an antique myself — but wheeled luggage, when used in an over-the-road environment, has got to be tough. The Kensington Contour Roller is pretty light in weight but definitely not a lightweight when it comes to being sturdy. The shoulder strap, handle, and contour design also make it pretty easy to carry when wheels are out of the question. You can get more information by visiting their Web site at `http://us.kensington.com`.

✔ **Samsonite Business One Mobile Office:** Besides the fact that it rolls, the thing I like best about this — and most of the Samsonite product line — is that it seems nearly indestructible. It also provides a lot of protection for my laptop and all the rest of the stuff that it has plenty of room to store. If I had one complaint, though, it would be this: If you're in an area where wheels won't work, this case isn't as easy to tote around as the Kensington Contour. I do like it, though, and if you're interested, you can get more information from (among other places) the Samsonite Web site at `http://us.samsonite.com`.

Maintaining Your Laptop

Granted, there's not a lot of external maintenance required for a laptop — or any electronic gadget, for that matter — but there are a couple things that need to be taken care of on a regular basis. For example, gadgets have batteries, and batteries run down. Gadgets also get dirty and need to be cleaned. Here are a couple of accessories that can keep you going and keep you clean — clean around the country.

Charging up

If you've got a built-in *inverter* (the gadget that changes battery current from 12V DC to 110-120V AC), it never hurts to have a backup — and if you don't have one, this one should fill the bill quite nicely. The Xantrex Pocket

Powerpack 100 combines a 100-watt inverter with a high-capacity, high-output battery pack that has a three-prong power outlet and USB charging port. The battery pack can power your laptop for up to two and a half hours, or you can plug the inverter into the DC power port on your vehicle, recharging both the Powerpack 100 battery and your laptop's battery.

The USB charging port can charge or power compatible cellphones, PDAs, or iPods in less than a half-hour, and if you don't think you really need the combination of a battery and inverter, you can instead choose the Xantrex XPower 100 or Xantrex XPower 175 DC-to-AC inverter. Both have a standard, three-prong, AC outlet as well as the USB charging port, and the 175 provides up to 175 watts of power. You can get more information about these devices from the Xantrex Web site at www.xantrex.com, and they're available at Crutchfield and other online retailers.

Keeping your laptop clean

A laptop can be a dirt magnet. Most of them are made of some combination of plastic and light metals — and with the spinning fans and electricity running through them, the static electricity that's created attracts dust, dirt, and hair at an alarming rate. I've heard of folks cleaning keyboards, fans, and ports with compressed air cans, but I really don't recommend that — and under no circumstances should you consider attacking your laptop with the air hose you might use to clean your cab. There are a couple of things I've found, however, that can help you keep your laptop spic'n'span.

Deferring dirt

Dust has a way of working its way into every nook and cranny — especially, it seems, in an over-the-road environment. Even with the lid closed, a laptop can become dusty, dirty, and grimy. As a matter of fact, while happily typing away, you deposit a little oil from your fingers on each of the keys you touch. I've found a product, though, that can help to keep that oil from being transferred to the screen when the lid's closed — and at the same time keep dust from getting on the keys.

The Notebook ScreensavRz, manufactured and sold by RadTech, can help to protect your laptop's LCD screen from body oils and dirt as well as from scratching and abrasion. The ScreensavRz (a 0.6-millimeter-thick polishing fabric that you lay on your keyboard before closing the lid) can help to maintain a clean keyboard and screen — *and* can actually polish and remove scratches from your screen! It was designed for use with Macs, but RadTech offers models made for PCs as well. You can get more information from their Web site at www.radtech.us.

Eradicating dirt

No matter how you try — with or without the ScreensavRz — your laptop is bound to get dirty. When it does, I recommend using a handy little product manufactured by LensPen — the Laptop-Pro. With an optical-grade chamois on one end and two brushes on the other end (one for removing dust from the screen and another for removing dirt and dust from the keyboard), it's the best tool for cleaning a laptop I've ever run across. By visiting the LensPen Web site at www.lenspen.com, you can get more information about the Laptop-Pro, as well as tips on the best methods of use.

Accessorizing Your Workspace

It just makes sense to make your workspace as comfortable and efficient as possible. Here I tell you about a few items that can make life and work on the road a little less taxing and a little more convenient.

Desks without legs

I use a portable laptop desk while traveling. I do so because, first, I sometimes prefer to use a mouse instead of the touch pad, and second, most laptop desks incorporate some method of cooling the laptop (besides insulating your lap from the heat generated by a laptop).

Now, I haven't owned or extensively tested a whole bunch of laptop desks, but recently, when I went shopping for a new one, I found the Targus Notebook Portable LapDesk — which was recommended in one magazine or another, so I thought I'd give it a go. The three things I like best about it are:

- ✔ **It's light.** Weighing in at a couple ounces less than a pound and a half, it's definitely not a burden to carry around.

- ✔ **It's small.** Like a lot of laptop desks, it folds in the middle and when folded, measures less than one square foot. It also fits in my laptop bag. What more could you want?

- ✔ **It's cheap.** It could go up in price — but I paid less than thirty bucks for mine, and I think that's a pretty good deal.

It's got ventilation channels under the laptop, similar to others, but — and this is the thing that sets it apart — it's also got an adjustable foot that raises the back edge of the laptop. Raising the back of the laptop accomplishes two things: First, by increasing airflow, it improves cooling; second, with the rear of the laptop raised, I find it easier to use the keyboard. You can get more information about the Targus LapDesk by visiting their Web site at www.targus.com.

Another laptop desk and pad manufacturer — one that you should most definitely take a look at when shopping for a laptop desk — is LapLogic. Their Traveler Series LapPads, although not rigid enough to be called *desks,* help to dissipate heat. And their Guardian Series Laptop Desks, which are made of the same material as the heat-dissipating pads, are both colorful and lightweight. You can get more information from their Web site at `http://laplogic.com`.

Mice without tails

My wife has finally convinced me that a mouse is better than a touch pad or pointing stick, and I'm sure there are myriad mice that do a great job. But in an effort to reduce the number of cords and wires hanging off of my laptop, I made the decision to opt for a Bluetooth wireless mouse. There are quite a number of them available, so I had no problem finding a few to choose from. When the shopping dust had settled, I'd narrowed the field to two, and I think either of these will do quite nicely.

- **Bluetake BT500:** The Bluetake Web site says you can use this mouse up to 10 meters away from a Bluetooth-enabled computer. That's just great, but if I'm 33 feet from my laptop, I can't possibly see the cursor. So what's the point? (Well, if you're giving PowerPoint presentations to illustrate the many benefits dock personnel will enjoy by getting you unloaded before anyone else, you can wander around and away from your laptop while doing so.) Anyway, the BT500's a mini mouse, and although I didn't think I'd want a small mouse, when I gave it a try, it felt fine, and I liked the fact that it took up less space in the bag. If you don't have integrated Bluetooth capability, you can buy their Combo Pack, which includes the USB-powered BT009X Bluetooth adapter. You can get more information from their Web site at `www.bluetake.com`, and it's also available from several online retailers.

- **Anycom Blue Mini Mouse BTM-100:** The Blue Mini Mouse BTM-100 is powered by AAA batteries that can be recharged while in use, with the included USB Power Clip. During recharging, the mouse works like a regular wired mouse, and once charged, the clip can be removed. This mouse boasts the ridiculous range of 30 meters. What are these people thinking? I don't know about you, but I've never had the urge to browse the Web through a pair of binoculars. Nonetheless, it's a great product, and if you need a Bluetooth adapter, the BTM-100 can be bundled with the Anycom Blue USB-120 or USB-130 adapter. More information's available at `www.anycom.com`, and it's available from quite a number of online retailers.

Phones without hands

I guess, technically speaking, no phone has hands, and I should have titled this section, "Hands-free phones," but . . . I've got a kind of theme going here. You understand, don't you? Sure you do, and I've got a couple of interesting phone accessories to tell you about that could cause you to say something like, "Look ma, no hands!" So, without any further ado. . . .

✔ **ClearOne Chat 50:** The ClearOne Chat 50 is a USB-powered speakerphone that really shines when it's connected to a laptop to make VoIP calls. (I introduce VoIP in Chapter 13.) But, provided you're using the optional external AC adapter for power, you can also connect it to a cellphone via the headphone jack. The Chat 50 also has *full-duplex capability,* meaning that you can both hear and speak to the person on the other end of the call at the same time. That's a feat most cellphones are incapable of performing. You can get more information by visiting their Web site at www.clearone.com.

✔ **Bluetake BT400 G5 Headset:** I've already mentioned Bluetake once in this chapter, and because they make some really good Bluetooth wireless products, I could probably mention them again. (But I won't.) The BT400 G5 Headset is among the best they offer. True, you've got to have a Bluetooth-capable cellphone to use this baby, but really, it's so good that, if you haven't already got one, you should run right out and get a cellphone with Bluetooth technology. I mean, you can actually be nearly 100 feet from your cellphone and still talk on it using this thing. Not only that, but the volume is also so loud and clear you can easily hear the other party in the noisiest of conditions. More information's available by visiting Bluetake at www.bluetake.com.

Entertaining Accessories

In the previous chapter, I gave you a few ideas about using your electronic wonders to enhance and expand your over-the-road entertainment choices. Here I've got a couple ideas about some accessories that can improve your enjoyment of that entertainment, as well as one that can help you share, save, and remember your experiences on the road.

MP3 players

Once you've got music on your laptop, it's really nice to be able to listen to it anytime and anywhere. All you need is an MP3 player. Everyone, it seems, is in love with their iPods — and if I'd ever had one, I probably would be too.

I'm a bit of a contrarian, so when I decided it was finally time to join the rest of the world and put hundreds of songs on a device that was just a little bit bigger than a pack of gum, I went looking for a non-iPod player.

I found, during my shopping, that there were actually quite a few really good non-iPods out there. Because I wasn't sure just how much use I was going to get out of this kind of gadget, I decided to go with the cheapest one I could find that was well reviewed. I came up with the Zen Nano Plus. It's manufactured by Creative, offered with a storage capacity of either 512MB or 1GB, and it's compatible with either MP3– or WMA–formatted music.

The 1GB version of the Nano Plus can store around 500 songs and comes complete with an FM tuner. The one thing that really caught my eye, however, is that it also includes Line-In encoding so that you can connect directly to — and record from — any audio source. The Nano Plus package includes a Line-in cable for recording from a CD or cassette player, and with a mini-plug-to-RCA-plug adapter, you can even record vinyl LPs directly from the turntable or amp. This player's available from Wal-Mart, Best Buy, or any number of online retailers, and more information's available on the Creative Web site at: www.creative.com.

Portable speakers

With the proliferation of MP3 players has come a nearly equal boom in the number of portable speakers capable of giving the little devices a big voice. For me, though, I wanted a set of portable speakers that could also be used as external laptop speakers. I found just what I was looking for in the Boomtube H2O1, manufactured by Think Outside. They're not, at around $250 a set, what I'd call inexpensive, but the sound is superb. If you're interested, you can find their Web site at www.thinkoutside.com.

Sharing your over-the-road life

I can't imagine traveling without a camera. Not, mind you, that I've always *had* a camera; I haven't. And because I haven't, I've missed out on the opportunity to share some amazing sights with my family and friends. No more, though — because I recently found a reasonably priced digital camera that can take wide angle shots as well as optical-zoom photos with up to 5X magnification. What is this amazing camera? Why, it's the Kodak EasyShare V570, of course.

The beauty of the Kodak EasyShare line of cameras is, as the moniker implies, the ease with which photos can be organized, edited, and shared. The EasyShare button on the back of the camera makes it a snap to tag photos that you want to print or e-mail; EasyShare software helps you make those photos look their absolute best, and the included EasyShare Photo Frame Dock 2 helps you transfer photos to your computer with a single touch. What more could you ask for? Well, you could ask that it be priced at less than $400 — and it is. More information's available at www.kodak.com.

Of course, the camera is king when it comes to accessories, and the Kodak EasyShare line is no exception. The V570 comes standard with enough stuff to get you started and keep you going, but after a while, you might start feeling the need to accessorize. And wouldn't you know it, Kodak is there to help. The EasyShare line looks like it's going to be around for awhile, so I'm sure they'll come up with a lot of cool stuff for you to drool over.

Chapter 18

Ten Fantastic Free Applications

In This Chapter

▶ Making your desktop work for you

▶ Keeping an eye on your computer

▶ Finding free office applications

▶ Having some fun with your computer

Chances are good, if you've read any part of this book, that you already know I'm enamored with almost anything that advertises itself as free. And even if this is the first chapter you're reading, I'm willing to bet that the word *free* has a special place in your heart as well. Now, I grant you, the word *free* doesn't always really mean free, and having studied economics, I believe TANSTAAFL (There Ain't No Such Thing As A Free Lunch) to be a truism.

All the above notwithstanding, I've gathered together, in this chapter, ten applications that — even if they're not perfectly polished — won't require you to whip out your credit card prior to installing them. And believe me, it wasn't easy to whittle the list of free stuff found on the Web down to ten items. The Web sites I visit regularly to shop for freeware include these:

✔ **Softpile.com:** www.softpile.com

✔ **SnapFiles:** www.snapfiles.com

✔ **Softpedia:** www.softpedia.com

✔ **FreewareFiles:** www.freewarefiles.com

✔ **Tucows:** www.tucows.com

As you might guess, enticing unsuspecting cheapskates like me with the promise of free software is one way Internet scoundrels manage to con folks into downloading malicious programs. Those sites I mention in the preceding list, as well as several others, do all they can to be sure the program applications they offer for download are virus-free. If you've got any doubt about the site or the program, play it safe and don't download.

Enhancing Your Desktop

If you spend a fair amount of time staring at your computer, it's nice to have your desktop organized and useful. It should also be easy on the eyes. To that end, developers around the world have written literally hundreds of program applications, some free and some not, that accomplish a range of productivity and organizational tasks and look good, too.

If you search around the Internet, you can find clocks, alarms, newsreaders, icon-makers, calendars, and personal information managers. You can even find several programs that create multiple virtual desktops. Because I don't like to clutter my desktop (or my hard drive) with a bunch of doodads, I don't grab every gadget that comes down the pike, but there are a couple I've found useful. (The fact that they're free doesn't hurt, either.)

Stickies

I've noticed a lot of people frame their computer monitors with colorful little sticky notes. These little reminders are really handy because, besides making one look very busy and efficient, they serve as a kind of external storage device for the brain. Because, however, I don't work in a traditional office and I don't use a desktop computer, I've always felt somewhat left out.

Now, I'm not really all that interested in looking busy or efficient, but the value of a deferred external memory system isn't lost on me at all — especially because I've been told I'm a fountain of useless information. Whether that's true or not, I know that given the choice between remembering the name of King Henry VIII's third wife or my wife's dental appointment, it seems I can instantly remember Jane Seymour (not Dr. Quinn), while the dental appointment takes me by surprise every time.

Enter a tiny little desktop utility called Stickies. This free program, created by Zhorn Software, allows you to put digital sticky notes all over your desktop. You can remind yourself of anything and everything. You can jot down phone numbers, addresses, names, appointments; you name it, and you can put it on a Stickies digital note. In addition to that, you can tell the note to go to sleep for a while and wake up whenever you want it to. You could even have it wake up month after month or year after year, reminding you to pay a bill or send a card. And, if you don't want the notes plastered all over the place, you can choose to hide them all.

If this sounds like a little gem you'd like to add to your arsenal of desktop tools, you can find it freely available at www.zhornsoftware.co.uk. To keep your Stickies looking fresh and interesting, you can also download your choice of several different skins.

Another free tool available from Zhorn, called Stickies Store, allows you to file away Stickies that have outlived their usefulness, but, for whatever reason, you want to keep. By the way, if you download the Stickies Store, you'll notice it's a zipped folder. The installation instructions are included in the folder, so all you need to do is read the instructions and extract the `.exe` and `.chm` files to the same program folder in which the Stickies program files reside.

Desktop Sidebar

Okay, I hear you asking: What in the world is a desktop sidebar? Well, one of the many features available with Vista (the newest Windows operating system) is a desktop panel loaded with a bunch of gadgets. Some access the Web and provide news headlines, weather updates, online slide shows, or stock prices; other gadgets give you easy access to your e-mail, contacts, calendar, or media player. Sounds pretty good, eh? Well, you don't have to wait for Windows Vista; you can have all that now — for no cost. Figure 18-1 gives you a look at a few views available.

Each panel, when the cursor hovers over it, displays details off to the side; if you right-click it, each panel is (to various extents) customizable. You can also undock panels and float them into any position on your desktop that you choose. A few of the panels available are

- ✔ **Clocks:** A number of clock styles are available within the hundreds of skins. Almost every skin gives you the option of a digital or analog clock. In most of the skins, I prefer the analog version even though it does take up a bit more space. Hovering over the clock usually brings up a calendar and (if you want) the time in various cities around the world.

- ✔ **Weather:** The weather panels are usually driven by The Weather Channel, and by entering a city name or Zip code, you can get local weather from anywhere in the world. It doesn't update itself as often as I'd like, but a quick right-click on the panel offers the option to refresh.

- ✔ **Performance Monitor:** This panel is one of the main reasons I installed the sidebar. You can monitor a number of areas within your computer. If, for example, your CPU monitor suddenly jumps, it might be an indication that someone's hacked into your system or some form of malware has found a new home on your hard drive.

- ✔ **Newsroom:** I like the news — always have, always will. With this panel, you can monitor headlines from a number of different news sources, and you can customize it with RSS feeds or blogs.

All these panels are standard issue when you choose to install the sidebar, but there are more than 50 others — some variations and some unique — available now, and developers are working on more all the time.

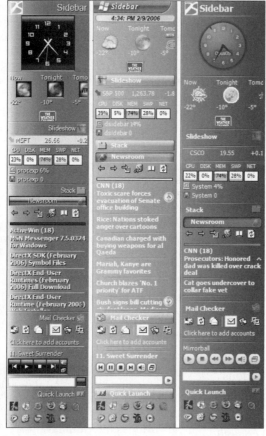

Figure 18-1:
The three
Desktop
Sidebar
views here
indicate a
fraction of
the skins,
panels, and
views
available
for use.

Slideshow is one of the standard-issue panels in Desktop Sidebar. You can use all kinds of photos; I've chosen to display Webcam views from around the world. I've got regularly updating photos ranging from Old Faithful to a penguin-research station in Antarctica. To save a webcam to Desktop Sidebar, just find the view you want, right-click it, choose Properties, and copy the Address. Open Panel Properties in the Slideshow panel, choose to Add a URL, configure the refresh time, click OK a couple of times, and you're done!

Now, I happen to really like the Desktop Sidebar, but you might also be interested to know that a similar product's available from TGT Soft called SpyderBar. It's also free, and, although it looks and operates much like Desktop Sidebar, it's not exactly the same, so you might want to check it out.

Another possibility for desktop enhancement is found at the Yahoo! Web site. During the summer of 2005, Yahoo! bought out Pixoria so they could get their hands on Konfabulator and their Widgets. What are Widgets? A few examples include alarm clocks, countdown clocks, calculators, performance monitors, day planners, news feeds, radio tuners, and weather stations. For the very paranoid among you, there's even a Werewolf Monitor that shows you the phases of the moon. You can place these Widgets anywhere on the desktop and configure them in a number of ways.

When Yahoo! purchased Konfabulator, they immediately ceased charging a fee. Widgets, once they were free, became instantly appealing to me. After downloading the Widget Engine from Yahoo!, you can choose from literally thousands of Widgets that can perform an incredible range of tasks. I use these more as an enhancement to the Desktop Sidebar than a replacement, but it's your computer, so *you* choose.

These program applications and their optional features can be freely downloaded at

 ✔ **Desktop Sidebar:** www.desktopsidebar.com

 ✔ **SpyderBAR:** www.tgtsoft.com

 ✔ **Widgets:** http://widgets.yahoo.com

Monitoring Your Computer

I'm normally pretty curious about stuff. I like to know just what it is, for example, that my computer's doing. Not that I understand all (or even most) of it. I don't, but that doesn't mean I don't like to snoop through the inner workings. I've found a couple of utilities that not only tell me considerably more than I ever thought I could find out about what my computer's doing, but also help me — slowly, very slowly — discover more about the way it does it.

The first utility I tell you about takes a snapshot of everything going on in your computer and generates a complete — and I really mean *complete* — report, detailing everything that's going on in there. The second utility is similar — it identifies the processes, indicating what's in use and how much of the available resources are being allocated to it — but it continually updates itself, giving you a real-time look at what's happening.

LookInMyPC

Created by Solid Oak Software, this little utility was recommended to me by a tech-support staffer. She told me that if I'd had this utility installed, I'd be able to take a snapshot of the internal workings of my computer, save it as a file, and e-mail it to her. She'd then be able to go through it and figure out exactly what was fouling up the works.

Of course, at that particular moment, I didn't have LookInMyPC loaded on my laptop, so I was out of luck. Because I am, however, one who believes in learning from my mistakes, I downloaded a copy of LookInMyPC just in case I ever needed it again. Every once in a while, especially if things seem a little sluggish or if the system monitors I use in Desktop Sidebar seem to be indicating something's happening, I run the utility and create a report.

A few of the hundreds of items you find by scanning a typical report include

- ✔ **Windows version:** You see the exact version of Windows installed on your computer, including build and serial numbers.

- ✔ **Hard-drive information:** The make and model number are identified along with the total capacity, number of partitions, and current status.

- ✔ **Installed hotfixes:** Creates a detailed list of all the Windows updates and hotfixes that have been installed on your computer. Each link opens the Microsoft Knowledge Base article for that particular fix.

- ✔ **Installed programs:** Although only registered programs are listed (meaning that malicious applications are unlikely to be represented), you can find out about some very obscure programs by following the links.

- ✔ **Installed services:** Creates a detailed list of all the programs running in the background. You can see the full path as well as their current status.

The report includes so much information concerning the hardware installed that it's probably a good idea to generate and print a report just so you have that information at your fingertips if you ever need it.

You can download a copy of your own at www.lookinmypc.com.

Process Explorer

Rather than give you a snapshot of the processes currently running in your computer, Process Explorer gives you a dynamic view. Process Explorer is a tremendously handy tool that's used by many professionals to troubleshoot computer problems. If you play around with the Process Explorer buttons and options a little bit, you can find out more about your computer than you ever thought possible.

Every process or application running on your computer, whether it's hidden or not, is shown in the upper window. If you click any item, the lower window displays information about that item's component. If you right-click an item, as shown in Figure 18-2, you can choose to display the Properties dialog box, kill or suspend the process, or click Google to open a browser window with search results related to the process name — if you just don't know what the item is.

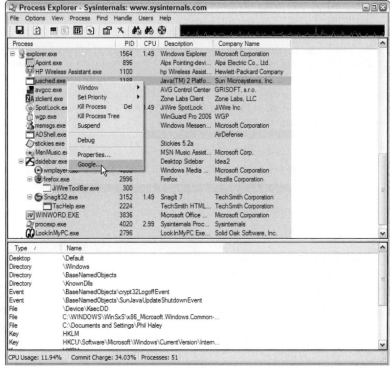

Figure 18-2:
Click Google
if you want
to search
for
information
on what a
process
does.

Downloading and using Process Explorer is a little different from how it is for most program applications you're probably familiar with. When you visit the Sysinternals Web site (www.sysinternals.com) to find Process Explorer, you navigate to the Processes and Threads page. Scroll down that page until you find Process Explorer (followed by a version number), and click the link.

The page that opens has a whole bunch of information (some important and some not-so-important) relating to Process Explorer. Scroll to the bottom of the page and click the link that lists your operating system. The download is a ZIP folder containing the help file, the README text, and the executable application. If you download the folder to your desktop or My Documents, you don't need to extract the files. You can simply open the folder and double-click the file you want to open. It's a good idea to read through the help file (procexp.chm) once before you begin working with the application.

Office Productivity Applications

Whether you need a whole suite of office applications or just a good word processor, you can get what you need without forking over a huge wad of cash. As a matter of fact, you can get what you need for no cost whatsoever, with two outstanding products that meet the needs of all but the most demanding users.

Both of these products are the result of open source projects that bring a wide variety of people and corporations together into a development community. This method of software development, wherein the source code is available to everyone and everyone can contribute, has been proven, time and again, to be both efficient and innovative. And, because many freely contribute, it's generally freely available.

When you visit these sites, you'll probably notice links to pages where donations of time, talent, or money are accepted. It's not required, and you're not a bad person if you don't contribute; but if you like the software, you might consider supporting, in some small way, to the well-being of the communities developing the software.

AbiWord

Microsoft Word 2003 is (at least in my opinion) the absolute best word processor available. It's unquestionably the standard by which all others are judged, and its lofty position is reflected in the equally lofty price tag. There is, however, a close runner-up that does nearly everything MS Word does — and has the added attraction of being absolutely free.

AbiWord can read and write to all the current document types, including Microsoft Word and Word Perfect, and because it has a user interface very similar to both of those, it's very easy to learn and use. Like any high-end processor, AbiWord allows you to embed images, format tables, and create bulleted or numbered lists — you can even create HTML Web pages.

Another nice thing about AbiWord is its small size. It doesn't take up a lot of space on your hard drive, and places fewer demands on memory resources when it's in use. When you download AbiWord, you get the basic word processor; then, after you install the basic program, you can go back and download any plug-in applications you might want.

If you select the check boxes next to *Associate .doc with AbiWord* and *Associate .rtf with AbiWord* during the installation process, any MS Word documents you have currently saved — as well as any Rich Text Format documents — are forever after displayed as AbiWord documents. However, you don't need to select those check boxes in order to save AbiWord documents as .doc or .rtf files.

AbiWord is produced by AbiSource and can be downloaded from their site, located on the World Wide Web at www.abisource.com. The plug-ins must be downloaded and installed separately from — and after — the basic program application.

OpenOffice

Do you need a complete office suite, but for some obscure reason, you don't feel like spending $400 or more? Well, here's the solution to your problem. In October of 2000, OpenOffice.org opened to the public the source code for StarOffice by Sun Microsystems. Since that time, thousands of contributors have helped develop a world-class, office productivity suite.

Open Office is compatible with all the major office productivity suites and includes the following components:

- **Word processor:** Known as Writer, this word processor is quite good. I like AbiWord a bit better, but if you only want one, this does the job.

- **Spreadsheet program:** I've always found Excel a bit daunting. Calc, as the spreadsheet component is known, is somewhat easier to use. The Scenario Manager lets me do a lot of hypothetical forecasting; I like that.

- **Presentation creator:** Impress is the OpenOffice answer to PowerPoint, and it does a remarkable job. You can create 3-D or Flash presentations, and you can save your work in PowerPoint format.

- **Graphics tools:** You can import graphics from common formats or use Draw to create your own. You can easily create charts and diagrams, and the 3-D controller helps to give depth to your designs.

- **Database program:** I have to admit, I've never created a database, but if you want (or need) to do so, you can accomplish your goal with Base.

- **Equation program:** Complex equations can be rendered within Math for use in text documents. Do I have a need for this? No. Do you? Well, if you do, this is the tool for you. The equations can be inserted into Writer, Calc, or Impress. If they could then be printed on coffee-shop napkins, my dad would've loved this tool.

OpenOffice, commonly referred to as OOo, is available from OpenOffice.org at, appropriately enough, www.openoffice.org. You can find complete setup and installation instructions there, linked from the download page.

Viewing Your Destination from Space

Mapping software combined with GPS can easily get you to your destination, but it's less capable of showing you what the area surrounding your destination might look like. It certainly would be nice if you could get a preview, wouldn't it? Just think, by getting a look at the roads leading into your pickup or delivery location, you might be able to anticipate difficult turns or intersections. Or you might be able to see, ahead of time, whether an onramp is accessed from the right or left lane.

Likewise, if you're traveling to a new RV park or campground, it'd be nice to get a bird's-eye view of the layout and terrain, as well as the surroundings, wouldn't it? Well, now you can. A couple of free applications give you access to satellite imagery.

Google Earth

Rarely have I found something I thought was as flat-out great as Google Earth. With an Internet connection and Google Earth, you can virtually fly to nearly every city in the U.S. and get a pretty good view of buildings, parking lots, intersections, roads, highways, parks, campgrounds, and a whole bunch of other stuff. Just enter an address or intersection into the text field of the search tool, click the search icon, and you're off.

Once you get a look at your chosen location, you can zoom in for a closer view or zoom out to get some perspective. Another nice feature is the ability to tilt the view down by using the controls to the right of the directional buttons. In this view, you can actually feel like you're flying over an area. By using the different layers, you can add names and labels for roads, businesses, hospitals, pharmacies, fire stations, and a whole lot more. In some cases, mostly in the larger cities, you can even get 3-D views of the buildings.

As great as Google Earth is, however, it's far from perfect. Some smaller towns are a blur, and the satellite images are up to three years old. Still, even three-year-old images can give you a good idea of what to expect. Most larger towns are well covered, as are many smaller and more remote locations.

The Google Earth home page is located at `http://earth.google.com`, and you can find links there for the download page, as well as pages that'll help you get the most out of Google Earth. You can do a lot with this program, so don't expect to have total mastery of it in an hour or two.

World Wind

World Wind is one of the most powerful programs available on the Internet today. That it's free just amazes me. World Wind was developed by NASA, so as you might imagine, it's not quite as user-friendly as Google Earth. As a matter of fact, there's little doubt that an entire book could be written covering just this application. But don't let that scare you out of downloading World Wind. There's lots of information available to help you get proficient with the program, and just because it was developed by *actual* rocket scientists doesn't mean you have to be one to use and enjoy World Wind.

World Wind is available for download from NASA at `http://worldwind.arc.nasa.gov`, and some invaluable information about how it works and ways to use it is available from World Wind Central at `www.worldwindcentral.com/wiki/Main_Page`.

Make sure you take the Walkthrough Tour when you visit World Wind Central. It'll give you a good idea of what you can do right away with the program, and you can find out about add-on and plug-in programs that can further enhance your enjoyment of World Wind.

Making Music

It took me awhile, but after I realized what my laptop was capable of, I started using it in ways I'd never imagined I might. For example, I started ripping my CD collection onto the hard drive, and after reading an article in a magazine, I decided to try transferring my wife's vinyl LP collection onto CDs. In both cases, I found free software to help me do the job.

Audiograbber

I download a lot of music from places like MSN Music, iTunes, and others, but I also like to rip CDs. I can then transfer all this music to an MP3 player or just listen to it while I'm surfing the Web. When I first began loading my CD collection onto my hard drive, I noticed a distinct difference in the quality of the sound. The music I downloaded seemed to sound somewhat better than the music I ripped from my CDs, and my CDs sounded better on my stereo.

After doing a little research, I found that the problem might be due to media player software, which I used to copy CDs to my hard drive, using the sound card as a translator. I just figured I was going to have to accept this difference in sound quality, but then I stumbled across Audiograbber.

Because Audiograbber copies a CD digitally and directly, you can make a perfect digital audio copy. Even though this utility is very versatile and includes a lot of features, it's relatively easy to use, takes up very little space on your hard drive, and makes very little demand on resources when in use.

Audiograbber is available free of charge, and you can obtain it by pointing your browser to `www.audiograbber.com-us.net`.

After downloading Audiograbber, take advantage of the Guide for Newbies and the Guided Tour pages found on the Audiograbber Web site. Both of these guides will provide a solid foundation for using the utility. Another great resource for Audiograbber info is Tom's Audioguides, located on the Web at `http://ripping.v33.org/`.

Downloading and installing the LAME MP3 encoder

With most MP3 utilities — at least the free ones — it's necessary to download and install an MP3 encoder. The one most often recommended is the LAME encoder, and you can find it widely available on the Web by searching the term "LAME MP3 encoder." A couple sites I can recommend to download from are

✔ **Free-codecs.com:** The link for the LAME encoder is `www.free-codecs.com/download/Lame_Encoder.htm`.

✔ **Softpedia:** The encoder can be found here `www.softpedia.com/get/Multimedia/Audio/Audio-CD-Rippers-Encoders/LAME-MP3-Encoder.shtml`.

This download is in the form of a ZIP folder, so I suggest you download it to your desktop. (This just seems to work best for me.) Once the folder's finished downloading, you can open it with WinZip or the Windows XP utility and extract the contents to the location, such as `C:\Program Files\audiograbber`, at which the Audiograbber or any other MP3 utility resides.

Audacity

After reading an article in *Popular Mechanics,* I decided I'd try my hand at transferring my wife's aging LP collection onto CD. The advantages of digitizing our vinyl collection seemed obvious, so I began to collect the pieces and parts necessary to do the job. After spending a couple hundred bucks on the hardware — mainly due to the fact that the old turntable just wasn't up to the job — I was desperate for a free software solution.

Buried in the article was a reference to Audacity, so I jumped at the opportunity to save a few bucks. The only thing missing in the program — which only makes its presence felt when you want to export your MP3s — is the LAME MP3 encoder. Audacity offers a host of other features as well; you can find out about them by visiting their Web site at `http://audacity.sourceforge.net`. The Help page includes links to the FAQs, Documentation, and Tutorials. Once you make it through those sections, you'll have a good working knowledge of the program.

If, like me, you're interested in converting your vinyl collection into a CD collection, you can read the article that sparked my interest by visiting `www.popularmechanics.com/technology/audio/1552397.html` and reading the "Vinyl to Go-Go" article.

Index

• N •

• O •

USINESS, CAREERS & PERSONAL FINANCE

Grant Writing
FOR DUMMIES

0-7645-5307-0

Home Buying
FOR DUMMIES

0-7645-5331-3 *†

Also available:
- Accounting For Dummies †
  0-7645-5314-3
- Business Plans Kit For Dummies †
  0-7645-5365-8
- Cover Letters For Dummies
  0-7645-5224-4
- Frugal Living For Dummies
  0-7645-5403-4
- Leadership For Dummies
  0-7645-5176-0
- Managing For Dummies
  0-7645-1771-6

- Marketing For Dummies
  0-7645-5600-2
- Personal Finance For Dummies *
  0-7645-2590-5
- Project Management For Dummies
  0-7645-5283-X
- Resumes For Dummies †
  0-7645-5471-9
- Selling For Dummies
  0-7645-5363-1
- Small Business Kit For Dummies *†
  0-7645-5093-4

ME & BUSINESS COMPUTER BASICS

Windows XP
FOR DUMMIES

0-7645-4074-2

Excel 2003
ALL-IN-ONE DESK REFERENCE
FOR DUMMIES

0-7645-3758-X

Also available:
- ACT! 6 For Dummies
  0-7645-2645-6
- iLife '04 All-in-One Desk Reference
  For Dummies
  0-7645-7347-0
- iPAQ For Dummies
  0-7645-6769-1
- Mac OS X Panther Timesaving
  Techniques For Dummies
  0-7645-5812-9
- Macs For Dummies
  0-7645-5656-8

- Microsoft Money 2004 For Dummies
  0-7645-4195-1
- Office 2003 All-in-One Desk Reference
  For Dummies
  0-7645-3883-7
- Outlook 2003 For Dummies
  0-7645-3759-8
- PCs For Dummies
  0-7645-4074-2
- TiVo For Dummies
  0-7645-6923-6
- Upgrading and Fixing PCs For Dummies
  0-7645-1665-5
- Windows XP Timesaving Techniques
  For Dummies
  0-7645-3748-2

OD, HOME, GARDEN, HOBBIES, MUSIC & PETS

Feng Shui
FOR DUMMIES

0-7645-5295-3

Poker
FOR DUMMIES

0-7645-5232-5

Also available:
- Bass Guitar For Dummies
  0-7645-2487-9
- Diabetes Cookbook For Dummies
  0-7645-5230-9
- Gardening For Dummies *
  0-7645-5130-2
- Guitar For Dummies
  0-7645-5106-X
- Holiday Decorating For Dummies
  0-7645-2570-0
- Home Improvement All-in-One
  For Dummies
  0-7645-5680-0

- Knitting For Dummies
  0-7645-5395-X
- Piano For Dummies
  0-7645-5105-1
- Puppies For Dummies
  0-7645-5255-4
- Scrapbooking For Dummies
  0-7645-7208-3
- Senior Dogs For Dummies
  0-7645-5818-8
- Singing For Dummies
  0-7645-2475-5
- 30-Minute Meals For Dummies
  0-7645-2589-1

ERNET & DIGITAL MEDIA

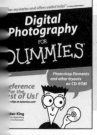

Digital Photography
FOR DUMMIES

0-7645-1664-7

Starting an eBay Business
FOR DUMMIES

0-7645-6924-4

Also available:
- 2005 Online Shopping Directory
  For Dummies
  0-7645-7495-7
- CD & DVD Recording For Dummies
  0-7645-5956-7
- eBay For Dummies
  0-7645-5654-1
- Fighting Spam For Dummies
  0-7645-5965-6
- Genealogy Online For Dummies
  0-7645-5964-8
- Google For Dummies
  0-7645-4420-9

- Home Recording For Musicians
  For Dummies
  0-7645-1634-5
- The Internet For Dummies
  0-7645-4173-0
- iPod & iTunes For Dummies
  0-7645-7772-7
- Preventing Identity Theft For Dummies
  0-7645-7336-5
- Pro Tools All-in-One Desk Reference
  For Dummies
  0-7645-5714-9
- Roxio Easy Media Creator For Dummies
  0-7645-7131-1

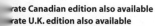

rate Canadian edition also available
rate U.K. edition also available

e wherever books are sold. For more information or to order direct: U.S. customers visit www.dummies.com or call 1-877-762-2974.
tomers visit www.wileyeurope.com or call 0800 243407. Canadian customers visit www.wiley.ca or call 1-800-567-4797.

SPORTS, FITNESS, PARENTING, RELIGION & SPIRITUALITY

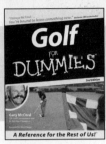

0-7645-5146-9

0-7645-5418-2

Also available:
- Adoption For Dummies
  0-7645-5488-3
- Basketball For Dummies
  0-7645-5248-1
- The Bible For Dummies
  0-7645-5296-1
- Buddhism For Dummies
  0-7645-5359-3
- Catholicism For Dummies
  0-7645-5391-7
- Hockey For Dummies
  0-7645-5228-7

- Judaism For Dummies
  0-7645-5299-6
- Martial Arts For Dummies
  0-7645-5358-5
- Pilates For Dummies
  0-7645-5397-6
- Religion For Dummies
  0-7645-5264-3
- Teaching Kids to Read For Dummies
  0-7645-4043-2
- Weight Training For Dummies
  0-7645-5168-X
- Yoga For Dummies
  0-7645-5117-5

TRAVEL

0-7645-5438-7

0-7645-5453-0

Also available:
- Alaska For Dummies
  0-7645-1761-9
- Arizona For Dummies
  0-7645-6938-4
- Cancún and the Yucatán For Dummies
  0-7645-2437-2
- Cruise Vacations For Dummies
  0-7645-6941-4
- Europe For Dummies
  0-7645-5456-5
- Ireland For Dummies
  0-7645-5455-7

- Las Vegas For Dummies
  0-7645-5448-4
- London For Dummies
  0-7645-4277-X
- New York City For Dummies
  0-7645-6945-7
- Paris For Dummies
  0-7645-5494-8
- RV Vacations For Dummies
  0-7645-5443-3
- Walt Disney World & Orlando For Dummies
  0-7645-6943-0

GRAPHICS, DESIGN & WEB DEVELOPMENT

0-7645-4345-8

0-7645-5589-8

Also available:
- Adobe Acrobat 6 PDF For Dummies
  0-7645-3760-1
- Building a Web Site For Dummies
  0-7645-7144-3
- Dreamweaver MX 2004 For Dummies
  0-7645-4342-3
- FrontPage 2003 For Dummies
  0-7645-3882-9
- HTML 4 For Dummies
  0-7645-1995-6
- Illustrator CS For Dummies
  0-7645-4084-X

- Macromedia Flash MX 2004 For Dummies
  0-7645-4358-X
- Photoshop 7 All-in-One Desk Reference For Dummies
  0-7645-1667-1
- Photoshop CS Timesaving Techniques For Dummies
  0-7645-6782-9
- PHP 5 For Dummies
  0-7645-4166-8
- PowerPoint 2003 For Dummies
  0-7645-3908-6
- QuarkXPress 6 For Dummies
  0-7645-2593-X

NETWORKING, SECURITY, PROGRAMMING & DATABASES

0-7645-6852-3

0-7645-5784-X

Also available:
- A+ Certification For Dummies
  0-7645-4187-0
- Access 2003 All-in-One Desk Reference For Dummies
  0-7645-3988-4
- Beginning Programming For Dummies
  0-7645-4997-9
- C For Dummies
  0-7645-7068-4
- Firewalls For Dummies
  0-7645-4048-3
- Home Networking For Dummies
  0-7645-42796

- Network Security For Dummies
  0-7645-1679-5
- Networking For Dummies
  0-7645-1677-9
- TCP/IP For Dummies
  0-7645-1760-0
- VBA For Dummies
  0-7645-3989-2
- Wireless All In-One Desk Reference For Dummies
  0-7645-7496-5
- Wireless Home Networking For Dummies
  0-7645-3910-8